Schriftenreihe
der Historischen Kommission bei der Bayerischen
Akademie der Wissenschaften

Band 114

Digitale Edition und vormoderner Parlamentarismus / Digital Scholarly Edition and Pre-modern Parliamentarism

Eine interdisziplinäre Annäherung an frühneuzeitliche Quellen / An Interdisciplinary Approach to Early Modern Sources

Herausgegeben von / Edited by
Florian Zeilinger, Roman Bleier, Josef Leeb

VANDENHOECK & RUPRECHT

Die Schriftenreihe wird herausgegeben
vom Sekretär der Historischen Kommission:
Bernhard Löffler

Gedruckt mit Unterstützung der Franz Schnabel Stiftung.

Bibliografische Information der Deutschen Nationalbibliothek:
Die Deutsche Nationalbibliothek verzeichnet diese Publikation in der
Deutschen Nationalbibliografie; detaillierte bibliografische Daten sind
im Internet über https://dnb.de abrufbar.

© 2025 Vandenhoeck & Ruprecht, Robert-Bosch-Breite 10, D-37079 Göttingen,
ein Imprint der Brill-Gruppe
(Koninklijke Brill BV, Leiden, Niederlande; Brill USA Inc., Boston MA, USA;
Brill Asia Pte Ltd, Singapore; Brill Deutschland GmbH, Paderborn, Deutschland;
Brill Österreich GmbH, Wien, Österreich)
Koninklijke Brill BV umfasst die Imprints Brill, Brill Nijhoff, Brill Schöningh,
Brill Fink, Brill mentis, Brill Wageningen Academic, Vandenhoeck & Ruprecht,
Böhlau und V&R unipress.

Alle Rechte vorbehalten. Das Werk und seine Teile sind urheberrechtlich
geschützt. Jede Verwertung in anderen als den gesetzlich zugelassenen Fällen
bedarf der vorherigen schriftlichen Einwilligung des Verlages.

Umschlagabbildung: Reichstagssitzung 1598 im Regensburger Rathaus
(»Verissima delineatio AUGUSTISSIMI CONSESSUS LEGATORUM S.R. IMPERII
INCOMITIIS RATISBONENSIBUS ANNO CHRISTI [M] D XCVII [...]«). Kupferstich von
Wilhelm Peter Zimmermann, 1598. Bildrechte: Bayerische Staatsbibliothek, https://mdz-nbn-resolving.de/details:bsb00098770. Digitalisat unter der CC-Lizenz BY-NC-SA (Namens-
nennung – Nicht-kommerziell – Weitergabe unter gleichen Bedingungen) 4.0 International.

Satz: SchwabScantechnik, Göttingen
Druck und Bindung: ⊕ Hubert & Co, Ergolding
Printed in the EU

Vandenhoeck & Ruprecht Verlage | www.vandenhoeck-ruprecht-verlage.com
E-Mail: info@v-r.de

ISSN 0568-4323
ISBN 978-3-525-30292-7

Inhalt

Gabriele Haug-Moritz, Georg Vogeler (Graz)
Einführung 7

Praxisbeispiele I:
Foren politischer Mitsprache im frühneuzeitlichen Europa

Tim Neu (Wien)
Teilhabegefüge, oder: Wie lässt sich die europäische Beratungskultur
der Vormoderne konzeptionell fassen (und was könnte daraus für
Editionsprojekte folgen)? 19

Paulina Kewes (Oxford)
Representative Assemblies in the Political Thought of Jean Bodin 43

Petr Maťa (Wien)
Wege und Irrwege der Erschließung ständischer Landtagsakten
in der Habsburgermonarchie
Bestandsaufnahme – Relevanz – Perspektiven 71

Paul Seaward (London)
The English Parliament in the Sixteenth and Seventeenth Centuries:
Sources and Digitisation 97

Krzysztof Fokt, Maciej Mikuła (Cracow)
The Digitalisation of the Oldest Legacy of the Polish and Polish-Lithuanian
Seym in the Framework of the IURA Project
Dilemmas, Limitations, Prospects 111

Rik Hoekstra, Marijn Koolen, Joris Oddens, Ronald Sluijter
(Amsterdam)
Structure-Derived Incremental Modelling
The Case of the Resolutions of the Dutch States General 121

Praxisbeispiele II:
Digitale Editionen frühneuzeitlicher Quellen

Ronald G. Asch (Freiburg im Breisgau)
Die Tagebücher Christians II. von Anhalt und ihre digitale Edition 145

Andreas Zecherle (Mainz), Kevin Wunsch (Darmstadt)
Das Projekt »Europäische Religionsfrieden Digital – EuReD«
Projektvorstellung und exemplarische Analyse des Augsburger Interims (1548) 161

Andreas Wagner (Frankfurt am Main)
Die Integration von Editionen frühmoderner Rechtstexte in eine
Linked-Open-Data-Landschaft 177

Martin de la Iglesia (Wolfenbüttel)
Besondere Herausforderungen des digitalen Edierens frühneuzeitlicher Texte
am Beispiel der Reiserelationen Philipp Hainhofers 195

Marius Hug, Linda Kirsten (Berlin)
Historische Texte der neuhochdeutschen Sprachstufe als Forschungsdaten
*Das »Deutsche Textarchiv« im Kontext der Nationalen Forschungsdaten-
infrastruktur (NFDI)* 205

Roman Bleier (Graz), Elisabeth Brantner (Graz),
Josef Leeb (Oberpöring/München), Eva Ortlieb (München/Bonn),
Constanze Rammer (Graz), Florian Zeilinger (Graz)
Der Reichstag zu Regensburg 1576
Eine digitale Edition 221

Abkürzungen 245

Autorinnen und Autoren 249

Register 255

GABRIELE HAUG-MORITZ, GEORG VOGELER (GRAZ)

Einführung

Unaufhaltsam schreitet der digitale Wandel, auch und gerade in den Geisteswissenschaften, voran. Er transformierte und transformiert epistemische Konfigurationen, bietet neue Chancen und stellt (auch) die historischen Disziplinen vor neue methodologische Herausforderungen[1]. Lange bevor im deutschen Sprachraum die ersten Professuren für »Digital Humanities« (DH) ausgeschrieben wurden (2008 ff.) und in der Geschichtswissenschaft diese Teildisziplin 2012 mit der Gründung der »AG Digitale Geschichtswissenschaft« des Verbandes der Historiker und Historikerinnen Deutschlands endgültig institutionelle Konturen annahm[2], reflektierten Kolleginnen und Kollegen, die editionswissenschaftlich arbeiteten, das Potential, das der Digitalität für ihr wissenschaftliches Tun eignet[3]. Und so konnte, als wir im Frühsommer 2018 unser, von den nationalen Forschungsförderern in Österreich und Deutschland finanziertes »Pilotprojekt zum digitalen Edieren frühneuzeitlicher Quellen« am Beispiel des Regensburger Reichstages von 1576 in Angriff nahmen, kein Zweifel mehr bestehen, dass editorische Grundlagenforschung nur unternommen werden kann, wenn Expertinnen und Experten der Digitalen Geisteswissenschaften eng mit Historikerinnen und Historikern zusammenarbeiten[4]. Konkret: Wenn die Expertise der »Abteilung Deutsche Reichstagsakten. Reichsversammlungen 1556–1662« und diejenige des Grazer Instituts »Zentrum für Informationsmodellierung«[5] gebündelt wird. Im Rahmen dieses Vorhabens veranstalteten wir im April 2022 in Graz eine internationale und interdisziplinäre Tagung, um uns mit Kolleginnen und Kollegen über Arbeitserfahrungen auszutauschen und Projektergebnisse mit ihnen zu diskutieren[6]. Dieser Band dokumentiert deren Beiträge. Finanziert wurde unser Gedankenaustausch von der Historische Kommission bei der Bayerischen Akademie der Wissenschaften, die die Edition der »Deutschen Reichstagsakten« seit 1858 und diejenige der Abteilung »Reichs-

---

1 *Hiltmann*, Medienwandel.
2 Professuren für Digital Humanities | DHd-Blog: https://www.historikerverband.de/mitglieder/arbeitsgruppen/ag-digitale-geschichtswissenschaft/ (01.02.2024); vgl. auch *Zey*, Edieren.
3 Z.B. *Schwob/Kranich-Hofbauer/Suntinger*, Historische Edition und Computer; *Thaller*, Reproduktion, Erschließung, Edition, Interpretation; *Sahle*, Digitales Archiv – Digitale Edition; *Price*, Edition, Project, Database, Archive, Thematic Research Collection. Eine Übersicht über die Frühgeschichte der digitalen Edition geben auch *Sahle*, Digitale Editionsformen, Teil II, S. 1–124.
4 Einen Überblick über die DH in der Frühneuzeitforschung geben: *Estill/Jakacki/Ullyot*, Early Modern Studies After the Digital Turn; *Loffman/Phillips* (Hg.), Handbook of Editing Early Modern Texts.
5 Ab 1. August 2024: »Institut für Digitale Geisteswissenschaften«.
6 *Brantner/Rammer*, Tagungsbericht.

versammlungen« seit 1986 verantwortet, und von der Karl-Franzens-Universität Graz (Vizerektorat für Forschung).

In nuce spiegelt die Editionsgeschichte der »Reichsversammlungen 1556–1662« den »Weg ins Digitale« wider. Er kann als Weg von medialer zu konzeptioneller Digitalität beschrieben werden[7]. Noch unter der Abteilungsleitung Maximilian Lanzinners (bis 2014) wurden mit der digitalisierten Edition des Reichstages von 1556/57 erste Schritte gesetzt. Dabei handelt es sich um eine hybride, d. h. als Druckmanuskript erarbeitete und als Buch 2013 publizierte, 2014 online im Open Access zur Verfügung gestellte Edition. Mit einer solchen Editionsform verbunden sind viele Vorteile des Digitalen – Zugänglichkeit, Recherchierbarkeit, Hypertextualität –, um nur einige zu nennen, doch von der Pfadabhängigkeit des gedruckten Buches vermag sich ein der medialen Digitalität verpflichtetes Edieren nicht zu lösen. Anders die digitale Edition, wie wir sie in unserem Pilotprojekt erarbeitet haben[8].

Digitale Editionen konzeptualisieren Edieren immer noch als bewährten wissenschaftlichen Standards gehorchendes Bearbeiten von – im Falle des Reichstages und anderer Ständeversammlungen – Texten (transkribieren, kollationieren, kommentieren etc.), aber nicht mehr nur. Die auf uns gekommenen, textlich verfassten materiellen Substrate der europäischen kirchlich-politischen Beratungskultur werden zu Datenstrukturen. Diese Datenorientierung nötigt zu formalisierten sowie zu definitorisch eindeutigen, menschen- wie maschinenlesbaren Beschreibungen der Quellen, und sie macht Textfassungen, Dokumentationen und Register zu Datenbanken. Konzeptioneller Digitalität verpflichtete Editionen können zudem von einem Textverständnis ausgehen, das über die Abbildung des wörtlich Gesagten in geschriebenem Text hinausgeht. Sie können Schriftlichkeit sowohl in ihrer Dokumenthaftigkeit und Visualität selbst der Erklärung zugänglich machen als auch die in den Texten vermittelten Informationen[9]. So z. B., wenn die Grenzen der gedruckten Edition aufgebrochen werden und Quellenmaterial nicht nur integraler (Volltext) und umfänglicher, sondern auch vielgestaltiger, z. B. als Faksimiles, repräsentiert wird und damit verschiedenartigeren Erkenntnisinteressen Rechnung tragen kann. Schließlich – last, but not least – erlaubt ein so verstandenes digitales Edieren den Bearbeiterinnen und Bearbeitern, die gerade im Archiv- und Bibliotheksbereich immer umfänglicher zur Verfügung stehenden digitalen Daten wie Faksimiles und Metadaten in die Edition zu integrieren sowie die eigenen Daten

---

7 Editorische Einführung: https://gams.uni-graz.at/o:rta1576.bt2563p2 (01.02.2024); vgl. auch *Hiltmann*, Medienwandel, v. a. S. 35 (Schaubild), sowie *Sahle*, Digitale Editionsformen, v. a. Teil II, S. 148–155.
8 https://gams.uni-graz.at/context:rta1576 (01.02.2024).
9 *Sahle*, Digitale Editionsformen, Teil III, S. 45–60 hat die Pluralität der Textdimensionen in einem radförmigen Diagramm zu beschreiben versucht, das »Textrad«, das inhaltliche, werkhaft-strukturelle, generell linguistische, konkret verschriftlichte, dokumentarische und visuell zeichenhafte Eigenschaften von Text zu fassen versucht.

mit den Methoden des Semantic Web anzureichern[10]. Indem sie so verfahren, erarbeiten sie sog. assertive Editionen[11], d. h. Editionen, die von den Texten vermittelte Inhalte als hochstrukturierte Daten an die Texte anfügen. Im Semantic Web wird die eigene Edition mit anderen Datenbanken verbunden, die wiederum ihrerseits, vice versa, die eigenen Projektdaten nachnutzen können.

Für Nutzerinnen und Nutzer potenzieren digitale Editionen die bereits digitalisierten Editionen gegenüber dem Buch eignenden Vorteile, vor allem was die Recherchierbarkeit betrifft. Doch dies begründet nicht die qualitative Andersartigkeit dieser editorischen Praxis. Deren grundsätzliche Verschiedenheit liegt darin, dass der editorische Inhalt transmedial abstrahiert wird und damit qualitativ neue Nutzungsmöglichkeiten eröffnet, auch wenn die Edition immer noch in einer, an altüberkommene Rezeptionsmodi anschließenden Form begegnet. Diese Aneignungspraktiken lassen in der Wahrnehmung der Rezipierenden zunächst den Bildschirm zu einer, um nützliche Features (Hyperlinks, Pop-ups etc.) erweiterten, digitalen Buchseite werden (Präsentationsebene). Doch nun sind Inhalte auch in ihrer abstrakteren, aus der Perspektive der Nutzenden betrachtet: voraussetzungsvolleren, Form als standardisiert beschriebene digitale Daten präsent. Diese Datenebene ist Software zugänglich und erschließt sich deshalb nur der- bzw. demjenigen, die bzw. der die entsprechenden Programme beherrscht, mit denen man z. B. die Auszeichnungssprache XML (eXtensible Markup Language) und die in den Standards der Textkodierung der Text Encoding Initiative (TEI) erfassten Daten auslesen und verarbeiten kann. XML wie TEI gewährleisten dabei die Langzeittauglichkeit der Editionsdaten, da sie quelloffen dokumentierte Standards sind und die Dateien in einem einfachen Textformat vorliegen. Sie erfüllen damit die Nachnutzbarkeitsanforderungen der FAIR-Prinzipien[12]. Wer über mehr als rudimentäre Kenntnisse dieser Technologien verfügt und sich des methodischen Instrumentariums der DH zu bedienen vermag, dem eröffnen sich dergestalt ganz neue Optionen im Umgang mit dem Edierten. Sie oder er kann die Daten z. B. über Schnittstellen oder in Form von Databankauszügen, in seine eigene digitale Arbeitsumgebung integrieren und für seine Forschungsfragen fruchtbar machen, die auch ganz unabhängig vom ursprünglichen inhaltlichen Entstehungszusammenhang der Daten sein können.

Der Grazer Gedankenaustausch verfolgte mehrere Ziele. Ein Ziel war es, Forscherinnen und Forscher zusammenzubringen, die, in interdisziplinärem Dialog, das Forschungsfeld beleuchten, dem die erarbeitete digitale Edition inhaltlich zuzurechnen ist, d. i. die Geschichte politischer Mitsprache im vormodernen Europa.

---

10 Zur Bedeutung des Semantic Web für geschichtswissenschaftliche Daten und Editionen vgl. *Ciula/Spence/Monteiro Viera*, Expressing complex associations; *Wettlaufer*, Semantic Web und digitale Editionen; *Beretta*, Making data FAIR; *Borek* u. a., Technical and Methodological Foundations of Digital Indexing; *Vogeler*, The ›Assertive Edition‹; *Heßbrüggen-Walter*, Tatsachen im semantischen Web; *Hinkelmanns*, Semantic Web; das KONDE Weißbuch (https://www.digitale-edition.at/ [01.02.2024]) liefert generell einen guten und knappen Zugang zu Fachtermini der DH.
11 *Vogeler*, The ›Assertive Edition‹.
12 *Wilkinson* u. a., The FAIR Guiding Principles.

Das andere bestand darin, die eigene editorische Arbeit als editorische Arbeit zu kontextualisieren, indem aktuelle Editionsvorhaben, die in den gleichen raum-zeitlichen Zusammenhang gehören wie die »Reichsversammlungen«, präsentiert und diskutiert wurden. Ganz besonders wichtig war uns, dass, was die inhaltliche Seite des Themas betrifft, Expertise aus ganz verschiedenen europäischen Ländern in unsere Gespräche eingebracht wurde. Denn jeder und jedem, die sich mit Fragen politischer Teilhabe beschäftigt oder der editorisch arbeitet, ist bewusst, wie national geprägte Deutungs- und Editionstraditionen einer integraleren Sicht auf die Erscheinungsformen von Mitsprache im frühneuzeitlichen Europa entgegenstehen[13]. Nicht zuletzt in dieser Hinsicht scheinen uns die neuen digitalen Möglichkeiten ein erhebliches Potential zu bieten, das wir ausloten wollten.

Am Ende der Tagung waren sich die Tagungsteilnehmerinnen und -teilnehmer einig, dass sich dieses Ausloten gelohnt hat, aber auch darin, dass es sich dabei nur um einen ersten, vielversprechenden Schritt in die richtige Richtung handelt. Richtig erschien uns die Richtung deswegen, weil deutlich wurde, wie ertragreich der Einsatz des Werkzeugkastens der DH für das frühneuzeitliche Quellenmaterial ist, aber auch wie unterschiedlich er gehandhabt wird und welches Potential daher intensiverem Erfahrungsaustausch zukommen könnte. Auch deswegen waren wir überzeugt, auf dem richtigen Weg zu sein, weil in unseren Diskussionen deutlich wurde, was die Prämisse der gesamten Tagung war: Forschen und Edieren stellen zwei Seiten einer Medaille dar. Hat doch die vergleichende Betrachtung digitaler Editionspraxis, präziser: die Notwendigkeit formalisierter Beschreibung, ein fundamentales Defizit historiographischen Bemühens um die Foren politischer Mitsprache im frühneuzeitlichen Europa offengelegt. Es mangelt an einem – kollaborativ zu erarbeitenden – kontrollierten Vokabular, um die phänomenologisch vielfältigen Erscheinungsformen, in denen politische Mitsprache in der Frühen Neuzeit begegnet, kategorial zu fassen und in einer transnationalen Perspektive beschreiben zu können.

Würde im Rahmen künftigen editorischen Arbeitens die Beseitigung dieses Defizits in Angriff genommen, so könnte es zu einem Kristallisationskern werden, um länderübergreifende Forschungsgemeinschaft zu verstetigen. Der Konjunktiv freilich ist bewusst gewählt. Denn eine Conditio sine qua non eines solchen Unterfangens ist, dass die Entscheidungsträgerinnen und -träger, sei es an Universitäten, sei es bei Akademien oder Forschungsförderern, bereit sind, die notwendigen Mittel für Kooperationen zur Verfügung zu stellen. Dass dies im Zeichen knapper Kassen schwierig ist, ist einer der roten Fäden, der sich durch zahlreiche Beiträge zieht. Doch die Aufsätze verdeutlichen auch, dass gerade die neuen Wege, die eine dem Digital-first verpflichtete editorische Herangehensweise eröffnet, die Chance bietet, aus dem Konjunktiv einen Indikativ zu machen.

Die ersten beiden Beiträge nähern sich, aus ganz unterschiedlichen Perspektiven, der Aufgabe, Phänomene politischer Mitsprache analytisch neu zu kon-

---

13 Vgl. neben den Literaturnachweisen in den Beiträgen von Kewes und Neu jetzt auch *Blockmans*, Political Participation before the Revolutions.

zeptualisieren. *Paulina Kewes*, PI der Oxforder Forschungsgruppe »Recovering Europe's Parliamentary Culture, 1500–1700« untersucht an einem Fallbeispiel, das mit Jean Bodins »Les Six Livres de la République« (auch) in das Frankreich des Jahres 1576 führt, die transnationale Dimension der parlamentarischen Beratungskultur der Vormoderne, die zwar Bodin, die längste Zeit jedoch nicht der Forschung selbstverständlich war. *Tim Neu* stellt sich der identischen Herausforderung, indem er methodologische Überlegungen zum Ausgangspunkt seines Nachdenkens macht und vorschlägt, parlamentarische Beratungsforen als »Teilhabegefüge« zu charakterisieren. Dieser Begriff, so sein Argument, erlaube es, das in Alltags- wie Wissenschaftssprache überfrachtete Repräsentationskonzept ad acta zu legen und durch das Konzept der assemblage/Assemblage zu ersetzen. Dessen erkenntnisförderndes Potential liege darin begründet, dass es den Fokus auf die Art und Weise lenke, wie aus heterogenen Elementen, Menschen wie Dingen, Neues, ein Gefüge, werde, und dass es damit das Erklärte und das der Erklärung Bedürftige nicht verwechsle.

Beispielhaft stehen beide Artikel dafür, wie unterschiedlich die wissenschaftlichen Suchbewegungen nach einem neuen »Sehepunkt« sind, der eine integralere Sicht auf die lateineuropäische Versammlungskultur eröffnet, als sie einer geschichts- wie sozialwissenschaftlichen Forschung möglich war, die primär an der Funktion der Stände im Prozess der Staatsbildung interessiert war und ist. Die beiden Abhandlungen veranschaulichen demzufolge die Dynamik des Forschungsfeldes, aber auch das, was den Tagungsteilnehmerinnen und -teilnehmern durch zwei Tagungsvorträge, die hier leider nicht als schriftliche Ausarbeitungen dokumentiert werden können, noch offenkundiger war[14] – Forschungen zur Geschichte politischer Mitsprache in der Frühen Neuzeit konstituieren ein Forschungsfeld, aber sie haben bis dato kein Forschungsgefüge hervorgebracht. Einen der vielen Gründe, warum dem so ist, gibt der Beitrag von Tim Neu zu erkennen, der ein Teilkapitel mit »Spekulationen: Teilhabegefüge und Editionsprojekte« übertitelt. Edieren und Forschen erscheinen hier als allenfalls locker gekoppelte, wissenschaftsintern unterschiedlich prämierte Modi geisteswissenschaftlicher Erkenntnisproduktion. Gerade die Editionsgeschichte der Reichstagsakten aber, die den Reichstag editorisch erschufen, lange bevor er existierte[15], belehrt eines Besseren. Editorische Arbeit kann nur gelingen, wenn sie um Forschungskonzepte weiß, und diese sind, umgekehrt, maßgeblich davon geprägt, welche Materialien in Editionen bereitgestellt werden und welche nicht.

Dass gerade konzeptionelle Digitalität die Chance eröffnet, beide Manifestationen geisteswissenschaftlicher Grundlagenforschung neu zueinander in Beziehung zu setzen, haben wir zuvor argumentiert. Die in diesem Band versammelten Bei-

---

14 Zu einer Ausarbeitung ihrer Vorträge sahen sich leider Rachel Renault (Le Mans), Europäische Versammlungskultur und politische Repräsentation. Ein Vergleich der französisch- und deutschsprachigen Historiographie, und Lars Behrisch (Utrecht/Berlin), The Genesis of Democracy in Early Modern Europe, außerstande.

15 Hierzu immer noch, wenn auch in manchem Detail überholt, *Moraw*, Versuch über die Entstehung des Reichstags.

träge zeigen aber auch die damit einhergehenden Herausforderungen, die zugleich die Herausforderungen der alltäglichen Projektarbeit waren und vom Herausgeberteam dieses Bandes sowie den anderen Projektmitarbeiterinnen und -mitarbeitern[16] herausragend bewältigt wurden. Akzentuieren die folgenden Beiträge doch das Spannungsfeld zwischen Editionsgegenstand, -praxis und den, dem Digital-first-Prinzip entsprechenden, digitalen Werkzeugen ganz unterschiedlich. Diese Akzentuierungen künden von den unterschiedlichen Expertisen der Autorinnen und Autoren (Philologie, Geschichtswissenschaft, Informatik), davon, dass geschichtswissenschaftliches digitales Arbeiten nur einen Teilaspekt geisteswissenschaftlicher Digitalität darstellt, und vor allem davon, dass es einer kontinuierlichen, engen und vertrauensvollen Zusammenarbeit bedarf, um konzeptionelle Digitalität erfolgreich zu operationalisieren.

Vor diesem Hintergrund ordnete der zweite Teil der Tagung und ordnet der erste Teil dieses Sammelbandes die editorische Arbeit des Projektes (*Roman Bleier, Josef Leeb, Eva Ortlieb, Florian Zeilinger*) in die aktuelle Editionslandschaft zur Geschichte politischer Mitsprache im frühneuzeitlichen Europa ein. Auch hier wurde und konnte nur exemplarisch verfahren werden. Es war uns aber daran gelegen, den (nord-)westeuropäischen Bias ständegeschichtlicher Forschung nicht zu reproduzieren. Demzufolge ist sowohl die komplexe Ständelandschaft der Herrscher (und auch einer Herrscherin) des Hauses Österreich (*Petr Maťa*) und der polnische Sejm (*Krzysztof Fokt, Maciej Mikuła*) repräsentiert als auch das englische Parlament (*Paul Seaward*) und die Niederländischen Generalstaaten (*Rik Hoekstra, Marijn Koolen, Joris Oddens, Ronald Sluijter*). Alle Beiträge geben zu erkennen, dass, auch und gerade editorisches Bemühen, gesellschaftliche Mitsprache(ansprüche) in ihrer historischen Tiefendimension zu dokumentieren, weit in die geschichtliche Zeit zurück reicht – im Falle der Ständevertretungen der Habsburgermonarchie und des Reichstages bis in die Mitte des 19. Jahrhunderts. In diesen beiden Geschichtslandschaften sind die Anfänge der Editionsgeschichte, die Institutionalisierung der Geschichtswissenschaft als eigenständige Wissenschaftsdisziplin und kulturelle Nationsbildungsprozesse unauflöslich miteinander verwoben[17]. Ganz unterschiedlich aber ist diese Longue Durée des Edierens in der Gegenwart präsent.

In den Nachfolgestaaten der Habsburgermonarchie ist das wissenschaftliche Edieren de facto abgebrochen. Eine Situation, die es auch erlaubt, neue, die Möglichkeiten des Digitalen ausschöpfende Perspektiven aufzuzeigen, wie sie z.B. unter dem Begriff »Protoedition« angedacht sind[18]. Demgegenüber ist das bisher im Druck Publizierte, in mehr oder weniger großem Umfang, die Basis gegenwärtig erarbeiteter digitaler Editionen. So bilden für den polnischen Sejm, das englische Parlament sowie die Niederländischen Generalstaaten die gedruckten Akten den Ausgangspunkt ihrer Arbeit. Jedoch in ganz unterschiedlichen, nicht sachlich, sondern in den verfügbaren materiellen Ressourcen begründeten digitalen Repräsentationsformen.

---

16 https://gams.uni-graz.at/o:rta1576.bt4354p1 (01.02.2024).
17 *Wolgast*, Deutsche Reichstagsakten.
18 *Vogeler*, Edition – Protoedition – Reproduktion.

Als durchsuchbare, größtenteils hinter einer Paywall befindliche PDFs im Falle des englischen Parlamentes, als hybride Edition im Falle des Reichstages (seit 2014) und als digitale Editionen im Falle des Sejms, der Generalstaaten und, nun auch, des Reichstages. Anschaulich illustriert der Beitrag zu den Generalstaaten die Entwicklung der Digitalen Geisteswissenschaften. Zunächst als rein gedruckte Edition konzipiert, wird die Edition der Beschlüsse seit 1998 als XML kodierte Texte in Verbindung mit einer relationalen Datenbank für die Erschließung erstellt. Das Corpus (1576–1796) ist jedoch immens: allein die Zeit bis 1624 umfasst 21 Bände, sodass die Autoren des Beitrags mit einer Größenordnung von einer Million Beschlüsse rechnen, die insgesamt zu edieren sind. Zunehmend kommen deshalb automatische Verfahren zum Einsatz, mit denen die Texte transkribiert, strukturiert und erschlossen werden. Sie können dabei auf den formelhaften Texten aufbauen, die für die historische Auswertung uninteressant zu sein scheinen, für die automatische Erschließung aber einen sehr guten Ansatz bieten. Mit ihrem inkrementellen Ansatz zeigen sie zugleich einen der fundamentalen Unterschiede digitalen und analogen Edierens auf, d. i. seine Dynamik, Offenheit und Adaptierbarkeit an sich wandelnde Erkenntnisinteressen. Diese aber gestalten sich momentan, wie die Beiträge zeigen, vielgestaltig, wobei den Ergebnissen des gemeinsamen Beratens die besondere Aufmerksamkeit gilt, und weniger dem, unserem Herangehen zugrundeliegenden Interesse an deren Her- und Darstellung. Beide Herangehensweisen, diejenige, die in diachronem Längsschnitt eine einzelne Form parlamentarischer Schriftlichkeit fokussiert, wie diejenige, die das Zelebrieren und Deliberieren eines einzelnen Versammlungsereignisses integral digital abbilden möchte, liefern die Probe aufs Exempel dessen, was zuvor als national(staatlich) geprägte Editionstraditionen apostrophiert wurde. Dass sich beide Annäherungen in einer, sich vom Nationalstaatlichen lösenden Betrachtungsperspektive wechselseitig befruchten könnten, steht außer Zweifel.

Außer Zweifel steht aber auch – und dies verbindet die Beiträge des zweiten Teils mit denen des vorigen –, dass das forschungsgeleitete Erkenntnisinteresse für Form und Umfang der Datenmodellierung ausschlaggebend ist, divergieren doch das Wünschenswerte und das Machbare, wie *Andreas Wagner* explizit und damit auch trefflich unsere eigene Arbeitserfahrung beschreibt. Die in diesem Abschnitt präsentierten Abhandlungen stehen einmal mehr in einem zeitlichen, so die Anhalt-Tagebücher (*Ronald Asch*) und die Reiseberichte Hainhofers (*Martin de la Iglesia*), einmal mehr in einem inhaltlichen Zusammenhang, so die Editionen der frühneuzeitlichen Religionsfrieden (*Andreas Zecherle/Kevin Wunsch*) und Rechtstexte (*Andreas Wagner*), mit dem Gegenstandsbereich der »Reichsversammlungen«. Was sie von den Editionen zum vormodernen Parlamentarismus unterscheidet, ist, dass ihre Vorgeschichte allenfalls ins ausgehende 20. Jahrhundert zurückreicht. Pfadabhängigkeiten bei der Quellenerschließung, sei es handschriftlicher oder gedruckter Quellen, sind bei diesen Projekten daher in wesentlich geringerem Umfang gegeben als bei den Editionen zum vormodernen Parlamentarismus. Zugleich sind sie, vergleichend mit den Editionsvorhaben des ersten Teiles betrachtet, inhaltlich heterogener und methodisch homogener. Liegt ihre inhaltliche Heterogenität in der Natur der Sache begründet, d. i. in der Art und Weise, wie wir die Tagung und damit diesen Sammelband konzeptualisierten, so handelt es sich bei allen vorgestellten Arbeitsvorhaben um solche, die ihre Inhalte in einem dem Digital-first verpflichteten Zugriff erschließen. Anders formuliert: Zu Beginn des dritten Jahrzehnts des 21. Jahrhunderts ist datenorientiertes, sich der Instrumentarien des Semantic Web bedienendes wissenschaftliches Edieren in interdisziplinärer Zusammenarbeit State of the Art. Die für den fruchtbaren wissenschaftlichen Austausch nötigen Standards sind aber noch eher basal: Die TEI und die Verwendung von Normdatenreferenzen, z. B. auf die Gemeinsame Normdatei (GND), liefern eine gute Grundlage, sind aber vielfach für die spezifischen Anforderungen einer geschichtswissenschaftlichen Edition zu allgemein. So haben Normdaten einen bibliothekarischen Bias und die TEI hat sich lange eher auf literaturwissenschaftliche Textgattungen konzentriert.

Unterschiedlich wiederum fällt die Gewichtung der inhaltlichen wie digitalen Seite des Edierens bei den einzelnen Autoren und der Autorin aus, die ihre Vorhaben skizzieren. Für Christian II. von Anhalt und das Augsburger Interim von 1548 geben die Verfasser Einblicke in erste historische Forschungsergebnisse, die durch die digitale Edition systematischer sind und zu einem früheren Zeitpunkt der editorischen Arbeit möglich werden. Dass die Rezeption solcher Ergebnisse jedoch stets menschlicher Datenkritik unterworfen sein muss, denn es sind Menschen, die – bei frühneuzeitlichen Quellen vielfach in mühevoller Handarbeit – mit ihren Auszeichnungsgrundsätzen die Ergebnisse präformieren, auch das verdeutlicht die Lektüre der Artikel. Ermutigend auch die Einblicke, die die Beiträge in gelungenes Communitybuilding geben, d. h. eine regelmäßige, dauerhafte projekt- und disziplinenübergreifende Zusammenarbeit entlang bestimmter Gegenstandsbereiche, die das Potenzial konzeptioneller Digitalität nicht nur, wie auf unserer Tagung, punktuell, sondern nachhaltig fruchtbar macht.

Gleichsam als schließende Klammer rufen die Ausführungen *Martin Hugs und Linda Kirstens* zum »Deutschen Textarchiv« eine Gemeinsamkeit aller in diesem Sammelband präsentierten Editionsprojekte auf. Denn es sind Texte, die in ganz verschiedenen medialen wie textuellen Manifestationsformen auf uns gekommen sind, die editorisch bearbeitet werden. Das »Deutsche Textarchiv«, das als Referenzkorpus (auch) für die frühneuzeitliche deutsche Sprache firmiert, blickt seinerseits auf eine, inzwischen mehr als 15 Jahre währende Projektgeschichte zurück, vor allem aber ist es als Mitglied des Konsortiums Text+ der bundesrepublikanischen Nationalen Forschungsdateninfrastruktur (NFDI) in die Weiterentwicklung maschineller Texterkennung involviert. Dass sich hieraus, auch und gerade für geschichtswissenschaftliches Arbeiten mit frühneuzeitlichen Quellen, grundstürzende Optionen eröffnen könn(t)en, steht außer Zweifel[19]. Und auch die historisch arbeitenden Wissenschaften haben jüngst im Data-for-History-Konsortium[20] die Kommunikation über geteilte Datenmodelle begonnen. Den vormodernen Parlamentarismus

---

19 *Hodel*, Konsequenzen der Handschriftenerkennung und des maschinellen Lernens.
20 https://dataforhistory.org (01.02.2024).

zum Bestandteil dieser Überlegungen zu machen, ist daher eine Zukunftsaufgabe, die mit der Ontologie unseres Projektes[21] und dem in diesem Band dokumentierten Ertrag unserer Tagung hoffentlich einen Anfang genommen hat. Es bleibt also spannend.

Literaturverzeichnis

Beretta, Francesco: A challenge for historical research: making data FAIR using a collaborative ontology management environment (OntoME), in: Semantic Web, 12/2 (2021), o.S., https://doi.org/10.3233/SW-200416 (01.02.2024).

Blockmans, Wim: The Voice of the People? Political Participation before the Revolutions, übers. v. Michiel Horn, London 2024.

Borek, Arkadiusz u. a.: Technical and Methodological Foundations of Digital Indexing of Medieval and Early Modern Court Books, in: Digital Scholarship in the Humanities 35/2 (2020), S. 233–53, https://doi.org/10.1093/llc/fqz030 (01.02.2024).

Brantner, Elisabeth/Rammer, Constanze Maria: Tagungsbericht: Neue Wege der Edition frühneuzeitlicher Ständeversammlungen. Aktuelle geschichtswissenschaftliche Konzeptualisierungen ständischer Teilhabe und digitale Methoden, in: H-Soz-Kult, 2022, o.S., www.hsozkult.de/conferencereport/id/fdkn-129909 (01.02.2024).

Ciula, Arianna/Spence, Paul/Monteiro Viera, Jose Miguel: Expressing complex associations in medieval historical documents: The Henry III Fine Rolls Project, in: Literary and Linguistic Computing 23/3 (2008), S. 311–325.

Estill, Laura/Jakacki, Diane K./Ullyot, Michael: Early Modern Studies After the Digital Turn, 502. Medieval and Renaissance Texts and Studies, Toronto/Ontario 2016.

Haug-Moritz, Gabriele/Vogeler, Georg/Ortlieb, Eva/Zeilinger, Florian: PPAC-Datenmodell, in: *Josef Leeb/Christiane Neerfeld/Eva Ortlieb/Florian Zeilinger/Roman Bleier (Bearb.)*, Der Reichstag zu Regensburg 1576, hg. v. Gabriele Haug-Moritz/Georg Vogeler, Graz 2023, https://gams.uni-graz.at/o:rta1576.bt7825dm1 (01.02.2024).

Heßbrüggen-Walter, Stefan: Tatsachen im semantischen Web: Nanopublikationen in den digitalen Geisteswissenschaften?, in: Historyblogosphere. Bloggen in den Geschichtswissenschaften, Berlin/Boston 2013, S. 149–159, https://doi.org/10.1524/9783486755732.149 (01.02.2024).

Hiltmann, Torsten: Vom Medienwandel zum Methodenwandel: Die fortschreitende Digitalisierung und ihre Konsequenzen für die Geschichtswissenschaften in historischer Perspektive, in: *Karoline Dominika Döring u. a. (Hg.)*, Digital History: Konzepte, Methoden und Kritiken Digitaler Geschichtswissenschaft, Berlin/Boston 2022, S. 13–44, https://doi.org/10.1515/9783110757101-002 (01.02.2024).

Hinkelmanns, Peter: Semantic Web, in: *Helmut W. Klug (Hg.)*, KONDE Weißbuch, 2021, o.S., https://hdl.handle.net/11471/562.50.167 (01.02.2024), PID: o:konde.167.

Hodel, Tobias: Konsequenzen der Handschriftenerkennung und des maschinellen Lernens für die Geschichtswissenschaft. Anwendung, Einordnung und Methodenkritik, in: Historische Zeitschrift 316/1 (2023), S. 151–180, https://doi.org/10.1515/hzhz-2023-0006 (01.02.2024).

Loffman, Claire/Phillips, Harriet (Hg.): A Handbook of Editing Early Modern Texts, New York/London 2018.

Moraw, Peter: Versuch über die Entstehung des Reichstags, in: *Gabriele Haug-Moritz (Hg.)*, Verfassungsgeschichte des Alten Reiches, Stuttgart 2014, S. 133–170.

---

21 Haug-Moritz u. a., PPAC-Datenmodell.

Price, Kenneth M.: Edition, Project, Database, Archive, Thematic Research Collection. What's in a Name?, in: Digital Humanities Quarterly 3/3 (2009), o.S., http://digitalhumanities.org/dhq/vol/3/3/000053/000053.html (01.02.2024).

Sahle, Patrick: Digitales Archiv – Digitale Edition. Anmerkungen zur Begriffsklärung, in: *Michael Stolz u. a. (Hg.)*, Literatur und Literaturwissenschaft auf dem Weg zu den neuen Medien. Eine Standortbestimmung, Zürich 2007, S. 64–84 (= Literaturwissenschaft und neue Medien, Bd. 1).

Ders.: Digitale Editionsformen, Teil I: Das typografische Erbe, Teil II: Befunde, Theorie und Methodik, Teil III: Textbegriffe und Recodierung, Norderstedt 2013 (= Schriften des Instituts für Dokumentologie und Editorik), urn:nbn:de:hbz:38-53510, 8 = urn:nbn:de:hbz:38-53523, 9 = urn:nbn:de:hbz:38-53534 (01.02.2024).

Schwob, Anton/Kranich-Hofbauer, Karin/Suntinger, Diethard: Historische Edition und Computer. Möglichkeiten und Probleme interdisziplinärer Textverarbeitung und Textbearbeitung. Berichte von der Internationalen Tagung »Historische Edition und Computer«, Karl-Franzens-Universität Graz, 26.–30. Oktober 1988, Graz 1989.

Thaller, Manfred: Reproduktion, Erschließung, Edition, Interpretation. Ihre Beziehungen in einer digitalen Welt, in: *Brigitte Merta/Andrea Sommerlechner/Herwig Weigl (Hg.)*, Vom Nutzen des Edierens. Akten des internationalen Kongresses zum 150-jährigen Bestehen des Instituts für Österreichische Geschichtsforschung, 3.–5. Juni 2004, Wien/München 2005, S. 205–227.

Vogeler, Georg: The ›Assertive Edition‹, in: International Journal of Digital Humanities 1/2 (2019), S. 309–22, https://doi.org/10.1007/s42803-019-00025-5 (01.02.2024).

Ders.: Edition – Protoedition – Reproduktion: Der digitale Wandel, in: Geschichte in Wissenschaft und Unterricht 73/9–10 (2022), S. 498–511.

Wettlaufer, Jörg: Der nächste Schritt? Semantic Web und digitale Editionen, in: *Roland S. Kamzelak/Timo Steyer (Hg.)*, Digitale Metamorphose: Digital Humanities und Editionswissenschaft, 2, 2018, o.S. (= Zeitschrift für digitale Geschichtswissenschaften, Sonderbd. 1), http://zfdg.de/sb002_007 (01.02.2024).

Wilkinson, Mark D. u. a.: The FAIR Guiding Principles for Scientific Data Management and Stewardship, in: Scientific Data 3/1 (2016), Nr. 160018, https://doi.org/10.1038/sdata.2016.18 (01.02.2024).

Wolgast, Eike: Deutsche Reichstagsakten, in: *Lothar Gall (Hg.)*, ... für deutsche Geschichts- und Quellenforschung. 150 Jahre Historische Kommission bei der Bayerischen Akademie der Wissenschaften, München 2008, S. 79–120.

Zey, Claudia: Edieren ohne Ende? Editionen im Wandel am Beispiel der 200-jährigen Geschichte der Monumenta Germaniae Historica, in: SAGW-Bulletin 3/21 (Edieren/Éditer) (2021), S. 66–69.

Praxisbeispiele I:
Foren politischer Mitsprache
im frühneuzeitlichen Europa

Tim Neu (Wien)

Teilhabegefüge, oder: Wie lässt sich die europäische Beratungskultur der Vormoderne konzeptionell fassen (und was könnte daraus für Editionsprojekte folgen)?

Man könnte sich die Sache sehr einfach machen. Man könnte auf die Frage, wie sich die europäische Beratungskultur der Vormoderne konzeptionell fassen lässt, einfach antworten: Sie lässt sich gar nicht auf den Begriff bringen. Für eine solche Antwort könnte man sich beispielsweise auf eine bis heute vielzitierte Formulierung von Günter Birtsch berufen, der 1969 von der »Definitionsfeindlichkeit des Ständischen« sprach und statt Definition vielmehr »Differenzierung« als »eigentliches Lebenselement« des politischen Ständetums in Anschlag brachte[1]. Und noch 2001 eröffnete Michael Graves seine einschlägige Monographie mit dem Witz, die einzigen beiden Konstanten der frühneuzeitlichen Parlamentarismusgeschichte seien »variety in kind« und »variability over time«[2]. Würden sich die europäischen Ständeversammlungen also aufgrund ihrer ja unbestreitbaren empirischen Vielfältigkeit und Unterschiedlichkeit tatsächlich nicht konzeptionell fassen lassen, dann erübrigte sich auch die zweite im Titel dieses Beitrags aufgeworfene Frage nach möglichen Folgen für Editionsprojekte. So leicht aber kann man es sich eben nicht machen, denn wie schon Max Weber wusste: »*Scharfe* Scheidung ist in der Realität oft nicht möglich, klare *Begriffe* sind aber dann deshalb nur umso nötiger.«[3]

Die Tagungssektion, aus der dieser Beitrag hervorgegangen ist, trug den Titel »Ständeversammlungen und Parlamente: Aktuelle Forschungsperspektiven«. Dementsprechend werde ich mich im Folgenden zunächst dem Forschungsstand zuwenden und ihn unter Zuhilfenahme der formalen Unterscheidung von Funktionen und Funktionsweisen aufschließen (I.). Perspektiviert man auf diese Weise, so werde

---

1   *Birtsch*, Die landständische Verfassung als Gegenstand der Forschung, S. 42; zitiert etwa in *Bahlcke*, Landtagsakten, S. 357; *Krüger*, Die landständische Verfassung, S. 65; *Moraw*, Stand und Perspektiven der Ständeforschung, S. 5; *Buchholz*, Öffentliche Finanzen, S. 4; *Rühl*, Das ›freie Mandat‹, S. 26; *Fenske*, Der moderne Verfassungsstaat, S. 41.
2   *Graves*, The Parliaments of Early Modern Europe, S. 1.
3   *Weber*, Wirtschaft und Gesellschaft, S. 451 (Hervorhebung im Original); es handelt sich um ›idealtypische‹ Begriffsbildungen, vgl. *ders.*, Die »Objektivität« sozialwissenschaftlicher und sozialpolitischer Erkenntnis, S. 202–205; zu deren Erkenntnispotential als »counterfactual projection[s]« vgl. in geschichtstheoretischer Hinsicht etwa *Ringer*, Max Weber, S. 174, und in forschungspraktischer Hinsicht etwa *Pohlig*, Marlboroughs Geheimnis, S. 87–97, der am Beispiel der Unterscheidung von Infrastrukturen, Organisationen und Netzwerken ebenfalls deutlich macht, dass gerade die »Zuspitzung« der Begriffe sie überhaupt erst zu »heuristische[n] Instrumenten« macht, »um Abweichungen und Überlappungen überhaupt identifizieren zu können« (ebd., S. 89).

ich anschließend argumentieren, legt der Forschungsstand nahe, dass Ständeversammlungen – die Kernphänomene der europäischen Beratungskultur – stets sowohl instrumentell an der Steuerung des Gemeinwesens und symbolisch an seiner Integration beteiligt waren, und sich beide Dimensionen sinnvollerweise im Begriff der politischen Teilhabe zusammenführen lassen (II.). Drittens werde ich gegen die naheliegende Entscheidung, Ständeversammlungen dann konkret als Institutionen politischer Teilhabe zu fassen, plausibel zu machen versuchen, dass es heuristisch fruchtbarer sein könnte, sie – wie auch schon im Titel angekündigt – als Teilhabegefüge zu konzipieren (III.). Und abschließend werde ich an einem Beispiel kurz anreißen, worin der analytische Mehrwert des Gefügekonzepts besteht und einen sehr spekulativen Ausblick wagen, welche Folgen diese Begriffsarbeit für die Edition frühneuzeitlicher Ständeversammlungen haben könnte (IV.).

I. Forschungsstand: Funktionen und Funktionsweisen

Fragt man zunächst nach dem Forschungsstand, dann ist schon das nicht ohne Probleme möglich, denn welche Forschungsrichtung bzw. geschichtswissenschaftliche Subdisziplin ist hier eigentlich gemeint? Ständeforschung? Die Geschichte politischer Versammlungen (*histoire des assemblées politiques*)? Die Geschichte der Repräsentativinstitutionen (*storia delle istituzioni rappresentative*)? Oder etwa Parlamentsgeschichte (*parliamentary history*)[4]? Und ist die wechselseitige Rezeption von Forschungsergebnissen über staatliche und sprachliche Grenzen hinweg wirklich intensiv genug, um von ›einem‹ Forschungsstand hinsichtlich der europäischen Ständeversammlungen/Parlamente reden zu können[5]? Wim Blockmans hat beispielsweise immer wieder moniert, es gäbe im Grunde kaum wirklich vergleichende Forschung, stattdessen würden einzelne Versammlungen entweder als Ausnahmefälle vom europäischen Kontext isoliert oder im Gegenteil zu paradigmatischen Fällen ›der‹ europäischen Beratungskultur hypostasiert[6].

---

4 Vgl. jeweils zuletzt *Greindl*, Anmerkungen zur jüngeren deutschen Ständeforschung; *Hébert*, La voix du peuple; *Mattone*, Gli studi sulle istituzioni rappresentative in Italia; *Bentley*, Parliamentary History.

5 Zum Zwecke der Zusammenarbeit über politische und sprachliche Grenzen hinweg wurde 1936 auf maßgebliches Betreiben des Belgiers Émile Lousse und des Franzosen François Olivier-Martin die Commission Internationale pour l'Histoire des Assemblées d'États eingerichtet. Die Kommission, heute eher bekannt unter ihrem englischen Namen International Commission for the History of Representative and Parliamentary Institutions (ICHRPI) besteht bis heute und stellt mit ihren Jahrestagungen und der Zeitschrift »Parliaments, Estates & Representation – Parlements, États et Représentation« maßgebliche Infrastrukturen für die Forschungsvernetzung bereit, vgl. *Register*, Commission.

6 Vgl. *Blockmans*, Representation, S. 29, und noch jüngst wieder in *ders.*, Compairing Representative Institutions, S. 15.

Insofern ist es außerordentlich begrüßenswert, dass die vergleichende Forschung in den letzten Jahren wieder im Aufschwung begriffen ist: So haben neben Blockmans selbst etwa auch David Stasavage und Michel Hébert monographische Synthesen vorgelegt[7], denen eine Reihe von Sammelbänden mit europäisch-vergleichenden Perspektiven an die Seite gestellt werden kann[8]. Zudem intensiviert sich auch die wechselseitige Rezeption: So hat beispielsweise das international besetzte Forschungsprojekt »Recovering Europe's Parliamentary Culture, 1500–1700«[9] jüngst ein Blog initiiert, das schon jetzt Beiträge von Forscherinnen und Forschern aus ganz unterschiedlichen Kontexten enthält – darunter auch Beiträge aller bisher namentlich Genannten[10].

Dennoch ist die Forschungslage zu komplex und zu heterogen, als dass sie hier in ihrer Gesamtheit dargestellt werden könnte. Daher werde ich eine Perspektivierung vornehmen, um zumindest ›einen‹ Forschungsstand abbilden zu können, nämlich den Forschungsstand im Hinblick auf die *Funktionen und Funktionsweisen* der europäischen Ständeversammlungen, wobei ich diese hilfreiche Unterscheidung aus einem ebenso aktuellen wie wichtigen Aufsatz von Gabriele Haug-Moritz übernehme[11]. Aus funktionaler Perspektive schaut man auf die Bedeutsamkeit der Ständeversammlungen für andere Zusammenhänge, während eine an Funktionsweisen interessierte Betrachtung die Ständeversammlungen selbst fokussiert und ihre spezifische Eigenlogik ins Zentrum rückt[12]. Wie ein solcherart perspektivierter

---

7   Vgl. *Blockmans*, Medezeggenschap; *Stasavage*, The Decline and Rise of Democracy; *Hébert*, Parlementer.
8   Vgl. etwa *Neu/Sikora/Weller*, Zelebrieren und Verhandeln; *Ihalainen/Ilie/Palonen*, Parliament and Parliamentarism; *Genet/La Page/Mattéoni*, Consensu et représentation; *Hayat/Péneau/Sintomer*, La représentation-incarnation; *Damen/Haemers/Mann*, Political Representation; *Aerts u. a.*, The Ideal of Parliament; *Albareda/Herrero Sánchez*, Political Representation; *Hayat/Péneau/Sintomer*, La représentation avant le gouvernement représentatif; *Szijártó/Blockmans/Kontler*, Parliamentarism in Northern and East-Central Europe.
9   Beteiligt sind neben Projektleiterin Paulina Kewes (Oxford), Steven Gunn (Oxford), Joris Oddens (Amsterdam), Dorota Pietrzyk-Reeves (Krakau), Paul Seaward (London), Tracey Sowerby (Oxford) und Jim van der Meulen (Oxford). Für erste Ergebnisse vgl. *Kewes u. a.*, Early Modern Parliamentary Studies.
10 Vgl. Recovering Europe's Parliamentary Culture, 1500–1700.
11 Vgl. *Haug-Moritz*, Deliberieren, S. 116: »Neukonzeptualisierungen ständischer Institutionen, die weniger an deren Funktionen als an deren Funktionieren interessiert waren und sind, [...]«.
12 Die Einheit der Unterscheidung von Funktionen und Funktionsweisen lässt sich im Anschluss an Norbert Elias darin finden, dass in beiden Fällen auf Interdependenzen abgestellt wird, dies jedoch mit je unterschiedlichem Zuschnitt: Funktionale Perspektiven fragen nach Ständeversammlungen als Elementen in umfassenderen Interdependenzgeflechten (etwa denen der politischen Herrschaft), während nach Funktionsweisen dann gefragt wird, wenn Ständeversammlungen selbst als Interdependenzgeflechte perspektiviert werden, vgl. *Elias*, Was ist Soziologie?, S. 89 f.: »Das Modell weist darauf hin, daß auch der Begriff der Funktion [...] als *Beziehungsbegriff* verstanden werden muss. Von gesellschaftlichen Funktionen kann man nur reden, wenn man es mit mehr oder weniger zwingenden Interdependenzen zu tun hat«, in Verbindung mit *Elias*, Die höfische Gesellschaft, S. 218: »Wenn man bei der Untersuchung geschichtlich-gesellschaftlicher Probleme in Gedanken bei den Handlungen und Entscheidungen einzelner

Forschungsstand aussieht, lässt sich nun eindrücklich an den Beiträgen zum Blog von »Recovering Europe's Parliamentary Culture, 1500–1700« zeigen. Funktionale Analysen gehören nicht nur zu den ältesten Untersuchungsformen in der Erforschung der europäischen Beratungskultur überhaupt, sie erfreuen sich auch bis heute einer ungebrochenen Beliebtheit, zumal im englischen Sprachraum, wie mir scheint. Im Blog wird die funktionale Perspektive etwa von David Stasavage vertreten:

»One of the main reasons that economists and political scientists have shown increasing interest in the early history of European parliaments involves the idea that the presence of these bodies allowed rulers to make credible commitments to not interfere with the affairs of merchants. This could then help lead to good economic outcomes such as growth of incomes and the development of public finance.«[13]

Der größere Zusammenhang, um den es ihm hier geht, ist die Herausbildung öffentlicher Kreditfähigkeit, also ein Entwicklungsprozess bestimmter vormodern-europäischer Gemeinwesen, in dem Parlamenten bzw. Ständeversammlungen angeblich eine Schlüsselfunktion zukam[14]. Andere Fundamentalprozesse, zu denen Ständeversammlungen Leistungen beisteuerten (und das können natürlich auch negative Leistungen sein, wie etwa eine Bremsfunktion), wären etwa Staatsbildung oder Demokratisierung. Es müssen aber nicht nur solche ›großen‹ Prozesse sein: So stellt Stasavage in seiner wichtigen Globalgeschichte der Demokratie beispielsweise fest, dass Ständeversammlungen im Kontext der von ihm so genannten ›frühen Demokratie‹ regelmäßig als funktionales Äquivalent eines Verwaltungsapparats anzusehen seien, weil und insofern sie dem Herrscher Informationen lieferten und bei der alltäglichen Herrschaftsausübung unterstützend tätig waren[15]. Mit dem

---

Menschen stehen bleibt, als ob sie sich ohne Beziehung auf die Abhängigkeiten der betreffenden Individuen, ohne Beziehung auf das Netz der Interdependenzen, das sie mit anderen bilden, verstehen ließen, dann verstellt man sich gerade jene Aspekte der menschlichen Beziehungen, die das feste Rahmenwerk ihrer ›Interaktionen‹ bilden.«

13 *Stasavage*, Parliamentary Culture and Public Credit. Der Blogbeitrag basiert hier im Wesentlichen auf *Stasavage*, States of Credit; vgl. kritisch dazu *Neu*, Speaking in the Name of.

14 Vgl. zur Schlüsselfunktion von Parlamenten/Ständeversammlungen für die Entstehung (früh) modernen öffentlichen Kredits klassisch *North/Weingast*, Constitutions and Commitment, popularisiert u. a. durch *Acemoglu/Robinson*, Why Nations Fail, und *Ferguson*, The Great Degeneration, kritisiert erneut von den Beiträgen in *Coffman/Leonard/Neal*, Questioning Credible Commitment; in der Zusammenschau hat die Forschung die Bedeutsamkeit der Parlamente/Ständeversammlungen zugunsten herrschaftlich-bürokratischer und marktbezogener Faktoren erheblich relativiert, vgl. etwa *Coffman/Neal*, Introduction, S. 17, und *Desan*, Making Money, S. 288–290; vgl. auch *Stasavage*, Public Debt, *Macdonald*, A Free Nation Deep in Debt, und allgemein *Barreyre/Dealande*, A World of Public Debts, vor allem die Beiträge in »Part I: Political Crises and the Legitimacy of Public Debts (1770s–1860s)«, und *Beigel/Eckert*, Vom Wohl und Wehe der Staatsverschuldung.

15 *Stasavage*, The Decline and Rise of Democracy, S. 4f.

Politikwissenschaftler Gerhard Göhler ließen sich diese Funktionen auch unter dem Begriff der ›Steuerung‹ zusammenfassen[16].

Gegen solche funktionalen Analysen ist kritisch eingewandt worden, dass sie mit der Konzentration auf die Leistungen für andere Zusammenhänge die Ständeversammlungen selbst ungebührlich vernachlässigten. Träger dieser Kritik ist heute vor allem eine kulturwissenschaftlich gewendete Geschichtswissenschaft, im Blog etwa vertreten durch Barbara Stollberg-Rilinger:

»Yet if the assemblies of estates fulfilled the function of decision-making only in a limited way, why did they take place at all? The answer is, because they were also significant social and political rituals. They represented or embodied the political whole in the sense that they made it sensually perceptible – visible, audible, tangible. In the ceremonial convening of ruler and estates, the entire political body, consisting of head and members, came into existence.«[17]

Die vormodernen Ständeversammlungen seien vorschnell und im anachronistischen Vergleich mit modernen Parlamenten vor allem an ihrer politischen Entscheidungsfunktion gemessen worden. Damit aber werde ausgeblendet, dass sie für sich genommen mindestens auch als politische Rituale fungierten, in denen das Gemeinwesen verkörpert und damit überhaupt erst sinnlich wahrnehmbar hervorgebracht wurde[18]. In den Blick genommen werden damit Aspekte der Ständeversammlungen, die vor allem der ›Integration‹ dienen, wie man unter erneutem Bezug auf Göhler sagen könnte[19]. Wichtig ist in diesem Zusammenhang allerdings, dass Stollberg-Rilinger die funktionale Perspektive nicht vollständig zurückweist, sondern eher ihre Überziehung kritisiert, wenn sie etwa feststellt, dass die vormoderne Beratungskultur oft nur sehr überschaubare Entscheidungsleistungen erbrachte.

Überhaupt ist die integrierte Thematisierung von Funktionen und Funktionsweisen ein deutlich festzustellender Trend in der Forschung, wie das Beispiel eines dritten Forschenden aus einem dritten Sprachraum deutlich macht:

---

16 Der Begriff der ›Steuerung‹ nach *Göhler*, Politische Institutionen und ihr Kontext, S. 38. Göhlers Unterscheidung von ›Steuerung‹ und ›Integration‹ (s. u.) habe ich für die Ständegeschichte nützlich zu machen versucht in *Neu*, Die Erschaffung der landständischen Verfassung, S. 64–83.
17 *Stollberg-Rilinger*, Rituals of Consent or Procedures of Decision-Making?
18 Vgl. auch *Stollberg-Rilinger*, Vormoderne politische Repräsentation, S. 48; *Neu/Sikora/Weller*, Einleitung, S. 9; *Neu*, Rhetoric and Representation, S. 3; *Dücker*, Reichsversammlungen im Spätmittelalter, S. 20; *Peltzer/Schwedler/Töbelmann*, Einleitung, S. 9; *Weinfurter*, Versammlungen und politische Willensbildung, S. 276; *Helmrath/Feuchter*, Einleitung – Vormoderne Parlamentsoratorik, S. 10; *Hoffmann-Rehnitz/Krischer/Pohlig*, Entscheiden als Problem der Geschichtswissenschaft, S. 236; *Kewes u. a.*, Early Modern Parliamentary Studies; auch für moderne Parlamente ist die Berücksichtigung symbolisch-ritueller Aspekte eingefordert und analytisch fruchtbar gemacht worden, vgl. nur *Mergel*, Parlamentarische Kultur in der Weimarer Republik; *Crewe/Müller*, Rituals in Parliaments; *Hänni/Luginbühl*, Politische Geschichte, S. 87 f.
19 Vgl. *Göhler*, Politische Institutionen und ihr Kontext, S. 38 f.

»The history of medieval representative assemblies is largely dominated by a functional paradigm that tends to emphasize the study of their role in the institutional development of the states and principalities that were being formed during the closing centuries of the Middle Ages. [...] Nevertheless, and this is a key figure of early medieval political assemblies, they foreshadowed future developments of representation, inasmuch as they acted as impersonations of political communities, equating ritually formalized bodies to the featuring of the entire community of given regnal or seigneurial entities.«[20]

Auch Michel Hébert geht in seinem Blogbeitrag von der bisher dominanten funktionalen Analyse der Ständeversammlungen im Kontext der Staatsbildung aus, um dann – ganz ähnlich wie Stollberg-Rilinger – auf die auch seiner Ansicht nach zentrale Eigenschaft der mittelalterlichen Parlamente hinzuweisen, dass sie nämlich als im Modus des Rituals operierende Beratungskörperschaften das Gemeinwesen personifizierten und in dessen Namen handeln konnten, wie man mit Blick auf die Definition in Héberts grundlegendem Werk »Parlementer« hinzufügen könnte[21]. Der empirische Befund lautet also, dass sich in weiten Teilen der Forschung ein Ansatz durchgesetzt hat, der neben den (Entscheidungs-)Leistungen für das Gemeinwesen und die Prozesse, in die es verstrickt ist, also neben der Steuerungsfunktion von Ständeversammlungen auch ihre rituelle Funktionsweise thematisiert, die Verkörperung und damit effektive Hervorbringung des Gemeinwesens[22]. Wie lässt sich dieser Befund nun konzeptionell fassen und auf den Begriff bringen?

II. Begriffsarbeit: Politische Teilhabe

Der Sache nach verfolgen also inzwischen viele Forscherinnen und Forscher den Ansatz, sowohl die Funktionen als auch die Funktionsweisen der vormodernen Beratungskultur Europas zu untersuchen. Um nun aber eine engere Zusammenarbeit dieser Forscherinnen und Forscher zu ermöglichen und die schon erzielten Ergebnisse besser aufeinander beziehen zu können, bedarf es einer begrifflichen Explikation des Ansatzes. Und hier kommt man meines Erachtens nicht um die Feststellung herum, dass Barbara Stollberg-Rilinger mit der konzeptionellen Unterscheidung von instrumentellen und symbolischen Dimensionen die klarste Fassung dieses Ansatzes formuliert hat:

20 *Hébert*, Late Medieval Europe.
21 *Hébert*, Parlementer, S. 1: »À cette fin, on peut définir les assemblées représentatives comme la réunion, dans un espace-temps commun et normé, des individus ou des groupes qui, en personne ou par leurs représentants, figurant un ensemble politique, sont habilités à parler et à agir au nom de cet ensemble, dans une relation de négociation avec un prince territorial, sur tous les aspects de la recherche du bien commune.«
22 Vgl. auch, jeweils mit weiterführender Literatur, *Haug-Moritz*, Deliberieren, S. 117, 147; *Van Gelder*, Introduction, S. 12 f.; *Damen/Haemers/Mann*, Introduction, S. 2; *Hayat/Péneau/Sintomer*, La représentation-incarnation, S. 14; *Kewes u. a.*, Early Modern Parliamentary Studies.

»Dazu [zur Verfassungskultur, d. Vf.] gehörten an erster Stelle die Praktiken politischer Partizipation auf Ständeversammlungen. Diese Praktiken [...] hatten stets eine instrumentelle und eine symbolisch-expressive Dimension. [...] Ständetage, mit anderen Worten, repräsentierten das politische Ganze im doppelten Sinne des Wortes: Sie stellten es zum einen im technisch-instrumentellen Sinne her, insofern nämlich, als sie kollektiv verbindliche Entscheidungen für das politische Ganze trafen und es so erst handlungsfähig machten. Und sie stellten das politisch soziale Ganze zugleich im symbolischen Sinne dar, indem sie seine fundamentalen Gliederungsprinzipien immer aufs Neue anschaulich präsent machten und auf öffentlicher Bühne inszenierten. Beides hing untrennbar miteinander zusammen.«[23]

Wichtig dabei ist, dass es sich um analytische Kategorien handelt, die nicht nur konzeptionell zusammenhängen, wie Stollberg-Rilinger in diesem Zitat ja betont, sondern die vor allem auch in der historischen Wirklichkeit nicht ›rein‹ vorkommen. Vor allem lassen sich die beiden Dimensionen nicht umstandslos auf bestimmte Praktiken abbilden oder mit ihnen identifizieren, wie ein kurzer Blick auf das frühneuzeitliche Verständnis des Konzepts der ›Standschaft‹ zeigt. In Karl Friedrich Häberlins »Handbuch des Teutschen Staatsrechts« heißt es 1794:

»Das eigentliche Kennzeichen eines Reichsstandes besteht also in dem Sitz- und Stimmrechte auf allgemeinen Reichstagen. Wer dieses Recht nicht hat, ist kein Reichsstand, wenn er gleich sonst alle Rechte hätte, deren sich ein teutscher Reichsstand erfreuet.«[24]

Was aber ist mit ›Sitz und Stimme‹ konkret gemeint? Die entsprechenden Einträge in Johann Heinrich Zedlers »Universal-Lexicon aller Wissenschafften und Künste« aus der ersten Hälfte des 18. Jahrhunderts lauten folgendermaßen:

»Sitz, (Vor-) der Rang, die Präcedenz, siehe Rang, im XXX Bande, p. 802. u. ff. desgleichen Rang-Ordnungen ebend. p. 811. u. ff.«[25]

»Stimme, Lat. Vox, Votum, Suffragium, heißt in Gericht- und Raths-Stuben das Recht, zu denen vorgetragenen Sachen mit zu reden, und seine Meynung zu sagen. [...] Ein mehrers siehe Votum.«[26]

Als Kennzeichen der Standschaft, und nicht nur im Reich, denn für die Landstandschaft lassen sich leicht analoge Stellen finden, galten also gemeinhin ›Sitz und Stimme‹[27]. Gemeint war damit im Verständnis der Zeit, wie die Lexikoneinträge klar be-

---

23 *Stollberg-Rilinger*, Politische Partizipation als Inszenierung, S. 201 f.; vgl. auch *dies.*, Herstellung und Darstellung politischer Einheit, und erstmals *dies.*, Symbolische Kommunikation, S. 497 f.
24 *Häberlin*, Handbuch des Teutschen Staatsrechts, Bd. 1, S. 258.
25 Art. Sitz, (Vor-), Sp. 1870.
26 Art. Stimme, Lat. Vox, Votum, Suffragium, Sp. 114.
27 Vgl. Art. Stimme (V.): »[daz die] kurfursten rechte stimme und stat habin *um 1360* [...] als die [von stedten] ire session, stelle und stimme neben den landtstenden im rechten gehabt *1570* [...] ist ein reichs-stand eine person, die sitz und stimme auf dem reichs-tag hat *1751* [...] jeder immatrikulierte landstand, welcher 75 gulden kontribuzion entrichtet, hat das recht, dem landtage mit sitz und stimme beizuwohnen *1787*«.

legen, eine komplexe Eigenschaft, die zwei unterschiedliche Arten von Ansprüchen miteinander kombinierte: Zum einen Ansprüche im Hinblick auf die Rangordnung der Stände untereinander und zum anderen Ansprüche auf die Beteiligung an den Beratungsverfahren der Ständeversammlung als solcher[28]. Das darf aber nicht dazu führen, auch wenn das eine häufige Lesart der vorgeschlagenen Unterscheidung ist, nun Rangfragen der symbolischen und Abstimmungsfragen der instrumentellen Dimension zuzuordnen. Denn der Clou der analytischen Unterscheidung besteht gerade darin, ständisch strukturierte Versammlungen als Ganze daraufhin zu beobachten, wie sie als komplexe Phänomene des Ineinandergreifens von Rang- und Verfahrenspraktiken gleichermaßen instrumentell wie symbolisch wirksam waren[29].

Welcher Begriff eignet sich nun dazu, diese beiden Dimensionen zusammenzuführen? Bisher wird dazu vor allem der Begriff der ›politischen Repräsentation‹ genutzt, nicht zuletzt von Stollberg-Rilinger selbst[30]. Damit lässt sich der Sachverhalt, dass Ständeversammlungen stets sowohl instrumentelle Steuerungs- als auch symbolische Integrationsleistungen erbrachten, in der Tat angemessen auf den Begriff bringen, nämlich durch die Unterscheidung von Stellvertretungsrepräsentation einerseits und Identitätsrepräsentation andererseits[31]. Gleichwohl zieht diese begriffliche Entscheidung zwei nicht unerhebliche Folgeprobleme nach sich. Erstens kommt es damit zu einer verkomplizierenden Begriffsverdoppelung: Da es

28 Vgl. grundlegend *Stollberg-Rilinger*, Zeremoniell als politisches Verfahren, S. 108: »Die zeremonielle Ordnung des Reichstags war nun zugleich seine Verfahrensordnung und hatte als solche eine wichtige Funktion für seine technische Handlungsfähigkeit.« Für den Reichstag vgl. auch *Krischer*, Inszenierung und Verfahren, und *Annas*, Repräsentation, Sitz und Stimme. Für landständische Kontexte vgl. *Neu*, Sitzen, Sprechen und Votieren, S. 124–131, und im Anschluss daran jetzt etwa *Maťa*, Der steirische Landtag in Raum und Bild um 1730, S. 201–214; *Neu*, Zeremonielle Verfahren, S. 26–32, und im Anschluss daran *Hartmann*, Die Reichstage unter Karl V., S. 27–29.
29 Vgl. *Stollberg-Rilinger*, Symbolische Kommunikation, S. 497 f., und im Anschluss daran *Neu/Sikora/Weller*, Einleitung, S. 13, sowie ausführlicher *Neu*, Sitzen, Sprechen und Votieren, S. 120–124, und *Köhler*, Strategie und Symbolik, S. 30–36. Vgl. auch *Haug-Moritz*, Deliberieren, die jedoch nicht nach instrumentellen und symbolischen Dimensionen unterscheidet, sondern nach unterschiedlichen kommunikativen Logiken: »Die Repräsentanten sind einerseits der diskursiven Logik des Beratens unter Anwesenden, andererseits den positionalen Logiken, die sich aus der Stellvertretung externer Dritter ergeben, unterworfen.« (S. 126). Diese von *Schäfer*, Zwischen Repräsentation und Diskurs, übernommenen Logiken lassen sich dabei in konzeptioneller Hinsicht problemlos auf die Legitimationsmechanismen des ›zeremoniellen Verfahrens‹ beziehen: die positionale Logik auf den Korrespondenzmechanismus, die diskursive Logik auf den Mechanismus der prozeduralen Verstrickung, vgl. *Haug-Moritz*, Deliberieren, S. 126, 136–139, 141, 144, 154, in Verbindung mit *Neu*, Zeremonielle Verfahren, S. 26–32.
30 Vgl. nur zuletzt *Stollberg-Rilinger*, Vormoderne politische Repräsentation, S. 133–138; vgl. auch *Hayat/Péneau/Sintomer*, La représentation-incarnation, S. 10–12; *Neu*, Die Erschaffung der landständischen Verfassung, S. 40–55, 78–83.
31 Vgl. grundlegend *Hofmann*, Repräsentation, und *Podlech*, Repräsentation; vgl. neben *Stollberg-Rilinger*, Vormoderne politische Repräsentation, S. 137 f., auch *Sintomer*, Les sens de la représentation politique, S. 21, *Hébert*, La voix du peuple, S. 168–171, *Disch*, Introduction, S. 2, alle mit Verweis auf *Hofmann*, Repräsentation.

sich nämlich auch um einen quellensprachlichen Begriff der Vormoderne handelt, müsste im Grunde an jeder Textstelle angegeben werden, ob gerade vom quellen- oder forschungssprachlichen Begriff die Rede ist[32]. Und zweitens handelt es sich um einen Begriff, der sowohl in den frühneuzeitlichen Debatten über Ständeversammlungen als auch in den spätneuzeitlichen, also letztlich unseren Debatten über moderne Parlamente einen festen Platz hat – und zwar mit jeweils zum Teil sehr unterschiedlichen Bedeutungen und Assoziationen[33]. In der Summe führen diese zwei Faktoren dazu, dass der Begriff in Forschungskontexten häufig gerade nicht das gegenseitige Verständnis fördert, weil er gleichsam überdeterminiert ist.

Daher plädiere ich für den Begriff der *Teilhabe*, dessen Vorteil gerade darin besteht, eher unterbestimmt zu sein, und der daher sozusagen ›frei‹ ist, um ihn als Grundbegriff für den Zusammenhang der beiden analytischen Dimensionen zu nutzen und ihn so zu einem wissenschaftlichen Terminus technicus mit einer präzise bestimmten Bedeutung zu machen[34]. Denn ›Teilhabe‹ ist dafür semantisch offen genug, der normalsprachliche Begriff spezifiziert ja gerade nicht, worin die Teilhabe genau besteht oder auf was sie sich bezieht. Gleiches gilt mit Abstrichen auch für *Partizipation, participation* (engl. wie frz.), *participación* und *partecipazione*[35].

Meiner Ansicht nach könnte die europäisch-vergleichende Erforschung der vormodernen Beratungskultur also davon profitieren, einen Begriff politischer Teilhabe ins Zentrum zu stellen, der dazu anleitet, Ständeversammlungen sowohl hinsichtlich ihrer instrumentellen Steuerungsleistungen für das Gemeinwesen und ihrer symbolischen Hervorbringung des Gemeinwesens zu untersuchen. Bisher habe ich hier vor allem bekannte Forschungstrends und wohl ebenso bekannte konzeptionelle Vorschläge rekapituliert und zum Zwecke der Verdeutlichung aufbereitet. Im Anschluss soll es nun darum gehen, die konzeptionelle Debatte auch einen

---

32 Ein Beispiel: Analytisch gesehen lassen sich die Landtage der Territorien des Alten Reiches grundsätzlich als Phänomene politischer Repräsentation verstehen, weil sich zeigen lässt, dass sie durchgehend symbolische Integrations- und auch instrumentelle Steuerungsleistungen erbrachten. Gleichzeitig jedoch ist zu beobachten, dass die Landstände erst im 17. Jahrhundert dazu übergingen, ihre traditionelle Herrschaftsteilhabe auch selbst als politische Repräsentation zu explizieren, vgl. *Neu*, Die Erschaffung der landständischen Verfassung, S. 492f.
33 Vgl. etwa, um ein beliebiges Beispiel zu konstruieren, *Stollberg-Rilinger*, Was heißt landständische Repräsentation?, für die argumentative Verwendung von politischer Repräsentation in der Frühen Neuzeit mit *Mulieri*, Exploring the Semantics of Constructivist Representation, für die gegenwärtige Debatte über politische Repräsentation nach dem *constructivist turn*: Beide beziehen sich auf *Hofmann*, Repräsentation, und die Unterscheidung von Stellvertretungs- und Identitätsrepräsentation, aber die jeweils untersuchten Debatten weisen kaum Überschneidungen auf.
34 Für einen anderen Vorschlag zum Umgang mit diesem Problem vgl. *Neu*, Politisch partizipieren – aber in wessen Namen?
35 Vgl. *Ungern-Sternberg/Reinau*, Einleitung, S. 1: »Die Frage, was Partizipation konkret bedeutet, welche Elemente ihr notwendigerweise inhärent sind und wie diese im politischen Alltag realisiert werden sollen und können, wird offensichtlich ganz unterschiedlich beantwortet«; *Wimmer u. a.*, Introduction, S. 2: »The concept of participation has multiple meanings«; *Douillet*, Sociologie politique, S. 15: »Le principe de participation peut être traduit de multiples façons et la définition de la ›bonne façon de participer‹ est un enjeu de luttes continu.«

Schritt voranzutreiben – oder dies zumindest zu versuchen. Und hier kommt der ungewohnte Begriff des ›Gefüges‹ ins Spiel.

III. Was sind Teilhabegefüge?

Zunächst ist aber plausibel zu machen, dass es überhaupt weiterer Begriffsarbeit bedarf. Denn das liegt keineswegs auf der Hand, könnte man doch sehr leicht auf einen üblichen und eingeführten Begriff zurückgreifen und die Ständeversammlungen einfach als *Institutionen* politischer Teilhabe bezeichnen. Nun wird auch der Begriff der Institution sehr unterschiedlich gefasst, etwa als Struktur von Regeln und Ressourcen oder als System verallgemeinerter und stabilisierter Gewohnheiten oder auch als Komplex von Erwartungserwartungen[36], aber in allen Fällen werden damit Beziehungen zwischen menschlichen Akteuren beschrieben: Der Begriff der Institution ist, so könnte man sagen, anthropozentrisch. Das scheint nun auf den ersten Blick gerade ein Vorteil zu sein, stellen doch viele Definitionen von Ständeversammlungen wie selbstverständlich auf die beteiligten Menschen ab, wie etwa die von Michel Hébert: »[L]es assemblées représentatives« könnten definiert werden als »la réunion [...] des individus ou des groupes qui [...] figurant un ensemble politique, sont habilités à parler et à agir au nom de cet ensemble [...] avec un prince territorial«[37]. Ständeversammlungen sind in dieser Bestimmung spezifische Vereinigungen von menschlichen Individuen oder Gruppen von Menschen, die mit einem anderen Menschen, nämlich dem Fürsten, reden und verhandeln.

Die Wahl des Institutionenbegriffs leuchtet also unmittelbar ein, aber dennoch vergibt man sich damit Erkenntnischancen, was ich zunächst an einer völlig beliebigen Szene der europäischen Beratungskultur plausibel machen möchte. Am 20. April 1653 löste Oliver Cromwell das englische Parlament auf. In einer zeitnahen Quelle heißt es dazu:

»*Wednesday, 20th April*. The Parlement sitting as usually, and being on debate upon the Bill with the amendments, [...] the Lord Generall Cromwell came into the House [...] and sate down as he used to do in an ordinary place. After a while he rose up, putt of his hat, and spake; at the first and for a good while, he spake to the commendation of the Parlement, for theyr paines and care of the publick good; but afterwards he changed his style, told them of theyr injustice, delays of justice, self-interest and other faults; [...] then he putt on his hat, went out of his place, and walked up and down the stage or floore in the

---

36 Vgl. nur *Giddens*, Die Konstitution der Gesellschaft, S. 430, der »Institutionen als fortwährend reproduzierte Regeln und Ressourcen« konzipiert, *Gehlen*, Urmensch und Spätkultur, S. 20, der von »Systemen stereotypisierter und stabilisierter Gewohnheiten« spricht, und *Luhmann*, Legitimation durch Verfahren, S. 122, für den »Institutionalisierung heißt [...], daß Konsens über bestimmte Verhaltenserwartungen vermutet und als Handlungsgrundlage benutzt werden darf«. Für einen einführenden Überblick vgl. *Häußling*, Institution.
37 *Hébert*, Parlementer, S. 1.

middest of the House, with his hat on his head, and chid them soundly [...]. After this he sayd to Corronell Harrison, (who was a Member of the House) ›Call them in,‹ then Harrison went out, and presently brought in Lieutenant Collonell Wortley [...] with five or six files of musqueteers, about 20 or 30, with theyr musquets, then the Generall, pointing to the Speaker in his chayre, sayd to Harrison, ›Fetch him down;‹ Harrison went to the Speaker, and spoke to him to come down, but the Speaker sate still, and sayd nothing. ›Take him down,‹ sayd the Generall; then Harrison went and pulled the Speaker by his gowne, and he came down. [...] Then the Generall went to the table where the mace lay, which used to be carryed before the Speaker, and sayd, ›Take away these baubles;‹ so the soldiers tooke away the mace, and all the House went out; [...] All being gon out, the doore of the House was locked, and the key with the mace was carried away, as I Heard, by Corronell Otley.«[38]

Abb. 1: *John Hall* nach *Benjamin West*, Oliver Cromwell dissolving the Long Parliament, line engraving, published 1789 (1783) © National Portrait Gallery, London.

---

38 Journal of the Earl of Leicester, S. 139–141. Zu dieser Episode und zum politischen Kontext vgl. immer noch grundlegend *Worden*, The Rump Parliament, S. 317–341, und jetzt, mit weiterer Literatur, *Cunningham*, Divided Conquerors.

Cromwell betrat den Beratungsraum, hielt eine Rede voller Beleidigungen, ließ den *Speaker of the House* aus seinem (Vor-)Sitz vertreiben und ging dann zu dem Tisch, auf dem das *mace* lag, ein Amtsstab, der sich historisch aus dem Streitkolben entwickelt hatte und der von einem Lexikon des 19. Jahrhunderts noch kundig als »obrigkeitliches Machtzeichen«[39] umschrieben wurde. Und dort befahl er, das *mace* zu entfernen und bezeichnete es zudem herabwürdigend als »baubles«, was so viel heißt wie Tand oder Kinderspielzeug[40]. Es handelte sich um einen machtvollen performativen Akt, der genau das bewirkte, was er bezeichnete, nämlich die Schließung des Parlaments. Denn schon im 17. Jahrhundert verhielt es sich so, wie man auch heute noch der Webseite des Parlaments selbst in aller Deutlichkeit entnehmen kann: »The mace in Parliament is the symbol of royal authority and without it neither House can meet or pass laws.«[41] Daher ist es auch nur folgerichtig, dass im Zentrum von Abbildung 1, die den Titel »Oliver Cromwell dissolving the Long Parliament« trägt, die Entfernung des *mace* steht. Und das ist auch der Grund, warum Lloyd Russell-Moyle 2018 eigenmächtig das *mace* an sich nahm, um gegen den Brexit zu protestieren[42]. Sollte aber dann das Objekt, das Ding, das solche Wirkungen haben kann, nicht auch als zur Versammlung gehörig, als Element neben den menschlichen Elementen angesehen werden? Ich denke ja, aber dazu reicht der auf reine Sozialbeziehungen zentrierte Institutionenbegriff nicht aus, und sollte meines Erachtens durch ein offeneres Konzept ersetzt werden – das Gefüge.

Das hier gemeinte Konzept ist allerdings in der Regel unter einem anderen Namen bekannt, dem der Assemblage. Hier ist eine kurze terminologische Anmerkung notwendig: Gilles Deleuze und Félix Guattari, die das Konzept im Wesentlichen entwickelt haben, sprachen von *agencement*, und erst in der englischen Übersetzung wurde daraus in nicht unproblematischer Weise *assemblage*[43]. In der deutschsprachigen Forschung hat sich dann ebenfalls ›Assemblage‹ durchgesetzt, wobei das Wort allerdings – um die Verwirrung komplett zu machen – überwiegend französisch ausgesprochen wird, obwohl es die englische Begriffsverwendung nachbildet[44]. Ich halte mich jedoch lieber an die ursprüngliche Übersetzung, in der von ›Gefüge‹ die Rede ist[45].

---

39 Art. Mace, S. 1056.
40 Vgl. Art. bauble: »A small ornament, piece of jewellery, decorative accessory, etc., that is showy or attractive but typically inexpensive or of little value; a trinket, a knick-knack«, »An object for children to play with; a toy, a plaything«.
41 Art. Mace (The). Zum Stellenwert von *maces* vgl. auch *Strauß*, The Ceremonial Mace in the House of Commons and Great Maces of Cities and Boroughs in the 16th and Early 17th Century, und *Neu*, Inszenierte, vielfältige und vielzeitige Gefüge, S. 68 f.; zu Performativität vgl. grundlegend *Fischer-Lichte*, Performativität, und *Martschukat/Patzold*, Geschichtswissenschaft und »performative turn«.
42 *Elgot*, MP causes uproar in parliament by grabbing mace in Brexit protest.
43 Vgl. *Deleuze/Guattari*, Mille Plateaux, und *Phillips*, Agencement/Assemblage.
44 Vgl. etwa *DeLanda*, Assemblage Theory, und *Buchanan*, Assemblage Theory and Method.
45 Vgl. die Anmerkung der Übersetzerin und des Übersetzers Gabriele Ricke und Ronald Voullié in *Deleuze/Guattari*, Tausend Plateaus, S. 12.

Das Werben für dieses Konzept resultiert dabei nicht aus einer unkritischen Vorliebe für *french theory*, sondern steht im Kontext einer verstärkten Aufmerksamkeit für die Eigenheiten sozialer Praxis, die in den letzten Jahren quer durch viele Wissenschaftsbereiche massiv zugenommen hat[46]. In diesem Kontext plädiert etwa der Rechtswissenschaftler Jens Kersten dafür, die Verfassung als Assemblage bzw. Gefüge zu verstehen:

»Das Konzept der Assemblage eröffnet die Möglichkeit, die komplexen Relationen unter heterogenen und diversen Elementen als ein emergentes Ganzes zu verstehen, ohne es zu einer vorgegebenen Einheit idealisieren zu müssen oder zu können. Das bedeutet: Die kollektive Wirkung, die sich aus der Relation heterogener und diverser Elemente einer Assemblage ergibt, geht über die schlichte Summe deren Elemente hinaus.«[47]

Ich schließe also bereits an erste Vorarbeiten an, wenn ich mich ebenfalls auf dieses Konzept beziehe und vorschlage, Ständeversammlungen als Teilhabegefüge zu verstehen[48]. Aber was bedeutet das nun konkret? Für Gefüge sind zwei Eigenschaften wesentlich, Heterogenität und Emergenz[49]. Heterogenität meint, dass die Elemente, aus denen das Gefüge besteht, untereinander divers bzw. verschiedener Art sind. In Gefügen können also beispielsweise Menschen und Dinge miteinander verbunden sein. Zum Kontrast: Der Begriff der Institution ist durch Homogenität gekennzeichnet, weil er nur Elemente einer bestimmten Art umfasst, nämlich menschliche Beziehungen. Emergenz meint hingegen, dass die Effekte des Gefüges, darunter auch seine Einheit als Gefüge, sich nicht auf die einzelnen Elemente oder deren Addition zurückführen lassen, sondern aus dem Zusammenhang der Elemente überhaupt erst entstehen. Ein klassisches Beispiel für ein Gefüge ist etwa eine Fluggesellschaft. Diese bringt klarerweise den Effekt des Fliegens hervor, aber er kann nicht auf die Elemente als solche zurückgerechnet werden, weder Piloten noch Flugzeuge können für sich genommen fliegen, dieser Effekt entsteht erst aus der Assoziation der heterogenen Elemente des Gefüges: Neben menschlichen Piloten und Flugzeugdingen braucht es Bodenpersonal, Geldströme, Informationsketten, formale Regeln und vieles mehr[50].

46 Vgl. etwa *Schatzki/Knorr Cetina/Savigny*, The Practice Turn in Contemporary Theory; *Schäfer/Daniel/Hillebrandt*, Methoden einer Soziologie der Praxis.
47 *Kersten*, Die Notwendigkeit der Zuspitzung, S. 44; vgl. dazu jetzt *Neu*, Inszenierte, vielfältige und vielzeitige Gefüge.
48 Vgl. zum analytischen Einsatz des Konzepts weiterführend auch *Schritt*, Contentious Assemblages; *Liebsch*, Materialität, Interaktion und der Umgang mit der Lücke; *Wise*, Assemblage.
49 Vgl. *Kersten*, Die Notwendigkeit der Zuspitzung, S. 41, der zusätzlich noch Relationalität anführt. Vgl. auch *Bennett*, Vibrant Matter, S. 23 f.: »Assemblages are ad hoc groupings of diverse elements, of vibrant materials of all sorts.«
50 Das Beispiel stammt von *Latour*, Über technische Vermittlung, S. 490: »Fliegen ist eine Eigenschaft der gesamten Verbindung von Entitäten, die Flughäfen und Flugzeuge, Abflugrampen und Ticketschalter umfasst. Die B-52-Bomber fliegen nicht, sondern die ›U.S. Air Force‹. Handeln ist nicht einfach ein Vermögen von Menschen, sondern von einer Verbindung von Aktanten.« Zum heuristischen Nutzen der Akteur-Netzwerk-Theorie vgl. *Füssel/Neu*, Akteur-Netzwerk-Theorie und Geschichtswissenschaft.

Ständeversammlungen als Gefüge zu begreifen, hieße also erstens, sich verstärkt für ihre nicht-menschlichen Elemente zu interessieren, also etwa für materielle Dinge wie den erwähnten zeremoniellen Streitkolben[51]. Und zweitens würde es heißen, sich zu fragen, wie genau, durch welche Arten und Weisen der Verbindung, Verknüpfung und Verflechtung der menschlichen und nicht-menschlichen Elemente eigentlich die Effekte von Ständeversammlungen entstehen[52]. Wer neue Begriffe vorschlägt, der hat klarerweise die Bringschuld zu zeigen, dass ihre Übernahme nicht nur plausibel ist, sondern auch analytisch fruchtbar. Während eine erste Plausibilisierung hoffentlich schon mit diesem Beispiel gelungen ist, soll abschließend an einem weiteren Beispiel im Hinblick auf den Aspekt der Heterogenität darüber nachgedacht werden, was aus dieser Neuperspektivierung für Editionsprojekte folgen könnte. Aber noch mal: Weder ist der Begriff der Teilhabegefüge eingeführt, noch kenne ich mich mit Editionsprojekten aus. Die folgenden Ausführungen sind daher unbedingt als Gedankenspiele zu verstehen, nicht als Forderungen an Editorinnen und Editoren.

IV. Spekulationen: Teilhabegefüge und Editionsprojekte

Die Ständeversammlung, um die es abschließend geht, der Landtag des Herzogtums Steiermark[53], trat in der Frühen Neuzeit in Graz im sogenannten ›Landhaus‹ zusammen. Abbildung 2 zeigt eine idealisierte Darstellung dieses Landtags um 1730; es handelt sich dabei um eine absolute Seltenheit, denn es gibt praktisch keine bildlichen Darstellungen von frühneuzeitlichen Landtagssitzungen[54].

Petr Maťa hat diesen Kupferstich eingehend analysiert und ist zu dem Schluss gekommen, dass die steirischen Landstände hier die Absicht verfolgten, »mittels der idealisierten Landtagsszene die Sitz- und Stimmordnung der steirischen Ständeversammlung und damit also sowohl die ständeinternen Hierarchien als auch die Geschäftsordnung des Landtags zu visualisieren«[55]. Das ist zunächst einmal ein Beleg

---

51 Damit würde die Ständeforschung Anschluss finden an einen allgemeinen Forschungstrend, vgl. statt vieler nur *Füssel*, Die Materialität der Frühen Neuzeit, und *Schmidt-Funke*, Zur Sache.
52 Auch damit würde die Ständeforschung an einen wichtigen Forschungstrend anknüpfen, vgl. etwa *Brendecke*, Praktiken der Frühen Neuzeit; *Freist*, Diskurse, Körper, Artefakte.
53 Vgl. zur steirischen Ständegeschichte zuletzt *Steiner*, Die Landstände in Steiermark, Kärnten und Krain und die josephinischen Reformen; zur Ständegeschichte der Habsburgermonarchie insgesamt vgl. *Ammerer u. a.*, Bündnispartner oder Konkurrenten, und jetzt *Lahner/Schennach*, Zwischen Teilhabe, Revolte und Marginalisierung?
54 Vgl. *Maťa*, Der steirische Landtag in Raum und Bild um 1730, S. 165: »Die Einzigartigkeit der Darstellung besteht nicht in der – eher mittelmäßigen – künstlerischen Qualität des Kupferstiches, sondern sie ergibt sich aus der Tatsache, dass es sich hierbei um das wohl einzige komplexere in der Frühen Neuzeit entstandene Bild eines Landtags der österreichischen Länder, ja sogar der gesamten Habsburgermonarchie handelt.«
55 *Maťa*, Der steirische Landtag in Raum und Bild um 1730, S. 215f.

Abb. 2: *Johann Heinrich Störcklin*, Steirische Landtagsszene, Kupferstich, in: *Deyerlsperg*, Erb-Huldigung, zwischen S. 6 und S. 7.

dafür, dass mit der Unterscheidung symbolisch/instrumentell auch bildliche Darstellungen ertragreich analysiert werden können.

Wichtiger sind hier jedoch die dargestellten ›Dinge‹: die Tische und Stühle, die Tintenfässer, die Schreibfedern und Papiere, der Kachelofen und vor allem die acht merkwürdigen Rednerpulte, für die es ansonsten keine Belege gibt[56]. Nun macht es klarerweise einen erheblichen Unterschied, ob man an einer Versammlung stehend oder sitzend teilnimmt, ob man mitschreiben kann oder nicht, ob man sich Gehör verschaffen kann oder nicht. Alle diese Dinge sollten also als Elemente des steirischen Teilhabegefüges angesehen werden, denn sie machen einen Unterschied, ihnen kommt im Gefüge der Versammlung Wirkmacht zu[57].

---

56 Ebd., S. 205.
57 Vgl. *Bennett*, Vibrant Matter, S. IX: »I want to highlight what is typically cast in the shadow: the material agency or effectivity of nonhuman or not-quite-human things«, und S. XVII: »The locus of agency is always a human-nonhuman working group«. Handlungsträgerschaft oder Wirkmacht (*agency*) wird von den Sozial- und Kulturwissenschaften klassischerweise nur Menschen zugesprochen. Bennett verweist explizit auf den generalisierten *agency*-Begriff von Bruno Latour und der Akteur-Netzwerk-Theorie, für die »*jedes* Ding, das eine gegebene Situation verändert, indem es einen Unterschied macht, ein Akteur« ist (*Latour*, Eine neue Soziologie, S. 123 [Hervorhebung im Original]).

Was aber würde daraus für die Edition von einzelnen Ständeversammlungen folgen? Nun, man müsste darüber nachdenken, wie man die wirkmächtigen Dinge – wenn sie denn wirkmächtig waren, also eher die Rednerpulte als der Kachelofen – in die Edition einbindet. Das ist nun aber alles andere als einfach, denn Dinge produzieren nun einmal keine Texte, anders als die beteiligten Menschen – und auf diesen Texten beruhen ja die Editionen. Man könnte also erwägen, ob es zur Aufgabe von Editorinnen und Editoren gehören könnte, verstärkt eigene Texte zu schreiben, mit denen die Wirkmacht der stummen Dinge eingefangen werden könnte – und nicht nur in der Einleitung, sondern als Bestandteil der Edition selbst.

Wie das in der Praxis aussehen könnte, weiß ich nicht. Und daher ende ich hier mit einer Zusammenfassung dessen, was ich weiß: In der Forschung, so hat sich einleitend gezeigt, werden inzwischen regelmäßig sowohl die Funktionen als auch die Funktionsweisen von Ständeversammlungen untersucht. Dieser Ansatz lässt sich dahingehend begrifflich fassen, dass Ständeversammlungen stets sowohl instrumentell an der Steuerung des Gemeinwesens und symbolisch an seiner Integration beteiligt waren, was sich in einem weiten Sinn und ohne den Ballast des Repräsentationsbegriffs als politische Teilhabe bezeichnen ließe. Dann habe ich vorgeschlagen, Ständeversammlungen als Teilhabegefüge zu denken, um auch andere als menschliche Elemente einzuschließen. Und für Editorinnen und Editoren könnte das schließlich bedeuten, so mein Gedankenspiel, die Dinge selber durch Texte zum Sprechen zu bringen. Ob diese Gedankenspiele aber inspirierend oder gar umsetzbar sind, das müssen die Leserinnen und Leser entscheiden – freuen würde es mich.

Quellen- und Literaturverzeichnis

Quellen

Art. Sitz, (Vor-), in: *Johann Heinrich Zedler (Hg.)*, Grosses vollständiges Universal-Lexicon aller Wissenschafften und Künste, Bd. 37, Leipzig/Halle 1743, Sp. 1870.

Art. Stimme, Lat. Vox, Votum, Suffragium, in: *Johann Heinrich Zedler (Hg.)*, Grosses vollständiges Universal-Lexicon aller Wissenschafften und Künste, Bd. 40, Leipzig/Halle 1744, Sp. 114.

Edler von Deyerlsperg, Georg Jakob (Hg.): Erb-Huldigung, welche dem Allerdurchleuchtigist-Großmächtigisten und Unüberwindlichsten Römischen Kayser, Carolo dem Sechsten, zu Hispanien, Ungarn, und Böheim König, sc. sc. als Hertzogen in Steyer, von denen gesamten Steyrischen Land-Ständen den sechsten Julii 1728. in allerunterthänigster Submission abgeleget, Grätz 1740.

Häberlin, Karl Friedrich: Handbuch des Teutschen Staatsrechts nach dem System des Herrn Geheimen Justizrath Pütter, Bd. 1, Neue Aufl., Frankfurt/Leipzig 1794.

Journal of the Earl of Leicester, in: *R. W. Blencowe (Hg.)*, Sydney Papers, consisting of a Journal of the Earl of Leicester, and Original Letters of Algernon Sydney, London 1825, S. 1–161.

Literatur

Art. bauble, in: *Oxford University Press (Hg.)*, Oxford English Dictionary, Juli 2023, https://doi.org/10.1093/OED/6898056871 (31.07.2023).

Art. Mace, in: *Newton Ivory Lucas (Hg.)*, Englisch-Deutsches und Deutsch-Englisches Wörterbuch, Bd. 1: Englisch-Deutsch, 2. Abt., Bremen/London 1856, S. 1056.

Art. Mace (The), in: *UK Parliament (Hg.)*, Glossary, https://www.parliament.uk/site-information/glossary/mace/ (27.07.2023).

Art. Stimme (V.), in: *Heidelberger Akademie der Wissenschaften (Hg.)*, Deutsches Rechtswörterbuch. Wörterbuch der älteren deutschen Rechtssprache, bearbeitet von Andreas Deutsch, Bd. XIV, Heft 1/2, Stuttgart 2019, Sp. 307 f.

Recovering Europe's Parliamentary Culture, 1500–1700, https://intellectualhistory.web.ox.ac.uk/recovering-europes-parliamentary-culture-1500-1700 (27.07.2023).

Acemoglu, Daron/Robinson, James A.: Why Nations Fail. The Origins of Power, Prosperity and Poverty, London 2012.

Aerts, Remieg u. a. (Hg.): The Ideal of Parliament in Europe since 1800, Cham 2019 (= Palgrave Studies in Political History).

Albareda, Joaquim/Herrero Sánchez, Manuel (Hg.): Political Representation in the Ancien Régime, New York/London 2019 (= Routledge Studies in Renaissance and Early Modern Worlds of Knowledge).

Dies.: Introduction, in: dies. (Hg.), Political Representation in the Ancien Régime, New York/London 2019, S. 1–13 (= Routledge Studies in Renaissance and Early Modern Worlds of Knowledge).

Ammerer, Gerhard u. a. (Hg.): Bündnispartner oder Konkurrenten der Landesfürsten? Die Stände in der Habsburgermonarchie, Wien/München 2007 (= Veröffentlichungen des Instituts für Österreichische Geschichtsforschung, Bd. 49).

Annas, Gabriele: Repräsentation, Sitz und Stimme. Zur fürstlichen Stellvertretung auf Reichsversammlungen des späten Mittelalters, in: *Jörg Peltzer/Gerald Schwedler/Paul Töbelmann (Hg.)*, Politische Versammlungen und ihre Rituale. Repräsentationsformen und Entscheidungsprozesse des Reichs und der Kirche im späten Mittelalter, Ostfildern 2009, S. 113–150 (= Mittelalter-Forschungen, Bd. 27).

Bahlcke, Joachim: Landtagsakten (unter besonderer Berücksichtigung der Verhältnisse in der frühneuzeitlichen Habsburgermonarchie), in: *Josef Pauser/Martin Scheutz/Thomas Winkelbauer (Hg.)*, Quellenkunde der Habsburgermonarchie. Ein exemplarisches Handbuch, Wien/München 2004, S. 351–364 (= Mitteilungen des Instituts für Österreichische Geschichtsforschung, Ergänzungsband, Bd. 44).

Barreyre, Nicolas/Delalande, Nicolas (Hg.): A World of Public Debts. A Political History, Basingstoke 2020 (= Palgrave Studies in the History of Finance).

Beigel, Thorsten/Eckert, Georg (Hg.): Vom Wohl und Wehe der Staatsverschuldung. Erscheinungsformen und Sichtweisen von der Antike bis zur Gegenwart, Münster 2013.

Bennett, Jane: Vibrant Matter. A Political Ecology of Things, Durham/London 2010.

Bentley, Michael: Parliamentary History: An Oblique Glance, in: Parliamentary History 40 (2021), S. 228–244.

Birtsch, Günter: Die landständische Verfassung als Gegenstand der Forschung, in: *Dietrich Gerhard (Hg.)*, Ständische Vertretungen in Europa im 17. und 18. Jahrhundert, Göttingen ²1974, S. 32–55 (= Veröffentlichungen des Max-Planck-Instituts für Geschichte, Bd. 27).

Blockmans, Wim: Representation (Since the Thirteenth Century), in: *Christopher Allmand (Hg.)*, The New Cambridge Medieval History, Bd. 7: c. 1415–c. 1500, Cambridge 1998, S. 29–64.

Ders.: Medezeggenschap. Politieke Participatie in Europa vóór 1800, Amsterdam 2020.

Ders.: Comparing Representative Institutions. The Historiography and the Challenges, in: *István M. Szijártó/ders./László Kontler (Hg.)*, Parliamentarism in Northern and East-Central Europe in the Long Eighteenth Century, Bd. 1: Representative Institutions and Political Motivations, Abingdon/New York 2023, S. 14–49 (= Routledge Research in Early Modern History).

Brendecke, Arndt (Hg.): Praktiken der Frühen Neuzeit. Akteure, Handlungen, Artefakte, Köln/Weimar/Wien 2015 (= Frühneuzeit-Impulse, Bd. 3).

Buchanan, Ian: Assemblage Theory and Method, London 2019.

Buchholz, Werner: Öffentliche Finanzen und Finanzverwaltung im entwickelten frühmodernen Staat. Landesherr und Landstände in Schwedisch-Pommern 1720–1806, Köln/Weimar/Wien 1992 (= Veröffentlichungen der Historischen Kommission für Pommern, Bd. 5/Forschungen zur Pommerschen Geschichte, Bd. 25).

Coffman, D'Maris/Leonard, Adrian/Neal, Larry (Hg.): Questioning Credible Commitment. Perspectives on the Rise of Financial Capitalism, Cambridge 2013 (= Macroeconomic Policy Making).

Coffman, D'Maris/Neal, Larry: Introduction, in: *dies./Adrian Leonard/ders. (Hg.)*, Questioning Credible Commitment. Perspectives on the Rise of Financial Capitalism, Cambridge 2013, S. 1–20 (= Macroeconomic Policy Making).

Crewe, Emma/Müller, Marion G. (Hg.): Rituals in Parliaments. Political, Anthropological and Historical Perspectives on Europe and the United States, Frankfurt am Main 2006.

Cunningham, John: Divided Conquerors: The Rump Parliament, Cromwell's Army and Ireland, in: English Historical Review 129 (2014), S. 830–861.

Damen, Mario/Haemers, Jelle/Mann, Alastair J. (Hg.): Political Representation. Communities, Ideas and Institutions in Europe (c. 1200–c. 1690), Leiden/Boston 2018 (= Later Medieval Europe, Bd. 15).

Dies.: An Introduction: Political Representation. Communities, Ideas and Institutions in Europe (c. 1200–c. 1690), in: *dies. (Hg.)*, Political Representation. Communities, Ideas and Institutions in Europe (c. 1200–c. 1690), Leiden/Boston 2018, S. 1–15 (= Later Medieval Europe, Bd. 15).

DeLanda, Manuel: Assemblage Theory, Edinburgh 2016 (= Speculative Realism).

Deleuze, Gilles/Guattari, Félix: Mille Plateaux. Capitalisme et schizophrénie, Paris 1980.

Dies.: Tausend Plateaus. Kapitalismus und Schizophrenie, hg. v. *Günther Rösch*, Berlin 1992.

Desan, Christine: Making Money. Coin, Currency, and the Coming of Capitalism, Oxford 2014.

Disch, Lisa: Introduction. The End of Representative Politics?, in: *dies./Mathijs van de Sande/Nadia Urbinati (Hg.)*, The Constructivist Turn in Political Representation, Edinburgh 2019, S. 1–18.

Douillet, Anne-Cécile: Sociologie politique. Comportements, acteurs, organisations, Malakoff 2017.

Dücker, Julia: Reichsversammlungen im Spätmittelalter. Politische Willensbildung in Polen, Ungarn und Deutschland, Ostfildern 2011 (= Mittelalter-Forschungen, Bd. 37).

Elgot, Jessica: MP causes uproar in parliament by grabbing mace in Brexit protest. Lloyd Russel-Moyle waves symbol of Queen's authority to show anger over debate delay, in: The Guardian, 10. Dezember 2018, https://www.theguardian.com/politics/2018/dec/10/day-of-brexit-drama-ends-with-mp-grabbing-the-ceremonial-mace (27.07.2023).

Elias, Norbert: Die höfische Gesellschaft. Untersuchungen zur Soziologie des Königtums und der höfischen Aristokratie. Mit einer Einleitung: Soziologie und Geschichtswissenschaft, Frankfurt am Main [9]1999.

Ders.: Was ist Soziologie?, Weinheim/Basel [12]2014 (= Grundfragen der Soziologie).

Fenske, Hans: Der moderne Verfassungsstaat. Eine vergleichende Geschichte von der Entstehung bis zum 20. Jahrhundert, Paderborn 2001.

Ferguson, Niall: The Great Degeneration. How Institutions Decay and Economies Die, London 2012.

Fischer-Lichte, Erika: Performativität. Eine kulturwissenschaftliche Einführung, Bielefeld [4]2021.

Freist, Dagmar (Hg.): Diskurse, Körper, Artefakte. Historische Praxeologie in der Frühneuzeitforschung, Bielefeld 2015 (= Praktiken der Subjektivierung, Bd. 4).

Füssel, Marian: Die Materialität der Frühen Neuzeit. Neuere Forschungen zur Geschichte der materiellen Kultur, in: Zeitschrift für Historische Forschung 42 (2015), S. 433–463.

Ders./Neu, Tim (Hg.): Akteur-Netzwerk-Theorie und Geschichtswissenschaft, Paderborn 2021.

Gehlen, Arnold: Urmensch und Spätkultur. Philosophische Ergebnisse und Aussagen, Frankfurt am Main ⁶2004 (= Klostermann Seminar, Bd. 4).

Genet, Jean-Philippe/Le Page, Dominique/Mattéoni, Olivier (Hg.): Consensus et représentation. Le pouvoir symbolique en Occident (1300–1640), Paris 2017.

Giddens, Anthony: Die Konstitution der Gesellschaft. Grundzüge einer Theorie der Strukturierung, Studienaus., Frankfurt am Main/New York ³1997 (= Theorie und Gesellschaft, Bd. 1).

Göhler, Gerhard: Politische Institutionen und ihr Kontext. Begriffliche und konzeptionelle Überlegungen zur Theorie politischer Institutionen, in: *ders. (Hg.)*, Die Eigenart der Institutionen. Zum Profil politischer Institutionentheorie, Baden-Baden 1994, S. 19–45.

Graves, Michael A. R.: The Parliaments of Early Modern Europe, London/New York 2001.

Greindl, Gabriele: »Landstände im Alten Reich« – »Landschaft in Bayern«. Anmerkungen zur jüngeren deutschen Ständeforschung, in: Mitteilungen des Instituts für Österreichische Geschichtsforschung 127 (2019), S. 189–203.

Hänni, Adrian/Luginbühl, David: Politische Geschichte. Eine Einführung in Theorien und Methoden, Paderborn 2023.

Hartmann, Thomas Felix: Die Reichstage unter Karl V. Verfahren und Verfahrensentwicklung 1521–1555, Göttingen 2017 (= Schriftenreihe der Historischen Kommission bei der Bayerischen Akademie der Wissenschaften, Bd. 100).

Haug-Moritz, Gabriele: Deliberieren. Zur ständisch-parlamentarischen Beratungskultur im Lateineuropa des 16. Jahrhunderts, in: Historisches Jahrbuch 141 (2021), S. 114–155.

Häußling, Roger: Institution, in: *Johannes Kopp/Anja Steinbach (Hg.)*, Grundbegriffe der Soziologie, Wiesbaden 2018, S. 191–193.

Hayat, Samuel/Péneau, Corinne/Sintomer, Yves (Hg.): La représentation-incarnation, in: Raisons politiques 72 (2018), S. 5–164.

Dies. (Hg.): La représentation avant le gouvernement représentatif, Rennes 2020 (= Histoire).

Hébert, Michel: Parlementer. Assemblées représentatives et échange politique en Europe occidentale à la fin du Moyen Âge, Paris 2014 (= Romanité et modernité du droit).

Ders.: La voix du peuple. Une histoire des assemblées au Moyen Âge, Paris 2018.

Ders.: Late Medieval Europe. Founding a Parliamentary Culture, in: Recovering Europe's Parliamentary Culture, 1500–1700, 18. November 2021, https://intellectualhistory.web.ox.ac.uk/article/late-medieval-europe-founding-a-parliamentary-culture (27.07.2023).

Helmrath, Johannes/Feuchter, Jörg: Einleitung – Vormoderne Parlamentsoratorik, in: *dies. (Hg.)*, Politische Redekultur in der Vormoderne. Die Oratorik europäischer Parlamente in Spätmittelalter und Früher Neuzeit, Frankfurt am Main/New York 2008, S. 9–22 (= Eigene und fremde Welten, Bd. 9/Studies presented to the International Commission for the History of Representative and Parliamentary Institutions, Bd. 86).

Hoffmann-Rehnitz, Philip/Krischer, André/Pohlig, Matthias: Entscheiden als Problem der Geschichtswissenschaft, in: Zeitschrift für Historische Forschung 45 (2018), S. 217–281.

Hofmann, Hasso: Repräsentation. Studien zur Wort- und Begriffsgeschichte von der Antike bis zum 19. Jahrhundert, Berlin ⁴2003 (= Schriften zur Verfassungsgeschichte, Bd. 22).

Ihalainen, Pasi/Ilie, Cornelia/Palonen, Kari (Hg.): Parliament and Parliamentarism. A Comparative History of a European Concept, New York/Oxford 2016 (= European Conceptual History).

Kersten, Jens: Die Notwendigkeit der Zuspitzung. Anmerkungen zur Verfassungstheorie, Berlin 2020 (= Verfassungstheoretische Gespräche, Bd. 1).

Kewes, Paulina u.a.: Early Modern Parliamentary Studies. Overview and New Perspectives, in: History Compass 21 (2023), o.S., https://doi.org/10.1111/hic3.12757 (27.07.2023).

Köhler, Matthias: Strategie und Symbolik. Verhandeln auf dem Kongress von Nimwegen, Köln/Weimar/Wien 2011 (= Externa, Bd. 3).

Krischer, André: Inszenierung und Verfahren auf den Reichstagen der Frühen Neuzeit. Das Beispiel der Städtekurie und ihres politischen Verfahrens, in: *Jörg Peltzer/Gerald Schwedler/Paul Töbelmann (Hg.)*, Politische Versammlungen und ihre Rituale. Repräsentationsformen und Entscheidungsprozesse des Reichs und der Kirche im späten Mittelalter, Ostfildern 2009, S. 181–205 (= Mittelalter-Forschungen, Bd. 27).

Krüger, Kersten: Die landständische Verfassung, München 2003 (= Enzyklopädie deutscher Geschichte, Bd. 67).

Lahner, Julian/Schennach, Martin P. (Hg.): Zwischen Teilhabe, Revolte und Marginalisierung? Die Stände der österreichischen Länder in der Neuzeit (1500–1848/49). Beiträge zur Tagung an der Universität Innsbruck am 18. und 19. Juni 2021, Wien 2023.

Latour, Bruno: Über technische Vermittlung. Philosophie, Soziologie und Genealogie, in: *Andréa Belliger/David J. Krieger (Hg.)*, ANThology. Ein einführendes Handbuch zur Akteur-Netzwerk-Theorie, Bielefeld 2006, S. 483–528 (= Science Studies).

Ders.: Eine neue Soziologie für eine neue Gesellschaft. Einführung in die Akteur-Netzwerk-Theorie, Frankfurt am Main 2007.

Liebsch, Katharina: Materialität, Interaktion und der Umgang mit der Lücke. Von der Theorie der »assemblage« zu einer Methode der Erforschung psychosozial-kultureller Gefüge, in: *Erica Augello von Zadow u. a. (Hg.)*, Widerstand und Fürsorge. Beiträge zum Thema Psychoanalyse und Gesellschaft, Göttingen 2018, S. 217–232 (= Schriften des Sigmund-Freud-Instituts, Bd. 8).

Luhmann, Niklas: Legitimation durch Verfahren, Frankfurt am Main 1983.

Macdonald, James: A Free Nation Deep in Debt. The Financial Roots of Democracy, New York 2003.

Martschukat, Jürgen/Patzold, Steffen (Hg.): Geschichtswissenschaft und »performative turn«. Ritual, Inszenierung und Performanz vom Mittelalter bis zur Neuzeit, Köln/Weimar/Wien 2003 (= Norm und Struktur, Bd. 19).

Mat'a, Petr: Der steirische Landtag in Raum und Bild um 1730. Symbolische Ordnung und visuelle Darstellung, in: Zeitschrift des historischen Vereins für Steiermark 104 (2013), S. 163–218.

Mattone, Antonello: Gli studi istituzioni rappresentative in Italia fra erudizione e miti storiografici (XIX–XX secolo), in: *Laura Casella (Hg.)*, Rappresentanze e territori. Parlamento friulano e istituzioni rappresentative territoriali nell'Europa moderna, Udine 2003, S. 47–74 (= Strumenti di storia del Friuli).

Mergel, Thomas: Parlamentarische Kultur in der Weimarer Republik. Politische Kommunikation, symbolische Politik und Öffentlichkeit im Reichstag, Düsseldorf 2002 (= Beiträge zur Geschichte des Parlamentarismus und der politischen Parteien, Bd. 135).

Moraw, Peter: Zu Stand und Perspektiven der Ständeforschung im spätmittelalterlichen Reich, in: *Hartmut Boockmann (Hg.)*, Die Anfänge der ständischen Vertretungen in Preußen und seinen Nachbarländern, München 1992, S. 1–33 (= Schriften des Historischen Kollegs; Kolloquien, Bd. 16).

Mulieri, Alessandro: Exploring the Semantics of Constructivist Representation, in: *Lisa Disch/Mathijs van de Sande/Nadia Urbinati (Hg.)*, The Constructivist Turn in Political Representation, Edinburgh 2019, S. 205–223.

Neu, Tim: Zeremonielle Verfahren. Zur Funktionalität vormoderner politisch-administrativer Prozesse am Beispiel des Landtags im Fürstbistum Münster, in: *Stefan Haas/Mark Hengerer (Hg.)*, Im Schatten der Macht. Kommunikationskulturen in Politik und Verwaltung 1600–1950, Frankfurt am Main/New York 2008, S. 23–50.

Ders.: Sitzen, Sprechen und Votieren. Symbolische und instrumentelle Dimensionen landständischer Handlungssequenzen in Hessen-Kassel (17./18. Jahrhundert), in: *ders./Michael Sikora/Thomas Weller (Hg.)*, Zelebrieren und Verhandeln. Zur Praxis ständischer Institutionen im frühneuzeitlichen Europa, Münster 2009, S. 119–143 (= Symbolische Kommunikation und gesellschaftliche Wertesysteme, Bd. 27).

Ders.: Rhetoric and Representation: Reassessing Territorial Diets in Early Modern Germany, in: Central European History 43 (2010), S. 1–24.

Ders.: Die Erschaffung der landständischen Verfassung. Kreativität, Heuchelei und Repräsentation in Hessen (1509–1655), Köln/Weimar/Wien 2013 (= Symbolische Kommunikation in der Vormoderne/Studies presented to the International Commission for the History of Representative and Parliamentary Institutions, Bd. 93).

Ders.: Speaking in the Name of. Collective Action, Claim-making and the Development of Pre-modern Representative Institutions, in: *Mario Damen/Jelle Haemers/Alastair J. Mann (Hg.)*, Political Representation. Communities, Ideas and Institutions in Europe (c. 1200–c. 1690), Leiden/Boston 2018, S. 106–121 (= Later Medieval Europe, Bd. 15).

Ders.: Inszenierte, vielfältige und vielzeitige Gefüge – Bausteine einer Theorie der Verfassungsgeschichte, in: *Ino Augsberg/Michael W. Müller (Hg.)*, Theorie der Verfassungsgeschichte. Geschichtswissenschaft – Philosophie – Rechtsdogmatik, Tübingen 2023, S. 53–77 (= Recht – Wissenschaft – Theorie, Bd. 17).

Ders.: Politisch partizipieren – aber in wessen Namen? Politische Repräsentation als Argument in frühneuzeitlichen Ständekonflikten, in: *Anna Gianna Manca/Siegrid Westphal (Hg.)*, Politische Repräsentation und Partizipation. Vom Mittelalter bis heute/Rappresentanza politica e partecipazione. Dal medioevo a oggi, Berlin/Boston 2024, S. 81–105.

Ders./Sikora, Michael/Weller, Thomas (Hg.): Zelebrieren und Verhandeln. Zur Praxis ständischer Institutionen im frühneuzeitlichen Europa, Münster 2009 (= Symbolische Kommunikation und gesellschaftliche Wertesysteme, Bd. 27).

Dies.: Einleitung, in: *dies. (Hg.)*, Zelebrieren und Verhandeln. Zur Praxis ständischer Institutionen im frühneuzeitlichen Europa, Münster 2009, S. 9–19 (= Symbolische Kommunikation und gesellschaftliche Wertesysteme, Bd. 27).

North, Douglass C./Weingast, Barry R.: Constitutions and Commitment. The Evolution of Institutional Governing Public Choice in Seventeenth-Century England, in: Journal of Economic History 49 (1989), S. 803–832.

Peltzer, Jörg/Schwedler, Gerald/Töbelmann, Paul: Einleitung, in: *dies. (Hg.)*, Politische Versammlungen und ihre Rituale. Repräsentationsformen und Entscheidungsprozesse des Reichs und der Kirche im späten Mittelalter, Ostfildern 2009, S. 9–20 (= Mittelalter-Forschungen, Bd. 27).

Phillips, John: Agencement/Assemblage, in: Theory, Culture & Society 23 (2006), S. 108–109.

Podlech, Adalbert: Repräsentation, in: *Otto Brunner/Werner Conze/Reinhart Koselleck (Hg.)*, Geschichtliche Grundbegriffe. Historisches Lexikon zur politisch-sozialen Sprache in Deutschland, Bd. 5, Stuttgart 1984, S. 509–547.

Pohlig, Matthias: Marlboroughs Geheimnis. Strukturen und Funktionen der Informationsgewinnung im Spanischen Erbfolgekrieg, Köln/Weimar/Wien 2016 (= Externa, Bd. 10).

Ringer, Fritz: Max Weber on Causal Analysis, Interpretation, and Comparison, in: History and Theory 41 (2002), S. 163–178.

Rogister, John: The International Commission for the History of Representative and Parliamentary Institutions – Commission Internationale pour l'Histoire des Assemblées d'États: aims and achievements over seventy years, 1936–2006, in: Parliaments, Estates, and Representation 27 (2007), S. 1–7.

Rühl, Ulli F. H.: Das »freie Mandat«. Elemente einer Interpretations- und Problemgeschichte, in: Der Staat 39 (2000), S. 23–48.

Schäfer, Andreas: Zwischen Repräsentation und Diskurs. Zur Rolle von Deliberation im parlamentarischen Entscheidungsprozess, Wiesbaden 2017 (= Kritische Studien zur Demokratie).

Schäfer, Franka/Daniel, Anna/Hillebrandt, Frank (Hg.): Methoden einer Soziologie der Praxis, Bielefeld 2015 (= Sozialtheorie).

Schatzki, Theodore R./Knorr Cetina, Karin/Savigny, Eike von (Hg.): The Practice Turn in Contemporary Theory, London/New York 2001.

Schmidt-Funke, Julia A.: Zur Sache. Materielle Kultur und Konsum in der Frühen Neuzeit, in: *dies. (Hg.)*, Materielle Kultur und Konsum in der Frühen Neuzeit, Köln/Weimar/Wien 2019, S. 11–36 (= Ding, Materialität, Geschichte, Bd. 1).

Schritt, Jannik: Contentious Assemblages. Gefüge, Affekt, politische Situationen und die erweiterte Fallmethode als Analysewerkzeuge zum Verständnis urbaner Aufstände, in: *Judith Vey/Johanna Leinius/Ingmar Hagemann (Hg.)*, Handbuch Poststrukturalistische Perspektiven auf soziale Bewegungen. Ansätze, Methoden und Forschungspraxis, Bielefeld 2019, S. 138–151 (= Edition Politik, Bd. 82).

Sintomer, Yves: Les sens de la représentation politique: usages et mésusages d'une notion, in: Raisons Politiques 50 (2013), S. 13–34.

Stasavage, David: Public Debt and the Birth of the Democratic State. France and Great Britain, 1688–1789, Cambridge 2003.

Ders.: States of Credit. Size, Power, and the Development of European Polities, Princeton/Oxford 2011 (= The Princeton Economic History of the Western World).

Ders.: The Decline and Rise of Democracy. A Global History from Antiquity to Today, Princeton/Oxford 2020 (= The Princeton Economic History of the Western World).

Ders.: Parliamentary Culture and Public Credit. How Merchants Overcame Their Weak Position, in: Recovering Europe's Parliamentary Culture, 1500–1700, 14. Januar 2022, https://intellectualhistory.web.ox.ac.uk/article/parliamentary-culture-and-public-credit-how-merchants-overcame-their-weak-position (27.07.2023).

Steiner, Philip: Die Landstände in Steiermark, Kärnten und Krain und die josephinischen Reformen. Bedrohungskommunikation angesichts konkurrierender Ordnungsvorstellungen (1789–1792), Münster 2017.

Stollberg-Rilinger, Barbara: Zeremoniell als politisches Verfahren. Rangordnung und Rangstreit als Strukturmerkmale des frühneuzeitlichen Reichstags, in: *Johannes Kunisch (Hg.)*, Neue Studien zur frühneuzeitlichen Reichsgeschichte, Berlin 1997, S. 91–132 (= Zeitschrift für Historische Forschung; Beiheft 19).

Dies.: Was heißt landständische Repräsentation? Überlegungen zur argumentativen Verwendung eines politischen Begriffs, in: Zeitsprünge. Forschungen zur Frühen Neuzeit 4 (2000), S. 120–135.

Dies.: Symbolische Kommunikation in der Vormoderne. Begriffe – Thesen – Forschungsperspektiven, in: Zeitschrift für Historische Forschung 31 (2004), S. 489–527.

Dies.: Herstellung und Darstellung politischer Einheit. Instrumentelle und symbolische Dimensionen politischer Repräsentation im 18. Jahrhundert, in: *Jan Andres/Alexa Geisthövel/Matthias Schwengelbeck (Hg.)*, Die Sinnlichkeit der Macht. Herrschaft und Repräsentation seit der Frühen Neuzeit, Frankfurt am Main/New York 2005, S. 73–92 (= Historische Politikforschung, Bd. 5).

Dies.: Politische Partizipation als Inszenierung. Zur symbolisch-rituellen Dimension frühneuzeitlicher Ständeversammlungen am Beispiel des Reichstags von 1653/54, in: *Werner Daum u. a. (Hg.)*, Kommunikation und Konfliktaustragung. Verfassungskultur als Faktor politischer und gesellschaftlicher Machtverhältnisse, Berlin 2010, S. 201–221 (= Veröffentlichungen des Instituts für Europäische Verfassungswissenschaften, Bd. 7).

Dies.: Vormoderne politische Repräsentation als Abbildung und Zurechnung, in: *Paula Diehl/Felix Steilen (Hg.)*, Politische Repräsentation und das Symbolische. Historische, politische und soziologische Perspektiven, Wiesbaden 2016, S. 133–155 (= Staat – Souveränität – Nation).

Dies.: Rituals of Consent or Procedures of Decision-Making? Assemblies of Estates in Early Modern Europe, in: Recovering Europe's Parliamentary Culture, 1500–1700, 23. Dezember 2021, https://intellectualhistory.web.ox.ac.uk/article/rituals-of-consent-or-procedures-of-decision-making-assemblies-of-estates-in-early-modern-eu (27.07.2023).

Strauß, Kathrin: The Ceremonial Mace in the House of Commons and Great Maces of Cities and Boroughs in the 16th and Early 17th Century, in: Parliamentary History 41 (2022), S. 389–405.

Szijártó, István M./Blockmans, Wim/Kontler, László (Hg.): Parliamentarism in Northern and East-Central Europe in the Long Eighteenth Century, Bd. 1: Representative Institutions and Political Motivations, Abingdon/New York 2023 (= Routledge Research in Early Modern History).

Ungern-Sternberg, Jürgen von/Reinau, Hansjörg: Einleitung, in: *dies. (Hg.)*, Politische Partizipation. Idee und Wirklichkeit von der Antike bis in die Gegenwart, Berlin/Boston 2013, S. 1-2 (= Colloquium Rauricum, Bd. 13).

Van Gelder, Klaas: Introduction: Eighteenth- and Nineteenth-Century Coronations and Inaugurations in the Habsburg Monarchy. Why Do They Matter?, in: *ders. (Hg.)*, More Than Mere Spectacle. Coronations and Inaugurations in the Habsburg Monarchy during the Eighteenth and Nineteenth Centuries, New York/Oxford 2021, S. 1-28 (= Austrian and Habsburg Studies, Bd. 31).

Weber, Max: Wirtschaft und Gesellschaft. Soziologie. Unvollendet 1919-1920, hg. v. *Knut Borchardt/ Edith Hanke/Wolfgang Schluchter*, Tübingen 2013 (= Max Weber Gesamtausgabe, Abteilung I: Schriften und Reden, Bd. 23).

Ders.: Die »Objektivität« sozialwissenschaftlicher und sozialpolitischer Erkenntnis, in: *Gerhard Wagner (Hg.)*, Zur Logik und Methodik der Sozialwissenschaften. Schriften 1900-1907, Tübingen 2018, S. 142-234 (= Max Weber Gesamtausgabe, Abteilung I: Schriften und Reden, Bd. 7).

Weinfurter, Stefan: Versammlungen und politische Willensbildung zwischen Inszenierung und Ritual. Zusammenfassende Überlegungen, in: *Jörg Peltzer/Gerald Schwedler/Paul Töbelmann (Hg.)*, Politische Versammlungen und ihre Rituale. Repräsentationsformen und Entscheidungsprozesse des Reichs und der Kirche im späten Mittelalter, Ostfildern 2009, S. 273-279 (= Mittelalter-Forschungen, Bd. 27).

Wimmer, Jeffrey u. a.: Introduction, in: *dies. (Hg.)*, (Mis)Understanding Political Participation. Digital Practices, New Forms of Participation and the Renewal of Democracy, New York 2017, S. 1-13.

Wise, J. Macgregor: Assemblage, in: *Charles J. Stivale (Hg.)*, Gilles Deleuze. Key Concepts, London/ New York 2011, S. 91-102 (= Key Concepts).

PAULINA KEWES (OXFORD)

Representative Assemblies in the Political Thought of Jean Bodin[1]

For all that Jean Bodin has long been recognized as a founding father of comparative political science, historiography, and jurisprudence, the study of his thought routinely lacks a comparative dimension. It either exists at a stratospherically high level of abstraction or else remains resolutely Franco-centric. Nowhere is this truer than in respect of Bodin's approach to representative assemblies. The ever-proliferating treatments of Bodin's conception of indivisible sovereignty characteristically affirm the apparent subjection, subservience, and powerlessness of representative institutions vis-a-vis the sovereign prince. Meanwhile, the scholarship concerned with what we might anachronistically call Bodin's ›parliamentarism‹ focuses almost exclusively on the French Estates General and Bodin's own experience – and account – of participating in the 1576–1577 meeting at Blois as a delegate of the Third Estate from the baillage of Vermandois.

What, though, of Bodin's ambitious assessment of all manner of representative assemblies, both general and provincial, in a variety of political systems, ancient and modern, and its place within the larger framework of his thought? How and to what end does he invoke transhistorical and transnational comparisons in scrutinizing such bodies? Which of them and why does he hold in highest esteem or propose as a model? And, lastly, how far do his views evolve across the successive versions of his »Six livres de la République« from its first edition of 1576 right up to the expanded Latin »Republica« of 1586? While only a hefty monograph could address these questions in detail, this essay's far more modest aim is twofold. First, to provide a corrective to standard readings of Bodin's »République« which as a rule underestimate the importance Bodin accords to representative assemblies. And, secondly, to indicate how subtle textual differences between editions of Bodin's landmark treatise, in particular those affecting Book III, chapter vii – »De Corps et Colleges, Estats & Communautez« (»Of Corporations and Colleges, Estates and Communities«) – evince his changing vision of the utility and power of such

---

1   The argument presented here had an early outing at the Oxford History of Political Thought seminar in October 2022. I am grateful to the audience for their trenchant questions, and to Sue Doran, Ioannis Evrigenis, Mark Goldie, Mark Greengrass, Paul Seaward, Jim van der Meulen, and Blair Worden for valuable conversation and comments on subsequent versions. Work on this essay was generously supported by a major grant from the University of Oxford's John Fund and the award of a Leverhulme Trust Major Research Fellowship. Warm thanks are due to Christopher Archibald for editorial assistance and to the students who have lent a helping hand as part of the University of Oxford's Micro-Internship Programme: I could not have done this without you.

institutions, especially in what he defines as »just« or »royal« monarchies such as France, England, and Spain.

I.

This essay stems from a broader collaborative project seeking to develop a transnational history of early modern representative assemblies – parliaments, estates, diets, Cortes, to mention only some of the names they went under. Central to it is the novel concept of parliamentary culture – a common core of customs, ideas, symbols, and discourses that formed around such assemblies notwithstanding their legal and institutional diversity. Although parliaments and other representative assemblies are among the most familiar of political organizations, we were puzzled by how rarely they have been looked at as cultural phenomena, rather than as sites for formal legislation and political contention, or properly examined in comparative terms. One thing we emphasize in our recent overview of the field is the lack of in-depth, systematic engagement with the role of representative institutions by historians of political thought, including the Cambridge School and their followers[2]. J. G. A. Pocock's classic »The Ancient Constitution and the Feudal Law« (1957; 1987) did have a good deal to say about the English/British Parliament, and modern scholars regularly note the role attributed to political assemblies in sixteenth-century French and Dutch resistance writings by Protestants such as François Hotman, Theodore de Bèze, Philippe du Plessis Mornay, Marnix van St Aldegonde, and, later, by Catholics associated with the Holy League such as Jean Boucher[3]. But neither those studying early modern »republicanism«, whether civic, constitutional, or »monarchical«, nor those examining »sovereignty« and »absolutism« pay much attention to the actual institutional embodiment of these concepts[4].

Why such désintéressement? Intellectual historians see little or no correlation between political ideas and procedural formalities or practical policy formation. Meanwhile, parliamentary historians rarely venture into the province of political thought, let alone pursuing broader transnational comparisons. What the subject needs, and needs badly, is a rapprochement between intellectual and institutional and political history. It would also vastly benefit from taking on board, and consistently applying, the methods and techniques of textual criticism, histoire du livre,

---

2 *Kewes et al.*, Early Modern Parliamentary Studies, p. 6f. For an exposition of the term ›parliamentary culture‹ and our comparative interdisciplinary methodology, see *Kewes et al.*, Towards a History of Parliamentary Culture, forthcoming.
3 *Pocock*, Ancient Constitution and the Feudal Law; see esp. *Kingdon*, Calvinism and Resistance Theory, *Salmon*, Catholic Resistance Theory, *Mortimer*, Reformation, Resistance, and Reason of State.
4 See, among others, *Skinner*, Liberty before Liberalism; *Van Gelderen/Skinner (ed.)*, Republicanism; *McDiarmid (ed.)*, Monarchical Republic of Early Modern England; *Lloyd/Burgess/Hodson (ed.)*, European Political Thought 1450–1700.

and rhetorical analysis (as also of cultural history)[5]. For only then can we hope to avoid distortion in reconstructing the period's mental world. Briefly, we should not be privileging contemporaries' reading of say Cicero or Tacitus or command of the *Digest* at the expense of their first-hand knowledge and experience of representative institutions, whether local or national, and their often remarkably exact understanding of equivalent bodies elsewhere in Europe, understanding acquired not only from books or conversations with foreign envoys and visitors but also during diplomatic missions or personal travels abroad which might include witnessing actual deliberations, given that some Continental assemblies, such as the French Estates General or the Polish-Lithuanian Sejm, allowed spectators, both men and women, in the galleries[6]. Significantly, many of those who served in national or provincial assemblies were employed as official or informal diplomats and government advisors, as well as producing works of political philosophy, polemic, history, or imaginative literature[7].

Bodin's life and career perfectly epitomize this intersection of diverse spheres of intellectual and political activity. He was a jurist, lawyer, diplomat, counsellor, deputy to provincial and general estates, political thinker, translator, and author of numerous works on a tremendous range of themes[8]. In 1556 Bodin was present at the meeting of the Estates of Languedoc. In 1559, he spoke in the Senate of Toulouse. He practised as barrister in the highest court in the land – the Parlement of Paris. He translated into French – perchance even composed – the Latin oration of welcome delivered by Charles de Pérusse des Cars, Bishop of Langres to the Polish envoys, both Catholics and Calvinists, who, in 1573, brought the offer of their country's crown to Charles IX's younger brother and heir presumptive Henry of Valois following his election by the nobility assembled on Warsaw's fields in an electoral Sejm or diet, the first so-called *electio viritim*[9]. Bodin participated in the 1576–1577 Estates General summoned to Blois by Henry, now King of France, ostensibly to ratify the Edict of Beaulieu (Peace of Monsieur) granting freedom of worship to the Huguenots; he swiftly published a spirited account, in both French and Latin, of the assembly's fraught deliberations and his own heroic role therein[10]. He advised Henry's younger brother and heir, Francis Duke of Anjou, and, though not pres-

---

5   *Kewes et al.*, Towards a History of Parliamentary Culture, forthcoming.
6   *Kane et al.*, Parliamentary Culture and Exclusion.
7   *Kewes et al.*, Towards a History of Parliamentary Culture, forthcoming.
8   For a masterful reconstruction, see *Lloyd*, Jean Bodin.
9   *Bodin*, Harangue de Messire Charles des Cars. James B. Collins proposes that Bodin may have authored the oration in his »Birth of the Royal State 1561–1651«. I am grateful to Professor Collins for sending me his work before its publication. For the suggestion that the Polish example shaped Bodin's thought in the »République«, see *Collins*, Wpływ doświadczenia Henryka Walezjusza, p. 509 f. On the election of Henry of Valois to the Polish throne, see *Roşu*, Elective Monarchy in Transylvania and Poland-Lithuania, 1569–1587, ch. 1 passim.
10 *Greengrass*, A Day in the Life of the Third Estate; *id.*, Peace and Reform in the French Kingdom 1576–1585; *id.*, Experiential World of Bodin; *Holt*, Attitudes of the French Nobility at the Estates-General of 1576; *Bodin*, Recueil; *Bodin*, Commentarius.

ent at Plessis-lès-Tours in August 1580 during the negotiations with the Protestant Dutch for a leadership role for Anjou in their fight against Spain, he accompanied the Duke to London in 1581–1582 and then on his abortive – and for Bodin acutely hairy – mission in the Low Countries in 1582–1583[11]. Consorting throughout with politicians, diplomats, scholars, and lawyers both at home and abroad and reading avidly, Bodin was better informed than most about European affairs past and present.

Bodin's writing evinces the breadth of his knowledge and experience[12]. Yet, alongside the daunting linguistic and historiographic demands posed by his work, its sheer volume and the lack of a proper critical edition exacerbate the challenge of studying Bodin other than piecemeal. We badly need a hypertext digital edition of the »République« such as the one Professor Ioannis Evrigenis has long been trying to get off the ground[13]. This kind of resource would facilitate systematic comparison between and across the different versions of the text, and enable us to track the tiniest revision. As things stand, however, scholars cite either the first French edition of 1576 or that of 1583, both of which Bodin himself had readied for the press, or else that of 1591, sometimes also cross-referencing his expanded Latin version of 1586 or even the manifestly faulty 1606 English translation by Richard Knolles, an amalgam of French and Latin source-texts, reissued in facsimile in 1962 with a commentary by Kenneth McRae[14]. (There is no satisfactory English translation either of the French or of the Latin text, though Professor Evrigenis is at work on the latter[15].) The late Mario Turchetti's parallel-text French-Latin edition, of which Books I–III have now appeared, is thus welcome, identifying as it does the principal discrepancies between the 1593 French edition and the 1591 Latin one which are its copy-texts, though it too offers relatively little by way of explanatory or textual notes; unfortunately, whether the remaining three books will follow is unclear[16]. Anyone serious about analysing textual variation as an index of Bodin's changing outlook must therefore turn to the physical copies of the original sixteenth-century

---

11 *Griffiths*, Humanists and Representative Government in the Sixteenth Century; *Machielsen*, Bodin in the Netherlands.
12 *Greengrass*, Experiential World of Bodin. For a bibliography of Bodin's works printed in his lifetime, see *Bibliographie critique*; *Lloyd*, Jean Bodin, p. 117–129. For an online index of sources, see *McRae et al.*, Bodin Sources Index.
13 https://sites.tufts.edu/dynamicvariorum/archives/253 (01.02.2024); https://sites.tufts.edu/bodinproject/ (01.02.2024). See also *Evrigenis*, Digital Tools and the History of Political Thought. Evrigenis is at work on an English translation of the Latin text, and I am grateful for advance access to it.
14 *Bodin*, Republique 1576; *id.*, Republica 1586; *id.*, Commonweale 1606; *id.*, Commonweale 1962. To illustrate, in his Preface to *id.*, République Liber I 2013, Quentin Skinner cites the McRae-Knolles edition.
15 For an Italian translation, with notes and commentary, of the 1583 French edition, see *Bodin*, Stato.
16 *Bodin*, République Liber I; Liber II; Liber III. The editors list as their copy-texts several of the 1593 French editions and the 1591 Latin one which they cross-reference with a number of others (Introduction to Liber I, 101–111).

editions published in his lifetime or else to the digital ones accessible via the online resource Gallica (https://gallica.bnf.fr/).

Given the sweeping comparative scope of Bodin's work, it is odd that there is no study of the place of representative assemblies – estates, diets, parliaments, landtagen, ständen – in Bodin's thought. Such institutions are rarely mentioned in Bodin scholarship except in two contexts, both centred on the French Estates General. The first involves the argument that Bodin became more ›absolutist‹ by the time he wrote the »République«; the second – the attempt to square his political theory and practice and reconcile what he said in the first edition of the »République« with how he acted a few months later as a delegate, and then spokesman, of the Third Estate at Blois, and how he subsequently justified his actions in the journal of that assembly, as well as in later editions of the »République«. The idea of Bodin's alleged conversion from a constitutionalist in his »Methodus ad facilem historiarum cognitionem« (1566; rev. 1572), a seminal exposition of the ars historica and its implications for a comparative study of politics and public law, into an absolutist in the »République« had originated more than half a century ago with Julian Franklin and soon gained the status of orthodoxy[17]. Quentin Skinner, in his prefatory essay to Turchetti's 2013 edition of Book I, and Sophie Nicholls in her 2019 article on Bodin, are but the latest scholars to repeat it, albeit with some qualifications[18]. Skinner remarks on – though he does not explain – the apparent shift in Bodin's thinking about the Estates from seemingly attributing to them the power to limit what the monarch can do in the »Methodus« to disavowing that the Estates possess any such power ten years later in the »République«. In support of this claim, Skinner and others invoke Bodin's memorable formulation from the single most extensively scrutinized chapter of the treatise: »De la Souverainete« (»Of Sovereignty«), I.ix:

»Et en cela se cognoist la grandeur, & maiesté d'un vray Prince souverain, quand les estats de tout le people sont assemblez presentans requestes, & supplications à leur Prince en toute humilité, sans avoir aucune puissance de rien commander, ny decerner, ny voix deliberative: ains ce qui'il plaist au Roy consenter, ou dissentir, commander, ou defendre, est tenu pour loy, pour edit, pour ordonnance. En quoy ceux qui ont escrit du devoir des Magistrats, & autres livres semblables, se sont abusez de soustenir que les estats du people sont plus grands que le Prince: chose qui fait revolter les vrais sugets de l'obeïssance qu'ils doivent à leur Prince souverain [...].«[19]

»And in this the greatness and majesty of the true sovereign prince is seen when the estates of all the people are assembled to present their requests and supplications to their Prince in all humility, without having any power to command, grant, or decide anything: thus, what the King is pleased to consent to, or dissent from, command, or defend is held to be

---

17 *Franklin*, Jean Bodin and the Rise of Absolutist Theory.
18 *Skinner*, Preface, in »République« Liber I; *Nicholls*, Sovereignty and Government, p. 63–44.
19 *Bodin*, Republique 1576, I.ix, p. 136 f. This passage takes aim at recent Calvinist resistance writings, among them the lawyer Hotman's »Franco-Gallia« (1573) and the theologian de Bèze's »Du droit des magistrats« (1574).

law, edict, or ordinance. Therefore, those who have written of the duties of magistrates, and other similar books are wrong to claim that the estates of the people are greater than the Prince: such notions incite true subjects to revolt from the obedience they owe their sovereign prince. [...] All such ideas are absurd and incompatible.«

These lines, it is said, reinforce Bodin's conception of the sovereign as *solutus legibus*, unfettered by or free from all law, rendering Bodin an absolutist avant la lettre.

Such readings emphasizing ideological discrepancy between the »Methodus« and the »République« have now been challenged. In her 2013 edition of the »Methodus«, Sara Miglietti convincingly argues for greater continuity between the two works[20]. So, too, Richard Tuck, in his »The Sleeping Sovereign: The Invention of Modern Democracy« (2016), Daniel Lee in his two monographs, »Popular Sovereignty in Early Modern Constitutional Thought« (2016) and »The Right of Sovereignty: Jean Bodin on the Sovereign State and the Law of Nations« (2021), and Benjamin Straumann in his »Crisis and Constitutionalism: Roman Political Thought from the Fall of the Republic to the Age of Revolution« (2016) variously dispute Franklin's and his followers' contention that in the »République« Bodin abandoned his erstwhile constitutionalism[21]. However, neither Miglietti, nor Tuck nor Lee nor Straumann has much to say about the Estates General or other representative bodies. Nor do they engage with the detailed analyses by Mark Greengrass and others of Bodin's involvement with the Blois Estates which opened four months after the »République«'s publication, and his tenacious defence of the Third Estate against both manipulation by the king and threat of it being ›out-voted‹ by the other two estates, the Nobility and the Clergy[22].

Tuck denies the claim of Bodin's newly dismissive view of the Estates General not in the main body of his chapter but in a note appended to it. Besides, in doing so Tuck cites not the »République« but the »Receuil«. This in turn rather weakens his argument by presuming if not an outright contradiction, at least a considerable divergence between the two works. »Bodin«, says Tuck, »continued to believe that the fundamental laws of France could not be changed except with the consent of the Estates; he made that clear in the most concrete of circumstances the year after the ›Republic‹ was published, when as a delegate at the Estates General at Blois

---

20 *Bodin*, Methodus, p. 31–48.
21 *Tuck*, Invention of Modern Democracy, p. 31–35; *Straumann*, Roman Political Thought from the Fall of the Republic to the Age of Revolution, p. 278–302; *Lee*, Popular Sovereignty in Early Modern Constitutional Thought, p. 187; *id.*, Bodin on the Sovereign State and the Law of Nations, p. 95 f., p. 148–180. For an earlier assertion of continuity between the »Methodus« and the »République«, see *King*, Comparative Analysis of Bodin and Hobbes, p. 300–310.
22 *Greengrass*, A Day in the Life of the Third Estate; *id.*, Peace and Reform in the French Kingdom 1576–1585, ch. 3: »The Estates of Blois and the *Bien Public*«, p. 66–122; *id.*, The Experiential World of Bodin, p. 79–83. See also *Crahay*, Bodin aux États Généraux de 1576; *Ulph*, Bodin and the Estates-General of 1576. For the most recent discussion in relation to confessional divisions and citizenship, see *Jones*, Liberty of Conscience and the Boundaries of the Polity, ch. 3: 'Jean Bodin's Citizenship: Property, Pluralism, and the Polity', p. 138–201.

in 1577 he spoke out against the alienation of the royal domain (a constant theme of his writing and activity)«²³. Tuck's Bodin, it seems, is preoccupied only with the representative assembly of his native France and none other, registering his dissent in an occasional anonymous pamphlet not in his major treatise.

In resorting to Bodin's printed diary of the Blois Estates, moreover, Tuck never probes the significance of its simultaneous publication in French and Latin. Why had Bodin not confined himself to the vernacular but instantly brought out the »Recueil« in Latin too, in sharp contrast to the »République« which had to wait 10 years for a Latin translation? Why was he so keen for the European audience to learn what had transpired at Blois and advertise his own audacity in checking the machinations of the king and the ultra-Catholic warmongers? Tuck certainly has a point but that point needs to be argued with reference to Bodin's larger – and developing – treatment of political assemblies in the »République«. For, as Mark Greengrass has shown, Bodin incorporated a vignette of the Blois Estates into his discussion of such bodies in later editions of his treatise, tinkering with it right up until the Latin version of 1586[24].

Bodin was at once a committed universalist, empiricist, and comparatist, so we must ask how representative institutions fit into the overall structure of his thought, and assess how he conceptualized, and judged, the stature and authority of such bodies across diverse political systems. Not only did Bodin insist, I demonstrate, that representative assemblies were the target of both tyrants and colonial powers, and that their extensive web often worked best in aristocratic regimes. He was adamant that without them the state cannot long survive.

II.

Bodin's approach to representative institutions, this essay suggests, is at once bolder and more sophisticated than we have thought. His seemingly categorical assertion of the Estates' utter incapacity and abjection vis-à-vis their princely sovereign in »République« I.ix is, if not negated, at least considerably tempered, by what he says in III.vii about the corporate structure of the state and the Estates' place within it, no less than by how he says it. As Sarah Miglietti and Elisa Jones have variously shown, the sweeping juridical statements Bodin makes early on, above all in Books I and II, are not just fleshed out, but subtly refashioned, amended, and modulated in later sections of the work which have received far less critical attention[25]. And

---

23 *Tuck*, Invention of Modern Democracy, p. 57–58.
24 *Greengrass*, Experiential World of Bodin, p. 79 passim.
25 *Miglietti*, Sovereignty, Territory, and Population in Bodin's République, p. 22–23, p. 31; *Jones*, Liberty of Conscience and the Boundaries of the Polity, p. 197 passim. For earlier discussions along similar lines which, however, tend to overemphasize the tension between theory and practice, see *Denault*, Legitimation of the Parlement of Paris and the Estates General of France 1560–1614, p. 428 f.; *Keohane*, Philosophy and the State in France, p. 54–82.

this process of elaboration and adjustment, bringing in various extra-juridical elements, cannot be reduced to a mere juxtaposition of political theory and practice.

III.vii: »De Corps et Colleges, Estats & Communautez« is key to grasping Bodin's notion of representative assemblies. Bodin worked very hard at the underlying logic of the »République«. In order to understand III.7 one needs to put it in the context of Book III as a whole. In all the French editions brought out in Bodin's lifetime, it concludes a sequence of six chapters variously expounding the role, power, and duties of the council of state (also called a senate), officers, commissioners, and magistrates. How and why did Bodin find it necessary at that point in the text to confront the issue of corporate bodies?

In III.vii, Bodin articulates his vision of the state as made up of a plethora of smaller units, starting with what he defines as the natural community – the family[26]. Although he acknowledges that, in theory, the state could consist only of families, in practice this virtually never happens and, in any case, a state of this kind would be highly unstable. Rather, alongside families, states comprise a multitude of heterogeneous civil and religious bodies licensed by the sovereign: corporations, colleges, estates, and communities. These variously centre on politics or religion or education or professions and trades or the administration of justice or magistracy; their membership, accorded for life or a limited term, creates a web of mutual links and interdependencies, fostering and strengthening the fabric of any society. Among such bodies Bodin numbers universities and colleges, professional and trade associations, artisanal guilds, convents, abbeys, and churches, parlements (including the highest court of the land – the Parlement of Paris), and estates, whether provincial or general.

It would be difficult to overemphasize the significance of Bodin's inclusion of representative institutions along this variegated spectrum. Rather than setting them apart from other types of communal organization, Bodin sees such bodies as integral to the state's complex, pluralistic character. Yes, they have their own distinctive features, both formal and cultural, but they also share essential characteristics with other socio-political formations, whether educational, religious, judicial, magisterial, professional, or commercial; and their members typically belong to, or boast prior experience of, various other organizations[27]. Viewed from this perspective, the (power) relationship between the sovereign, whether princely, aristocratic, or popular, and the general assembly becomes far less straightforward than Books I and II might lead us to assume.

Bodin identifies four topics he intends to consider in III.vii: the origins of colleges, corporations, and other collective bodies; their power and privileges; the sys-

---

26 *Bodin*, République 1576, p. 381 passim. Bodin mostly speaks of »république« – which Knolles translates as »commonwealth«, and only sometimes »l'état«. In what follows, I use the modern term »state« for the sake of clarity.
27 For a brilliant analysis of Third Estate delegates to Blois in 1576, see *Greengrass*, A Day in the Life of the Third Estate, p. 77 f.

tem of punishment if they transgress; and their position in the state[28]. What follows illuminates his conception of the role of collective bodies, representative assemblies among them, in the socio-political order. He is unambiguous in placing God above all else, stressing that neither human laws nor princely edicts can derogate from divine law and natural law[29]. While he does argue that the sovereign possesses ultimate power, and that no collective body is legitimate unless licensed by the sovereign, he reconciles this with a firm belief in the critical value of such bodies for the proper operation of the state. He does not treat the French example in isolation. Rather, he draws numerous transnational parallels, and appeals to precedents found in Graeco-Roman sources, scripture, and medieval and contemporary history. Partly, he does this to hint at shortcomings in the French system. Above all, though, Bodin seeks to construct a universal model of state formation, examining the concept of the state from diachronic and synchronic perspectives. While it is beyond the scope of this essay to delve into all the characteristics of the state outlined in Bodin's treatise, from III.vii one can safely infer that he gave collective bodies at both national and sub-national level a vital place in his overarching scheme.

The state, Bodin argues, can be broken down into units of increasing breadth and scope. He identifies the family as the principal unit in any state, and suggests that groups of families form civil communities such as colleges and corporations, and that multiple such units in turn form a state. Within this scheme, the term community applies equally to family, college, and state. In the French edition(s), the terminology is somewhat ambiguous, and, for this reason, the Latin one (which I discuss below), offers clearer definitions of each of the units in his scheme. It defines a college as the »legitimate association of three or more persons of the same condition« (»legitima trium pluriumve personarum eiusdem conditionis consociatio«), a corporation as »the union of multiple colleges« (»plurium collegiorum coniunctio«), and a community as »the collection of all families, colleges, and corporations of a given town, which is united by a common right« (»omnium familiarum, collegiorum, & corporum eiusdem oppidi iuris communione sociata multitudo«)[30]. Bodin elucidates the make-up of the state in terms of multiple levels of organisation: individuals > families > colleges > corporations > communities > state. As societies develop, he argues, they acquire each of these wider levels of organisation, even though a state could in principle comprise families alone.

Bodin makes sovereign power central to the formation and survival of states. »[D]iverse corporations and communities united under sovereign power«, he avers, »make up the state« (»plusieurs corps, & communautez alliez par puissance souveraine, font une Republique«), and he goes on to define the state as »a community governed by sovereign power« (»une communauté gouvernee par puissance souveraine«)[31]. Early societies, he explains, were ignorant of any form of »republic or

---

28   Bodin, République 1576, p. 381.
29   Ibid., p. 387.
30   Bodin, Republica 1586, p. 327; cf. id., République 1576, p. 381.
31   Bodin, République 1576, p. 381.

sovereign power« (»republique ni puissance souveraine«), and as such fell prey to factional strife and violence. At the heart of his theory of the state is the concept of »l'amitié« (amity, friendship). He sees amity as the bedrock of communal organisation: »l'amitié est le seul fondement de toute société«. Amity helps create, and sustains, collective bodies: it is a glue that binds society together and ensures its survival and flourishing. Indeed, amity is more necessary than justice itself, for it fosters natural justice, that is, love between men and men's love of God[32]. For Bodin, »l'amitié et bienveillance« (»amity and kindness«) are at the core of communities, and he is adamant that states cannot exist »sans amitié« (»without amity«)[33]. No wonder the values a tyrant seeks to undermine first are »l'union« and »l'amitié« (»unity« and »amity«), knowing that crackdown on assemblies is the surest means to that end[34].

How then does Bodin view the nature, composition, and jurisdiction of the various collective bodies? More precisely, how autonomous does he think they are or should be? He emphasizes the power of the sovereign over them on numerous occasions, noting that neither a corporation nor a college can exist without »l'autorité du souverain« (»sovereign authority«), and that »les statuts du college« (»statutes of the college or collegium«) are either established by the sovereign, or by the founder of the college with the authority of the sovereign[35]. While acknowledging this limitation, Bodin underlines the power of collective bodies again and again. In particular, he identifies the judges and magistrates as the colleges with the most influence[36]. Provided they do nothing to subvert either their own statutes or the laws of the land, Bodin repeats after Solon, collective bodies are within their rights to devise any regulations they see as tending to the public good[37]. He goes on to defend the right of colleges to impose penalties upon those who disobey the relevant ordonnances, but stresses that colleges should concern themselves only with »ce qui leur est commun« (»what they share in common«) not »autres affaires« (»with other things«)[38]. In short, Bodin sees a crucial place for corporate bodies in the socio-political order, but stresses that they must be subject to the scrutiny of the sovereign and operate strictly within the established system.

Bodin shows keen interest in the internal organisation of colleges and other collective bodies. He notes the requirement of equality among members, with everyone entitled to a deliberative voice: all must be »egaux en puissance, pour le regard de la communauté, ayants chacun voix deliberative« (»equal in power in the eyes of the community, each having a deliberative voice«)[39]. However, he suggests that the leaders can be appointed to rule, correct, and punish colleagues. He then considers at length how the decision-making process should operate in such bodies. Regarding

32 Ibid., p. 383.
33 Ibid., p. 395.
34 Ibid., p. 398.
35 Ibid., p. 384.
36 Ibid., p. 386.
37 Ibid., p. 390.
38 Ibid., p. 391.
39 Ibid., p. 384.

matters which are of individual interest to members, he argues, decisions should be taken with unanimous consent, but regarding those which are common to all, a simple majority is sufficient; this stipulation, we shall see, is further elaborated in subsequent French editions, and again revised in the Latin one in the light of the author's participation in the Estates General[40]. Bodin next advances a legal framework for the punishment of collective bodies should they transgress. He maintains that if a regional assembly approves a criminal act, the whole community should be held responsible and punished accordingly – for example, in the case of an all-out rebellion. However, in the absence of such an institutional warrant, collective punishment is not appropriate[41].

Bodin is resolute that collective bodies are at the core of any state. Echoing a long line of thinkers, he describes communal organisation as a natural instinct and links this innate human sociability with the emergence of civil society. He identifies the formation of collective bodies as a key step in the development of the state. The state, he argues, cannot survive without them, just as society cannot survive without l'amitié[42]. There is no better means, Bodin contends, than estates, colleges, and corporations of preserving democracies and ruining tyrannies (»pour maintenir les estats populaires et ruiner les tyrannies«)[43]. But whereas democracies welcome them all, and tyrannies seek to abolish them all, aristocracies and just monarchies are best served by a moderate number of well-regulated collective bodies. This argument is illustrated with choice vignettes drawn primarily from ancient Roman history. Numa Pompilius stands as the originator of collective bodies, and Claudius the Tribune as their restorer; conversely, a series of tyrants or would-be tyrants from Tarquin to Julius Caesar and Nero are indicted for relentlessly striving to asphyxiate them, Nero, whom the Senate would later denounce as public enemy, in particular fearful of conspiracies against evil rulers fomented in assemblies[44].

Bodin moves seamlessly – and cannily – from Neronian Rome to contemporary France and Europe. He introduces his reflections on the Estates General within a broader discussion about the internal organisation of collective bodies, and devotes the chapter's closing pages to expounding the role and significance of representative institutions. As noted above, he accords a vital place to both sub-national and national collective bodies, from the smallest guild or college to general assemblies. He now declares, innocuously enough, that »just monarchy has no surer foundation than the estates of the people, corporations, and colleges« (»la juste Royauté n'a point de fondement plus asseuré que les estats du peuple, corps, & colleges«)[45]. Even as he underscores the fundamental importance of all these bodies to the proper functioning of the political order, Bodin makes another astute rhetorical move. For,

---

40 Ibid., p. 388 f.; *Greengrass*, Experiential World of Bodin, p. 80 f.
41 *Bodin*, République 1576, p. 391 passim.
42 Ibid., p. 399.
43 Ibid., p. 398.
44 Ibid., p. 398 f.
45 Ibid., p. 399.

quietly dropping »corps et colleges« (»corporations and collegia«), he argues that in an emergency it is only »the estates of the people, and of every province, town, and community« (»les estats du people, & de chacune province, ville, & communauté«) that make possible the raising of funds, assembling of forces, and defence against enemies. With a note of admonition in his tone, Bodin points out that even princes previously bent on abolishing the estates then realise they have no better protection than those very institutions[46]. The rhetorical crescendo reaches a climax with a passionate celebration of the general assembly, »estats generaux de tous les sugets« (»general estates of all the people«), the prince at its helm. It is there, Bodin gushes, that affairs touching each and every member of the commonwealth are communicated; it is there that just grievances of the poor subjects, which otherwise never reach the prince's ears, are heard; it is there that larcenies, thefts, and other crimes unknown to the prince are revealed[47]. The general assembly thus emerges as an ideal platform for airing public concerns and direct communication between ruler and ruled. Bodin's paean exemplifies what Mark Greengrass has dubbed the »beneficent myth« of the Estates General, shared by the French across the confessional spectrum, as the one institution capable of safeguarding the »bien publique« (»public good«)[48].

Bodin, having condemned unsavoury attempts to stifle representative institutions, thus seemingly reverts to a portrait of the general assembly akin to the one in I.ix which many see as glorifying royal absolutism. For he marvels at the subjects' excitement and pride whenever the monarch appears before them. Even if their pleas often go unrequited, Bodin concludes, the prince's attendance at the general assembly mightily boosts his standing with the people. As good as calling for more regular meetings of the Estates General, Bodin extols Spain where the estates are held every two or three years, and commends England where, he says, they meet often enough[49]; a transparent gibe at France where the Estates General have not met since 1561[50].

Bodin views representative bodies as cementing the sovereign's primacy; and seems committed to preserving a system which gives the people a political voice, albeit one that in theory can be ignored. Yet, contrary to what the historiography has long been telling us, Bodin does in fact envisage circumstances where the sovereign monarch can ill afford to disregard the people's complaints. He conveys the point through an arresting – and threatening – metaphor:

»& tout ainsi que plusieurs coups d'artillerie l'un apres l'autre, n'ont pas si grand effect, pour abattre un fort, que si tous ensemble sont delaschez: aussi les requestes particulieres s'en vont le plus souvent en fumee: mais quand les colleges, les communautez, les

---

46 Ibid.
47 Ibid.
48 *Greengrass*, Peace and Reform in the French Kingdom 1576–1585, p. 66.
49 *Bodin*, République 1576, p. 400.
50 In the run-up to the Estates set for December 1576 at Blois, some championed quinquennial meetings. See *Lloyd*, Jean Bodin, p. 161.

estats d'un pays, d'un people, d'un Royaume font leurs plaints au Roy, il luy est mal-aisé de les refuser.«[51]

»For, like discharging many pieces of artillery one after another does not have so great an effect in battering a fort as when they are discharged all at once, so the particular requests often vanish up in smoke: but when collegia, communities, estates of a country, a people, a kingdom make their pleas to the king together, he would be ill-advised to refuse them.«

Comparing the grievances of the people ventilated through colleges, communities, and estates to a formidable gun salvo – and, by implication, likening the king to a fort set to be battered by it, Bodin makes no bones about what he thinks the royal response to this barrage should be. At stake is not whether the king is within his rights to rebuff the subjects' pleas: he is. But it would be unwise – and imprudent – for him to do so. This is a daring and perhaps unexpected stance for Bodin to take. His simile comes across as ominous, not least given the trauma of France's blood-soaked and seemingly interminable civil wars. There is also another aspect of the trope. The metaphor of artillery fire presupposes absolute unanimity. A sudden discharge of shot in multiple directions would be pointless, whereas here the people are all aiming at the king. Could this be an oblique glance at the venerable practice of reconciling and amalgamating, at every geopolitical level, the hundreds of cahiers de doléances (lists of grievances), a process which by its very nature presumes flexibility, readiness to give way, compromise, and strive for consensus and unity[52]? In any case, one could be forgiven for supposing that even in a just monarchy such as France corporate bodies, above all the general assembly, offer subjects the chance to shape royal policy in a way that transcends the venerable concept of giving counsel to the monarch. And Bodin clearly sees this as a good thing, in the very next sentence hailing »a thousand *other* benefits of estates in every country« [emphasis mine] (»a mil autres utilitez des estats en chacun pays«)[53]. Among those, he lists effective raising of troops and money to fight enemies, ridding the country of thieves, and so on; all which tasks, Bodin submits, have been best carried out by the Estates of Languedoc. Theirs is an indispensable contribution to the well-being and administration of the state. Bodin's imaginative avowal of the force of the united remonstrances of the people assembled in the general estates and other collective bodies, notwithstanding there is no formal obligation on the monarch to call them, consult them, or adopt their views, is thus surely not reducible to a simple juxtaposition of juridical propriety versus counsel of prudence.

Switching once again from native to foreign assemblies, Bodin next lauds the estates structure of the Swiss cantons and the German Empire as the finest in Europe. According to the taxonomy developed elsewhere in the tract, the former is not a fully functioning state; the latter is classified as an aristocracy, sovereignty

---

51 Bodin, République 1576, p. 399 f.
52 For a masterful reconstruction of this »harmonisation and homologation« process of the cahiers of the Third Estate in 1576, see *Greengrass*, A Day in the Life of the Third Estate, p. 79 passim.
53 Bodin, République 1576, p. 400.

resting with the electors and imperial diet not the emperor. Of relevance for Bodin's case here is that the Swiss, as well as having an assembly in every village and canton, also have estates general; and that the intricate network of representative assemblies throughout the Empire is equally impressive:

»I'ay bien voulu coter en passant ces particularitez, pour faire entendre le grand bien qui reussist des estats, qui sont encores mieux reiglez és Republiques des Suisses, & de l'empire d'Almaigne, qu'en autres Republiques de l'Europe. car outre les estats de chacune ville, & canton, ils onte leurs estats generaux. les dix circuits de l'empire, ont leurs estats separez, ausquels se raportent les estats particuliers des villes imperiales, & contrees: & les estats des circuits, se raportent aux estats de l'empire: qui fust long temps-a ruyné sans ceste police.«[54]

»I wanted to mention these particularities in passing in order to demonstrate the great success of the estates, of which there is even better regulation in the Commonwealths of the Swiss and the German Empire than in other European states. Besides the estates of each city and canton, they have their central estates: the ten circuits of the Empire have their separate estates to which the particular estates of the imperial cities and counties report, and the estates of the circuit report to the estates of the Empire, without which this polity would have long since perished.«

Bodin then revisits the virtue of moderation. He reiterates that suppressing such bodies spells ruin of the state and its decline into barbarous tyranny (»d'oster tous les corps et communautez, c'est ruiner un Estat et en faire une barbare tyrannie«, i.e. »to suppress all bodies and communities is to ruin a state and make it a barbaric tyranny«), even as he cautions against permitting any and all such formations[55]. Just monarchies would do well, it seems, to emulate the dense multi-level estates structure of the Swiss and the Germans.

The overall effect of III.vii is to undermine some iconic pronouncements from I.ix on the asymmetrical power dynamic between the royal sovereign and his subjects. Bodin's analysis of the pluralistic structure of the state, epitomized by the supremely beneficial co-existence of diverse collective bodies, representative institutions prominent among them, culminates with a startling image of a faceoff between subjects and prince. If united and presenting their grievances together as a community, for Bodin subjects of a just monarchy possess far greater political agency than has been allowed. Meanwhile, his vindication of collective bodies as the surest bulwark against tyranny, and his advocacy both of higher frequency of the Estates General on the model of Spain and England and of wider spread of assemblies across the French socio-political system on the model of the Swiss Confederation and the Empire, point the way towards future reform.

But why has this been missed? Quite apart from the lack of sustained attention to III.vii, perhaps because political scientists and intellectual historians – as also

54 Ibid.
55 Ibid.

editors of Bodin – largely shun metaphors, preferring to focus on juridical formality and what they see as clear statements of principle. They are interested in the questions of the history of law, especially Roman law, and the history of big concepts, mostly inherited from Antiquity, seldom allowing Bodin's different writings to play off one against another or relating them to their immediate context. Yet, alongside his bravura argument that representative assemblies and other collective bodies are integral to the fabric of the state, Bodin's remarkable metaphor of artillery fire dictates a reappraisal of how he construed the relationship between monarch and estates. Or, to put it differently, it signals that scholarship based chiefly on I.ix is at best partial and at worst misleading.

III.

In later published writings, Bodin only reinforced his appreciation for representative institutions. Already in 1577, within a year of the »République«'s first outing in print, he brought out a trenchant diary of the recent Blois Estates convoked on 6 August 1576 to address the divisions in the kingdom, and the second, revised edition of the »République« (soon to be followed by a third and fourth and fifth and more). The former has been much if selectively studied, the latter has garnered next to no critical comment. In their different ways, we shall see, both evince Bodin's deepening sense of representative assemblies as the lifeblood of a political community.

Scholarship has long debated the impact of Bodin's service in the Blois Estates, set down in the »Receuil«, and variously informing subsequent editions of the »République«. These studies centre on how the vocal deputy for Vermandois thwarted Henry III's bid to enforce religious uniformity by war, so contrary to the provisions of the recent Edict of Beaulieu with its promise of religious pluralism and peace, that, moreover, would have lumbered the Third Estate with disproportionate exactions, and how he went on to rationalize his actions in print. Aside from alienating the crown lands which Bodin vehemently opposed as illegitimate, the royal plan entailed that each of the three estates nominate 12 out of their midst, and that those 36 commissioners then attend king and council's discussion of the cahiers de doléances[56]. While initially Nobility, Clergy, and the Third Estate all acceded, and the commission began its tense debate, going back and forth between their various constituents and the king, Bodin remonstrated against this kind of assembly-in-miniature, further arguing that in a corporate body such as the Estates General it is unacceptable for two estates to make a decision unfairly affecting the third, very much what Nobility and Clergy were on the cusp of doing. Bodin further objected that in the presence of king and council, the nominees of the Third Estate would feel overawed, and likely agree to whatever those more exalted than

---

56 *Greengrass*, Peace and Reform in the French Kingdom 1576–1585, p. 91 passim; *Lloyd*, Jean Bodin, p. 160 passim.

they proposed, even if detrimental to their own interests. His eloquent interventions carried the day, at once scuppering Henry's ploy and Bodin's own career prospects. His conduct cost him his credit with the king, a disgrace that was sealed by his publication of the »Recueil«.

All this is often taken as proof of dissonance between Bodin's political theory and practice, »République« and »Recueil«, or else, far more plausibly, explained as interdependence and mutual influence of ideas and lived experience[57]. Even this more nuanced approach, however, tends to overlook the »Receuil's« experimental form, steadfast promotion of good deliberative practice, and lasting legacy for French ›parliamentarism‹. Here one can but adumbrate a few of these themes. A multi-layered work of autobiography, history, counsel, and political thought, the »Receuil« belongs to a familiar genre: the parliamentary diary. While a few national historiographies, principally the English and Polish ones, have explored such texts in detail, the genre's transnational dimension has been strangely neglected[58]. Parliamentary diaries, comprising accounts of proceedings in a general or provincial assembly or just reproducing a few notable speeches, were intended for political patrons or allies or members of a local network, or even just as an aide memoir for the compiler himself. These were not public documents, and, unlike royal addresses printed by official command for wide distribution, at most circulated scribally. Deliberations of such bodies were as a rule meant to be confidential even if reports inevitably leaked out. Foreign diplomats sought to obtain copies for despatch to their masters or else, in countries where they could watch the proceedings, composed summaries themselves.

Bodin's journal is thus doubly unique. First, because he speedily arranged for its print publication, angling not just for domestic but also for international audience; and, secondly, because unlike most reporters, he gave himself a starring role, sedulously shaping the narrative to bolster his own agenda. Why, though, did Bodin want to publish in Latin and not just French, and do so anonymously? One purpose was surely to inform both homegrown and foreign readers about what happened at Blois, including the minutiae of the Estates' protracted, and eventually vain, struggle to work out a viable common stance in the face of escalating religious discord and civil war. Another, for which parading his name on the title-page would have been counterproductive, to establish his own credentials as a brave and effective political actor, confronting peers and social superiors and besting them through his intellectual clout, no matter the personal cost.

The crux at Blois was whether the Catholic deputies – there were only three reformed ones, all among the Nobility – would agree on a new war to root out reli-

---

57 For the former view, see *Ulph*, Bodin and the Estates-General of 1576; for the latter, *Crahay*, Bodin aux États Généraux de 1576; *Greengrass*, A Day in the Life of the Third Estate; *id.*, Experiential World of Bodin; *Collins*, Birth of the Royal State 1561–1651.
58 *Kewes et al.*, Towards a History of Parliamentary Culture; *Van der Meulen*, Parliamentary Diary. For the French ones from 1576–1577, see *Greengrass*, A Day in the Life of the Third Estate, p. 75–77; *id.*, Peace and Reform in the French Kingdom 1576–1585, p. 83 passim.

gious dissent. Bodin's diary is a valuable source for understanding the tensions that arose from the debates around religion, but it is also a story of the tensions among the different constituencies. First, there are tensions between the king and the three estates since the king tries to guide the deputies' decisions for his own benefit. Bodin introduces a new layer of tension by portraying Clergy and Nobility as the holder of power but also as often colluding against the Third Estate. While he characteristically figures the Third Estate as the most upright in working towards the public good, he does not shy away from disclosing internal conflicts between those pushing for war and those, such as Bodin and his allies, defending peace. A key goal of the »Receuil« then is to legitimize proper deliberative practice, one where participants remain open to changing their mind if weighty arguments are put to them, and to encourage good parliamentary practice in general.

Witness of and actor in a challenging political event, Bodin manipulates the conventions of history writing, embellishing his own role in ways that serve his self-presentation. Superficially, his is a dispassionate, humdrum account, filled with dates and lengthy descriptions of venues and ritual and debates. Despite its title's pretensions to comprehensiveness, »Recueil de tout ce qui s'est négotié en la compagnie du Tiers Estat« (»Account of all that was debated in the assembly of the Third Estate«), it is in fact highly selective. Throughout, Bodin the unnamed author refers to Bodin the deputy in the third person, recounting his maiden intervention thus:

»Bodin deputé de Vermandois, devant que opiner leut tout haut le premier & xii article du cayer general de Vermandois, qui portoit qu'il pleust au Roy maintenir ses suiets en bonne paix, & dedans deux ans tenir un Concile general ou national, pour regler le fait de la Religion: & puis, apres avoir longuement discouru sur les incommoditez de la guerre, fut interrompu par Versoris.«[59]

»Bodin, deputy of Vermandois [...] read aloud the first and seventh articles of the general *cahier* of Vermandois which asked if it would please the King to maintain the subjects in peace and to hold a general or national Council within two years to solve the problem of religion; and after a long speech on the inconveniences of war, he was interrupted by Versoris.«

Bodin styles himself an ardent defender of peace, a leitmotif in the rest of the »Recueil«, and a man who has enemies, with Versoris as his main opponent. Was the idea to include in the Vermandois cahier the demand for a national council to settle religion Bodin's? Certainly, the »République«'s valorization of all manner of assemblies makes it plausible, and we know that the Nobility discussed a Protestant petition for a council of this kind, to be convoked within three years, so presumably the proposal was well known[60].

In the end, the three estates urged Catholic re-unification; it was hardly possible to voice a different opinion in public given the confessional make-up of the del-

---

59 *Bodin*, Recueil, p. 9.
60 *Greengrass*, Peace and Reform in the French Kingdom 1576–1585, p. 78.

egate body[61]. The means of such a re-unification, however, were fiercely contested. Towards the end of December, the deputies hear that several cities in Guyenne have been occupied by Protestants which considerably heightens the stakes of the debate[62]. This, though, does not stop Bodin and the Third Estate from toning down ›sharp passages‹ in the letters addressed by the Nobility and Clergy to the Protestant King of Navarre[63]. As Bodin's account of the proceedings in February and March 1577 shows, the Third Estate will disagree over whether the king should start a new war or try to achieve unity through peaceful means. This will result in frictions within the Third Estate to the point that Bodin, supposedly fearing for his life, decides to carry a sword[64]. Meanwhile, the deputies' respect for religious rituals lessens with time: Bodin notes that on the day of Purification the assembly should have been adjourned, but the political questions now seem too pressing to the deputies[65]. While his advocacy of peace will not win the majority's approval, Bodin stresses that his voice influenced some decisions, including the message delivered to key political actors.

Bodin shows himself adept at exposing the other estates' self-interested motives, and this in turn strengthens his image as avid defender of the bien public. As the episode with the sword reveals, Bodin is far from an impartial witness. On the contrary, he works to present himself in a positive, even heroic light. He is the first to voice concerns that the king's demands would compromise the – mainly financial – interests of the Third Estate. In the absence of the Parisian deputies during several sessions, Bodin ends up presiding. He cleverly uses this opportunity to sway others regarding peace or the royal finances, not without hazard to himself:

»Il y ent un Seigneur qui dit en presence du Roy, que Bodin manioit les Estats à son plaisir, ainsi que ledit Bodin fut averti. Ce qui fut cause que le Roy ne regarda pas, deslors en avant, ledit Bodin, de si bon oeil qu'il avoit accoustumé, comme ledit Bodin presumoit.«[66]

»There was a Sir who said in the presence of the King that Bodin manipulated the Estates according to his desires, of which Bodin was warned. This caused the King to lose his former liking for Bodin, as the latter presumed.«

We hear of other instances of Henry expressing frustration with the actions of his erstwhile dinner companion, who even refuses to serve as an envoy of the Estates, preferring to stay where the decisions are made, and where he can make the greatest difference[67]. Bodin constructs his identity as a leading actor at the Estates, one whose prestige is only heightened by having powerful enemies.

---

61 *Holt*, Attitudes of the French Nobility at the Estates-General of 1576, p. 492.
62 *Bodin*, Recueil, p. 22.
63 Ibid., p. 25 f.
64 Ibid., p. 123.
65 Ibid., p. 57.
66 Ibid., p. 52, p. 78.
67 Ibid., p. 59, p. 65, p. 27.

It is no surprise then that Bodin carefully chooses which other voices to incorporate into his narrative. Take his treatment of the envoys' report of their reception by the Prince of Condé; Henry, King of Navarre; and Montmorency-Damville, Governor of Languedoc. Condé, a Huguenot noted for his bellicosity, refuses to recognize the envoys' legitimacy and charges them with selfish motives before declaring that since only the Nobles actively take part in war, they should be the ones deciding on it[68]. This discourse goes against everything Bodin himself stands for, and he spends little time on it. By contrast, he directly quotes the other Huguenot, the King of Navarre's letter urging the Estates to work towards peace. Navarre's missive is full of pathos in evoking the calamities of war, a trait it imparts to Bodin's text[69]. Thus, out of the sole two Protestant voices found in the »Recueil«, Bodin opts to highlight the one that corresponds to his own views. Later in the book, he also inserts the letter of Montmorency-Damville, a Catholic, which was read publicly at Blois. The rhetoric of this letter again echoes the one used by Bodin and his allies: Montmorency-Damville opens by professing readiness to sacrifice his life for the Catholic Church but then, in a stunning about-turn, makes an impassioned plea for peace. Like Navarre, he begs the deputies to reflect on the state's fragility before declaring a new war[70]. He even speculates that perhaps it is God's will to have the French divided into two religions, and proclaims that in Languedoc confessional co-existence works just fine[71]. Like others before him, Montmorency-Damville reminds his audience that no Protestant will peacefully give up their late won freedom of worship, the exact argument Bodin has used when exhorting the deputies to vote for unification by »the softest and holiest means his Majesty could have«[72]. By reproducing the discourses closest to his own position, Bodin bolsters his own stature as wise and public spirited.

The »Receuil«, as well as aligning him with the cause of peace, enables Bodin to illustrate how he applied his political knowledge at Blois. And that, we learn, was both to secure a desired outcome and to foster good parliamentary practice. For the Vermandois deputy guides the assembly to obey age-old precedents and customs or else to adopt new, better ones. In order to justify his recommendations, he looks to the example of other countries. He does so in three instances. The first pertains to recording date and time of legal documents:

»Ce mesme iour, Bodin depute de Vermandois requit la compagnie du tiers Estat, qu'il fust employé article au cayer, par lequel le Roy seroit supplié ordonner que les sergens & notaires deslors en avant seroyent tenus de dat ter les actes par les heures, du moins devant ou apres midi, & quant aux testaments, qu'il seroit mis ausi s'ils estoyent passez le iour ou la nuicte, remonstrant la coustume presques de tons les autres pays.«[73]

68 Ibid., p. 63f.
69 Ibid., p. 81–85.
70 Ibid., p. 106.
71 Ibid., p. 110f.
72 Ibid., p. 112, p. 37.
73 Ibid., p. 27.

»On that same day [January 3rd], Bodin, deputy of Vermandois, required from the assembly of the Third Estate to write an article in the *cahier* that begged the king to order that the sergeants and notaries from that moment be obliged to date their acts by hours, at least by morning or afternoon, and for wills that it must be written down whether they were made during the day or the night, following a custom found in almost every other country.«

His sensible proposal is approved forthwith. The new procedure will serve to validate a document's authenticity, as, for instance, assemblies' protocols prepared by clerks. Bodin himself will scold some deputies trying to cancel the article on peace for having met in secret, alleging that since the meeting has not been properly recorded, their decisions are invalid[74].

The second case relates to the proprieties of corporate decision-making. As chronicled in the »Recueil«, Bodin's performance at Blois involves successful application of the principle previously outlined in the »République« that in matters pertaining diversely to different segments of a corporate body consent by all is a sine qua non. Now, criticizing the undue influence Nobility and Clergy seek to exert over the Third, Bodin stresses the axiom's antiquity and universality: »la coustume ancienne de ce Royaume, gardee en tous les Royaumes de la Chrestienté, estoit que les deux Estats ne pouvoyent rien arrester, au preiudice du troisiesme« (»the ancient tradition of this State, kept by all the Christian States, was that the two estates could not decide anything to the prejudice of the third«)[75]. As well as blatant injustice to the Third Estate, the alternative would violate a rule long observed not just in France but throughout Christendom.

Lastly, Bodin brings up Roman laws of war when discussing the king's decision to declare war: »les loix des Romains ne permettoyent point que la guerre fust conclude, ny denoncee, que par les grands Estats du peuple, & ne ant moins que la paix se pouvoit conclure & arrester par le menu peuple, attendu les difficultez de la guerre & la douceur de la paix« (»the laws of the Romans did not allow a war to be concluded or denounced only by the great Estates of the people, but nevertheless that peace could be concluded and decided by the small people due to the difficulties of war and the softness of peace«)[76]. Bodin uses a clever rhetorical strategy in this remark: he humbly implies that the Estates do not have the power to make the final decision about war, but he still reminds the reader that the first victims of war are the common people and that that is why they should have a say in the matter.

As well mastermind of his estate's deliberations, Bodin portrays himself as guardian of honest and efficient parliamentary practice that he tries to instill in his colleagues. We have seen him object to the Nobility and Clergy's appointment of commissioners to co-author the final cahier with king and council. Since he is the one who orchestrated the negative vote on the issue in the Third Estate, Bodin is

---

74 Ibid., p. 112.
75 Ibid., p. 77.
76 Ibid., p. 123.

charged with letting the Clergy know about the Third Estate's refusal to comply[77]. He zealously undertakes this mission, and exploits it to teach the Clergy a lesson in policy making:

»Apres avoir fait une preface d'honneur, il commença son propos par une maxime politique, qu'il n'y a rien plus dangereux en matière d'Estat que de se tenir ferme & arresté en ses propos, ains qu'il faut changer & s'accommoder aux plus saines opinions.«[78]

»After having delivered an honorable preamble, he started his speech with a political maxim, that there is nothing more perilous in matters of state than to stay firm and unyielding in one's words and one thus should change and accept the soundest opinion.«

Sending a handful of commissioners, Bodin argues, would reduce the representative power of the assembly; worse yet, those from the Third Estate, intimidated by the presence of their social betters, might be led to modify their opinions[79]. He gives the example of Louis XI who skillfully manipulated his deputies by not letting them debate without him. Bodin holds that a general assembly is more robust and better equipped to work towards the public good; he even uses the very modern-sounding formulation »pluralité des voix« to praise the French Estates[80].

In fine, setting aside obvious differences in genre, form, and purpose, does the »Receuil« subvert the conception of representative institutions emanating from the »République«? Not, I suggest, if we take on board how the latter's III.vii envisions the role and function of such bodies. Far from reneging on anything in the treatise, the diary applies, clarifies, and develops its monumental predecessor's insights. We have seen this, for example, in relation to corporate decision-making: at Blois, as the »Recueil« narrates, Bodin triumphantly upholds the requisite of unanimity when what is at stake affects one estate differently. His redoubtable command of law and history likewise ensures the fiasco of the plan to alienate the royal domain, but nothing in his argument denies an iota of the »République«. Claims to the contrary typically fail to notice that Bodin persuades the Estates to reject the royal plan entirely in line with the principles enunciated in III.vii. Furthermore, the »Recueil« claims, variously echoing both I.i and III.vii, that once the cahiers de doléances have been submitted, the deputies can only make requests but have no actual say in the decisions which are reserved for the king and council, hardly a claim a closet republican or proponent of the mixed constitution would advance[81]. So, too, Bodin's valiant if ultimately futile pursuit of religious peace at Blois – and in the »Receuil« – is prefigured in the »République«, again in III.vii. There Bodin provides an overview of religious societies, warning against conspiracies hatched under the colour of religion and the danger secret ones pose to the state, his prime exhibits,

77 Ibid., p. 72.
78 Ibid., p. 72 f.
79 Ibid., p. 74.
80 Ibid., p. 72 f.
81 Ibid., p. 92.

respectively, Bacchanals and Munster Anabaptists. Quoting Cato, he insists that it is infinitely more expedient either to permit such bodies to meet publicly or else to ban them tout court[82]. Could this be a damning pointer to the cells of the Catholic League formed without royal warrant straight after the edict of pacification, and proliferating by stealth ever since[83]? And which the king later tried to hijack by making himself the League's head? Bodin does draw a flagrant parallel with contemporary France as he ruminates on how judiciously to manage religious divisions. Using his cherished metaphor of a ship tossed at sea, he argues that although religious uniformity is the ideal, a wise prince, rather than seeking to eradicate a sizeable confessional minority by force of arms, ought instead to accommodate it in order to preserve peace, imitating a seasoned pilot who trims his course in a storm safely to reach the shore[84]. By writing himself into the narrative of the »Receuil«, and by depicting his interventions at the Estates as often decisive and always animated by a concern about the public good, Bodin takes up his rightful place alongside illustrious public figures and law-makers named in the »République«, Cato among them.

In III.vii, we have seen Bodin expatiate on the internal regulation of collective bodies. The »Receuil« elaborates on this theme with reference to the French Estates General, proffering, like the »République«, suggestions for reform by analogy with foreign institutions. As evinced by its transmission in print, this facet of the »Recueil« was to have long-term bearing on the French parliamentary tradition. For Bodin's journal of a fruitless assembly, rather than perishing the way of other political ephemera, continued to be republished, read, and mined as a rare repository of information about the workings of the Estates General. It was reprinted in 1614 – with authorial attribution – to coincide with the first Estates General for over a quarter century, and in 1651, during the Fronde, when an Estates General was summoned but never actually met, and again in 1789, when, after more than 150 years of desuetude, the assembly reconvened fleetingly before being converted first into National Assembly and then into National Constituent Assembly[85]. Bodin's legacy as political writer thus remained inextricably linked with his lucid, engrossing, and at times acerbic appraisal of France's general assembly.

The »Receuil« does not relate the official ending of the Blois Estates[86]. Nor does it supply a coda. Why? Granted, the king's final decision to revoke the edict of pacification goes against all of Bodin's hopes and endeavours, so recounting it would do little to shore up his reputation as an influential deputy. But another, no less compelling reason could be his wish to focus the reader's attention on parliamentary process rather than the dispiriting outcome. And in this, he is doubtless successful.

---

82 *Bodin*, République 1576, p. 396.
83 Impeccably reconstructed in *Greengrass*, Peace and Reform in the French Kingdom 1576–1585, ch. 3.
84 *Bodin*, République 1576, p. 397. Elsewhere, Bodin uses a sailing metaphor to justify princely sovereignty, suggesting that the ship of state would be wrecked before the helmsman could consult those on board (i. e. estates).
85 *Bodin*, Relation; *Quinet (ed.)*, Recueil 1651; *Duval/Lalourcé (ed.)*, Recueil 1789.
86 *Crahay*, Bodin aux États Généraux de 1576, p. 113.

IV.

In 1577, when completing his diary of the Blois Estates, Bodin was also tinkering with the »République«, whose second edition coincided with the »Recueil«'s first. Among other revisions, he affixed a short but potent passage at the close of III.vii. This new finale uses the history of Roman imperialism to reaffirm the utility of corporate bodies:

»Or tout ainsi qu'il n'y a rien meilleur pour la force & union des sugets que les corps & communautez, aussi n'y a il rien plus expedient pour asservir les ennemis vaincus, que leur oster premierement les corps & communautez, comme tresbien pratiquerent les Romains apres avoir vaincu les Rois de Macedoine: & depuis encores les Acheans assugetis [...].«[87]

»And so it goes that there is nothing better for the power and unity of subjects than corporations and communities, and there is nothing more expedient to enslave vanquished enemies than to deprive them of their corporations and colleges, as the Romans excellently did after defeating the kings of Macedon, and also after subjugating the Achaeans [...].«

As ever, Bodin's lexical choices are revealing. He nimbly slides from »corps & communautez« to »antiqua concilia« (»ancient councils«), quite a different proposition, which the Romans restored to the conquered Achaeans, Phocaeans, Boeotians, and the rest of Greece, having subdued and turned them into obedient subjects[88]. Dismantling indigenous councils and other forms of assembly thus emerges as a tried and tested instrument of imperial control, as it enervates the political community that withers without them. Bodin does not decry the Romans for what they did. If anything, he is impressed by the efficacy of their modus operandi that, one suspects, a modern-day colonial empire would do well to copy. His ratiocination is eerily reminiscent of François Hotman's pungent resistance tract »Francogallia« (1573; rev. 1576). For, although the victims of Roman imperialism are different in each case, and although Bodin remains aloof whereas Hotman eviscerates the Romans for extinguishing the Gauls' ancient constitution and, with it, their manliness and liberty, the two authors converge in viewing public councils as the very lifeblood of a nation[89]. Unlike Hotman, Bodin at no time assigns a foundational role, either in historical or legal terms, to representative assemblies, yet both writers – Bodin implicitly, Hotman explicitly – equate those ancient assemblies with the French Estates General.

In the successive editions of the »République« that, starting with the third authorized one of 1580, were demoted from the imposing folio format to the more modest, and cheaper, octavo, Bodin continued to adjust his handling of corporate

---

87 *Bodin*, République 1577, p. 368. In the Latin version, Bodin stresses the Romans' prudence (Republica, p. 347).
88 *Bodin*, République 1577, p. 368.
89 Hotman speaks of »publicum gentis concilium« (»public council of the people«), Francogallia.

bodies, adding, and repeatedly tweaking, cameos of the Blois Estates. Yet it was not until the enlarged and revised Latin version of 1586 that he went full-on autobiographical, reciting in the first person his feats at Blois. Scholars have tracked the shifting story of Bodin's parliamentary adventure across the French and Latin texts[90]. Yet the broader resonance of the Latin for his treatment of representative institutions remains uncharted territory. How does Bodin translate the French »corps«, »communauté«, »États Généraux«, or »Tiers État« and what are the consequences of his lexical choices? Bodin was more than alive to the significance of language, famously analysing the phrasing of statutes and edicts to corroborate the prince's supremacy over the estates[91]; and so must we be.

To comprehend the reception of the »Republica« by people steeped in Latin writings and Roman history alike (an enterprise distinct from, if related to, charting his use of Roman law) would require a lengthy investigation, also taking in the »Methodus«, the Latin and French texts of the oration to the Polish ambassadors, and the self-translated »Commentarius«. For the moment, a handful of relevant examples from his master-text must suffice. Bodin uses different terms to denote the general assembly, ranging from »conventus« (»universae Galliae conventus«) and »comitia« (»Nostri reges non ita saepe ut Angli comitia cogunt«) to »senatus« (»senatus populique Anglici ordines«)[92]. Echoing the medieval ordo theory, the phrase »cuiusque civitatis ordinibus convocatis« corresponds to the French »les trois estats de France en general«; the Latin »populi tribus et ordines« corresponds to the French »les estats de tout le people«. Elsewhere, the Latin phrase describing the assembly of the three estates is expansive compared to the French one, running from »cuisque civitatis« to »legitime coactis«, where the French only describes »les trois estats de France en general, ou de chacun baillage en particulier«[93]. Is there a discernible trend across the »Republica«, and, if so, what are the overall connotations of Bodin's Latin? Would it be too much to say that the French editions predominantly refer to »estats«, while the Latin mostly refers to »comitiorum suffragiis« and »populi comitiis ac suffragiis«, thus highlighting a connection with the Roman assemblies of the people (»comitiae«) rather than the patrician senate? And what

---

90 *Greengrass*, Experiential World of Bodin, p. 80–82; for the autobiographical reference to Blois in the Latin Epistola prefaced to République 1583), sig. [a8]-vo, see *Blair*, Authorial Strategies in Bodin, p. 148. Mario Turchetti omits to address these larger implications in his Bodin as Self-Translator of his République.
91 Bodin stresses that if the estates had power over the king, the »leges ac edicta« would be published under their name and not the monarch's, which they are not, and demonstrates their subservience to the prince in the passages which follow. See I.viii in respectively Republica 1586, p. 89; République 1576, p. 137.
92 *Bodin*, Republica, p. 335, p. 346, p. 91.
93 *Bodin*, Republica 1586, I.viii, p. 89; *id.*, République 1576, p. 136. In the Commentarius, Bodin translates »estates« as »ordinum« and the third estate as »tertius ordo«: this rendition corresponds most closely to the institutional reality of 1570s France and, an added bonus, evokes no potentially misleading associations with ancient Roman institutions such as the popular assemblies or the senate.

to make of Bodin's extensive use of the word »consociatio« (whose equivalent is absent from the French) which has led some scholars proleptically to link his work with de Tocqueville, Montesquieu, and Guizot[94]? These and similar questions are ones that a future study would do well to answer.

The artillery metaphor in III.vii, which has persisted across all the French editions, disappears from the Latin one. With religious divisions compounded by uncertainty over the succession following the death of the Duke of Anjou, Bodin's decision to remove a trope conjuring the image of subjects firing at their monarch seems nothing if not sensible. But, contrary to what we might expect, the equivalent passage in the »Republica«, though stripped of a disturbing metaphor, is in some respects sharper than the original:

»Sed quam sint necessaria totius populi concilia, ex eo perspicitur, quod quibus populis sua concilia cogere licet, cum iis optime agitur, caeteri populi tributis ac servitute urgentur; nam singulourm voces minus exaudiuntur: totius vero provinciae clarissima vox est, & rogatio efficax, quam ne princeps quidem ipse, si velit, repudiare possit.«[95]

»But how necessary are councils of the whole people is obvious from the fact that for people who are allowed to call together their councils things go very well, while all the others are oppressed by taxes and servitude; for each voice alone is less clearly heard; but the voice of an entire province is most clear, and its request effective, and not even the prince himself, even if he wanted to, would be able to reject it.«

Not only does the sentence underscore the necessity of public councils or assemblies (something the original French does not do), but, rather than mincing words, states bluntly that the prince cannot reject the collective voice of the people even if tempted to do so. The original, we recall, only said that this would be unwise.

So too Bodin's increasing exasperation with the French political system comes across loud and clear. For whereas the French text simply hints at the benefits of regular estates by praising the frequency of Spanish and English ones, now that the Estates General have gone into abeyance for a decade, Bodin unfavourably compares the reluctance of French kings (»nostri reges«) to summon and work with their Estates unlike their counterparts in Spain and England[96]. And, his ethos boosted by recent ambassadorial service, he further notes the English kings' reliance on parliament for monies. For once, let us quote Knolles's translation which nicely conveys the contemporary flavour of Bodin's aperçu:

»All which is better obserued and kept in Spayne, than in any place of the world, where the assemblies of the estates heretofore haue beene holden euery two or three yeares one. And in England also, for that the people graunt no payments, if the Estates be not assembled: as I remember was done, when as I passed ouer into England embassadour from

---

94 *Lee*, Bodin on the Sovereign State and the Law of Nations, p. 58.
95 *Bodin*, Republica 1586, p. 346 f.
96 Ibid., p. 346.

Frauncis duke of Aniou. Our kings do not so often call together the assemblies of their estates, as doe the kings of England.«[97]

What is this if not a call on Henry III to convoke the Estates? More generally, how can we reconcile Bodin's emphatic insistence in I.ix, persisting across the French and Latin editions, that in a royal or just monarchy the prince need not listen to or even summon the estates with a no less emphatic insistence in III.vii, which, if anything, grows stronger in the »Republica«, on the estates' enormous significance, inestimable benefit, and collective force that the sovereign prince cannot – should not – ignore? Perhaps the answer has to do with Bodin's use of contemporary transnational comparisons, and in 1586, also his own first-hand knowledge not just of the French Estates but also the English Parliament and, even more, his concern about amity and harmony that underpin the new chapter, III.viii, »De ordinibus civium«. At the very least, I hope to have persuaded you that far from undervaluing or dismissing the role of representative institutions, Bodin championed their utility at both general and provincial level, and that he firmly believed that a wise, prudent prince must foster and encourage them.

Bibliography

Sources

Bèze's, Théodore de: Du droit des magistrats, n.pl. 1574.
Bodin, Jean: La Harangue de Messire Charles des Cars prononcée aux magnifiques Ambassadeurs de Poulongne, estans à Metz, le huictieme iour d'Aoust 1573. Tournee de Latin en François par Iean Bodin, Aduocat, Lyon 1573.
Id.: Les six livres de la République, Paris 1576.
Id.: Commentarius de iis omnibus quae in Tertii Ordinis conventu acta sunt, generali Trium Ordinum concilio Blesis a rege indicto ad 15 novembris diem 1576, Rignaviae [fictitious place of pub.] 1577.
Id.: Recueil de tout ce qui s'est négotié en la compagnie du Tiers Estat de France en l'assemblée géneralle des trois Estats, assignez par le Roy en la ville de Bloys, au xv. Nouembre 1576, Paris 1577.
Id.: De republica libri sex, Lyon/Paris 1586.
Id.: The Six Bookes of a Commonweale, transl. by Richard Knolles, London 1606.
Id.: Relation journalière de tout ce qui s'est négotié en l'assemblée générale des États, assignez par le roy en la ville de Blois, en l'an 1576 pris des Mémoires de M. J. Bodin, Paris 1614.
Id.: The Six Bookes of a Commonweale: A Facsimile Reprint of the English Translation of 1606, Corrected and Supplemented in the Light of a New Comparison with the French and Latin Texts, ed. by Kenneth Douglas McRae, Cambridge, Mass. 1962.
Id.: I sei libri dello stato, ed. and transl. by Diego Quaglioni/Margherita Isnardi Parente, 3 vol., Torino 1988–1997.
Id.: Methodus ad facilem historiarum cognitionem, ed. by Sara Miglietti, Pisa 2013.

---

97 *Id.*, Commonweale, p. 384.

Crahay, Roland/Isaac, Marie Thérèse/Lenger, Marie-Thérèse (ed.): Bibliographie critique des éditions anciennes de Jean Bodin n.pl. 1992 (= Académie royale de Belgique), https://projects.iq.harvard.edu/bodinproject/bibliography (01.02.2024).
Duval, François-Alexis/Lalourcé, Charlemagne (ed.): Recueil des pièces originales et authentiques, concernant la tenue des états généraux, 9 vol., Paris 1789.
Hotman, François: Franco-Gallia, n.pl. 1573.
Quinet, Toussaint (ed.): Recueil general des Estats tenus en France, Sous les Rois, Charles VI. Charles VIII. Charles IX. Henry III., et Louis XIII., Paris 1651.

Literature

Blair, Ann: Authorial Strategies in Jean Bodin, in: *Howell A. Lloyd (ed.)*, The Reception of Bodin, Leiden 2013, p. 137–156.
Collins, James B.: Wpływ doświadczenia Henryka Walezjusza w Polsce na jego rządy we Francji, in: *Adam Kaźmierczyk/Andrzej Link-Lenczowski/Mariusz Markiewicz (ed.)*, Rzeczpospolita wielu wyznań, Krakow 2004, p. 499–516 (= Księgarnia Akademicka).
Id.: The Empire of Fear: France, the Birth of the Royal State, 1561-1651, Cambridge 2024.
Crahay, Roland: Jean Bodin aux États Généraux de 1576, in: Assemblee di stati e istituzioni rappresentative nella storia del pensiero politico moderno (secoli XV–XX), Atti del convegno internazionale tenuto a Perugia 1982, Perugia 1983, p. 85–120 (= Annali della Facoltà di Scienze Politiche).
Daussy, Hugues: Les assemblées et le système politique huguenot (1562-1598), in: *Philippe Chareyre/id. (ed.)*, La France Huguenote: Histoire institutionelle d'une minorité religieuse (XVIe–XVIIIe siècle), Rennes 2024, p. 229–72.
Denault, Gerard Francis: The Legitimation of the Parlement of Paris and the Estates General of France, 1560-1614, PhD dissertation, Ann Arbor Mich. 1975.
Evrigenis, Ioannis D.: Digital Tools and the History of Political Thought: The Case of Jean Bodin, in: Redescriptions, 18 (2015), p. 181–201.
Franklin, Julian H.: Jean Bodin and the Rise of Absolutist Theory, Cambridge 1973.
Greengrass, Mark: A Day in the Life of the Third Estate: Blois, 26 December 1576, in: *Adrianna Bakos (ed.)*, Politics, Ideology and the Law in Early Modern Europe: Essays in Honour of J. H. M. Salmon, Rochester NY 1994, p. 73–90.
Id.: Governing Passions: Peace and Reform in the French Kingdom, 1576-1585, Oxford 2007, p. 66–123.
Id.: The Experiential World of Jean Bodin, in: *Howell A. Lloyd (ed.)*, The Reception of Bodin, Leiden 2013, p. 67–96.
Griffiths, Gordon: Humanists and Representative Government in the Sixteenth Century: Bodin, Marnix, and the Invitation to the Duke of Anjou to become Ruler of the Low Countries, in: *id. (ed.)*, Representative Institutions in Theory and Practice, Brussels 1970, p. 59–83.
Holt, Mack P.: Attitudes of the French Nobility at the Estates-General of 1576, in: The Sixteenth Century Journal 18 (1987), p. 489–504.
Hotman, Franciscus: Francogallia, ed. by Ralph E. Giesey, transl. by J. J. M. Salmon, Cambridge 1972.
Jones, Elisa J.: Liberty of Conscience and the Boundaries of the Polity: Toleration, Sovereignty, and Citizenship in Sixteenth-Century France, unpublished PhD dissertation, Chicago 2019.
Kane, Brendan et al.: Unrepresentative Assemblies? Parliamentary Culture and Exclusion, in: *Dorota Pietrzyk-Reeves/Paulina Kewes/Paul Seaward (ed.)*, Early Modern Parliamentary Culture of Poland-Lithuania and the Kingdoms of Britain and Ireland, forthcoming.
Keohane, Nannerl O.: Philosophy and the State in France: The Renaissance to the Enlightenment, Princeton 1980.

Kewes, Paulina et al.: Early Modern Parliamentary Studies: Overview and New Perspectives, in: History Compass 21/1 (2023), e12757, p. 6 f., https://doi.org/10.1111/hic3.12757 (01.02.2024).

Kewes, Paulina et al.: Towards a History of Parliamentary Culture in the Early Modern World: Concept, Geopolitical Scope, and Method, in: Parliaments, Estates and Representation, forthcoming.

King, Preston: The Ideology of Order: A Comparative Analysis of Jean Bodin and Thomas Hobbes, New York 1974, p. 300–310.

Kingdon, Robert M.: Calvinism and Resistance Theory, 1550–1580, in: *J. H. Burns/Mark Goldie (ed.)*, The Cambridge History of Political Thought, 1450–1700, Cambridge 1991, p. 193–218.

Lee, Daniel: Popular Sovereignty in Early Modern Constitutional Thought, Oxford 2016, p. 159–224.

Id.: The Right of Sovereignty: Jean Bodin on the Sovereign State and the Law of Nations, Oxford 2021.

Lloyd, Howell A.: Jean Bodin, ›This Pre-eminent Man of France‹: An Intellectual Biography, Oxford 2017.

Id./Burgess, Glenn/Hodson, Simon (ed.): European Political Thought 1450–1700: Religion, Law and Philosophy, New Haven/London 2007.

Machielsen, Jan: Bodin in the Netherlands, in: *Howell A. Lloyd (ed.)*, The Reception of Bodin, Leiden 2013, p. 157–192.

McDiarmid, John F. (ed.): The Monarchical Republic of Early Modern England: Essays in Response to Patrick Collinson, Aldershot 2007.

McRae, Kenneth D./McCann, Alastair D./Andreads, Catherine: Bodin Sources Index, https://projects.iq.harvard.edu/bodinproject/sources-index (01.02.2024).

Miglietti, Sara: Sovereignty, Territory, and Population in Jean Bodin's *République*, in: French Studies 72 (2018), p. 17–34.

Mortimer, Sarah: Reformation, Resistance, and Reason of State, Oxford 2021.

Nicholls, Sophie: Sovereignty and Government in Jean Bodin's *Six Livres de la République* (1576), in: Journal of the History of Ideas 80 (2019), p. 47–66.

Pocock, John G. A.: The Ancient Constitution and the Feudal Law: A Study of English Historical Thought in the Seventeenth Century. A Reissue with a Retrospect, Cambridge 1987.

Roşu, Felicia: Elective Monarchy in Transylvania and Poland-Lithuania, 1569–1587, Oxford 2017.

Salmon, J. H. M.: Catholic Resistance Theory, Ultramontanism, and the Royalist Response, 1580–1620, in: *J. H. Burns/Mark Goldie (ed.)*, The Cambridge History of Political Thought, 1450–1700, Cambridge 1991, p. 219–253.

Skinner, Quentin: Liberty before Liberalism, Cambridge 1998.

Id.: Preface, in: *Jean Bodin*, Les Six Livres De La République Liber I (French and Latin Edition), ed. by Mario Turchetti/Nicolas de Araujo, Paris 2013, p. 25–30.

Straumann, Benjamin: Crisis and Constitutionalism: Roman Political Thought from the Fall of the Republic to the Age of Revolution, Oxford 2016.

Tuck, Richard: The Sleeping Sovereign: The Invention of Modern Democracy, Cambridge 2016.

Turchetti, Mario: Bodin as Self-Translator of his *République*: Why the Omission of »Politicus« and Allied Terms from the Latin Version?, in: *Martin Burke/Melvin Richter (ed.)*, Why Concepts Matter: Translating Social and Political Thought, Leiden 2012, p. 109–118.

Ulph, Owen: Jean Bodin and the Estates-General of 1576, in: *Julian H. Franklin (ed.)*, Jean Bodin, Aldershot 2006, p. 201–209.

Van der Meulen, Jim: Parliamentary Diary as a Transnational Genre, forthcoming.

Van Gelderen, Martin/Skinner, Quentin (ed.): Republicanism: A Shared European Heritage, 2 vol., Cambridge 2002.

PETR MAŤA (WIEN)

Wege und Irrwege der Erschließung ständischer Landtagsakten in der Habsburgermonarchie

Bestandsaufnahme – Relevanz – Perspektiven

Editionen historischer Quellen sind bekanntlich zeit-, arbeits- und kostenaufwändige Unternehmen, deren Relevanz und Wirkung sich im Voraus nicht leicht kalkulieren lassen. Ob ein Editionsprojekt einen häufig und langfristig benutzten Behelf hervorbringt, der zu einem beträchtlichen Zugewinn an inhaltlicher Erkenntnis führt, oder ob das Ergebnis – etwa infolge eines Paradigmenwechsels oder des gewandelten Forschungsinteresses – ohne größere Wirkung bleibt, hängt von vielen Faktoren ab und lässt sich oft erst im Rückblick aus hinreichend großer Distanz einschätzen. Dass Editionen durch die Auswahl bestimmter wiedergegebener Texte den Blick lenken und unser Bild der Vergangenheit beträchtlich gestalten, ist jedoch schwer zu leugnen und lässt sich auch exemplarisch am Gegenstand dieses Aufsatzes vor Augen führen. Der höchst unausgeglichene, streckenweise dürftige Forschungsstand zur ständischen Partizipation in der Habsburgermonarchie lässt freilich umgekehrt auch die Frage zu, inwiefern gerade die – editorische oder andersartige – Quellenerschließung eine notwendige Voraussetzung für eine systematische Annährung an traditionell vernachlässigte Bereiche und für neue Fragestellungen bildet. Anhand einer Reflexion der Leistungen und Stolpersteine editorischer Erschließung ständischer Akten aus der Habsburgermonarchie seit dem 19. Jahrhundert möchte ich in vier Schritten einige Vorüberlegungen dazu anstellen, wie man auf diesem Feld am sinnvollsten neue Perspektiven eröffnen könnte.

Zum Ersten werde ich wesentliche Merkmale der ständisch-korporativen Vertretung in der Habsburgermonarchie skizzieren. Das ist wichtig, um das Verständnis für die vielfach unterschätzte, wenn nicht gänzlich ignorierte, Eigenart des Forschungsgegenstandes im Vergleich zu anderen frühmodernen Herrschaftsbildungen mit ständisch-repräsentativen Institutionen und für die daraus resultierenden Herausforderungen zu vermitteln. Daran anschließend werde ich, zweitens, auf einige Besonderheiten der bisherigen Erforschung ständischer Partizipationsformen im habsburgischen Länderverband hinweisen. Für die Konkretisierung der Bedürfnisse und Ziele der künftigen Ständeforschung und der entsprechenden Quellenerschließung ist nämlich auch die Berücksichtigung früherer Forschungspräferenzen und der Eigenart der Forschungslandschaft von großer Relevanz. Im dritten Schritt werde ich bisherige Zugänge zur Erschließung von Stände- und Landtagsakten und verwandten Quellengattungen im Bereich der Habsburgermonarchie exemplarisch skizzieren. Eine Gesamtschau der methodisch vielfältigen Herangehensweisen sowie der politischen, fachwissenschaftlichen und organisatorischen Kontexte, die die editorische Aufarbeitung dieser Quellen ermöglichten oder aber verhinderten, ist eine Voraussetzung für realistische Zielsetzungen. Schließlich werde ich, viertens, von dieser Erfahrung ausgehend, meinen eigenen Vorschlag entwerfen: Von welcher Art der Quellenerschließung könnte im Bereich der Ständeforschung in der Habsburgermonarchie ein Zugewinn an Erkenntnis erwartet werden, der in einem vertretbaren Verhältnis zum Aufwand stünde? Wie könnten neue Wege der Quellenbearbeitung unser Verständnis der Transformation ständischer Partizipationsformen in der Habsburgermonarchie steigern?

I. Eine Vielzahl ständischer Versammlungen in der Habsburgermonarchie

Was die ständische Mitsprache betrifft, stellt die Habsburgermonarchie einen hochinteressanten Fall dar, dessen Eigenart und Signifikanz im gesamteuropäischen Vergleich noch keineswegs angemessen beachtet und gewürdigt worden sind. Das ist nicht zuletzt darauf zurückzuführen, dass das vielschichtige und unübersichtliche politische System dieser in der Mitte des Kontinents 1526/27 durch dynastisches Erbrecht sowie ständische Wahl- und Anerkennungsakte ins Leben gerufenen und bis 1918 bestehenden Union von Ländern und Ländergruppen viel zu oft unter der Wahrnehmungsschwelle der internationalen Forschung liegt – im auffälligen Kontrast zur wahrhaft internationalen Aufmerksamkeit, der sich sein Herrscherhaus erfreut. Dafür ist einerseits die mehrsprachige historiographische Aufarbeitung entlang der nationalen und Landesgrenzen verantwortlich, andererseits wird das politische System der Habsburgermonarchie vielfach durch die zahlreichen und wissenschaftsorganisatorisch wesentlich besser abgesicherten Forschungen, Veröffentlichungen und Forschungsprojekte zum Verfassungssystem des Alten Reiches (mit dem die Habsburgermonarchie verflochten, aber keineswegs deckungsgleich war) überschattet, nicht selten sogar mit diesem verwechselt. Vielfache Fehlannahmen erschweren es, sich von der ständischen Verfasstheit des habsburgischen Länderkomplexes ein adäquates Bild zu machen. Dazu gehört etwa die weit verbreitete und in höchstem Maße missverständliche Tendenz, dem Länderkonglomerat der österreichischen *Erblande* die beiden übrigen konstitutiven Teile der Monarchie als vermeintliche Einheiten (»Böhmen« und »Ungarn«) gegenüberzustellen. Dadurch wird das Bild der dynastischen Union von asymmetrisch verfassten und strukturell durchaus heterogenen Ländergruppen entscheidend deformiert, indem wesentliche Teile der Habsburgermonarchie in ihrer Beschaffenheit verkannt und – so herkömmlich die böhmischen »Nebenländer« Mähren, Schlesien und die beiden Lausitzen, die alle mit Böhmen untrennbar verbunden, aber eben keine Teile Böhmens waren – ausgeblendet werden[1].

---

1 Der Forschungsstand zu einzelnen Bereichen ist resümiert (vorerst unvollständig) in: *Hochedlinger/Maťa/Winkelbauer (Hg.)*, Verwaltungsgeschichte der Habsburgermonarchie.

Wenn wir die Habsburgermonarchie – also eine dynastische Union von zunächst drei asymmetrisch gewachsenen Ländergruppen (der böhmischen, der österreichischen und der ungarischen) – aus der Perspektive der ständischen Mitsprache strukturell-vergleichend einordnen wollen, so ist vorweg darauf hinzuweisen, dass sie vor 1848 nie eine ihre Territorien überwölbende ständisch-parlamentarische Institution hervorbrachte. Es entstand hier kein gemeinsames ständisches Forum, das man mit dem Reichstag des Heiligen Römischen Reichs, dem polnisch-litauischen Sejm oder den Niederländischen Generalstaaten vergleichen und dem man ähnlich konzentrierte Forschungsaufmerksamkeit widmen könnte. Zudem besaß die Habsburgermonarchie, im Gegensatz zu anderen zusammengesetzten Monarchien Europas, nicht einmal ein starkes einheitliches Kerngebiet, dessen ständisch-korporative Institution eine dominante Stellung wie der Riksdag im schwedischen Reich oder das englische Parlament in der Union der Kronen hätte einnehmen können. Der ungarische Landtag (bereits zeitgenössisch auch »Reichstag« genannt) hätte dazu angesichts seiner Größe, Struktur (als eine Zwei-Kammer-Versammlung) und seines ausgedehnten – im 18. Jahrhundert infolge der Rückeroberung Ungarns noch vielfach vergrößerten – Einzugsgebiets am ehesten die institutionellen Voraussetzungen gehabt[2]. Diese Option stand jedoch infolge der prononcierten Randposition Ungarns im habsburgischen politischen System gar nicht zur Wahl. Ständische Versammlungen im eigentlichen habsburgischen Kernland, von dem die Dynastie ihren Namen ableitete (»Erzhaus von Österreich« oder einfach »Haus Österreich«), sind mit dem englischen Parlament schwer zu vergleichen, ganz davon zu schweigen, dass das Erzherzogtum de facto in zwei Länder – Österreich unter der Enns und Österreich ob der Enns – mit jeweils einem Landtag (einem in Wien und einem in Linz) geteilt war.

So finden ständische Institutionen der Habsburgermonarchie adäquatere Vergleichspartner in anderen zusammengesetzten politischen Systemen Europas mit ähnlich dezentralen Strukturen ständischer Vertretung. Doch sowohl die Verbreitung als auch die Persistenz der Landtage lassen die Habsburgermonarchie in diesem Vergleichskontext wiederum markant hervortreten. In Frankreich waren die Provinzialstände (États provinciaux) in der Frühen Neuzeit ein Phänomen der Randgebiete, die etwa ein Viertel des Königreichs ausmachten. Im Gegensatz dazu bestanden Ständeversammlungen in allen Teilen der frühmodernen Habsburgermonarchie; mitunter (außer Ungarn mit seiner Komitatsstruktur vor allem in Schlesien) sogar auf mehreren Ebenen. Als ständelose Ausnahmen bildeten sich lediglich kleine Randgebiete der Militärgrenze und des Banats von Temesvár im Südosten heraus sowie die kommunalistisch geprägten Territorien in der Lombardei, die erst im 18. Jahrhundert aus dem spanischen Erbe übernommen wurden. Die auf gleiche Art und Weise mit der Habsburgermonarchie verbundenen Österreichischen Niederlande waren hingegen (mit der einzigen Ausnahme der flandrischen Grenzstriche, der sog. pays rétrocédés) ein weiteres Konglomerat von Fürstentümern mit Provinzialständen. Die Regelmäßigkeit der ständischen Versammlungen und Be-

---

2   *Szijártó*, A Diéta; *ders.*, Estates and Constitution.

willigungen (wenngleich nicht ohne regionale Ausnahmen) sowie die einmalige Kontinuität der Landtage über politische Brüche hinweg, sogar über die napoleonische Zeit, unterscheiden gleichzeitig die Länder der Habsburgermonarchie von den Königreichen Spaniens sowie von den Provinzen Brandenburg-Preußens, in denen korporative Versammlungen entweder eingingen oder ihren Anteil an der Steuerbewilligung frühzeitig einbüßten.

Die im europäischen Vergleich einzigartige Vielzahl paralleler Rituale der Herrschereinsetzung in der Habsburgermonarchie[3] findet in der großen Zahl von Ständeversammlungen ihre Entsprechung. Wie viele Landtage gab es eigentlich in der Habsburgermonarchie? Selbst wenn wir uns auf die drei zentraleuropäischen Ländergruppen beschränken, fällt eine Zählung schwer. In den österreichischen Ländern sind zu den beiden bereits erwähnten Ständeversammlungen des zweigeteilten Erzherzogtums (später wird man sie als den nieder- und den oberösterreichischen Landtag bezeichnen) vier Landtage der von 1564 bis 1619 unabhängig regierten innerösterreichischen Ländergruppe (die Herzogtümer Steiermark, Kärnten und Krain und die Grafschaft Görz) zu zählen; dann freilich der strukturell eigenartige Landtag in Tirol sowie die drei landständische Korpora in den »Vorlanden«, die u. a. als Klammer für den verstreuten habsburgischen Besitz im süd- und südwestdeutschen Gebiet dienten: die Landstände und Landtage der elsässisch-vorderösterreichischen, der schwäbischen und der vorarlbergischen Herrschaften, die mit Tirol von 1564 bis 1665 ebenfalls eigenen habsburgischen Landesfürsten unterstanden. Damit kommen wir nur für die österreichische Ländergruppe auf zehn eigenständige Landtage.

Das Bild, das die böhmischen Länder abgeben, wirkt ähnlich unübersichtlich, wenn nicht noch verwirrender. Neben dem böhmischen Landtag muss man zunächst die Ständeversammlungen in den vier dem Königreich bzw. der Krone »inkorporierten«, de facto aber mit völlig eigenständigen landständischen Strukturen ausgestatteten Ländern berücksichtigen: den (bis zum Dreißigjährigen Krieg in den beiden Landeshauptstädten, Brünn und Olmütz, abwechselnd zusammentretende) Landtag in Mähren, den schlesischen Fürstentag in Breslau sowie die strukturell unähnlichen Landtage in der Ober- und der Niederlausitz, die sich jedoch zwischen 1620 und 1635 aus dem habsburgischen Länderverband verabschiedeten. Komplett ist das Bild damit aber noch keineswegs. Im »zusammengesetzten« Herzogtum Schlesien müsste man zusätzlich zu den Versammlungen der »Fürsten und Stände« auch eine wandelbare Zahl von Landtagen der einzelnen Fürstentümer (davon einige in direktem habsburgischen Besitz) und anderer nicht-fürstlicher Herrschaften (der sogenannten Freien Standesherrschaften) berücksichtigen; mit etwa 15 bis 20 können wir nur eine Orientierungszahl dieser (auch in ihrer Größe voneinander markant unterschiedlichen) Landtage ansetzen. Dabei gibt der Landtag im Fürstentum Troppau, dessen Adel im ersten Jahrhundert der Habsburgerherrschaft eine Schaukelpolitik zwischen Schlesien und Mähren betrieb, ein ziemlich selbständiges Bild ab. Doch erst mit dem Landtag der Grafschaft Glatz, einer

---

3   Maťa, The Care of Thrones.

Brückenlandschaft zwischen Böhmen und Schlesien, und mit den ständischen Zusammenkünften im »Egerischen Bezirk«, einem nichteingelösten Reichspfand Böhmens, wird das Bild der Landtage der böhmischen Ländergruppe halbwegs komplett.

Im Vergleich dazu erscheint das Königreich Ungarn mit seiner *Diaeta* erleichternd übersichtlich, aber nur unter der Bedingung, dass wir die methodisch nicht unumstrittene Entscheidung treffen, die *Congregationes generales* in den zahlreichen (im 16. Jahrhundert etwa 35[4]) Komitaten, den adeligen Selbstverwaltungsbezirken, in die das Königreich eingeteilt war, außer Acht zu lassen. Das ließe sich jedoch zumindest im Falle des kroatisch-slawonischen Landtags, der auf eine im habsburgischen Kontext einmalige, Ende der 1550er Jahre erfolgte *union of parliaments* zurückging, schwer rechtfertigen – unangesehen der Tatsache, dass diese aus der Verbindung der früher unabhängigen Ständeversammlungen der Königreiche Kroatien und Slawonien entstandene Körperschaft als *Congregatio generalis* firmierte und aus der Perspektive des ungarischen Landtags/Reichstags sich daher eben nur auf der untergeordneten Ebene der Komitatsversammlungen befand. Nachdem Leopold I. in den 1690er Jahren das Fürstentum Siebenbürgen übernommen hatte, gelangte eine weitere, vielfach eigenartige und bis ins 19. Jahrhundert völlig unabhängig gehaltene Ständeversammlung ungarischer Herkunft in die Galaxie der habsburgischen Landtage. Ihre Gesamtzahl blieb im 18. Jahrhundert veränderlich infolge der Territorialverluste (der Großteil Schlesiens – doch in Rest-Schlesien wurde der Kontinuität halber ein reorganisierter »Fürstentag« auf die Beine gestellt) und Territorialgewinne: Außer den oben bereits erwähnten wäre auf den neu konstituierten Landtag im »Königreich Galizien und Lodomerien« hinzuweisen.

Mehrzahl, Omnipräsenz und Kontinuität sind somit definierende Merkmale ständischer Versammlungen in der Habsburgermonarchie. Wir haben es hier mit einem dezentralen, schwer durchschaubaren System ständischer Teilhabe zu tun, das aus mehreren Landtagen bestand, die unterschiedlich große Einheiten vertraten und einen durchaus unterschiedlichen Grad der Herrschaftsnähe bzw. -ferne aufwiesen.

Das macht die Ständeforschung in diesem Bereich zwar potenziell spannend, es hat aber auch gravierende Folgen sowohl methodischer als auch rein praktischer Natur. Im Kontext dieses Bandes heißt es zunächst: Der Vorteil der Fokussierung auf eine zentrale ständische Institution mit überragender Bedeutung ist hier nicht gegeben – vorbehaltlich des ungarischen Landtags, der auch unverhältnismäßig mehr Aufmerksamkeit erhielt und erhält. Stattdessen steht man als Forscher einer vielschichtigen Kommunikationssituation gegenüber: Strebt man ein gründlicheres Verständnis der ständischen Mitsprache in der Habsburgermonarchie an, muss eine Unzahl von parallel wirkenden Institutionen berücksichtigt werden. Denn – und das wiegt schwer – selbst mangels eines gemeinsamen Forums agierten die Landtage in der Habsburgermonarchie (trotz ihrer gängigen Rhetorik) nicht voneinander isoliert. Seitens der Regierung wurden sie mit ähnlichen Propositionen konfron-

---

4 *Pálffy*, The Kingdom of Hungary, S. 177.

tiert und sie trafen grundsätzliche Entscheidungen in der Regel mit Rücksicht auf jene der Nachbarländer. Zwischen den Ländern bestanden gemeinsame Interessen (einige – insbesondere jene in Innerösterreich – pflegten sogar regelmäßig direkte schriftliche Kontakte miteinander), gleichzeitig standen sie aber in permanenter Konkurrenz zueinander in der zentralen Frage der Aufteilung von Lasten, die periodisch wiederkehrte und mit der Transformation der Habsburgermonarchie in eine kriegführende Großmacht die Länder, ihre Stände, Grundherren und lokale Bevölkerung immer wieder vor neue Herausforderungen stellte. Bei den regional unterschiedlichen Ständewelten der Habsburgermonarchie handelte es sich also nicht nur um distinkte, voneinander unabhängige und gegeneinander abgeschottete Ausprägungen einer landständischen Verfassung, die man isoliert voneinander untersuchen und miteinander vergleichen kann, sondern auch um Körperschaften, die sich langfristig in einem Handlungs- und Kommunikationszusammenhang befanden und entsprechend wirkten.

Im ersten Jahrhundert der Habsburgermonarchie gingen sowohl vom Monarchen als auch von den Ständegemeinden Bemühungen um Koordination im Bereich der Defension und der Lastenverteilung in Form von länderübergreifenden Kongressen (den »Ausschusslandtagen« österreichischer Provinzen sowie den »Generallandtagen« der böhmischen Länder) aus. In den ersten Jahrzehnten des 17. Jahrhunderts erwies sich strategische Zusammenarbeit der Stände im Konfessionskonflikt mit dem Landesherrn als brandgefährlich für die Dynastie[5]. Nachdem die 1619/20 geschlossenen Konföderationen der protestantischen Stände aus den böhmischen, österreichischen und ungarischen Ländern militärisch niedergeworfen worden waren, wurden die ständischen Versammlungen in der Habsburgermonarchie strikt separat gehalten. Doch die kriegsbedingt intensivierte Ressourcenmobilisierung seit der zweiten Hälfte des 17. Jahrhunderts ließ neue Formen der Koordination der Landtage entstehen, bis hin zu Versuchen, ein regelrechtes Quotensystem zur Lastenverteilung zu etablieren – ein Grad der administrativen Verdichtung, dem man in anderen europäischen *composite monarchies* der gleichen Zeit (etwa in den spanischen Königreichen, in Brandenburg-Preußen oder in Großbritannien) nicht begegnet, den man aber sehr wohl aus den Vereinigten Niederlanden kennt, dort allerdings verbunden mit der Institution der Generalstände[6]. Hand in Hand mit der Koordination ständischer Bewilligungen erfolgte die Herausbildung eines aus acht Ländern der Habsburgermonarchie (von Schlesien bis Krain) geformten Kerngebiets der intensivierten Ressourcenextraktion zu militärischen Zwecken, das William Godsey und ich als *fiscal-military core* der Habsburgermonarchie bezeichnet haben[7]. Ähnlich wie sich das militärische System Großbritanniens auf England stützte, stützte sich die Kriegsfinanzierung sowie die Heeresergänzung der Habsburgermonarchie auf diesen Länderkomplex, der jedoch zusammengesetzt

---

5 *Krofta*, Snahy; *Volf*, Pokusy; *Bahlcke*, Durch »starke Konföderation wohl stabilisert«; *Mout*, Der Löwe und die Ameisen.
6 *Maťa*, Negotiating Fiscal-Military Coordination.
7 *Godsey/Maťa (Hg.)*: The Habsburg Monarchy, S. 27 f., 198, 206, 276.

blieb und daher die Koordination von acht Landtagen und ihren jährlichen Bewilligungen voraussetzte.

Ein ständiges Aufeinanderabstimmen in der Beschlussfassung der habsburgischen Landtage ist somit nicht nur ein Nebenaspekt unter vielen, sondern ein für das adäquate Verständnis sowohl der ständischen Entscheidungsfindung als auch der Kommunikation zwischen den Landtagen und dem Herrschaftszentrum ganz zentrales Merkmal. In der bisherigen Forschung fand diese kommunikative Situation nur höchst ungenügend Berücksichtigung. Die Landesgeschichte, der bei der Erforschung ständischer Landtage eine zentrale Rolle zukam, war von dieser Dimension ständischer Vertretung zumeist überfordert, auch weil sie in der Regel auf regional vorhandenen Quellenbeständen aufbaute. Auch das in der Forschung lange Jahrzehnte dominierende Modell eines ständisch-monarchischen Dualismus half dabei, die polyzentrische Dimension auszublenden: Das Nebeneinander der Ständegemeinden in der Habsburgermonarchie wurde freilich nicht in Abrede gestellt, methodische Rückschlüsse wurden daraus allerdings eher selten gezogen. Statt der Ständeforschung in der Habsburgermonarchie eine realitätsferne idealtypische dualistische Modellsituation zugrunde zu legen, in der der jeweilige Habsburgerherrscher nur einem isolierten Landtag gegenübergestellt wird, erscheint es vielversprechender, einen »pluralistischen«, stärker vergleichenden Ansatz zu erwägen, der der komplexen kommunikativen Situation des habsburgischen Länderverbands gerecht wird.

II. Zwei Ständeforschungen

Wiewohl sich die Stände und ihre Institutionen in der Habsburgermonarchie als Phänomene der langen Dauer – vom Spätmittelalter bis 1848 – präsentierten, werden sie nur selten als solche untersucht. Zu den Rahmenbedingungen der Ständeforschung in der Habsburgermonarchie, genauer: in dessen böhmisch-österreichischer Ländergruppe, gehört nämlich neben der regionalen Vielfalt auch eine Art antithetische fachwissenschaftliche Wahrnehmung der Stände vor und nach der Zäsur der 1620er Jahre bzw. des Dreißigjährigen Krieges. Ohne große Übertreibung kann man von zwei aneinander vorbeilaufenden, sich nur selten begegnenden Ständeforschungen sprechen, denen jeweils unterschiedliche Vorannahmen, Leitfragen, Forschungstraditionen und Zeitpräferenzen zugrunde liegen und die auch von unterschiedlichen Forscherinnen und Forschern in Angriff genommen wurden und werden.

Der eine, deutlich robustere und traditionsstärkere Forschungsstrang fokussiert nahezu ausnahmslos das erste Jahrhundert der Habsburgermonarchie, also den Zeitraum des konfessionspolitischen Konflikts. Als Orientierungsrahmen wurde dabei in der Regel weniger die Habsburgermonarchie herangezogen, oft dienten Ständewelten des Heiligen Römischen Reichs oder des partizipationsstarken Ostmitteleuropas als Referenzgebiete der zumeist auf einzelne Länder oder Ländergruppen fokussierten Untersuchungen. Erforscht werden vorzugsweise korporativer Widerstand, ständische Oppositionsbildung, das Ringen um Absicherung protestantischer Konfessionen sowie von den Ständen entwickelte Libertas-Vorstellungen und politische Alternativkonzepte zur monarchischen Herrschaft[8]. Vertreter dieser Forschungsrichtung interessierten sich in der Regel selten für das spätere knappe Vierteljahrtausend der ständischen Existenz (nach dem Desaster der protestantisch-ständischen Konföderationen zu Beginn des Dreißigjährigen Krieges) und sie fassten diese oft in Kategorien der Entmachtung, des Niedergangs und einer bloß formalen Existenz ständischer Mitsprache auf. Erst das kurze politische »Erwachen« der Stände um 1790 und die letzten Jahre des Vormärz finden gelegentlich Aufmerksamkeit[9]. Ungarn und seine Teile bzw. Nebenländer bilden freilich, dank der eigenständigen politischen Entwicklung, eine Ausnahme: Hier wird der dualistische (von einem prinzipiellen Antagonismus von Landesherren und Ständen ausgehende) Forschungsblick bis ins 19. Jahrhundert gerichtet, weshalb etwa den ungarischen Landtagen im 18. Jahrhundert als einer politischen Arena große Aufmerksamkeit gewidmet wurde[10]. Die Forschung brachte hier in der jüngeren Zeit Überblickswerke zum Landtagswesen quer durch die Jahrhunderte hervor[11].

Die andere Ständeforschung orientiert sich an anderen Leitfragen: Sie fragt nach Handlungsräumen der Stände jenseits der prinzipiellen Oppositionsbildung und des Widerstands im langen Zeitabschnitt zwischen dem Dreißigjährigen Krieg und dem Vormärz. Die paradigmatische Wirkung des Absolutismus-Konzepts kombiniert mit der dualistischen Betrachtungsweise verhinderte lange die Entwicklung tragfähiger Fragestellungen und ließ die Erforschung der Stände in dieser Periode als wenig attraktiv erscheinen. Gelegentliche Initiative blieben vereinzelt und fanden keine Fortsetzung[12]. Erst die Begriffe der *composite monarchy* und des *fiscal-military state* sowie Vergleiche mit anderen zusammengesetzten Monarchien ermöglichten eine neue Konzeptualisierung der ständischen Relevanz. In den Ständen wurde eine Kraft erkannt, die den Charakter der Habsburgerherrschaft bis in den Vormärz wesentlich mitprägte. Eine starke Komponente dieser Forschung bildet die Hinwendung zum Fragenkomplex der kriegsbedingten Ressourcenmobilisierung

---

8 Zu den wichtigsten Veröffentlichungen gehören (in strenger Auswahl): *Schulze*, Landesdefension; *Eberhard*, Monarchie und Widerstand; *Pánek*, Ständewesen; *ders.*, Stavovská opozice; *Evans/Thomas (Hg.)*, Crown, Church and Estates; *Bahlcke*, Regionalismus und Staatsintegration; *Strohmeyer*, Konfessionskonflikt und Herrschaftsordnung; *Bahlcke/Bömelburg/Kersken (Hg.)*, Ständefreiheit und Staatsgestaltung; *Jeřše*, Glaube, Hoffnung, Herrschaft.
9 Vgl. *Cerman*, The Estates Opposition; *Steiner*, Landstände; und *Lahner*, Stände; jeweils mit Hinweisen auf frühere Literatur.
10 *Szijártó*, A Diéta; *ders.*, Estates and Constitution; *Forgó*, Egyház – Rendiség – Politikai kultúra; *Szijártó/Blockmans/Kontler (Hg.)*, Parlamentarism.
11 *Fazekas/Gebei/Pálosfalvi*, Rendi országgyűlések; *Szijártó*, A 18. századi Magyarország rendi országgyűlése; *Dobszay*, A rendi országgyűlés utolsó évtizedei; *ders. u. a. (Hg.)*, Rendiség és parlamentarizmus; *Révész*, Anfänge; *Bérenger/Kecskeméti*, Parlement.
12 Vgl. den vielzitierten Aufsatz von *Hassinger*, Landstände, eine mehrfach nachgedruckte Gelegenheitsarbeit.

durch die Stände und Landtage, die von der erstgenannten Ständeforschung zwar mitbedacht, aber in der Regel nur peripher wahrgenommen wurde[13]. Diese doppelte Ausrichtung der Ständeforschung in den Territorien der ehemaligen Habsburgermonarchie ist zu berücksichtigen, wenn über Aktenerschließung nachzudenken ist. Denn zum einen trägt die Vielfalt der editorischen Zugänge dem insgesamt beträchtlichen Wandel der Struktur und des Umfangs landständischer Quellen Rechnung: Während aus den frühen Jahrzehnten der Habsburgermonarchie das Quellenmaterial zumeist nur fragmentarisch und verstreut vorliegt, schließen kompakte Bestände aus dem 17. und 18. Jahrhundert Volltexteditionen von vornherein aus. Und zum anderen hatte jede der beiden Ständeforschungen jeweils eine andere Forschungsagenda und deshalb quellenmäßig etwas andere Präferenzen. Die bisherige Quellenerschließung erfolgte zumeist aus der Perspektive der ersten der beiden Forschungsstränge und bevorzugte überproportional – Ungarn ausgenommen – das erste Jahrhundert der Habsburgermonarchie[14].

III. Sechs Wege der Erschließung von Landtagsquellen

Im Folgenden möchte ich in einem gerafften Überblick exemplarisch, ohne Anspruch auf Vollständigkeit, sechs methodisch unterschiedliche Zugänge der Erschließung ständischer Akten umreißen, die in verschiedenen Ländern der Habsburgermonarchie seit dem 19. Jahrhundert von verschiedenen Forscherinnen und Forschern angewendet wurden. Das Ziel ist, die Vielfalt der editorischen Vorgehensweisen vor Augen zu führen sowie ihren Nutzen und ihre Nachteile abzuwägen. Ganz unbeachtet lasse ich analytische und monographische Veröffentlichungen, selbst wenn einige von ihnen in Fußnoten oder Textbeilagen wichtige Quellen in Auswahl zugänglich machten. Als solche wäre etwa die dreibändige Erfassung der ständischen Versammlungen und Institutionen in Mähren im ersten Jahrhundert der Habsburgerherrschaft von František Kameníček (1856–1930) zu nennen[15]. Ich konzentriere mich hingegen nur auf verschiedene Formen editorischer Erschließung bzw. systematischer Erfassung von Angaben aus den Landtagsakten.

(1) *Editionen der Landtagsakten* stellten das meiste bisher edierte Quellenmaterial zu habsburgischen Landtagen zur Verfügung und bilden bis heute unverzichtbare Nachschlagewerke. Gleich zu vier Ständeversammlungen wurden mehrbändige Editionswerke von mehrheitlich im Volltext abgedruckten Aktenstücken erarbeitet: zum schlesischen Fürstentag aus den Jahren 1618 bis 1629 in

---

13 *Ammerer u. a. (Hg.)*, Bündnispartner und Konkurrenten; *Maťa*, Landstände und Landtage; *Rauscher (Hg.)*, Kriegführung und Staatsfinanzen; *Godsey*, The Sinews of Habsburg Power; *David*, Nechtěné budování státu; *Godsey/Maťa (Hg.)*, The Habsburg Monarchy as a Fiscal-Military State.
14 Vgl. exemplarisch die Überlegungen von *Bahlcke*, Landtagsakten.
15 *Kameníček*, Zemské sněmy a sjezdy moravské.

acht zwischen 1865 und 1906 herausgegebenen Bänden[16], zum ungarischen Landtag (von 1526 bis 1606) in zwölf Bänden (erschienen zwischen 1874 und 1917)[17], zum böhmischen Landtag (von 1526 bis 1605 und 1611) in dreizehn Bänden (erschienen zwischen 1877 und 1929)[18] und zum kroatisch-slawonischen Landtag (von 1526 bis 1630) in fünf Bänden (erschienen zwischen 1912 und 1918)[19]. Alle vier Quellensammlungen wurden für das erste Jahrhundert der Habsburgermonarchie konzipiert, wobei außer den eigentlichen »Landtagshandlungen« auch ergänzende Aktenstücke, Korrespondenzen und chronikalische Nachrichten berücksichtigt wurden.

Obwohl eigenständig realisiert und wechselseitig, wenn überhaupt, nur unzureichend koordiniert, fällt ein zeitlicher Zusammenhang dieser Editionswerke auf. Sie wurden nacheinander in einer Zeitspanne von knapp drei Jahrzehnten nach der Mitte des 19. Jahrhunderts in die Wege geleitet und allesamt in den fünf Jahrzehnten vor dem Zusammenbruch der Habsburgermonarchie zum Druck gebracht. Zum Teil handelte es sich hierbei um Prestigeprojekte, die legitimatorische und identitätsstiftende Funktionen – Betonung der staatlichen Kontinuität: so insbesondere im böhmisch/tschechischen, ungarischen und kroatischen Fall – erfüllten und daher entsprechende Finanzierung und institutionelle Verankerung erhielten[20]. Es war offenbar die einzige Zeitspanne, in der günstige Rahmenbedingungen für die erfolgreiche Realisierung voluminöser Landtagsakteneditionen bestanden, wenn auch die Edition der schlesischen Fürstentagsakten eher auf das Interesse und Engagement zweier Geschichtslehrer und die Unterstützung seitens des Breslauer Geschichtsvereins zurückzuführen ist[21]. Des Weiteren ähnelten alle vier Editionsprojekte einander in ihrem Verlauf: Auf eine dynamische Anfangsphase, die etwa ein Jahrzehnt,

---

16 *Palm/Krebs (Hg.)*, Acta Publica.
17 *Fraknói/Károlyi (Hg.)*, Magyar országgyűlési emlékek. Die Bände sind digitalisiert unter: https://library.hungaricana.hu/hu/collection/ogyk_orszaggyulesi_emlekek (13.09.2023). Zur Einordnung: *Bessenyei*, Magyar országgyűlési emlékek. Parallel erfolgte die noch umfangreichere Herausgabe der Akten des siebenbürgischen Landtags aus den Jahren 1540–1699: *Szilágyi (Hg.)*, Erdélyi országgyűlési emlékek.
18 Dazu wäre noch ein Registerband (1939) sowie zwei zusätzliche, in ihrer Anlage anders gestaltete Bände von 1941 und 1954 zu rechnen, die sich als eine neue, der Durchführung der ständischen Beschlüsse gewidmete Reihe verstanden, Sněmy české.
19 *Šišić (Hg.)*, Acta comitialia regni Croatiae.
20 Schlesische Fürstentagsakten: Herausgabe seitens des Breslauer Vereins für Geschichte und Alterthum Schlesiens seit 1855 vorgesehen; Subventionierung der Druckkosten durch den schlesischen Provinziallandtag seit den 1860er Jahren, *Palm/Krebs (Hg.)*, Acta publica, Bd. 1, S. VI, *Kersken*, Breslau, S. 104, 117. Ungarische Landtagsakten: Beschluss der Ungarischen Akademie der Wissenschaften wegen Herausgabe der Landtagsakten: 1871, *Bessenyei*, Magyar országgyűlési emlékek, S. 7. Böhmische Landtagsakten: Antrag des Direktors des böhmischen Landesarchivs Anton Gindely auf die Gründung der Edition: 1873; Beschluss des böhmischen Landtags wegen der Finanzierung des Vorhabens: 1874, *Pánek*, Sněmy české, S. 23. Kroatische Landtagsakten: Beschluss der Jugoslawischen Akademie der Wissenschaften und Künste wegen der Herausgabe der Landtagsakten: 1884; Finanzierung der Herausgabe durch die Landesregierung: 1911, *Šišić (Hg.)*, Acta comitialia regni Croatiae, Bd. 1, S. VIf.
21 *Bahlcke*, Gemeinsame Vergangenheit, S. 413–415.

seltener auch mehr, dauerte, folgten Verzögerung und Überforderung, und schließlich wurde das Editionsprojekt unvollendet abgebrochen.

Die Einstellung des böhmischen, vom 1862 gegründeten Königlich Böhmischen Landesarchiv getragenen, in zwei parallelen Sprachausgaben (einer tschechischen und einer deutschen) herausgegebenen Editionswerks »Sněmy české«, des ambitioniertesten unter allen vier Unternehmen, lässt die Umstände erkennen, unter denen das »Fenster der Gelegenheit« für umfassende Landtagsakteneditionen sich zu schließen begann: Nachdem der Archivdirektor Anton Gindely (1829–1892) und sein fleißiger, doch weniger begabter Nachfolger František Dvorský (1839–1907), sich auf weitere Mitarbeiter stützend, aufgrund pragmatischer Entscheidungen über die Auswahl des Materials und dessen editorische Bearbeitung in vergleichsweise zügigem Tempo zehn Bände herausgegeben hatten, geriet die Quellenedition in die vehemente Kritik der jüngsten, kritisch geschulten Historikergeneration, die an die editorische Arbeit höhere Maßstäbe anlegte. Die Übertragung des Projekts auf Herausgeber mit erhöhten Ansprüchen führte jedoch zur Verzögerung, zum Aufblähen des Materials, zu strategischer Verwirrung und schließlich zur Aufgabe des Projekts: Nachdem das ursprüngliche Team Aktenstücke aus nahezu 80 Jahren (1526–1604) in knapp einem Jahrhundertviertel editorisch aufbereitet und damit der Forschung eine der bedeutendsten editorischen Leistung zur böhmischen Frühneuzeit hinterlassen hatte, konnten die besser geschulten Nachfolger nur mehr Landtage aus zwei (zugegebenermaßen ereignisreichen) Jahren, 1605 und 1611, wenn auch auf einem sehr hohen Niveau, zur Publikation zu bringen[22].

Auf ähnliche Art und Weise blieb die Edition der ungarischen Landtagsakten 1917 beim Jahr 1606 und jene der kroatischen Landtagsakten 1918 beim Jahr 1630 stecken, während die ursprüngliche Absicht, bei der Herausgabe der schlesischen Fürstentagsakten vom Dreißigjährigen Krieg bis zum Anfang der Habsburgerherrschaft zurückzuschreiten[23], nie umgesetzt wurde. Der seit 1960 unternommene Versuch, die Edition der ungarischen Landtagsakten an der Ungarischen Akademie der Wissenschaften wiederzubeleben und bis 1790 in 14 Bänden (perspektivisch sogar bis 1848 in weiteren 15 Bänden) fortzuführen (gleichzeitig sollte ein Register zu den früher erschienen zwölf indexlosen Bänden erarbeitet werden), hatte zwar beachtliche Sammel- und Katalogisierungsarbeiten zur Folge, führte jedoch infolge ungenügend abgesicherter administrativ-institutioneller Rahmenbedingungen zu keiner Veröffentlichung[24]. Die rezente Ergänzung zu der hundert Jahre früher aufgelassenen Quellenreihe um Akten des längsten ungarischen Landtags 1646/47 ist als ein Sonderfall einzuordnen[25].

Das ›kurze‹ 20. Jahrhundert war den Landtagsakteneditionen in den Nachfolgestaaten der Habsburgermonarchie nicht förderlich. Das im Auftrag der 1892 ge-

---

22 *Pánek*, Sněmy české. Ständeakten aus den besonders dramatischen Jahren 1606–1610 und 1612–1620 sind daher bis heute nicht ediert.
23 *Palm/Krebs (Hg.)*, Acta Publica, Bd. 1, S. VI.
24 *Benda*, A Magyar Országgyűlési Emlékek; *Bessenyei*, Magyar országgyűlési emlékek.
25 *Bessenyei (Hg.)*, Magyar országgyűlési emlékek 1646–1647.

gründeten Historischen Landeskommission für Steiermark bereits um 1900 ins Auge gefasste, doch erst seit 1975 aktiver bearbeitete Editionsprojekt »Die steirischen Landtagsakten 1519–1637« unter der Leitung Berthold Sutters (1923–2004), das mit Abstand ambitionierteste Unterfangen dieser Art aus den österreichischen Ländern, erbrachte zwar eine große Sammlung von Fotokopien, Transkriptionen und Hinweisen auf verstreute Aktenstücke aus der ersten Hälfte des 16. Jahrhunderts, gedruckte Ergebnisse sind jedoch nicht in Sicht[26]. Übrigens ist das seit der Gründung der Landeskommission energischer vorangetriebene Vorgängerprojekt »Die ältesten steirischen Landtagsakten« nach wie vor nicht abgeschlossen und wurde, mit zwei 1953 und 1958 erschienen Bänden, nur bis 1493 geführt[27]. Ebenso kam die in den 1980er Jahren in Angriff genommene Edition der Krainer Landtagsakten nicht über das Jahr 1519 hinaus[28].

(2) Als einer der gangbaren Auswege erwies sich daher die Verengung des Fokus auf bestimmte Quellengattungen. So wurde die am Ende des Ersten Weltkriegs beim Jahr 1630 abgebrochene Edition der kroatischen Landtagsakten zwischen 1958 und 1980 wieder aufgenommen und in der Form einer zwölfbändigen *Edition der Landtagsbeschlüsse*, die in handschriftlichen Foliobänden der kroatisch-slawonischen Stände vorlagen, bis 1847 erfolgreich weitergeführt[29]. Möglicherweise spielte dabei das ungarische Beispiel eine Rolle, denn die Beschlüsse der ungarischen Landtage, überliefert in der besonderen Form der durchnummerierten und wiederholt im Druck herausgegebenen Gesetzartikel, wurden bereits um 1900 in fünf Bänden der sogenannten »Millenniumausgabe« sämtlicher ungarischer Gesetze veröffentlicht[30]. Einen ähnlichen Zugang wählte der tschechische Historiker Dalibor Janiš, der 2010 mit dem ersten Band der Gedenkbücher des mährischen Landtags (*Pamětní knihy*; später als »Landtags-Pamatken« bezeichnet) dessen Beschlüsse aus den Jahren 1518 bis 1546 edierte[31]. Die geplante Fortsetzung bis 1570 geriet jedoch mangels institutioneller Absicherung ins Stocken[32].

Während alle diese Werke sehr hilfreich sind, als universeller Zugang kann die Edition der Landtagsbeschlüsse, wie jene der Landtagsakten, nur bedingt empfohlen werden, denn auch dieses Material wird in den späteren Jahrhunderten enorm umfangreich und editorisch nicht bewältigbar. Vom böhmischen und mährischen

---

26 *Sutter*, Die steirischen Landtagsakten 1519–1637; *ders.*, Steirische Landtagsakten (1519–1637). Die Materialien sind im Steiermärkischen Landesarchiv in Graz aufbewahrt.
27 *Seuffert*, Über die Veröffentlichung von Landtagsakten; *Cerwinka*, Die ältesten steirischen Landtagsakten.
28 *Verbič (Hg.)*, Deželnozborski spisi kranjskih stanov.
29 Zaključci Hrvatskog sabora.
30 *Desző (Hg.)*, Corpus Juris Hungarici, Bd. 4 (1526–1608), 5 (1608–1657), 6 (1657–1740), 7 (1740–1835), und 8 (1836–1868). Beschlüsse des siebenbürgischen Landtags füllen einen weiteren Band: ebd., Bd. 3 (Siebenbürgen 1540–1848).
31 *Janiš (Hg.)*, Moravský zemský sněm.
32 Eine bis heute nützliche Beschreibung der im ehemaligen Archiv der mährischen Stände überlieferten Gedenkbücher aus dem ersten Jahrhundert der Habsburgerherrschaft bietet *Kameníček*, Archivní rozhled.

Landtag liegen etwa von der ersten Hälfte des 16. Jahrhundert bis 1848 durchgehend gedruckte Beschlüsse im Quartformat (seit 1619 in Böhmen und seit 1628 in Mähren in jeweils zwei sprachlichen Varianten) vor, die einige Dutzend, manchmal aber auch deutlich über hundert Druckseiten umfassen und zum guten Teil von verschiedenen Bibliotheken bereits digitalisiert worden sind[33]. Deutlich schwieriger zugänglich sind die Patente der Verordneten, die seit dem Ende des 17. Jahrhunderts nach dem Schluss der niederösterreichischen Landtage ebenfalls im Druck vervielfältigt wurden[34]. Für die Einsichtnahme in das meistens nur handschriftlich überlieferte Vergleichsmaterial aus anderen Ländern muss man allerdings nach wie vor Landesarchive bereisen.

(3) Eine vielfach zentrale Quelle zur Erforschung der Landtage wurde von den bisherigen Erschließungsmaßnahmen (aber auch von der Forschung) fast vollständig ignoriert: Es sind *Protokolle* einzelner Sitzungen, die von den meisten Landtagen seit dem 17. Jahrhundert in verschiedener Form überliefert sind: offiziell und privat; als Mitschriften oder als redigierte Reinschriften; manchmal sogar in mehreren parallelen Reihen. Während die Sitzungsprotokolle aus Kärnten, der Steiermark und Niederösterreich in gebundenen, chronologisch geordneten Reihen überliefert sind, liegen Protokolle des mährischen, böhmischen, Krainer und oberösterreichischen Landtags verstreut vor und sind nicht immer leicht im ständischen Schriftgut auffindbar. Aus Nieder- und Oberösterreich muss man zudem Protokolle der Separatsitzungen der drei oberen ständischen Kurien (der Prälaten, des Herren- und des Ritterstands) berücksichtigen.

Es sind eben diese Quellen, die den besten Aufschluss über den Verlauf und die Dynamik des ständischen Beratens (bis zu den Voten einzelner Teilnehmer) geben und außerdem auch die Teilnahme am Landtag zuverlässig zu rekonstruieren erlauben. Die Erschließung erfolgte bisher nur ansatzweise und zufällig. Von offiziellen Landtagsprotokollen steht praktisch nur eine 2018 online sowie in wenigen Druckexemplaren publizierte umfangreiche Transkription aus den allerletzten ständischen Landtagen in der Steiermark (1835–1848) zur Verfügung[35]. Die Form eines Sitzungsprotokolls haben die vorwiegend aus den 1670er und 1680er Jahren überlieferten und in einfacher Transkription nahezu ohne kritischen Kommentar veröffentlichten Berichte der Abgesandten der Stadt Jauer zu den gesamtschlesischen

---

33 Die umfangreichsten, bereits digitalisierten Sammlungen dieser Drucke sind jene der Národní knihovna [Nationalbibliothek] in Prag (https://www.manuscriptorium.com [13.09.2023]) und der Österreichischen Nationalbibliothek in Wien (https://usearch.univie.ac.at [13.09.2023]). Für weitere digitalisierte Exemplare siehe https://books.google.com (13.09.2023). Alle nachweisbare Exemplare sprachlich tschechischer Landtagsbeschlüsse aus Böhmen und Mähren bis einschließlich des Vormärz sind mit bibliographisch minutiösen Angaben erfasst durch: *Tobolka*, Knihopis, Sp. 56a–197a (Böhmen) und 197a–267a (Mähren). Dieses Grundlagenwerk ist digitalisiert unter: https://ndk.cz/uuid/uuid:0cdd01d0-fd48-11e3-97de-5ef3fc9ae867 (13.09.2023).
34 Die Wienbibliothek im Rathaus digitalisierte etwa Einzelexemplare von 1732 (https://www.digital.wienbibliothek.at/id/3675222 [13.09.2023]) und 1742 (https://www.digital.wienbibliothek.at/id/3474169 [13.09.2023]).
35 *Khull-Kholwald* (Hg.), Protokolle des Steiermärkischen Landtages 1835 bis 1848.

Zusammenkünften der Fürsten und Stände[36]. Jüngst wurde das Privatprotokoll der außerordentlichen Vollversammlung der Tiroler Stände im Sommer 1790 ediert[37]. Ansonsten steckt die Forschung bezüglich der Sitzungsprotokolle der habsburgischen Landtage in den Anfängen[38]. Selbst eine Verzeichnung des überlieferten Materials bleibt ein wichtiges Desiderat[39].

Im Zusammenhang mit dem ungarischen Landtag, der unter den habsburgischen Ständeversammlungen infolge seiner Größe, der ununterbrochenen politischen Bedeutung, der niedrigen Frequenz, der hohen Zahl der Abgesandten in der Unteren Tafel (Deputierte der Komitate, der königlichen Städte und einiger Klöster) und des daraus resultierenden infrastrukturellen Aufwands bei jeder Einberufung mehr ein Ereignis als eine Institution blieb, fanden anstatt Sitzungsprotokolle *Landtagsdiarien* Verbreitung. Sie sind als eine besondere Quellengattung zu betrachten. Beginnend mit dem bedeutenden Landtag 1790/91 pflegten die ungarischen Stände, offizielle Diarien im Druck herauszugeben. Seit derselben Zeit datieren die ersten Veröffentlichungen von privaten Landtagsdiarien aus den früheren Jahrhunderten, die meisten davon wurden jedoch erst im Zuge der fachwissenschaftlichen Erforschung der ungarischen Vergangenheit in den Jahrzehnten um 1900 erschlossen[40]. Die unsystematische editorische Aufbereitung dieser Quellengattung wird bis heute fortgesetzt, wie die vor einem Jahrzehnt herausgegeben »Acta et observata penes diaetam Hungaricam« 1712 zeigen, verfasst vom Bevollmächtigten des Zisterzienserabtes von Wellehrad in Mähren (der gleichzeitig Abt von Pásztó in Ungarn war)[41]. Die umfangreiche Sammlung wichtiger ungarischer Landtagsdiarien von 1637/38 bis 1790/91 aus dem Nachlass des Beisitzers der Pressburger Gerichtstafel György Gyurikovits (1780–1848) in der Ungarischen Parlamentssammlung

---

36 *Orzechowski (Hg.)*, Relacje deputatów miasta Jawora.
37 Der Offene Tiroler Landtag von 1790. Vgl. die anlässlich der Konstituierung des gewählten Tiroler Landtags 1861 anonym erfolgte Edition eines anderen, von Franz von Goldegg und Lindenburg verfassten Privatprotokolls des Landtags von 1790: Journal des offenen Tiroler Landtages.
38 In diesem Zusammenhang erscheint als eine Pionierleistung die wenig bekannte, auf einer von 1902 bis 1916 unternommenen Durchsicht beruhende ausführliche Inhaltsangabe der Protokolle des Troppauer Landtags von 1557 bis 1741: *Kürschner*, Bericht.
39 Als einzige Ausnahme und ein mögliches Vorbild ist die penible Bestandsaufnahme aller nachweisbaren schlesischen Privatprotokolle (überliefert vorwiegend aus der zweiten Hälfte des 17. Jahrhunderts) sowie des offiziellen, aus den Jahren 1700–1741 überlieferten Protokolls der Ständeversammlungen (»Landes-Diarium«) zu nennen: *Orzechowski*, Diariusze śląskie.
40 Vgl. (ohne Anspruch auf Vollständigkeit) Diarium Conventus Regnicolarum Posonium Anno 1608; *Komáromy (Hg.)*, Berényi György naplója; *Thaly (Hg.)*, Gr. Erdődy Sándor vasi főispán naplója; *Thury (Hg.)*, Lányi Pál gömöri alispán naplója; *Dongó-Gy[árfás] (Hg.)*, Szemere Pál diétai követ Diáriuma 1681-ből; *Paulinyi (Hg.)*, Az első magyar országgyűlési napló.
41 *Forgó (Hg.)*, Az 1712. évi Pozsonyi diéta, S. 179–272. Dem Herausgeber, *András Forgó*, ist eine wichtige Edition zu den beiden folgenden unter Karl VI. abgehaltenen ungarischen Landtagen zu verdanken: Auf Ihrer Kaiserlichen Majestät. Zwei weitere Landtagsdiarien wurden ediert in: *Bessenyei (Hg.)*, Magyar országgyűlési emlékek 1646–1647, S. 301–442. Ferner wäre auf eine rezente Edition der Instruktionen für die Deputierten zum ungarischen Landtag hinzuweisen: *Kiss/Nagy/Kapitány (Hg.)*, Pest-Pilis-Solt vármegye országgyűlési követutasításai.

(Magyar Parlamenti Gyűjtemény) der Bibliothek des Ungarischen Parlaments (Országgyűlési könyvtár) in Budapest ist zumindest in Form von Digitalisaten (einfache PDF-Dateien) erschlossen[42]. Hinweise auf weitere Diarien und andere Quellen zu den Landtagen des 18. Jahrhunderts lassen sich in der Bibliographie finden, die die von 2004 bis 2011 aktive Forschungsgruppe für die Geschichte des Ungarischen Landtags im 18. Jahrhundert (»Diaeta. A 18. századi magyar országgyűlések történetét kutató csoport«) unter der Leitung von István Szijártó erarbeitete[43].

(4) Einen weiteren wichtigen Zugang zu Landtagsakten stellt ihre Erschließung in Form von *Regestenwerken* dar. Sie erschien überall dort angezeigt, wo die Forschung sich nicht auf Vorarbeiten stützen konnte und der schiere Umfang des Materials eine editorische Bearbeitung von vornherein ausschloss. Beides trifft insbesondere auf die österreichischen Länder zu – und in der Tat kamen gerade hier Regestenkataloge der Landtagsakten wiederholt zur Anwendung. Das bekannteste und umfangreichste Beispiel stellt eine vom Archivar und Wiener Professor Karl Gutkas (1926–1997) um 1970 angeregte unvollständige Reihe von maschinschriftlich vorliegenden Dissertationen der Universität Wien dar, in denen die chronologisch geordneten Akten der niederösterreichischen »Landtagshandlungen« aus den Jahren 1530 bis 1705 (mit zwei Lücken in den Zeiträumen 1608–1634 und 1649–1682), unter Heranziehung von in der ständischen Registratur angefertigten handschriftlichen Regesten, nach einem ähnlichen Muster erschlossen wurden[44]. Diese Dissertationen lassen zumeist eine elaborierte Fragestellung vermissen, ihre Qualität ist unterschiedlich und die Nützlichkeit der Ergebnisse durch das beschränkte Verständnis der oft mechanisch arbeitenden Bearbeiterinnen und Bearbeiter für das mitunter komplizierte Steuersystem des Landes bedingt. Bei allen diesen Einschränkungen bleiben die Regestenteile ein nützlicher Behelf, dessen Wert all jenen deutlich wird, die nach vergleichendem Material von jenen Landtagen suchen, die nicht auf diese Art und Weise erschlossen worden sind[45].

(5) Als *systematische Erfassung von landtagsrelevanten Angaben* bezeichne ich einen weiteren überlegungswerten Zugang, der sogar auf sehr ferne Versuche zurückblicken kann. Bereits 1691 erschien im Druck ein übersichtliches Verzeichnis aller schlesischen Fürstentage seit 1623 einschließlich der postulierten und bewilligten Summen sowie der Namen der Fürstentagskommissare[46]. Handschriftlich überliefert finden sich ähnliche Aufstellungen als nützliche Nachschlagewerke in manchen Landesarchiven. Im 19. Jahrhundert stellte der oben bereits erwähnte Anton Gindely als Grundlage für eine seiner Abhandlungen die Steuerbewilligungen

---

42 https://mpgy.ogyk.hu/mpgy/gyurikovits (13.09.2023). Zur Sammlung *Vértes, Az Országgyűlési Könyvtár Gyurikovits-gyűjteménye*.
43 http://szijarto.web.elte.hu/diaeta-index.html (13.09.2023).
44 *Hametner*, Landtage 1530–1564; *Herold*, Hauptprobleme der Landtagshandlungen 1564–1576; *Neugebauer*, Landtage 1577 bis 1592; *Stangler*, Landtage von 1593 bis 1607; *Ortner*, Landtage 1635–1648; *Hummer*, Landtage von 1683 bis 1705.
45 Bis zur Drucklegung gelangte eine ähnlich angelegte Doktorarbeit auf Basis der steirischen Landtagsakten: *Ziegerhofer*, Ferdinand I.
46 *Neudorff und Mertzdorff*, EXTRACT.

aller böhmischen Landtage aus dem ersten Jahrhundert der Habsburgerherrschaft in übersichtlicher chronologischer Form zusammen[47]. Ähnliches versuchte vor wenigen Jahren für den niederösterreichischen Landtag der japanische Forscher Shuichi Iwasaki. Zusätzlich wertete er in tabellarischer Form die Teilnahme an einzelnen Landtagssitzungen in allen vier Kurien aus[48]. Auch diese Darstellungsform hatte unbewusstermaßen Vorläufer: Bereits 1947 fasste der tschechische Forscher Antonín Okáč (1908–1986) Angaben über die Teilnahme an böhmischen Landtagen und anderen ständischen Sitzungen des Vormärz tabellarisch zusammen[49]. Der Wert dieser anschaulichen Datenreihen würde freilich wachsen, wenn sie systematisch auch von anderen Landtagen erhoben würden und sich miteinander vergleichen ließen.

(6) Als letztes Beispiel der Zugänge zur Erschließung habsburgischer Ständeversammlungen möchte ich den Anhang in der bahnbrechenden Monographie über die Entwicklung des schlesischen Fürstentags unter der Habsburgerherrschaft (1526–1740) nennen. Kazimierz Orzechowski (1923–2009), von der profunden polnischen Forschung über den polnisch-litauischen Sejm angeregt[50], stellte hier aufgrund seiner systematischen Forschungen einen umfangreichen *Quellenkatalog* zu den einzelnen ständischen Zusammenkünften von 1339 bis 1740 zusammen[51]. Seine Aufstellung enthält außer der Angabe zur Eröffnung der Versammlung Hinweise auf die Überlieferung der Proposition, der abgegebenen Voten der einzelnen Kurien und der Beschlüsse. Angesichts des über zahlreiche Bestände mehrerer schlesischer Archive und Bibliotheken verstreuten Materials hat diese Aufstellung einen großen Wert, stellt sie doch der Forschung zum überhaupt ersten Mal ein Grundgerüst zur Verfügung. Im Kontext der Habsburgermonarchie ist dieser Versuch eines erschöpfenden Quellenverzeichnisses, wenn ich es richtig sehe, bisher einmalig geblieben. Da jedoch Orzechowskis dichte, überwiegend auf Polnisch veröffentlichte Untersuchungen zu gesamtschlesischen Zusammenkünften bisher überraschend wenig Beachtung und keine Nachfolger fanden, bleibt diese Leistung in der Forschung beinahe unsichtbar.

IV. Eine Perspektive

Eincinhalb Jahrhunderte methodisch diverser Bemühungen um die Erschließung der Landtagsquellen aus verschiedenen Territorien der Habsburgermonarchie hinterließen eine offene Baustelle und unzählige Lücken. Welche Lehre kann man

---

47 »Die jährlichen Budgets von 1527–1617, dargestellt nach den Landtagsverhandlungen und sonstigen officiellen Actenstücken«, *Gindely*, Geschichte der böhmischen Finanzen, S. 47–78.
48 *Iwasaki*, Stände und Staatsbildung, S. 344–351.
49 *Okáč*, Český sněm, Tab. 3: eine minutiöse Übersicht der Teilnahme an 75 ständischen Sitzungen von 1842 bis 1847.
50 Ein Überblick über Orzechowskis reiches Oeuvre zum schlesischen Fürstentag: *Maťa*, Verwaltungs- und behördengeschichtliche Forschungen, S. 467–474.
51 *Orzechowski*, Ogólnośląskie zgromadzenia stanowe, S. 371–459.

aus dem gebotenen Überblick ziehen? Welche der genannten Zugänge haben noch Zukunft? Kann digitales Edieren neue Perspektiven eröffnen und mit welchen Erschließungsmaßnahmen könnte man die Ständeforschung in der Habsburgermonarchie sinnvoll vorantreiben?

Ich fürchte, dass die Erfahrungen des letzten Jahrhunderts und die fehlende Infrastruktur weitere editorische Erschließungen der Landtagsakten aus der Habsburgermonarchie im Volltext illusorisch erscheinen lassen. Nicht einmal die Fertigstellung der eingefrorenen Editionsprojekte und die Schließung der Lücken, wie sehr sie auch sinnvoll wäre, lässt sich in absehbarer Zeit realistisch erwarten. Ich denke daher, man wäre gut beraten, die Fixierung auf zeitaufwendige aussichtslose Editionsprojekte zugunsten der Formulierung neuer, der Zeit, den technischen Möglichkeiten und dem Erkenntnisstand entsprechenden Ziele aufzugeben. Dabei sollte nach meinem Dafürhalten die oben besprochene Eigenschaft der Habsburgermonarchie – die Vielzahl unterschiedlich starker Landtage anstatt einer dominierenden Ständeversammlung – nicht als lähmende Beschränkung verstanden, sondern als erkenntnisversprechende Chance, methodische Anregung und motivierende Herausforderung aufgenommen werden: Gerade in der Vielfalt persistenter, nur partiell und ungenügend erforschter und miteinander interagierender Ständewelten besteht das Faszinosum des habsburgischen Länderkonglomerats.

Die im 19. Jahrhundert angeregten, bis heute unersetzlichen Volltexteditionen umfassender Bestände waren wichtige Hilfsmittel eines analogen Zeitalters, in dem hand- und maschinschriftliche Abschriften sowie analoge Kopien die einzigen Alternativen der Vervielfältigung darstellten. Die Digitalisierung bietet die Möglichkeit, in der Untersuchung des dezentralen Systems der ständischen Repräsentation in der Habsburgermonarchie neue Wege zu beschreiten. Denn wesentlich mehr als Volltexteditionen bräuchte die habsburgische Ständeforschung angesichts der umfassenden, aber hoffnungslos verstreuten Bestände eine Vereinfachung des Zugangs zu den wichtigsten Quellenserien sowie flexiblere Formen von deren Erschließung, die die Vorteile der oben exemplarisch vorgestellten Zugänge kombinieren, ohne unendliche Bearbeitungszeiten zu induzieren. Die Herausforderungen heißen: Zugangserleichterung und Orientierungshilfe.

Was die habsburgische Ständeforschung wirklich vorantreiben könnte, wäre ein Behelf in Form eines ausbaufähigen *digitalen Registers aller Landtage und Ständeversammlungen* in den Ländern der Habsburgermonarchie, über politische Brüche hinweg, von Ferdinand I. bis zum Ende der ständischen Verfassungen 1848, das eine Zusammenschau und schnelle Orientierung in der Materie und in (ausgewählten) Quellen ermöglichen würde. Es mag seltsam anmuten, aber ein derartiger Überblick fehlt – und sein Fehlen vermag zu erklären, warum die langfristige Transformation ständischer Landtage bislang bestenfalls partiell analysiert und beschrieben worden ist.

Ein systematisch aufgebautes Register sollte einerseits die wichtigsten vergleichbaren Angaben zu einzelnen Ständeversammlungen erfassen, andererseits den Zugang zu einschlägigen – edierten, digitalisierten oder nur katalogisierten – Quellen aller Art vereinfachen. Der Behelf sollte zu einem Forschungsportal ausbaufähig sein, würde aber bereits dann gute Dienste leisten, wenn er die bisher hoffnungslos verstreuten Grundinformationen zugänglich macht. Solche wären für den Anfang vor allem die Termine (und, wo notwendig und sinnvoll, auch Orte), die Namen der Landtagskommissare sowie bibliographische Hinweise. In einem weiteren Schritt könnten dann detailliertere Angaben ergänzt werden. Im Blick auf gegenwärtige und auch künftige Forschungen bieten sich als solche insbesondere: (1) Angaben zum Verlauf der Landtage bis hin zu einzelnen Sitzungen; dadurch könnten Sitzungsprotokolle exzerpiert werden; (2) Angaben zur Teilnahme an den Landtagen bis zu den Namen nachweisbarer Teilnehmer; (3) Angaben zu Beschlüssen, insbesondere die postulierten sowie die bewilligten Summen und Leistungen. Von allen diesen Angaben sind die Termine am einfachsten zu erheben, aber auch am wichtigsten für einen Überblick: Denn gerade aus den »Landtagszeiten« lassen sich eine Typologie habsburgischer Landtage sowie deren struktureller Wandel ablesen.

Ein wichtiger Mehrwert eines derartigen Behelfs wäre die Verbindung der Angaben über die gesamte ›Galaxie‹ der ständischen Versammlungen in der Habsburgermonarchie. Damit könnte man einerseits die herkömmliche landesgeschichtliche Verengung der Ständeforschung aufbrechen, andererseits den vergleichenden Blick stärken. Denn eine isolierte Betrachtung und Bearbeitung habsburgischer Landtage scheint den heutigen Anforderungen kaum mehr zu entsprechen.

Ein »Landtagsregister« würde der habsburgischen Ständeforschung nicht nur einen guten Dienst leisten, sondern es würde auch einen wichtigen Schritt in Richtung Verknüpfung, Systematisierung, Professionalisierung und Internationalisierung der habsburgischen Ständeforschung darstellen. Es würde zudem neue, länderübergreifende Fragestellungen ermöglichen. Drei Beispiele möchte ich hier abschließend in aller Kürze andeuten.

(1) Bekanntlich erschienen einzelne Mitglieder der Dynastie im ersten Jahrhundert der Habsburgermonarchie nicht nur auf Reichstagen, sondern sie bereisten auch Landtage. Inwiefern dadurch ihre Itinerare geprägt wurden, ist jedoch noch nicht methodisch verlässlich untersucht worden. Eine von mir probeweise unternommene Zusammenstellung von Angaben über die landesfürstliche Anwesenheit bei den Landtagen der bedeutendsten Länder in der Regierungszeit Ferdinands I. aus den bisher erschlossenen Beständen (Tab. 1) hat eine klare Hierarchisierung gezeigt und die zentrale Rolle Böhmens erhellt: Im Durchschnitt nahm Ferdinand persönlich an drei von vier böhmischen Landtagen teil, aber nur an jedem zweiten ungarischen, an jedem dritten niederösterreichischen und jedem vierten mährischen Landtag. Ein Landtagsregister würde zeigen, wie eng die Termine der Landtage und das Itinerar einzelner Habsburger – Herrscher sowie nicht regierender Vertreter – zusammenfielen.

Tab. 1: Anwesenheit Ferdinands I. und anderer Familienmitglieder bei Landtagen (1526–1564).

Land	Ferdinand I. persönlich	vertreten durch Familienmitglieder	vertreten durch Landtagskommissare	Gesamtzahl der Landtage
Böhmen	34 (= 77 %)	1	9	44
Ungarn	13 (= 50 %)	3	10	26
Niederösterreich*	20 (= 32 %)	3	40	63
Mähren	14 (= 23 %)	1	ca. 45	ca. 60
Steiermark	5	?	?	?

* Im Land abgehaltene Ausschusslandtage der österreichischen Länder werden nicht berücksichtigt.

(2) Die Aufteilung finanzieller und militärischer Lasten auf einzelne Länder – von der Finanzierung der ungarischen Feldzüge und des Grenzverteidigungssystems gegen die Osmanen im 16. Jahrhundert über die Verpflegung des stehenden Heeres seit dem Dreißigjährigen Krieg bis hin zur Stellung der Rekruten und zur Beschaffung von Hochzeitsdonativen – stellte ein Dauerthema im Dialog zwischen dem Regierungszentrum und den Landtagen dar. In den Quellen tauchen regionale sowie globale Aufteilungsschlüssel auf, auf die sich einzelne Akteure und Interessengruppen beriefen. Der Mechanismus der Lastenverteilung und sein Wandel sind jedoch beim gegenwärtigen Stand der Quellenerschließung schwer rekonstruierbar, da die postulierten und bewilligten Geldsummen nur punktuell vorliegen[52]. Das Zusammentragen dieser Angaben würde unsere Kenntnisse auf ein ganz neues Niveau heben.

(3) Die Landtage in der Habsburgermonarchie machten im Verlauf der Jahrhunderte einen tiefgreifenden, bisher aber kaum untersuchten strukturellen Wandel durch. Eine der auffälligsten Tendenzen im 17. Jahrhundert, die jene Landtage betraf, die sich im *fiscal-military core* der Habsburgermonarchie befanden, erscheint auf den ersten Blick als eine enorme Verlängerung ihrer Sitzungsperioden: Die Zeitspanne zwischen der Eröffnung und der Schließung eines Landtags verlängerte sich um ein Vielfaches[53]. Ein genauerer Blick lässt gleichzeitig regional unterschiedliche Lösungen für den Bedarf des häufigeren ständischen Beratens erkennen[54]. Der als Kalenderansicht visualisierte, zur Probe unternommene diachrone Vergleich zweier Landtage lässt etwa die tiefe strukturelle Transformation der steirischen

---

52 *Maťa*, Negotiating Fiscal-Military Coordination.
53 Für die Landtage in Böhmen, Mähren und Niederösterreich: *Maťa*, Český zemský sněm, S. 56–58; *Iwasaki*, Stände und Staatsbildung, S. 130 f.
54 Für Schlesien: *Orzechowski*, Geneza. Für Kärnten und Oberösterreich ansatzweise: *Maťa*, Landstände, S. 378 f.

Ständerversammlung von einer außeralltäglichen Zusammenkunft zu einem ausschussähnlichen Gremium erkennen. Dabei fällt unter anderem auf, dass die durchschnittliche Zahl der Landtagssitzungen sich nur unbeträchtlich änderte, diese sich jedoch regelmäßiger im Jahr verteilten (Abb. 1). Die weitere Entwicklung im letzten Jahrhundert der ständischen Landtage, in den Jahrzehnten der Reformen, der Napoleonischen Kriege, der Restauration und des Vormärz, ist bislang nicht einmal ansatzweise untersucht worden. Eine systematische, synchron und diachron vergleichende Analyse der »Landtagszeiten« würde es erlauben, den strukturellen Wandel dieser Institutionen über die Jahrhunderte nicht nur besser zu verstehen, sondern überhaupt erst in den Blick zu bekommen.

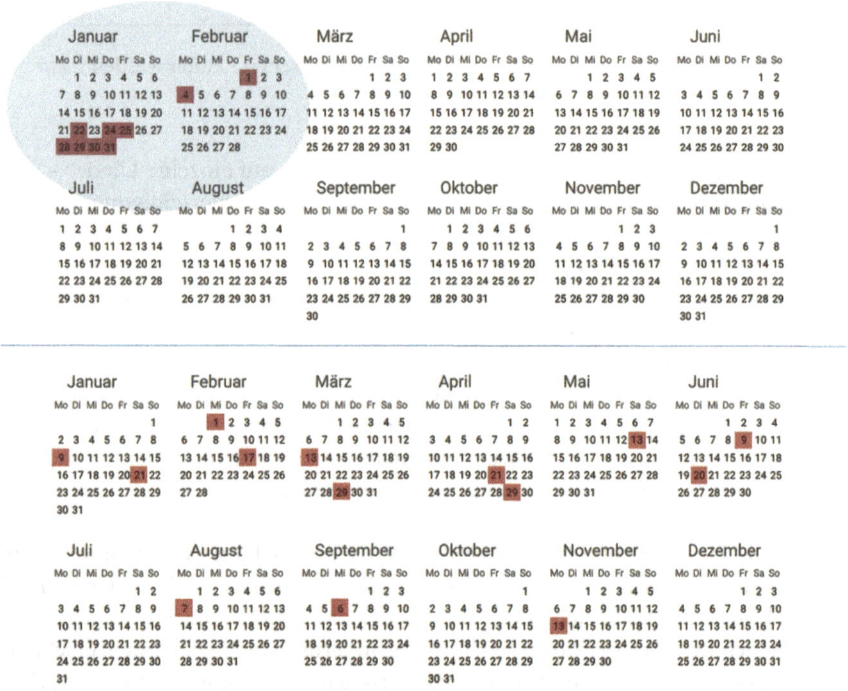

Abb. 1: Sitzungen des steirischen Landtags im Jahre 1630 (oben) und 1713 (unten). Quellen: Steiermärkisches Landesarchiv, Landschaftliches Archiv Antiquum, III, Karton 113, Heft 442; Karton 145, Heft 499.

Voraussetzungen, die für die Verwirklichung der hier entworfenen Vision essenziell wären, und Rahmenbedingungen, die dafür geschaffen werden müssten – von Kooperationen über Landes- und Staatsgrenzen hinweg über die aktive Zusammenarbeit seitens der Landes- bzw. Staatsarchive bei der Digitalisierung bedeutender Quellenserien bis zu Strategien der notwendigen Drittmittelfinanzierung –, müssen an anderer Stelle diskutiert werden. Hier ging es nur darum zu zeigen, inwiefern der länderübergreifende Rückblick auf Erfolge und Mißerfolge bei der Bearbeitung der Akten habsburgischer Landtage Inspiration und Denkanstöße für die Eröffnung neuer Horizonte und das Einschlagen neuer Wege liefert, die den Besonderheiten der Habsburgermonarchie gerecht würden. Um neue Impulse bei der Erforschung des habsburgischen Landtagswesens zu setzen, sollte man nämlich nicht epigonenhaft auf schwer vergleichbare und vielfach gründlicher erforschte »Zentralparlamente« anderer Herrschaftsbildungen blicken. Vielmehr geht es darum, einen eigenen Zugang zu entwickeln, um die historisch eigenartige, aus einer Mehrzahl von Landtagen im Handlungs- und Kommunikationszusammenhang herauswachsende ständische Beratungskultur im habsburgischen politischen System in den Blick zu bekommen und zu erklären.

Quellen- und Literaturverzeichnis

Quelleneditionen

Bessenyei, József (Hg.): Magyar országgyűlési emlékek 1646–1647 [Denkmale der ungarischen Landtage 1646–1647], Bd. 1, Eger 2017.

Desző, Márkus (Hg.): Corpus Juris Hungarici/Magyar Törvénytár 1000–1895, 21 Bde., Budapest 1896–1900.

Diarium Conventus Regnicolarum Posonium Anno 1608 […], in: G[eorgius] M[artinus] Kovachich (Hg.), Scriptores rerum Hungaricarum minores […], Bd. 1, Budae, 1798, S. 211–245.

Dongó-Gy[árfás], Géza (Hg.): Szemere Pál diétai követ Diáriuma 1681-ből [Das Diarium des Landtagsabgesandten Pál Szemere aus dem Jahre 1681], in: Adalékok Zemplén-vármegye történetéhez 11 (1905), S. 51–54, 113–114, 174–175, 237–238, 268–269; 12 (1906), S. 160–161, 226–229; 13 (1907), S. 36–38, 136–139, 246–247.

Forgó, András (Hg.): Az 1712. évi Pozsonyi diéta egy ciszterci szerzetes szemével [Der Preßburger Landtag von 1712 aus der Sicht eines Zisterziensermönchs], Pannonhalma–Veszprém 2013 (= Fontes ex Archivio Sancti Martini editi, Bd. 1; A Veszprém Megyei Levéltár kiadványai, Bd. 32).

Ders. (Hg.): Auf Ihrer Kaiserlichen Majestät allergnädigsten Befehl. Hofrat Johann Georg von Mannagettas Berichte über den ungarischen Landtag, 1722–1723 und 1728–1729, Wien 2021 (= Publikationen der ungarischen Geschichtsforschung in Wien, Bd. 20).

Fraknói, Vilmos/Károlyi, Árpád (Hg.): Magyar országgyűlési emlékek/Monumenta comitialia regni Hungariae, 12 Bde., Budapest 1874–1917.

Janiš, Dalibor (Hg.): Moravský zemský sněm na prahu novověku. Edice Památek sněmovních z let 1518–1570 [Der mährische Landtag an der Schwelle der Neuzeit. Edition der Landtagspamatken aus den Jahre 1518–1570], Bd. 1: Památky sněmovní [Landtagspamatken], Tbd. 1, Praha 2010 (= Prameny k českým dějinám 16.–18. století, Reihe A, Bd. I/1).

Journal des offenen Tiroler Landtages zu Innsbruck 1790. Aus den Papieren eines Zeitgenossen, Bozen 1861.

Khull-Kholwald, Martin (Bearb.): Protokolle des Steiermärkischen Landtages 1835 bis 1848, hg. v. *Gernot Peter Obersteiner*, Graz 2018 (= Forschungen und Darstellungen zur Geschichte des Steiermärkischen Landtages, Bd. 2).

Kiss, Anita/Nagy, János/Kapitány, Adrienn (Hg.): Pest-Pilis-Solt vármegye országgyűlési követutasításai a 18. században [Anweisungen den Landtagsabgordneten aus dem Komitat Pest-Pilis-Solt im 18. Jahrhundert], Budapest 2015 (= Pest Megyei Levéltári Füzetek, Bd. 38).

Komáromy, András (Hg.): Berényi György naplója az 1634/5-ik soproni és az 1637/8-ik évi pozsonyi országgyűlésekről [György Berényis Diarium über die Landtage in Ödenburg 1634/35 und Pressburg 1637/38], in: Történelmi tár, ohne Jg. (1885), S. 118–143.

Lahner, Julian (Hg.): Der Offene Tiroler Landtag von 1790. Nach den Tagebuchaufzeichnungen des Bozner Deputierten Andreas Alois Dipauli (1761–1839), Innsbruck 2021 (= Schlern-Schriften, Bd. 374).

Neudorff und Mertzdorff, Heinrich Wentzel von: EXTRACT Aus denen Käyser- und Königlichen FürstenTags-PROPOSITIONen / und darauf erfolgten Schlüssen / auch theils engen Zusammenkünfften / Was darinnen ihre Käyserliche Majestät an das allgmeine Land begehren lassen / und von denen Herren Fürsten und Ständen dieses Herzogthums Schlesien gewilliget worden [...], Breßlau 1691.

Orzechowski, Kazimierz (Hg.): Relacje deputatów miasta Jawora z lat 1669–1685 [Berichte der Delegierten der Stadt Jauer aus den Jahren 1669–1685], Wrocław 1991.

Palm, Hermann/Krebs, Julius (Hg.): Acta Publica. Verhandlungen und Correspondenzen der schlesischen Fürsten und Stände, 8 Bde., Breslau 1865–1906.

Paulinyi, Oszkár (Hg.): Az első magyar országgyűlesi napló. Feller Miklós naplója az 1546. évi pozsonyi országgyűlésről [Das erste ungarische Landtagsdiarium. Das Tagebuch von Miklós Feller über den Pressburger Landtag von 1546], in: A Gróf Klebelsberg Kuno Magyar Történetkutató Intézet évkönyve 4 (1934), S. 204–230.

Sněmy české od léta 1526 po naši dobu/Die böhmischen Landtagsverhandlungen und Landtagsbeschlüsse vom Jahre 1526 an bis auf die Neuzeit, Bd. 1–11/1–2, 15/1–3, Praha/Prag 1877–1954.

Szilágyi, Sándor (Hg.): Erdélyi országgyűlési emlékek. Monumenta comitialia regni Transylvaniae, 21 Bde., Budapest 1875–1898.

Šišić, Ferdo (Hg.): Acta comitialia regni Croatiae, Dalmatiae et Slavoniae/Hrvatski saborski spisi, 5 Bde., Zagreb 1912–1918.

Thaly, Kálmán (Hg.): Gr. Erdődy Sándor vasi főispán naplója az 1708-iki országgyűlésről [Das Diarium von Graf Sándor Erdődy, Obergespann von Eisenburg, über den Landtag von 1708], in: Történelmi tár 19 (1896), S. 385–400.

Thury, Etele (Hg.): Lányi Pál gömöri alispán naplója. Az 1712. évi pozsonyi országgyűlésről [Diarium von Pál Lányi, Vizegespann von Gömör. Über den Pressburger Landtag 1712], in: Történelmi tár N. F. 4 (1903), S. 395–413; 5 (1904), S. 1–34.

Verbič, Marija (Hg.): Deželnozborski spisi kranjskih stanov [Landtagsakten der Krainer Stände], Bd. 1: 1499–1515, Bd. 2: 1516–1519, Ljubljana 1980–1986 (= Publikacije Arhiva Socialistične republike Slovenije, Viri, Bd. 1–2).

Zaključci Hrvatskog sabora/Prothocolla Generalium congregationum Statuum et Ordinum regnorum Dalmatiae, Croatiae et Slavoniae, 12 Bde., Zagreb 1958–1980.

Literatur

Ammerer, Gerhard u. a. (Hg.): Bündnispartner und Konkurrenten der Landesfürsten? Die Stände in der Habsburgermonarchie, Wien/München 2007 (= VIÖG, Bd. 49).

Bahlcke, Joachim: Durch »starke Konföderation wohl stabiliert«. Ständische Defension und politisches Denken in der habsburgischen Ländergruppe am Anfang des 17. Jahrhunderts, in: Thomas Winkelbauer (Hg.), Kontakte und Konflikte. Böhmen, Mähren und Österreich: Aspekte eines Jahrtausends gemeinsamer Geschichte, Horn/Waidhofen an der Thaya 1993, S. 173–186 (= Schriftenreihe des Waldviertler Heimatbundes, Bd. 36).

Ders.: Regionalismus und Staatsintegration im Widerstreit. Die Länder der Böhmischen Krone im ersten Jahrhundert der Habsburgerherrschaft (1526–1619), München 1994 (= Schriften des Bundesinstituts für ostdeutsche Kultur und Geschichte, Bd. 3).

Ders.: Landtagsakten (unter besonderer Berücksichtigung der Verhältnisse in der frühneuzeitlichen Habsburgermonarchie), in: *Josef Pauser/Martin Scheutz/Thomas Winkelbauer (Hg.)*, Quellenkunde der Habsburgermonarchie (16.–18. Jahrhundert). Ein exemplarisches Handbuch, Wien/München 2004, S. 351–365 (= Mitteilungen des Instituts für Österreichische Geschichtsforschung, Erg.-Bd. 44). Neudruck unter dem Titel: Böhmische Landtagsakten im ostmitteleuropäischen Kontext. Genese, Quellenwert und historioprahiegeschichtliche Bedeutung, in: *ders. (Hg.)*, Erinnerungskonkurrenz. Geschichtsschreibung in den böhmischen Ländern vom 16. Jahrhundert bis zur Gegenwart, Frankfurt am Main 2016, S. 45–70 (= Forschungen zu Geschichte und Kultur der böhmischen Länder, Bd. 3).

Ders.: Gemeinsame Vergangenheit, selektive Erinnerung. Forschungen schlesischer Historiker zur böhmisch-mährischen Geschichte vor dem Ersten Weltkrieg, in: *Joachim Bahlcke/Roland Gehrke (Hg.)*, Epochen – Themen – Methoden. Geschichtsschreibung in Schlesien vom späten 18. Jahrhundert bis 1914, Wien/Köln/Weimar 2021, S. 383–447 (= Neue Forschungen zur schlesischen Geschichte, Bd. 30).

Ders./Bömelburg, Hans-Jürgen/Kersken, Norbert (Hg.): Ständefreiheit und Staatsgestaltung in Ostmitteleuropa. Übernationale Gemeinsamkeiten in der politischen Kultur vom 16.–18. Jahrhundert, Leipzig 1996.

Benda, Kálmán: A Magyar Országgyűlési Emlékek. Beszámoló egy forráskiadvány-sorozat munkálatairól [Denkmale der ungarischen Landtage. Ein Bericht über die Arbeit an einer Quelleneditionsreihe], in: Történelmi Szemle 17 (1974), S. 650–655.

Bérenger, Jean/Kecskeméti, Charles: Parlement et vie parlementaire en Hongrie. 1608–1918, Paris 2008.

Bessenyei, József: Magyar országgyűlési emlékek – egy vállalkozás története, néhány tanulsággal [Denkmäler der ungarischen Landtage – die Geschichte eines Unternehmens, mit einigen Lektionen], in: *Dániel Ballabás (Hg.)*, Országgyűlések – országos gyűlések, Eger 2011, S. 7–21.

Cerman, Ivo: The Estates Opposition in the Habsburg Reform Monarchy (1748–1790), in: *Harald Heppner/Peter Urbanitsch/Renate Zedinger (Hg.)*, Social Change in the Habsburg Monarchy, Bochum 2011, S. 155–174 (= Das Achtzehnte Jahrhundert und Österreich. Internationale Beihefte, Bd. 3).

Cerwinka, Günter: Die ältesten steirischen Landtagsakten (1396 bis 1518), in: 100 Jahre Historische Landeskommission für Steiermark 1892–1992. Bausteine zur Historiographie der Steiermark, hg. v. *Othmar Pickl*, bearb. v. *Robert F. Hausmann*, Graz 1992, S. 229–242 (= Forschungen zur geschichtlichen Landeskunde der Steiermark, Bd. 26).

David, Jiří: Nechtěné budování státu. Politika, válka a finance na Moravě ve druhé polovině 17. století [Unbeabsichtigte Staatsbildung. Politik, Krieg und Finanzen in Mähren in der zweiten Hälfte des 17. Jahrhunderts], Brno 2018 (= Knižnice Matice moravské, Bd. 46).

Dobszay, Tamás: A rendi országgyűlés utolsó évtizedei (1790–1848) [Die letzten Jahrzehnte der ständischen Nationalversammlung (1790–1848)], Budapest 2019.

Ders. u. a. (Hg.): Rendiség és parlamentarizmus Magyarországon. A kezdetektől 1918-ig [Ständewesen und Parlamentarismus in Ungarn. Von den Anfängen bis 1918], Budapest 2013.

Eberhard, Winfried: Monarchie und Widerstand. Zur ständischen Oppositionsbildung im Herrschaftssystem Ferdinands I. in Böhmen, München 1985 (= Veröffentlichungen des Collegium Carolinum, Bd. 54).

Evans, R. J. W./Thomas, T. V. (Hg.): Crown, Church and Estates. Central European Politics in the Sixteenth and Seventeenth Centuries, London 1991.

Fazekas, István/Gebei, Sándor/Pálosfalvi, Tamás: Rendi országgyűlések a Magyar királyságban a 18. század elejéig [Ständische Landtage im Königreich Ungarn bis zum Anfang des 18. Jahrhunderts], Budapest 2020.

Forgó, András: Egyház – Rendiség – Politikai kultúra. Papok és szerzetesek a 18. század országgyűlésein [Kirche – Stände – politische Kultur. Priester und Ordensleute auf den Landtagen des 18. Jahruhunderts], Budapest 2017.

Gindely, Anton: Geschichte der böhmischen Finanzen von 1526–1618, Wien 1868.
Godsey, William D.: The Sinews of Habsburg Power. Lower Austria in a Fiscal-Military State 1650–1820, Oxford 2018.
Ders./Maťa Petr (Hg.): The Habsburg Monarchy as a Fiscal-Military State. Contours and Perspectives 1648–1815, Oxford 2022 (= Proceedings of the British Academy, Bd. 247).
Hametner, Angelika: Die niederösterreichischen Landtage von 1530–1564, Diss. Wien 1969.
Hassinger, Herbert: Die Landstände der österreichischen Länder. Zusammensetzung, Organisation und Leistung im 16.–18. Jahrhundert, in: Jahrbuch für Landeskunde von Niederösterreich N.F. 36 (1964), S. 989–1035.
Herold, Hannelore: Die Hauptprobleme der Landtagshandlungen des Erzherzogtums Österreich unter der Enns zur Zeit der Regierung Kaiser Maximilians II. (1564–1576), Diss. Wien 1970.
Hochedlinger, Michael/Maťa, Petr/Winkelbauer, Thomas (Hg.): Verwaltungsgeschichte der Habsburgermonarchie in der Frühen Neuzeit, Bd. 1/1, Wien 2019, S. 29–62 (= Mitteilungen des Instituts für Österreichische Geschichtsforschung, Erg.-Bd. 62/1).
Hummer, Maria: Die niederösterreichischen Landtage von 1683 bis 1705, Diss. Wien 1976.
Iwasaki, Shuichi: Stände und Staatsbildung in der frühneuzeitlichen Habsburgermonarchie in Österreich unter der Enns 1683–1748, St. Pölten 2014 (= Studien und Forschungen aus dem Niederösterreichischen Institut für Landeskunde, Bd. 53).
Jerše, Sašo: Glaube, Hoffnung, Herrschaft. Die »imaginaires politiques« Innerösterreichs im Zeitalter des religiös-politischen Konflikts, in: Mitteilungen des Instituts für Österreichische Geschichtsforschung 121 (2013), S. 352–373.
Kameníček, František: Archivní rozhled [Achivalische Umschau], in: Časopis Matice moravské 15 (1891), S. 44–50, 142–148, 242–253, 341–345; 16 (1892), S. 49–57, 139–144, 238–243, 312–318; 17 (1893), S. 49–55, 150–154, 244–253, 344–353; 18 (1894), S. 48–53, 158–164, 245–254, 340–345.
Ders.: Zemské sněmy a sjezdy moravské. Jejich složení, obor působnosti a význam. Od nastoupení na trůn krále Ferdinanda I. až po vydání Obnoveného zřízení zemského (1526–1628) [Die mährischen Landtage und Ständeversammlungen. Ihre Zusammensetzung, ihr Wirkungsbereich und ihre Bedeutung. Von der Thronbesteigung König Ferdinands I. bis zum Erlass der Verneuerten Landesordnung (1526–1628)], 3 Bde., Brno 1900–1905.
Kersken, Norbert: Breslau als Zentrum landesgeschichtlicher Forschung: Der »Verein für Geschichte und Alterthum Schlesiens«, in: *Joachim Bahlcke/Roland Gehrke (Hg.)*, Institutionen der Geschichtspflege und Geschichtsforschung in Schlesien. Von der Aufklärung bis zum Ersten Weltkrieg, Köln/Weimar/Wien 2017, S. 87–120 (= Neue Forschungen zur schlesischen Geschichte, Bd. 26).
Krofta, Kamil: Snahy o společný sněm zemí domu rakouského v letech 1526–1848 [Bemühungen um einen gemeinsamen Landtag der Länder des Hauses Österreich in den Jahren 1526–1848], Prag 1917.
Kürschner, Gottlieb: Bericht über die wissenschaftliche Tätigkeit im schlesischen Landesarchiv zu Troppau, in: Zeitschrift für Geschichte und Kultur Österreichisch-Schlesien 13 (1918), S. 1–73; 14/15 (1919/20), S. 1–73.
Lahner, Julian: Stände und landesfürstliche Herrschaft in Tirol, 1756–1790, Diss. Innsbruck 2019.
Maťa, Petr: Český zemský sněm v pobělohorské době (1620–1740). Relikt stavovského státu nebo nástroj absolutistické vlády? [Der böhmische Landtag in der Zeit nach der Schlacht am Weißen Berg (1620–1740). Relikt des Ständestaates oder Instrument absolutistischer Herrschaft?], in: *Marian J. Ptak (Hg.)*, Sejm czeski od czasów najdawniejszych do 1913 roku, Opole 2000, S. 49–67.
Ders.: Landstände und Landtage in den böhmischen und österreichischen Ländern (1620–1740). Von der Niedergangsgeschichte zur Interaktionsanalyse, in: *ders./Thomas Winkelbauer (Hg.)*, Die Habsburgermonarchie 1620 bis 1740. Leistungen und Grenzen des Absolutismusparadigmas, Stuttgart 2006, S. 345–400 (= Forschungen zur Geschichte und Kultur des östlichen Mitteleuropa, Bd. 24).

Ders.: Verwaltungs- und behördengeschichtliche Forschungen zu den böhmischen Ländern in der Frühen Neuzeit. Ein kurzer Überblick über vier lange Forschungstraditionen, in: *Michael Hochedlinger/Thomas Winkelbauer (Hg.)*, Herrschaftsverdichtung, Staatsbildung, Bürokratisierung. Verfassungs-, Verwaltungs- und Behördengeschichte der Frühen Neuzeit, Wien/München 2010, S. 421–477 (Veröffentlichungen des Instituts für Österreichische Geschichtsforschung, Bd. 57).

Ders.: The Care of Thrones. The Plethora of Investitures in the Habsburg Composite Monarchy and Beyond from the Sixteenth to the Eighteenth Century, in: *Klaas Van Gelder (Hg.)*, More Than Mere Spectacle. Coronations and Inaugurations in the Habsburg Monarchy during the Eighteenth and Nineteenth Centuries, New York/Oxford 2021, S. 29–66 (= Austrian and Habsburg Studies, Bd. 31).

Ders.: Negotiating Fiscal-Military Coordination: Provincial Tax Quotas for the Habsburg Army 1648–1748, in: *William D. Godsey/ders. (Hg.)*, The Habsburg Monarchy as a Fiscal-Military State. Contours and Perspectives 1648–1815, Oxford 2022, S. 183–210 (= Proceedings of the British Academy, Bd. 247).

Mout, Nicolette: Der Löwe und die Ameisen. Der böhmische Aufstand (1618–1620) im europäischen Kontext, in: *Kopetz, Hedwig/Marko, Josef/Poier, Klaus (Hg.)*, Soziokultureller Wandel im Verfassungsstaat. Phänomene politischer Transformation, Bd. 2, Wien/Graz 2004, S. 899–910 (Studien zu Politik und Verwaltung, Bd. 90/2).

Neugebauer, Gabriele: Die niederösterreichischen Landtage von 1577 bis 1592, Diss. Wien 1979.

Okáč, Antonín: Český sněm a vláda před březnem 1848. Kapitoly o jejich ústavních sporech [Der böhmische Landtag und die Regierung vor dem März 1848. Kapitel über ihre Verfassungskonflikte], Praha 1947 (Knihovna Sněmů českých, Bd. 11).

Ortner, Gunther: Die niederösterreichischen Landtage von 1635–1648, Diss. Wien 1974.

Orzechowski, Kazimierz: Diariusze śląskie [Schlesische Landes-Diarien], in: Śląski kwartalnik historyczny Sobótka 27 (1972), S. 397–412.

Ders.: Geneza i istota śląskiega »Conventus publicus« [Genese und Wesen des schlesischen »Conventus publicus«], in: Śląski kwartalnik historyczny Sobótka 27 (1972), S. 561–577.

Ders.: Ogólnośląskie zgromadzenia stanowe [Die gesamtschlesischen Ständeversammlungen], Warszawa/Wrocław 1979.

Pálffy, Géza: The Kingdom of Hungary and the Habsburg Monarchy in the Sixteenth Century, New York 2009 (= East European Monographs, Bd. 735).

Pánek, Jaroslav: Das Ständewesen und die Gesellschaft in den Böhmischen Ländern in der Zeit vor der Schlacht am Weißen Berg (1526–1620), in: Historica 25 (1985), S. 73–120.

Ders.: Stavovská opozice a a její zápas s Habsburky 1547–1577. K politické krizi feudální třídy v předbělohorském českém státě [Die Ständeopposition und ihr Kampf mit den Habsburgern 1547–1577. Zur politischen Krise der Feudalklasse im böhmischen Staat in der Zeit vor der Schlacht am Weißen Berg], Praha 1982 (= Studie ČSAV, Bd. 2).

Ders.: Sněmy české. Naděje a ztroskotání edice k dějinám raného novověku [Die böhmischen Landtagsverhandlungen und Landtagsbeschlüsse. Hoffnungen und Scheitern einer Edition zur Geschichte der Frühen Neuzeit], in: *Alena Pazderová (Hg.)*, 130 let Zemského archivu, Praha 1993, S. 23–33.

Rauscher, Peter (Hg.): Kriegführung und Staatsfinanzen. Die Habsburgermonarchie und das Heilige Römische Reich vom Dreißigjährigen Krieg bis zum Ende des habsburgischen Kaisertums 1740, Münster 2010 (= Geschichte der Epoche Karls V., Bd. 10).

Révész, László: Die Anfänge des ungarischen Parlamentarismus, München 1968 (= Südosteuropäische Arbeiten, Bd. 68).

Schulze, Winfried: Landesdefension und Staatsbildung. Studien zum Kriegswesen des innerösterreichischen Territorialstaates (1564–1619), Wien/Köln/Graz 1973 (= VKNGÖ, Bd. 60).

Seuffert, Burkhard: Über die Veröffentlichung von Landtagsakten, in: Historische Vierteljahrschrift 24 (1929) S. 573–587.

Stangler, Gottfried: Die niederösterreichischen Landtage von 1593 bis 1607, Diss. Wien 1972.

Steiner, Philipp: Die Landstände in Steiermark, Kärnten und Krain und die josephinischen Reformen. Bedrohungskommunikation angesichts konkurrierender Ordnungsvorstellungen (1789–1792), Münster 2017.

Strohmeyer, Arno: Konfessionskonflikt und Herrschaftsordnung. Widerstandsrecht bei den österreichischen Ständen (1550–1650), Mainz 2006 (= Veröffentlichungen des Instituts für europäische Geschichte Mainz, Abteilung für Universalgeschichte, Bd. 201; Beiträge zur Sozial- und Verfassungsgeschichte des Alten Reiches, Bd. 16).

Sutter, Berthold: Steirische Landtagsakten (1519–1637), in: XXI. Bericht der Historischen Landeskommission für Steiermark, Graz 1982, S. 87–91.

Ders.: Die steirischen Landtagsakten 1519–1637. Ein Beitrag zur Geschichte der Erforschung der steirischen Landtage, in: *Orthmar Pickl (Hg.)*, 100 Jahre Historische Landeskommission für Steiermark 1892–1992. Bausteine zur Historiographie der Steiermark, bearb. v. Robert F. Hausmann, Graz 1992, S. 243–264 (= Forschungen zur geschichtlichen Landeskunde der Steiermark, Bd. 26).

Szijártó, István M.: A Diéta. A magyar rendek és az országgyűlés 1708–1792 [Die Diaeta. Die ungarischen Stände und der Landtag 1708–1792], Budapest 2005.

Ders.: A 18. századi Magyarország rendi országgyűlése [Der ständische Landtag Ungarns im 18. Jahrhundert], Budapest 2016.

Ders.: Estates and Constitution. The Parliament in Eighteenth-Century Hungary, New York/Oxford 2020.

Ders./Blockmans, Wim/Kontler, László (Hg.): Parliamentarism in Northern and East-Central Europe in the Long Eighteenth Century, Bd. 1: Representative Institutions and Political Motivation, London/New York 2022.

Tobolka, Zdeněk Václav: Knihopis českých a slovenských tisků od doby nejstarší až do konce XVIII. století [Bibliographie tschechischer und slowakischer Drucke von der ältesten Zeit bis zum Ende des XVIII. Jahrhunderts], T. 2: Tisky z let 1501–1800 [Drucke aus den Jahren 1501–1800], Bd. 1, Praha 1939.

Vértes, György: Az Országgyűlési Könyvtár Gyurikovits-gyűjteménye [Die Gyurikovits-Sammlung der Bibliothek des Parlaments], in: Századok 98 (1964), S. 334–338.

Volf, Miloslav: Pokusy o společnou defensi České koruny v poslední třetině 16. věku. Příspěvek k politickovojenské historii [Versuche einer gemeinsamen Verteidigung der Böhmischen Krone im letzten Drittel des 16. Jahrhunderts. Ein Beitrag zur Politik- und Militärgeschichte], in: K dějinám československým v období humanismu. Sborník prací věnovaný Janu Bedřichu Novákovi k šedesátým narozeninám, Praha 1932, S. 315–342.

Ziegerhofer, Anita: Ferdinand I. und die steirischen Stände. Dargestellt anhand der Landtage 1542 bis 1556, Graz 1996 (= Dissertationen der Karl-Franzens-Universität Graz, Bd. 102).

PAUL SEAWARD (LONDON)

The English Parliament in the Sixteenth and Seventeenth Centuries: Sources and Digitisation

The Parliament of England was, by the beginning of the sixteenth century, already an institution with a substantial history. Its origins were dated by the Italian historian Polydore Virgil precisely to 1116 and the reign of Henry I, though many others believed that it was much older than that, and by the end of the century the topic of parliament's antiquity was controversial; in the seventeenth century the controversy was elevated into a key issue of debate in contemporary politics as some historians insisted on a thirteenth-century origin for parliament, the reign of Henry III[1]. But it is difficult to identify a real origin to Parliament, since the institution is now seen as a development of many earlier practices, including the councils of pre-Norman England, albeit one whose key elements were considerably changed in the fourteenth and fifteenth centuries[2].

By then, parliaments, if not regular, were fairly frequent: seventy meetings were held over the course of the fifteenth century, and although in the last forty years of the century they were held at longer intervals and during the early sixteenth century had become almost purely occasional, the years of the Reformation saw a rapid increase in activity and the number of meetings. By 1500 parliament's essential structure and forms of procedure had become fairly stable; many of them are still recognisable at least vestigially in the operations of the modern UK Parliament[3]. Most obviously it was a bicameral body, with two chambers meeting mostly concurrently and separately. One contained the nobility, undifferentiated between prelates of the church and a secular nobility made up of those increasingly claiming to serve by hereditary right, though always renewed by new royal appointments to the peerage. The other contained the knights (lower nobility), and citizens and burgesses (representatives of cities and towns), all of whom were elected for each parliament at local courts or assemblies. No plenary sessions were held except for

---

1 See the discussion by *Cavill*, Polydore Vergil, and for the controversy in the later sixteenth century see *Gajda*, Elizabethan church and parliament.
2 The most recent scholarly discussion (by *Maddicott*, Origins) argues – against the previous consensus – for the essential continuity between the English Parliaments of the thirteenth century and afterwards and their Anglo-Saxon predecessors. See *Davies/Denton (ed.)*, English Parliament, for a useful summary of the earlier scholarship.
3 The most recent discussions of the form and functions of parliament in the fifteenth century may be found in *Dodd*, Justice and Grace, and *Clark (ed.)*, History of Parliament I. For a lucid account of parliament right at the end of the fifteenth century, see *Cavill*, English Parliaments of Henry VII. For a general history of the English/British/United Kingdom Parliament, see *Jones (ed.)*, Short History of Parliament.

formal proceedings at the beginning and the end of each parliament. Earlier in the century meetings were held between delegations of each House in a practice known as »intercommuning«, and while evidence of these is lacking for the later fifteenth century, it seems likely that contacts of this kind, which are well-established later in the sixteenth century, did continue.

The business of parliament by 1500 had become principally the making of public laws. This process had developed out of the practice of receiving and summarising and transmitting petitions to the king for his consideration. By now the process turned the petition, or what was increasingly a draft »bill«, into a formal »act« via the approval of both chambers and a royal assent. However, a substantial element of parliament's time was taken up by what are called private bills/acts, which sometimes functioned in similar ways to legal proceedings between parties and could be seen as an alternative to litigation in the royal courts, achieving a legal settlement of land or determining other disputes. While they were private business, they were dealt with in essentially the same way as public acts, but increasingly with certain procedural distinctions. They would result in a law that would be respected by the king's courts. Otherwise, parliament had largely ceased to deal with business in a way we would recognise as a judicial court, making judgements on the basis of existing laws. Most of the conventional judicial activity of early parliaments had moved to the royal courts in the fourteenth century. What remained was a very occasional hearing of appeals from other courts, although the continued existence of the function provided a basis for the revival of appellate judicial business by the House of Lords in the seventeenth century, for it to become a major preoccupation of that House by the eighteenth.

The way in which parliament's proceedings were formally recorded underwent – apparently – a significant change around the beginning of the sixteenth century, as the formal record of the medieval parliament – the Parliament Rolls – was largely (though not wholly) supplanted, at least as a useful and substantive source for understanding what happened, by the separate and formal journals of either House[4]. The reality and significance of this change, though, is difficult to assess. What are collectively known as the Parliament Rolls are the oldest records of the English Parliament, known as such because most of them consist of large rolls of parchment stitched together end to end and are kept together by the royal chancery in a series now deposited in The National Archives[5]. The first material to which the label is applied dates to the reign of Edward I, in the 1270s, around 40 years after the word »parliament« started to be used for some of the assemblies of magnates summoned by the king. But they are very patchy records, variable in form and completeness, predominantly consisting of petitions and sometimes responses, put together sub-

---

4   For a general overview of the parliamentary records, see *Bond*, Guide.
5   The series is catalogued as C65. A catalogue description can be found through The National Archives' website at https://discovery.nationalarchives.gov.uk/details/r/C3625 (13.09.2023).

sequently as an artificial collection[6]. The main series begins from 1322; and from the 1360s the series is almost continuous.

What is on them[7]? The rolls take on a more standard format quite rapidly in the 1340s, in the reign of Edward III. This standardisation coincides with some changes in parliament's role and prominence, but has also been attributed to the clerk of the parliament at the time[8]. As the formal record of a Parliament, the Rolls were treated as an authoritative document of reference. There was clearly anxiety about the scope for manipulation of the record particularly in the reigns of Richard II, Henry IV and Henry V: the Commons demanded the opportunity to check it in 1406[9]. The rolls constitute a very basic summary of the proceedings throughout the meeting, largely limited to the formal proceedings in the plenary sessions at the beginning and end of each parliament. By now the two elements of parliament were meeting separately: but the Parliament Rolls do not record the proceedings of the individual chambers, nor do they make it possible to follow proceedings day-by-day. They are highly selective, concentrating mainly on the outcomes of parliament, the conclusion of all proceedings, rather than the process of getting there. The Rolls would routinely record the »charge«, or an opening speech usually made by the chancellor at the beginning of a parliament; the appointment of the receivers and triers of private petitions (a committee of royal, rather than parliamentary, officials appointed to deal with the flood of petitions received around parliament time); the presentation to the king of the speaker chosen by the Commons, and his protestation and acceptance by the king. At the end of the parliament they record grants of taxation, the »common petitions« – the requests of the Commons, and the king's answers to them. Sometimes they record the statutes – the formal legislative enactment – concluded as a result – though statutes were more commonly enrolled in a separate series, known as the statute rolls. The Rolls would record other requests of the Commons and occasionally, especially in some of the parliaments of the 1380s and during the reign of Henry IV, a summary of debates to which they gave rise; they might include legal cases heard as a result of private petitions; and great matters of state or judgments concerning the peers, including notices of state trials such as the impeachments in Good Parliament of 1376, or in the parliament of 1450.

---

6   This is the collection of miscellaneous records in The National Archives referred to as the »Exchequer series«, or SC9. The name refers to the fact that these records originated in the royal exchequer: in the 1320s chancery appears to have taken on responsibility for recording the business of parliament. There is a catalogue entry covering them at https://discovery.nationalarchives.gov.uk/details/r/C13527 (13.09.2023). Another important, but understudied, source is the collection of private petitions known as the »Ancient Petitions« held at SC8. For this source, see *Dodd*, Justice and Grace, p. 7–9, 13. See also the discussion of other sources in the the edition of »The Rolls of Parliament« published in 2005: »General Introduction« in *Given-Wilson et al. (ed.)*, PROME.

7   For a fuller discussion, see the »General Introduction« in PROME, and the individual introductions to each section of that resource, and also *Clark (ed.)*, Parchment and People.

8   See *Ormrod*, Rolls of Parliament.

9   See *Given-Wilson*, Rolls of Parliament.

A change comes over the Parliament Rolls in the late fifteenth and sixteenth century. At first, they became more comprehensive, absorbing the separate category of the statute rolls, which ceased to exist in 1469[10]. But then the detail of private acts started to be omitted from the Rolls, and from 1593 they included only their titles. In general, through the sixteenth century the Rolls became much more formulaic. They were still used for recording some proceedings which are seen as of particular significance – for example the proceedings against Mary Queen of Scots in 1586 which resulted in her execution; or the detailed narrative of the trip to Spain by Prince Charles and the Duke of Buckingham in 1623. But after the parliament of 1629 all proceedings are recorded on them other than the acts themselves disappear – all the other material is no longer recorded in this series, which essentially just becomes the record copy of the statutes – the legislation itself, with no other proceedings recorded[11].

I. The Journal of the House of Lords

The gradual downgrading of the Parliament Rolls seems to be partly because the clerical service of parliaments in the sixteenth century became increasingly distanced from the royal chancery[12]; and because a different type of record – the House of Lords Journal – came to be treated as more important and authoritative. An almost complete series of Journals of the Lords exists from 1510 onwards in the Parliamentary Archives (there are some gaps in the sixteenth century), but they were not new in 1510. Fragments of Journals from 1449 and 1461 survive, looking remarkably similar to the text in the first volumes in the Parliamentary Archives[13]. By the time the main series of Journals was put together in the late sixteenth century (perhaps at the same time as a building was being created for a parliamentary record office in the old Jewel Tower of the Palace of Westminster, with new timber presses and bookcases) the earlier ones had disappeared[14].

In one way it is easy to see the difference between the Parliament Rolls and the Journal. The Journal is – as the name implies – very much what the Parliament Rolls are not: a day by day summary of proceedings. We can see that the basic daily format established by 1449 was still being followed in the sixteenth and seventeenth centuries. Indeed, there is much of it that remains today. Each day's entry was headed with the date, and a presence list, indicating the attendance on the day. There would be a brief (often only a line or two) summary of business transacted, particularly

---

10 These form the series C74 in The National Archives. A catalogue entry can be found at https://discovery.nationalarchives.gov.uk/details/r/C3634 (13.09.2023).
11 *Elton*, Rolls of Parliament.
12 See Ibid.
13 See *Dunham*, Lords' Journal.
14 *Thrush*, House of lords' records repository; *Foster (ed.)*, Proceedings in parliament 1610.

in terms of bills read and approved. Occasionally there are fuller details, particularly later on, of individual items; by later in the century the entries would include details of the appointment of committees and their reports. But many of the other elements of the Journal are very similar to the Parliament Rolls, with the formal elements at the beginning and end of a parliament recorded in essentially the same way to those in the Parliament Rolls. For the opening of a parliament, they routinely include a brief description of the opening of parliament and the presence of the king; the Lord Chancellor's opening speech; the instruction given to the Commons to choose a speaker; the appointment of the receivers and triers of petitions. For the last day, they would come to incorporate a note of speeches exchanged by the Speaker of the Commons and the Lord Chancellor, an account of the process of the king giving his assent or withholding assent to bills, and the prorogation of parliament. Perhaps the Journal was originally constructed as a business record and as a tool out of which the eventual Parliament Roll was put together, but it came ultimately to supersede it as a formal record. From 1621 the Lords were recording their Journal on parchment, rather than paper, and this, together with the downgrading of the information provided in the parliament roll after 1629 indicates a raising of the status of the Journal: that this was now the formal record of the proceedings of the parliament as a whole, as well as of the House of Lords in particular[15].

II. The House of Commons Journal

No corresponding Journal for the Commons has been found from before 1547, when the series as printed in the 1740s begins. There is a reference in a statute of 1515 to »the book of the clerk«, which some have construed as evidence of the pre-existence of the Journal.[16] And there probably was some document of the kind, if only because it is difficult to see how one could keep track of what was going on in business without some sort of record. The surviving early so-called »Journals« probably reflect such a basic record-keeping function, consisting essentially of a mere list of business considered on each day.

The beginning of the Journal series in 1547 coincides with the appointment of a new clerk, John Seymour, and it looks as if, as with the Lords, the series is down to a changed approach to keeping records either on the part of him or his successor. Those who originally bound the early Journals collected together all of those written during his tenure into a single volume marked on the spine with his name. The

---

15 See the discussion of the Lords Journal in the early seventeenth century in *Thrush (ed.)*, House of Lords 1604–1629, p. 69–72.
16 The reference comes from a statute of 6 Henry VIII c. 16, referring to the attendance of Members. There is a discussion of it in *Hawkyard*, House of Commons 1509–1558, p. 218 f. For discussions of the early House of Commons Journals see *Neale*, Commons' journals; *Pollard*, Under-clerks and the commons' journals, p. 151; *Pollard*, Queen Elizabeth's under-clerks, and *Hawkyard*, House of commons 1509–1558, p. 219–24.

Journals become a little more elaborate over the years of his clerkship; but it was during the period of office of his successor, Fulk Onslow, that they became much fuller and more informative. Onslow was the brother of the speaker elected in 1567. Onslow's later Journals, from 1584 to 1601, have not survived, though what appear to be partial copies of them are included in the great collection of the proceedings of the Elizabethan parliaments made by the politician and historian Sir Simonds D'Ewes in the early seventeenth century[17]. These suggest that Onslow was providing a much fuller and more descriptive record than Seymour's very bare minutes, with some key debates and proceedings extensively described. We do not know why parts of Onslow's record are so much fuller than was Seymour's, or that of his contemporaries in the lords. Possibly they are rough drafts, rather than the final, formal, production. Or Onslow may have conceived of the business of recording parliament in a different way than his colleagues in the lords. The business of minuting settles down into a rather more formal and standardised structure during the clerkship of Onslow's successor, Ralph Ewens, from 1607, by when the Journal is increasingly seen as an authoritative and precious record of the House's proceedings, constantly used to find procedural precedents[18].

The Commons Journal by then provides a far from perfect, but broadly coherent minute, very similar to that available in the House of Lords. It notes the business transacted on each day including readings of bills, the appointment of committees to consider bills in detail, dealings with the other House, and incidental proceedings – increasingly matters of alleged breaches of privilege against individual members. Unlike the Lords Journal there is no record of attendance: no such register was ever kept. It also lacks most of the formal details that were provided in the Lords Journal concerning the plenary meetings at the opening and ending of each parliament.

III. Private Accounts

Alongside these formal official records were the informal, private records. Very few substantial accounts of parliamentary proceedings exist from before the late sixteenth century. There is a famous and very circumstantial account of a debate in the so-called »Good parliament« of 1376 in a chronicle which may have been linked to one of the Chancery clerks responsible for parliament[19]. There is a detailed summary of the proceedings of the first few days of the parliament of 1485 in a letter from the members representing one town in the East of England back to their town gover-

---

17 *D'Ewes (ed.)*: Compleat Journal. For D'Ewes, see *McGee*, Industrious Mind.
18 There are numerous discussions of the Commons Journal in the seventeenth century. Andrew Thrush provides a general account in *Thrush (ed.)*, House of Commons 1604–1629, p. 233–236; see also *Seaward*, Institutional memory.
19 The so-called »Anonimalle Chronicle«: see *Pollard*, »Anonimalle« Chronicle.

nors[20]. Perhaps more of these were written: certainly letters from members to those whom they were representing giving some account of proceedings – albeit usually only concerning business that interested them – survive in greater numbers from the later seventeenth century. But no other substantial eyewitness reports survive until the 1560s and 1570s. These are by individual, usually identifiable members. They summarise speeches and describe in more narrative form the proceedings in the chamber. By 1610 takers of notes in the House of Commons chamber were a familiar sight, when in a speech James I slowed down and spoke more distinctly to allow them to catch up. These »parliamentary diaries« became more common in the 1620s. They were based on notes made in the chamber by individual members working away either in notebooks or waxed tablets[21]. Many of these accounts were widely circulated in manuscript, sometimes in an edited version, incorporating several different accounts. One in particular, an account of the 1629 session of the 1628–1629 parliament known as »The True Relation«, is now very commonly found[22]. There are similar, later productions, of which the most sustained was the diary maintained by the MP Anchitell Grey during his membership of several parliaments over 27 years, between 1667 and 1694.

These were far from the only material that related to parliamentary proceedings, for these by the seventeenth century were generating a huge amount of paper. Were it not for the destruction of the Commons archive (apart from the Journals) in the 1834 fire that burnt down much of the Palace of Westminster, the volume of material – draft bills and petitions, the records of committees, papers collected in the course of the work of the House would be much larger than it is today[23]. The House of Lords archive, stored separately, survived the fire, and remains (for the moment) at Westminster: its collections are probably considerably smaller than those of the House of Commons would have been – but they are nevertheless a large and important collection which makes it possible to put together the debates and formal records of parliament with some of the documents to which they referred[24].

IV. The Publication of Accounts of Parliamentary Proceedings

All of these documents came to be regarded in the seventeenth century as key political material: precious evidence of the status, history and privileges of parliament as these became controverted in the 1620s. The Parliament Rolls, held in the state

---

20 *Pronay/Taylor*, Parliamentary Texts, p. 175–189.
21 *Kyle*, Theater of State, p. 59–83.
22 *Millstone*, Manuscript Circulation; *Seaward*, Institutional Memory, p. 218–223.
23 For a recent account of the 1834 fire and its impact on the archives of the House of Commons, see *Shenton*, The Day Parliament Burned Down, p. 173–192.
24 The archive is in the process of being transferred to The National Archives at Kew, in outer London. This should be completed by 2025. The collection is described in *Bond*, Guide, and may be searched via the online catalogue at https://archives.parliament.uk/ (13.09.2023).

record repository then in the Tower of London, and the Journals, held by the clerks of each House of Parliament, were frequently copied to supply details of past precedents to inform current arguments. One of the great libraries of seventeenth-century London, that of Sir Robert Cotton (which ultimately formed the core of the British Library), was based in the middle of the parliamentary buildings in the 1620s and became a centre for the dissemination of copies of the fourteenth- and fifteenth-century parliamentary material[25].

It was the unofficial material, though, the records of debates taken down informally by individual members, that first found its way into print. Already widely circulated in manuscript, the »True Relation« of the 1628–1629 parliament was published in print in 1654, and was reprinted in a collection of material relating to the Civil War in the 1680s. The collection of material relating to the reign of Queen Elizabeth I put together by Simonds D'Ewes was published in 1682[26]. D'Ewes's collection had originally been compiled in the early seventeenth century as the basis of a much larger project to compile a parliamentary history of England: nearly a century later a number of historians and publishers were realising this ambition with the publication of other collected records, covering later periods (and in doing so entered into a contemporary controversy about whether debates and speeches from contemporary parliaments should also be made available to the public). Richard Chandler's »History and Proceedings of the House of Commons«, was published in 1742–1744 with the assistance of the historian James Ralph; Richard Timberland's »History and Proceedings of the House of Lords« appeared in 1742–1743. Both were designed to become continuous accounts of parliamentary debates up to the present day. The publication of Anchitell Grey's debates was proposed as a follow-up to the series, although they did not actually appear in print until 1763[27]. These texts were reprinted in various different formats during the eighteenth century, sometimes with additional historical and contemporary material. This process culminated in a collection prepared by the political journalist and businessman William Cobbett »Cobbett's Parliamentary History of England, from the Norman Conquest in 1066 to the year 1803«. It was published from 1812 by T. C. Hansard – the owner of the business that would eventually become synonymous with the publication of the current parliamentary debates.

These eighteenth and nineteenth century editions were uncritical and poorly produced, and recovering a more accurate record of the sixteenth- and especially seventeenth-century debates became the focus of an enormous effort of modern scholarship from the late 1920s. Wallace Notestein, the great American scholar of seventeenth century parliamentary history initiated a project or series of projects in 1921 to produce an edition of this material, beginning with the 1629 debates – the »True Relation« – in 1921[28]. Other volumes followed: Notestein, with his collabora-

---

25   *Tite*, Cotton library.
26   See *D'Ewes (ed.)*: Compleat Journal, n. 17.
27   *Patterson*, The Long Parliament of Charles II, p. 240–260.
28   *Notestein/Relf*, Commons Debates for 1629.

tors was responsible for a much more comprehensive edition of the accounts of the 1621 parliament, published in seven volumes in 1935[29]. In 1965 the establishment by J. H. Hexter of the Yale Center for Parliamentary History promoted an enormous effort to produce modern scholarly accounts of all of the seventeenth-century debates at Yale University. By the time the Center effectively closed, in 2007, eighteen volumes had been produced to add to those published by Notestein in the 1920s and 1930s[30]. A parallel edition of the Elizabethan material, replacing much of what was contained in Simonds D'Ewes's collection, was edited by T. E. Hartley in 1981–1995[31].

Editing and publication of the formal records of parliament was initiated at the same time, and under a similar impetus, as the publication of the diaries by Chandler and Timberland in the 1740s. The preparation for publication of the House of Commons Journal was begun after an inquiry by a House of Commons committee in 1742. A major task, probably the first state-funded historical research project and the biggest exercise in the editing of English historical documents yet attempted, the publication of the Journals from 1547 to date took more than twenty years. From 1762 the sessional Journal was printed annually after the end of each session. The Lords Journals followed thereafter: similar inquiry in the Lords in 1767 after that in the Commons resulted in the publication initially of the historical Journals from 1510, and then, likewise annually, at the end of each session. The editing and publication of the Parliament Rolls was proposed by the same House of Lords committee in 1767: these appeared as the Rotuli Parliamentorum in six volumes between 1767 and 1777.

V. Digitisation

These key documents for British history were not unnaturally early targets for the effort that went into the digitisation of historical sources in the early 2000s. In the case of »The Rolls of Parliament« this went together with the opportunity to edit these to modern standards, and incorporate material that was omitted from the eighteenth-century volumes, as well as providing a translation of the Latin, Norman-French and early English texts. Re-edited by a large academic team, the new edition was published in book and CD-ROM form in 2005, and is now available on-

---

29 *Notestein/Relf/Simpson*, Commons Debates.
30 There is a useful history of the work of the Yale Center at https://archives.yale.edu/repositories/12/resources/2743 (13.09.2023).
31 *Hartley (ed.)*, Proceedings in the Parliaments of Elizabeth I.

line[32]. The early Journals – the Commons up to 1699[33], the Lords up to 1790[34] – were included in the digitisation of a large collection of historical sources undertaken by the History of Parliament and the Institute of Historical Research in the early 2000s, based on an earlier project by the History of Parliament and Sheffield University covering the earliest volume of the Commons Journal only. Various other material has also been digitised and presented in the online collection British History Online along with the Journals: the material edited by Sir Simonds D'Ewes[35]; the seventeenth-century edition of Hayward Townshend's important Elizabethan diary[36]; Grey's Debates[37]; the nineteenth-century edition of the diary of Thomas Burton, covering the parliaments of the Cromwellian Protectorate in the 1650s[38]. Much less of the other material has been digitised, largely because the volumes edited by Wallace Notestein and his successors remain in copyright, although The History of Parliament Trust also has completed and put online the parliamentary diaries of 1624, a project begun by the Yale Center but left unfinished in 2007[39].

The digitisation of these sources has been an enormous help to historical research, and can perhaps be said to have assisted with a revival of interest in the political history of sixteenth- and seventeenth- century England[40]. »The Parliament Rolls of Medieval England« is one of the greatest scholarly contributions of the last century to the study of the Medieval English parliament. But for the moment we have ended up with a very haphazard and disjointed corpus of digitised texts, which largely reproduce the problems that existed with their printed predecessors: their main value is purely their accessibility and their searchability. They allow us to do little more than speed up the things we already were doing with the printed texts. We do not have as yet digitised versions of most of the more recent editions of parliamentary material, particularly the Yale editions of the seventeenth-century parliamentary diaries or T. E. Hartley's editions of the Elizabethan material (though some of the earliest of the former editions are already showing their age, and could not be said to live up to modern standards of editorial scholarship). The Journals – the spine text of English and British parliamentary history – remain in eighteenth-century editions. These were, by and large, efficient transcriptions of

32 Available through Scholarly Digital Editions http://www.sd-editions.com/PROME/home.html (13.09.2023), and via British History Online https://www.british-history.ac.uk/no-series/parliament-rolls-medieval (13.09.2023). Both versions require subscription.
33 https://www.british-history.ac.uk/search/series/commons-jrnl (13.09.2023). The Journal for 1830 is also available.
34 https://www.british-history.ac.uk/search/series/lords-jrnl (13.09.2023). Also available are the Journals for 1830, 1830–1831, and 1831–1832.
35 https://www.british-history.ac.uk/no-series/jrnl-parliament-eliz1 (13.09.2023).
36 https://www.british-history.ac.uk/no-series/parliament-proceedings-eliz1 (13.09.2023).
37 https://www.british-history.ac.uk/search/series/greys-debates (13.09.2023).
38 https://www.british-history.ac.uk/search/series/burton-diaries (13.09.2023).
39 https://www.british-history.ac.uk/no-series/proceedings-1624-parl (13.09.2023).
40 It is worth mentioning the digitisation of the records of the parliament of Scotland, available at https://www.rps.ac.uk/ (13.09.2023), a new edition of the material for the (up until 1707) separate parliament of Scotland, which was prepared between 1814 and 1875 in twelve volumes.

the words on the pages of the original volumes. However, they provide little of the additional evidence that would be commonly recorded in a modern edition, including a comparison with draft versions of the text, or a scholarly apparatus or assessment of the text.

Perhaps most importantly, this corpus of material is still only part of a vast body of those other papers that relate to parliamentary proceedings – most obviously the texts of bills and petitions, and evidence collected by the two Houses and their committees. The texts of most Acts of Parliament, which were actually agreed to, are usually available online, but similarly only here and there, in different editions and through different websites[41]; and the vastly greater category of bills, which were not passed, remain in manuscript and almost completely unpublished. Of course, creating anything better will involve the expenditure of a very large amount of time and money, and there are formidable conceptual and technical problems in the way of creating a more integrated, more interactive version of these materials. The History of Parliament Trust's experiment around twenty years ago with the first volume of the Commons Journal quickly showed us that manual tagging was very time consuming: subsequent experience with other texts has shown many of the difficulties with more automated data mining of such complex texts.

Nevertheless, the vision of an integrated edition of these materials remains a very enticing one, and we continue to work with partners on seeking funding to move towards it. Suggestive models exist, in the case of the British Isles notably in Ireland's Virtual Record Treasury of Ireland project, an attempt to bring together surrogates for the records lost in the destruction of the Record Office of Ireland in 1922[42]. For us, in practice this is likely to mean working on an incremental basis, seeking funding for projects that will fill in the gaps in the current coverage of digitised texts, broadly using the existing editions of the Journals and the parliamentary diaries, and build tagging into these texts, both new and old, creating linkages that can bring together different texts covering proceedings on the same day; linking named individuals to their History of Parliament biographies; geo-linking places; and trying to develop a trail for the proceedings on an individual piece of legislation, tracking its passage through both Houses of Parliament and the debates on it; and so on. Ultimately it would be desirable to re-edit some of the key texts – in particular the early Journals – to modern critical standards.

Working on an incremental basis could, in some ways, make our problem worse, giving us an even greater number of incompatible and non-standard texts. That makes it important to try to establish ways of creating a standard system of editing and tagging that will enable us to move in modular way. The History of Parliament Trust has been involved in several projects seeking to establish this in relation to the Hansard debates from after 1800 (the DILIPAD and LIPARM projects); the PPAC system developed for the Imperial Diet project looks like it may provide a

---

41 The »Statutes« Project website (http://statutes.org.uk/site/ [13.09.2023]) provides a bibliography of the statutes that are available online.
42 https://virtualtreasury.ie (13.09.2023).

solid basis for the development of this in relation to our early modern texts. There is much here that needs to be developed much more elaborately by both historians and digital specialists; but there are also many possibilities for sharing questions and approaches in relation to the digitisation of parliamentary material and its presentation.

Bibliography

Bond, Maurice F.: Guide to the Records of Parliament, London 1971.
Cavill, Paul: The English Parliaments of Henry VII, 1485–1504, Oxford 2009.
Id.: Polydore Vergil and the first English parliament, in: *id./Alexandra Gajda (ed.)*, Writing the History of Parliament in Tudor and early Stuart England, Manchester 2018, p. 37–59.
Clark, Linda (ed.): Parchment and People: Parliament in the Middle Ages, Edinburgh 2004.
Id. (ed.): The History of Parliament: the House of Commons 1422–61, vol. I: Introductory Survey, Cambridge 2020.
Davies, R. G./Denton, J. H. (ed.): The English Parliament in the Middle Ages, Manchester 1981.
D'Ewes, Sir Simon (ed.): A Compleat Journal of the Votes, Speeches and Debates, both of the House of Lords and House of Commons Throughout the whole Reign of Qyeen Elizabeth of Glorious Memory Collected by that Eminent Member of Parliament, Sir Simonds D'Ewes, Baronet, London 1682.
Dodd, Gwilym: Justice and Grace: Petitioning and the English Parliament in the late Middle Ages, Oxford 2007.
Dunham, William H.: The Fane Fragment of the 1449 Lords' Journal, New Haven 1935.
Elton, Geoffrey Rudolph: The Rolls of Parliament, 1449–1547, in: *id. (ed.)*, Studies in Tudor and Stuart Politics and Government, vol. III: Papers and Reviews 1973–1981, Cambridge 1983, p. 110–142.
Foster, Elizabeth R. (ed.): Proceedings in parliament 1610, vol. 2, Yale 1610, p. xxvii–xxviii.
Gajda, Alexandra: The Elizabethan church and parliament in: *Paul Cavill/id. (ed.)*, Writing the History of Parliament in Tudor and early Stuart England, Manchester 2018, p. 77–105.
Given-Wilson, Chris: The Rolls of Parliament 1399–1421, in: *Linda Clark (ed.)*, Parchment and People: Parliament in the Middle Ages, Edinburgh 2004, p. 58–59.
Id. et al. (ed.): The Parliamentary Rolls of Medieval England (PROME), Woodbridge 2005.
Hawkyard, Alasdair D. K.: The House of Commons 1509–1558: Personnel, Procedure, Precedent and Change, Chichester 2016 (= Parliamentary History Texts and Studies, vol. 12).
Hartley, T. E. (ed.): Proceedings in the Parliaments of Elizabeth I, 3 vol., Leicester 1981–1995.
Jones, Clyve (ed.): A Short History of Parliament: England, Great Britain, the United Kingdom, Ireland and Scotland, Woodbridge 2009.
Kyle, Chris: Theater of State: Parliament and Political Culture in Early Stuart England, Stanford CA 2012.
Maddicott, John Robert: The Origins of the English Parliament 924–1327, Oxford 2010.
McGee, J. Sears: An Industrious Mind: the Worlds of Sir Simonds D'Ewes, Stanford CA 2015.
Millstone, Noah: Manuscript Circulation and the Invention of Politics in Early Stuart England, Cambridge 2016.
Neale, John Ernest: The commons' journals of the Tudor period, in: Transactions of the Royal Historical Society, 3 (1920), p. 136–170.
Notestein, Wallace/Relf, Frances Helen: Commons Debates for 1629, critically edited and with an Introduction dealing with Parliamentary Sources for the early Stuarts, Minneapolis 1929.
Notestein, Wallace/Relf, Frances Helen/Simpson, Hartley: Commons Debates, 1621, 7 vol., New Haven/Oxford 1935.

Ormrod, William Mark: On- and off-the Record: The Rolls of Parliament, 1337–1377, in: *Linda Clark (ed.)*, Parchment and People: Parliament in the Middle Ages, Edinburgh 2004, p. 40–43.
Patterson, Annabel: The Long Parliament of Charles II, New Haven/London 2008.
Pollard, Albert Frederick: The Authorship and Value of the »Anonimalle« Chronicle, in: The English Historical Review 53 (1938), p. 577–605.
Id.: Queen Elizabeth's under-clerks and their commons' journals, in: Bulletin of the Institute of Historical Research 17 (1939), p. 1–12.
Id.: The under-clerks and the commons' journals (1509–1558), in: Bulletin of the Institute of Historical Research 16 (1939), p. 144–167.
Pronay, Nicholas/Taylor, John: Parliamentary Texts of the Later Middle Ages, Oxford 1980.
Seaward, Paul: Institutional memory and contemporary History in the House of Commons, 1547–1640, in: *Paul Cavill/Alexandra Gajda (ed.)*, Writing the History of Parliament in Tudor and early Stuart England, Manchester 2018, p. 215–219.
Shenton, Caroline: The Day Parliament Burned Down, Oxford 2012.
Thrush, Andrew: The house of lords' records repository and the clerk of the parliaments' house: a Tudor achievement, in: Parliamentary History 21/3 (2002), p. 367–373.
Id. (ed.): The History of Parliament: the House of Lords 1604–29, vol. 1, Cambridge 2021.
Tite, Colin G. C.: The Cotton library in the seventeenth century and its manuscript records of the English parliament, in: Parliamentary history 14/2 (1995), p. 121-38.

Krzysztof Fokt, Maciej Mikuła (Cracow)

The Digitalisation of the Oldest Legacy of the Polish and Polish-Lithuanian Seym in the Framework of the IURA Project

Dilemmas, Limitations, Prospects

In our paper, we would like to present the ongoing project of digitalisation of sources concerning the activities of the Seym (Diet) of the Kingdom of Poland and, from 1569 on, of the Polish-Lithuanian Commonwealth in the »long« 16th century (1492–1609). It was the formative era of early modern political constitution of Poland and later of Poland-Lithuania, which brought about, i.a., most important acts defining the shape and modes of operation of those polities. Therefore, the digital edition of the legal acts produced in and around the Seym – which in that period became the supreme governmental body – is one of the most important tasks for legal historians in the field of digital humanities in Poland, which deserves also much attention from everyone interested in constitutional and legal history of not only Poland but also Ukraine, Lithuania, Belarus, and Latvia.

The digitisation and digitalisation of the oldest legacy of the Polish and Polish-Lithuanian Seym is being carried out by legal historians from the Jagiellonian University who are also responsible for the most recent, still being continued, major paper edition of those sources, the »Volumina Constitutionum«. In fact, the digitisation of the first two volumes of this edition should be the starting point of any project of digital edition and elaboration of the legacy of the Seym from its »Golden Age«, i.e. the »long 16th century«. Therefore, in the following paragraphs of our paper we would like to bring some basic details concerning the history and principles of the »Volumina Constitutionum« edition. Subsequently, we will present the IURA knowledge base, and the way we decided to upload the digitised paper edition into it. Finally, the opportunities of further development of the digital edition of the legacy of the Seym with the means of the IURA project will be discussed.

I. The »Volumina Constitutionum« Edition

The »Volumina Constitutionum« edition is a result of decisions which were made in pre-digital technical environment, in the 1970s and 1980s. At that time, there were two radically different concepts discussed among the scholars in Poland concerning the ways of edition of the oldest legal acts of the Seym. The one was to reprint the oldest full but uncritical edition of the constitutions of the Seym: the »Volumina Legum«, which was edited in the 18th century by the Jesuits and re-printed in the 19th century by Jozafat Ohryzko. The other was to continue the total edition of Polish normative acts, which was started by Oswald Balzer[1]. As soon as Professor Stanisław Grodziski managed to create an organisational and personnel base for a new edition – the Laboratory of Source Editions at the Facuty of Law and Administration of the Jagiellonian University in Cracow[2] – a compromise solution was elaborated by him, which is neither a simple re-print of the old, uncritical edition, nor a total edition of all the normative material[3].

The idea of Stanisław Grodziski was to produce original work that would contain different variants of normative acts but with possibly modest apparatus that would not undermine the feasibility of carrying out the project in a reasonably acceptable period of time. That is why in the »Volumina Constitutionum« not all the existing versions of particular texts were published but only the ones that could be conceived as official – which were either inscribed into the Crown Metrica (official books of records which contain entries of charters issued on behalf of the king) or printed under Royal privilege – compared only with selected versions from most prominent castrensial (castle) court books. On the other hand, the objective of Grodziski and his team (Wacław Uruszczak and Irena Dwornicka) was to add to their edition some acts that had been previously neglected, as temporary constitutions and some executive documents, which sometimes contained the only traces of such temporary resolutions (the *litterae restium*)[4].

Beginning with the first part of the first volume, published in 1995, the »Volumina Constitutionum« have been printed by the Seym Publishing House (Wydawnictwo Sejmowe) in Warsaw (at present, part 1 of vol. 6 is being prepared)[5]. The first two volumes of the edition, which are of special interest for us, were prepared according to the edition guidelines sketched above (later volumes have been edited on a limited basis, with a reduced archival query). In the meantime, however, the scope of technical means available for source editions expanded rapidly. In the digital environment limitations concerning the amount of text virtually disappeared, thus turning irrelevant many of the technical concerns that Professor Grodziski and his team had to take seriously. Nevertheless, other factors which influenced the decisions of Grodziski and his co-editors – as the lack of adequate stable funding of ambitious edition projects – did not disappear since the 1980s or 1990s, and new problems appeared, e.g. the shortage of qualified staff at disposal. That is why it seemed reasonable to us not to plan any ambitious extension or transformation of

---

1   Balzer (ed.), Corpus Iuris Polonici.
2   On the begginings of the Laboratory, see: *Fokt*, Czterdzieści lat, p. 451.
3   *Grodziski*, Wstęp, p. 28–30.
4   Ibid., p. 37–38.
5   The Seym Publishing House has printed all the volumes of the edition at their costs, all of them being prepared on behalf of the Jagiellonian University by the team headed by Stanisław Grodziski (until 2020), and then Marcin Kwiecień; the preparation of the vol. 5–7 was also aided by the Ministry of Science and Higher Education of the Republic of Poland through the NPRH Programme.

the »Volumina Constitutionum« when digitising it, but rather to make it quickly available to broader public and at the same time open for further elaboration. To achieve both those goals, we used the means available to us, which was the IURA knowledge base.

II. The IURA Knowledge Base

The »IURA: Sources of Law from the Past« service (https://iura.uj.edu.pl) is a strategic project of the Faculty of Law and Administration of the Jagiellonian University in Cracow. It was designed as a comprehensive knowledge base with interlinked and easily searchable contents concerning the historical law, which encompasses not only normative texts but also legal literature and sources of legal practice. It runs upon the DiNGO dLibra software, developed by the Poznań Supercomputing and Networking Centre, which was originally designed to serve Polish digital libraries. That is why the basic form of IURA is a plain repository of sources in PDF and HTML format, be they already edited in other form or not. The sources published or re-published in IURA are being aggregated into interconnected collections. A default but not compulsory feature of the IURA database is that a photograph of a source may be published along with its transcript. The items presented in the IURA knowledge base may be structured hierarchically into »multiply objects«, which turned very useful when it came to practical digitisation of the »Volumina Constitutionum«, vol. 1–2 (see below).

The basic DiNGO dLibra software has been adopted to the specific requirements and needs of the IURA knowledge base by being supplemented with a few specific features. The content search engine was enhanced to take note of spelling variants, and a special CollateX tool was added, which enables the user to compare several text samples at the same time and save the results of comparation for the sake of further study. An important element of IURA that is not embedded in the texts published there but related to them are the standardised metadata descriptions. They function as source identifiers for the Semantic Web (Web 3.0) network and as indexes for search engines. While the scope of the IURA metadata is compliant with the Dublin Core Standard 1.1, the IURA software has its own application profile characterised by a set of key elements (attributes)[6].

---

[6] Detailed description of the features of the IURA may be found in: *Mikuła*, Repository. See also: https://www.dublincore.org/specifications/dublin-core/dces/ (29.08.2022).

III. Digital Re-edition of the »Volumina Constitutionum«, Vol. 1–2

The starting point of the process of digitalisation of the »Volumina Constitutionum«, vol. 1–2, was the consent of the Seym Publishing House for the digital representation of those volumes of the edition on 10 April 2019. Financial support for the project was obtained through the »Excellence Initiative – Jagiellonian University« (ID.UJ), operated by the Jagiellonian University and funded by the Ministry of Science and Higher Education of the Republic of Poland through the »Initiative of Excellence – Research University« (IDUB) competition. The external partner of the project is the »Księgarnia Akademicka« Publishing House in Cracow, which conducts most of the technical work. Final corrections, description, conversion and uploading of particular files are being done by Krzysztof Fokt and Marcin Z. Kwiecień in the Laboratory of Source Editions of the Faculty of Law and Administration of the Jagiellonian University Cracow.

During the planning phase, in which not only Fokt and Kwiecień took part but also Maciej Mikuła and Kacper Górski, various concepts have been discussed, concerning the mode of operation which would best fit into the technical framework and allow for further development of the planned collection of digital representations of the legal acts produced by the Seym. The basic choice we had to make was whether our goal would be a special collection of the acts produced by the Seym of the Kingdom of Poland and later of Poland-Lithuania, or just the digital representation of the existing paper edition. We agreed that with the technical and personal means at our disposal it is not the best moment to prepare a huge new digital edition project, which would build on the »Volumina Constitutionum«, but rather to make the existing edition digitally available as a piece of a broader collection named »Legislation of Polish Seym 15th–18th c.« (https://iura.uj.edu.pl/dlibra/publication/1124).

It appeared reasonable to us to divide the digital representation of the edition into smaller parts that would be stored as separate objects and quotable with their own permalinks, but with the page numbering of the paper original preserved for the ease of quotation. And indeed, the structure and interface of IURA allows to repeat the structure of the paper edition by using the multiply objects. Those correspond with particular Seym sessions, and contain lower-range single objects, which are digital representations of particular texts published in the »Volumina Constitutionum«. The texts were not divided further into particular prescriptions, which would be sometimes extremely short. It may be embarrassing when it comes to searching or quoting a single prescription from a longer text. They are, however, searchable and contain the page numbering of the paper edition as well.

We have also resigned from separate publication of differing versions of particular texts. The first reason for that was that the text would not be divided into short phrases (single prescriptions), which practically excludes the use of the CollateX tool (which was designed to compare versions of short texts rather than longer ones). The second, more important reason was that it would take really much workload and time only to explicate the versions of texts placed together in the printed edition, not even thinking about them being compared with the original texts. In fact, in order to explicate original text versions from the main edition and its apparatus, the work already put in by the editors of the »Volumina Constitutionum« would have to be redone without bringing almost any added value. Therefore, we decided to remain by the original layout of the paper edition, although its one-to-one searchable copy could not have been produced due to technical limitations (no original files or matrices were available for us). Nevertheless, wherever the versions of particular texts were presented in neighboring columns, the layout of original paper edition was preserved and thus the texts may be easily compared.

The project of digitalisation of the »Volumina Constitutionum«, vol. 1–2, is still running; for now, vol. 1 (parts 1 and 2), covering the years 1493–1549, was digitised and uploaded into the IURA knowledge base. Thus, the primary aim of the project will be probably soon achieved. From the viewpoint of the availability of the paper edition, most of which was already sold out (with vol. 1, part 2 being a real *rara avis*), this would be the happy end of the project. However, looking through the prism of studies on the parliamentarism and constitution of Poland and Poland-Lithuania, this may be seen only as a beginning of a new phase of research, which would be digital and computer-aided to a wider extent than ever.

IV. The Prospects

The digital re-edition of the »Volumina Constitutionum«, vol. 1–2, must be seen on the background of general studies on the functioning of Polish and Polish-Lithuanian Seym in the late Middle Ages and the early modern period. From such a viewpoint, it should not be overlooked that the »Volumina Constitutionum« do not even cover the whole period of its regular functioning. Recently Wacław Uruszczak has reminded, using both well-known and quite new arguments, that regular sessions of the Seym in Poland, visited by the envoys of the nobility (*szlachta*) from particular areas of the realm, date back not to the year 1493, as was for long accepted among scholars, but as early as 1468[7]. It seems, therefore, that also acts concerning the proceedings of the Seym between 1468 and 1492 should be gathered and critically commented. Whoever would do that, should also take into consideration the just being created digital re-edition of the »Volumina Constitutionum«, vol. 1–2, in the IURA service.

It is also well known that apart from the constitutions (laws) and tax resolutions there were other sources created before (especially the Royal legacies, through which the Seyms were summoned, and the instructions of particular dietines/seymiks for their envoys), during (e. g., the diaries, vota of parcicular chambers) or just after the Seym (the executive acts) which are of importance for the study of governmental and parliamentary practice but were never published in the »Volumina Legum« or »Volumina Constitutionum«. Should they find their place in a special collection in

---

7   *Uruszczak*, Najstarszy sejm; *id.*, Czy rok 1468.

IURA? Or rather should they be linked to from the IURA knowledge base? How should the original prints and manuscripts be linked to their digital representations in IURA? The answer to those questions is highly dependent on the further development of the IURA knowledge base. The work on that issue is carried out on two main levels: A) feeding the base with new resources, B) organising and semantically linking the objects introduced into the base.

(A) The legislation of the Seym was the most prominent source of law in the Kingdom of Poland and later in Poland-Lithuania. The laws passed by the Seym (constitutions) were often related to some older legislative acts and were themselves a base for creation of further legal acts. Therefore, they played a prominent role in a quasi-system, consisting of a conglomerate of different types of sources, functionally interlinked. The necessity of linking different types of sources in editions of legal sources was emphasised more than a century ago by Oswald Balzer, an outstanding publisher of the Polish Royal legislation of the 16th century[8]. Let us note, for example, that although the Sejm enacted a tax, its collection depended on the dispatch from the Royal chancellery of a series of executive acts (mandates), addressed mainly to officials, especially tax collectors. The same tax law may have suffered restrictions as a result of the king issuing privileges exempting their addressees from paying the tax. This was a not uncommon relief instrument, especially in the face of natural disasters. Naturally, parliamentary laws were also the subject of commentaries in the writings of lawyers.

The list of the types of sources interlinked with the constitutions of the Seym may naturally be further expanded, taking into account practice-oriented sources in particular. Unfortunately, the prospects of their edition are not imminent. However, there are already some sources uploaded into IURA that are somehow related to the parliamentary legislation. These include the collection »Works of Polish Lawyers 16th–18th C.«, still undergoing intensive preliminary work (https://iura.uj.edu.pl/dlibra/publication/1273). Furthermore, some *leges speciales*, i.e. Royal privileges which excluded the power of Diet laws, will be uploaded into the IURA collection »Polish Municipal Law« (in the section concerning the documents: https://iura.uj.edu.pl/dlibra/publication/1704), where editions of regulations for cities of the Kingdom of Poland are being prepared. Also, several printed works of jurisprudence are going to be published, along with the marginal notes of their users.

(B) Searching the content in the IURA base is possible through three main means: through the search box (which scans resource content and metadata), through indexes (i.e. metadata) and through browsing the content within the collection. With the introduction of new functionalities (including a new content display interface), object linkages via hyperlinks will become more important, such as from relevant printed works of lawyers to parliamentary laws. The ordering and semantic linking of objects, however, takes place primarily on the metadata level. While the attributes in digital editions developed according to the TEI standard are linked directly to the edited text, the scope of metadata in IURA, as defined by

---

8   Cf. his perfect edition quoted in footnote 1.

the DublinCore 1.1 standard, is somewhat external from the resource. This makes it much easier for the database administrator to manage the metadata.

The following attributes are of paramount importance in the description of legal and historical sources in the IURA base: date of origin of the original source, creator, territorial scope and topics (subject headings). While determining the value for ›date‹ is no problem (it is introduced according to the ISO 8601 standard), the standardisation of values for the remaining three attributes is far from clear and beset with difficulties. So, in order to establish and maintain the necessary degree of consistency and uniformity in these areas IURA has enlisted the help of researchers specialising in databases and standard setting. In effect, it has been decided that the values for the attribute Spatial Coverage would adopt the nomenclature of some authoritative reference works, namely the historical and geographical dictionaries of Poland compiled at the Institute of History of the Polish Academy of Sciences[9] and entries in Poland's »State Register of Geographical Names« (Państwowy Rejestr Nazw Geograficznych) and in »GeoNames« (currently, references to GeoNames are guaranteed through API protocols). Work on the standardisation of data for persons is still in progress, but the appropriate shortlist includes the database of Jagiellonian University alumni »Corpus Academicorum Cracoviense«[10], compiled by the Archives of the Jagiellonian University, and the »Internet Polish Biographical Dictionary«[11].

As there is no authoritative dictionary (thesaurus) of legal terms for history of Polish law, the job of developing a thesaurus for the attribute Subject in that field has a high priority. There are, of course, various legal thesauri. As the example, the dictionary for the »Policeyordnungen« project is one of the most interesting and instructive, also available in the form of a Simple Knowledge Organisation System (SKOS) document[12]. The so-called police orders from the early modern period, which we could call today administrative acts, were analyzed by Max-Planck-Institute for Legal History and Legal Theory for over 25 years[13]. They were also edited in paper book form. Semantic ontology has been developed for this very large collection of sources, but at the same time defined in terms of its content[14]. In the case of IURA, it will be necessary to develop a thesaurus covering a much larger semantic scope – resulting from the thematic and chronological range of the objects included in IURA. For this reason, the thesaurus will consist of a series of controlled vocabularies, dedicated to particular issues and periods in the history of law in the Polish lands. It may not be possible to compile a uniform dictionary – for example, for criminal law of the medieval period and 20th century criminal codes – hence the idea of developing the thesaurus in parts. In the case of parliamentary legislation,

---

9 http://www.slownik.ihpan.edu.pl/index.php (29.08.2022); https://atlasfontium.pl (29.08.2022).
10 https://cac.historia.uj.edu.pl (29.08.2022).
11 http://www.ipsb.nina.gov.pl:8080 (29.08.2022).
12 https://github.com/rg-mpg-de/vocabs-polmat/blob/main/polmat.ttl (29.08.2022).
13 https://policey.rg.mpg.de/web/ (29.08.2022).
14 https://policey.rg.mpg.de/web/assets/03_systematik_index_policeymaterien.pdf (29.08.2022).

it may prove crucial to make use of the valuable »indices rerum« to the »Volumina Constitutionum«. It might be assumed that the creation of such a thesaurus is necessary not only for the proper functioning of the IURA knowledge base – searching for objects (resources) related to each other in terms of content – but also for the whole domain. It will constitute a standard, or at least an important reference point, for the description of digital objects in this category for other databases. Undoubtedly, a consistent description of objects at the IURA metadata level will ensure even more efficient and effective content retrieval by users.

Further development of the IURA knowledge base with new resources will make it possible to semantically link sources of parliamentary provenance, originally published in the »Volumina Constitutionum«, with other legal sources. In turn, work on the infrastructure of the base – including the organisation of metadata with regard to the Topic attribute – will make the description of resources in the base more relevant and thus access to the desired content even faster and more efficient. It is worth mentioning that the new functionalities planned for the IURA in the near future include above all the introduction of alternative ways of displaying content (for now, the default way, resulting from the adaptation of digital library software for the needs of IURA, is PDF or HTML files and image files). This will allow easier semantic linking of resources. In addition, the new tools will facilitate the standardisation of geographic data description.

V. Conclusions

The edition of the legislation of the Old Polish Seym has been lasting for almost three hundred years by now. Launched in 1732, the »Volumina legum« had an eminently practical purpose. Nearly 250 years later, Stanisław Grodziski and his team undertook a critical edition of the Seym legislation in the new »Volumina Constitutionum« series. The vol. 1 and 2 of this series are the most recent critical edition of the legal acts issued in the prominent representative and governmental body of Poland and later Poland-Lithuania in their »Golden Age«, when all the foundations of the Commonwealth were laid, which lasted practically until its end in the 18th century. The ongoing digitalisation of these volumes through the »IURA. Sources of Law from the Past« service should bridge the gap between the paper edition that is for now hard to find in bookstores and the requirements of the digital era, where open-access searchable PDF files are a minimum standard of availability of scholarly data. It will certainly facilitate the use of the »Volumina Constitutionum« edition but also keep them open for further elaboration with upcoming facilities of the developing IURA project and other web services.

Bibliography

Sources

Balzer, Oswald (ed.): Corpus Iuris Polonici. Sectionis primae: privilegia statuta constitutiones edicta decreta mandata Regnum Poloniae spectantia comprehendentis (Księgi prawa polskiego. Dział pierwszy: przywileje, statuty, konstytucye, dekrety, mandaty koronne), vol. 3: 1506–1522, Kraków 1906.

Id. (ed.): Corpus Iuris Polonici. Sectionis primae: privilegia statuta constitutiones edicta decreta mandata Regnum Poloniae spectantia comprehendentis (Księgi prawa polskiego. Dział pierwszy: przywileje, statuty, konstytucye, dekrety, mandaty koronne), vol. 4: 1523–1534, fasc. 1, Kraków 1906, 1910.

Literature

Fokt, Krzysztof: Czterdzieści lat Pracowni Wydawnictw Źródłowych przy Katedrze Historii Prawa Polskiego UJ, in: Czasopismo Prawno-Historyczne 2/70 (2018), p. 451–455.

Grodziski, Stanisław: Wstęp, in: *id. (ed.)*, Volumina Constitutionum, tom. I: 1493–1549, vol. 1: 1493–1526, Warszawa 1996, p. 7–40.

Mikuła, Maciej: Repository for Digital Editions of Legal Historical Sources: »IURA. Sources of Law from the Past«, in: Zeitschrift der Savigny-Stiftung für Rechtsgeschichte: Germanistische Abteilung 140 (2023), im Druck.

Uruszczak, Wacław: Najstarszy sejm walny koronny »dwuizbowy« w Piotrkowie w 1468 roku, in: *Waldemar Bukowski/Tomasz Jurek (ed.)*, Narodziny Rzeczypospolitej: studia z dziejów średniowiecza i czasów wczesnonowożytnych, vol. 2, Kraków 2012, p. 1033–1056.

Id.: Czy rok 1468 można uznać za początek polskiego parlamentaryzmu i z jakich powodów?, in: Przegląd sejmowy 1/144 (2018), p. 194–208.

Quoted Online Resources

Corpus Academicum Cracoviense, https://cac.historia.uj.edu.pl (29.08.2022).
Dublin Core Standard, https://www.dublincore.org/specifications/dublin-core/dces/ (29.08.2022).
Max-Planck Institut für Rechtsgeschichte und Rechtstheorie (ed.): Repertory of early modern *Policeyordnungen*, https://policey.rg.mpg.de/web/ (29.08.2022).
Polish Academy of Sciences (ed.): Atlas of Sources and Materials, https://atlasfontium.pl (29.08.2022).
Polish Biographical Dictionary on-line (iPSB), http://www.ipsb.nina.gov.pl:8080 (29.08.2022).
Semantic Ontology of the repertory of early modern *Policeyordnungen*, https://policey.rg.mpg.de/web/assets/03_systematik_index_policeymaterien.pdf (29.08.2022)
Simple Knowledge Organization System of the *Policeyordnungen* project, https://github.com/rg-mpg-de/vocabs-polmat/blob/main/polmat.ttl (29.08.2022).
Tomasz, Jurek (ed.): Słownik historyczno-geograficzny ziem polskich w średniowieczu: Edycja elektroniczna, digitally ed. by *Stanisław Prinke*, http://www.slownik.ihpan.edu.pl (29.08.2022).

Rik Hoekstra, Marijn Koolen, Joris Oddens, Ronald Sluijter (Amsterdam)

Structure-Derived Incremental Modelling

The Case of the Resolutions of the Dutch States General

The REPUBLIC (an acronym for »REsolutions PUBlished In a Computational Environment«) project at the Huygens Institute in Amsterdam, was set up to make a digital publication of the corpus of the decisions that were taken by the States General of the Dutch Republic from 1576 to 1796, a large administrative resource of key importance for Dutch history[1]. We use largely automatic processes to make the resource accessible in a method of incremental modelling, which we describe in this essay.

Administrative corpora are characterised by constantly repeated phrases and elements. For readers repetition makes administrative text collections exhausting and boring and in research these elements are also usually neglected because researchers are interested in information that is varied. Nevertheless, these repetitive elements have several functions: they structure the corpus and are intended to make information easier to detect. Furthermore, the standardised mode of expression has an exact (administrative) meaning and prevents differences in interpretation. Therefore, they do contain important information that can be used as interpretive tools to make administrative corpora accessible.

We want to use these interpretive tools to convert the analogue corpus structure into a model usable for digital access and retrieval. This is a complex process because analog structuring employs a variety of devices ranging from volume division, sections, page and paragraph arrangement, use of different fonts and formulaic phrases. The analogue structure is often at least partly visually encoded and its meaning is usually implicit, which makes that the process of converting them to a model involves recognising and often decoding and interpreting their meaning to make them explicit.

The motivation to publish historical sources is always to make a documental corpus accessible to a larger audience because the initiators of the publication find it important that it is wider known and it is part of historical knowledge. This is not so much a definition as an observation with several implications. It implies that the publication of sources is based on an evaluation of its historical importance and by the desire to make it most effectively usable by the intended audience, regardless of whether this consists of historians or a wider public. Choices about the form of

---

[1] REPUBLIC (2019–2024), a project funded by the Netherlands Organisation for Scientific Research (NWO). See https://goetgevonden.nl (13.09.2023).

publication, that is, the medium and what is made accessible in which way, influence the usefulness for the users. Different publication forms have different implications for usability. The publication of the resolutions of the States General of the Dutch Republic (1576–1796) has a long history that has gone through a series of different editing methods, all of which had consequences for the way they were usable by the users. This essay is about the digital edition of the resolutions we are currently preparing, but we will put it in the perspective of the previous editions and evaluate the ways that subsequent editors have tried to make the same source available for their audience. As this essay is primarily about the current digital publication, we will go into detail about what we make accessible and how. We start with an introduction of the resolutions and why they are important and we continue with a short edition history, with an eye on possibilities for use and how this translates to edition requirements and their relation to the publication medium. In the second part of the essay, we go deeper into the incremental modelling method we develop in REPUBLIC.

I. From Paper to Digital Editions

The REPUBLIC project is about the online publication of the decisions (resolutions) of the States General, the supreme ruling body of the Dutch Republic, that existed from 1576 to 1796. From the end of the sixteenth century, they met six days a week (and exceptionally on Sundays and holidays) and recorded their resolutions in handwritten volumes. Dutch historians have long recognised the resolutions as a key resource for Dutch history as well as for European and world history and for different historical domains, because of the wide range of the States General's decisions and the Dutch Republic's powerful position in the early modern world[2].

REPUBLIC aims to publish all the resolutions issued by the States General online. This is not the first effort to make the resolutions available in an edition. Starting from the early twentieth century, there have been two book series (the Old Series 1576–1609 and the New Series 1609–1624, 21 volumes in total) and an earlier born-digital, partial edition[3]. Together, they cover the period from 1576 to 1630.

---

2   See for a summary of the nineteenth-century history leading up to the project: *Japikse (ed.)*, Resolutiën 1576–1577, p. IX–XXI.
3   *Japikse (ed.)*, Resolutiën 1576–1577; *id. (ed.)*, Resolutiën 1578–1579; *id. (ed.)*, Resolutiën 1580–1582; *id. (ed.)*, Resolutiën 1583–1584; *id. (ed.)*, Resolutiën 1585–1587; *id. (ed.)*, Resolutiën 1588–1589; *id. (ed.)*, Resolutiën 1590–1592; *id. (ed.)*, Resolutiën 1593–1595; *id. (ed.)*, Resolutiën 1596–1597; *id. (ed.)*, Resolutiën 1598–1599; *id. (ed.)*, Resolutiën 1600–1601; *Rijperman (ed.)*, Resolutiën 1602–1603; *id. (ed.)*, Resolutiën 1604–1606; *id. (ed.)*, Resolutiën 1607–1609; *Van Deursen (ed.)*, 1610–1612; *id. (ed.)*, Resolutiën 1613–1616; *Smit (ed.)*, 1617–1618; *id. (ed.)*, Resolutiën 1619–1620; *Roelevink (ed.)*, 1621–1622; *id. (ed.)*, Resolutiën 1623–Juni 1624; *id. (ed.)*, Resolutiën Juli 1624–1625. Digitized versions of all volumes are available at http://resources.huygens.knaw.nl/retroboeken/statengeneraal (13.09.2023).

Obviously, changing historical views and editing policies have left their traces in the respective series. Just fifty-four years of resolutions were published in almost a century which was the main incentive to consider digital publishing. The assumption was that digital editing would be faster than manual editing, but the XML edition process took just as much time and effort. It made clear that digital editing is not per definition faster or cheaper than paper publication, and also that considerations of time, money and capacity make choices in editing inevitable.

The desire to speed up the editing work may raise the question whether the new digital editing process does not influence quality in a negative way, a reason to examine the digital edition and its underlying process more closely, because faster publishing shifts the weight to the digital publishing methods at the expense of manual elaboration and checking. The evaluation of editing methods should, in our opinion, be considered not only from the point of view of editing, but also from the point of view of users. In Table 1 the edition characteristics of the different phases in the publication of the resolutions are compared[4].

Tab. 1: edition characteristics of the different phases in the publication of the resolutions.

Feature	Old Series	New Series	Digital Edition 1626–1630	REPUBLIC
Archive	official resolutions	official resolutions	official resolutions	official resolutions
Selection	selection	all resolutions summary	all resolutions summary	all resolutions
Digitisation	–	–	XML attendance lists; session days; resolutions; separate database of persons	all resolutions, indices
Description (Metadata)	dates, no attendance lists	dates, attendance lists summarised	dates, attendance lists separate	dates, attendance lists
Transcription	manual, verbatim and summary	manual, summary	manual, summary	automatic, verbatim
Text Structuring	by subject	by session, resolutions numbered	session, attendants, president, resolutions numbered by day	sessions, attendance lists

---

4   *Sluijter et al.*, Opening the Gates.

Feature	Old Series	New Series	Digital Edition 1626–1630	REPUBLIC
Annotation	notes, attendance lists, presidents	notes, attendance lists, presidents	persons, places, institution, ship names, books published	persons, places, institutions (ship names, books published)
Structured Data (contextualisation)	index, book divisions, subjects	sessions, book divisions, sessions	sessions, persons, function, places	sessions, persons, places, institutions
Publication	book: index, subject, (date)	book: index, date, (subject)	online: date, person, function, institution, place, resolution, attendants, presidents	online: date, person, function, institution, place, resolution, attendants, presidents
	transcriptions/ summaries	summaries	summaries	automatic transcriptions, images, structured text

The paper edition process was designed for a paper paradigm, with its strengths and its constraints. Many of the constraints of paper are well-known: space is expensive, and this often leads to selective editions. Indeed, in the introduction to the old series the editor writes that »It is not necessary to print, summarise or even mention all resolutions«[5]. Furthermore, the resolutions are spread over many volumes, it is hard to find specific texts or subjects if they are not in the indexes and users have to have physical access to the books. And book publications are static, forcing a particular view of the published sources on the users. But the books also have advantages: they are a sustainable resource especially if they are in libraries, referencing them is straightforward and persistent, and the organisation of books is static but familiar to everyone and optimised in a thousand years of book publication. Books are also the frame of reference for everyone, even for digital users. Some disadvantages of books, such as the difficulty of searching for specific text parts, were remedied when they were digitised[6].

The first editors of the resolutions always had the user in mind. Japikse writes in his introduction that the editing rules were formulated to make it as easy as possible for the user to consult resolutions on a particular subject. In the original resolution books, resolutions are listed in order of discussion at the meeting of the States General, and are not arranged by subject. The second purpose of the rules was to restrict the editors in tracing the origin of resolutions in supporting archi-

5 *Japikse (ed.)*, Resolutiën 1576–1577, p. XVIII; subsequent volumes list changed rules if applicable.
6 See on this *Van Zundert*, Scholarship.

val material, presumably to speed up the process[7]. When the editing process of the resolutions changed in 1971, the purpose was still to serve the »convenience of the user«. It was later decided to publish the guidelines for making summaries also in the editions. Previously, they were intended for internal use only, but the editor felt that their publication could help users understand what to expect from the edition[8]. This so-called New Series ran until 1624, but in 1998 it was decided that the manual editing process was too time-consuming and that the future was in a digital edition[9]. In retrospect, this edition is an in-between edition that is halfway between the manual editing tradition and digital editing paradigm. It consisted of manually edited XML files (one per meeting session day) and a relational database (from here: the XML edition). In the introduction to this edition, the editors wrote that the institute had determined that the editors should limit themselves to making the text accessible to keep the project feasible in terms of time and cost. Unlike the printed editions, no research was done on the archival appendices of the resolutions, nor are there internal references between resolutions. The editors claim that the online publication also offers »significant advantages« over the print edition: fulltext search of the resolution text that could be combined with searching a »variety of indices«, in this case a (selective) index on persons, places and ships. While ships and places were uniformised in the XML files, a relational database was used for the person index. It contained not only names, but also offices held by these individuals. This makes it possible to look up, for instance, who was ambassador of France over the years. The most remarkable continuity with the printed editions was that the resolutions were summarised in modern Dutch instead of making transcriptions. The editors state that this edition could still be used as a book by browsing meeting sessions sequentially[10].

In the transition from a book to a digital edition, much was learned, and key parts of the corpus (meeting sessions, attendance lists, resolutions) had been identified and modelled, as well as the indices we wanted to create. These were the persons, institutions and geographic names. Subject indexing was a much more difficult issue, as the approach to this was changed several times over the course of the book editions. The Old Series of the book edition had a selection of resolutions organised by theme, breaking the meeting order, and back-of-book indices of all resolutions, person names and subjects. The New Series had back-of-book »general« indices (per volume) with mixed subjects, persons, institutions, ship names and geographical names. In the digital 1626–1630 edition, assigning subjects to resolutions was deemed unnecessary because controlling consistency was judged to be

---

7 *Japikse (ed.)*, Resolutiën 1576–1577, p. XXf.
8 Respectively *Van Deursen (ed.)*, Resolutiën 1610–1612, p. V, and *Smit (ed.)*, Resolutiën 1619–1620, p. VII.
9 Available at https://resources.huygens.knaw.nl/besluitenstatengeneraal1576-1630/BesluitenStaten-generaal1626-1651 (13.09.2023). Also see *Nijenhuis*, Besluiten ontsloten.
10 Introduction to the web publication of the resolutions of the States General 1626–1630 available at https://resources.huygens.knaw.nl/besluitenstatengeneraal1576-1630/BesluitenStaten-generaal1626-1651/inleiding (13.09.2023).

too time consuming. While this was never explicitly stated, the idea also was that fulltext search together with a strict policy for summarising should make it possible for users to find the required information. As an example of how this might work, the edition's website included an essay that pointed out how six example subjects in three themes could be researched in the publication[11].

The efforts of the XML edition in many ways offered a good starting point for the digital edition we were to set up, but it was clear that the previous policies of editing had been too time-consuming. Overall, we estimated the number of resolutions over the 220-year period of the Dutch Republic at around one million, containing roughly 1.5 million persons, 850,000 geographical names and 350,000 institution names. Most of these (80–90 %) occur only once, which is a common feature of these types of resources[12]. So, from the onset, we knew that we had to automate as much of the process as possible. Obviously, this would produce a completely different publication than the previous series of editions. Even with the considerable grant we received from the Dutch Research Council, it remains impossible to either identify or check the data manually. It was therefore clear to us that this digital edition required a new editing process that was largely geared towards digital methods, although we made sure that at all times humans stayed ›in the loop‹ for decisions and for checks. If only by the editing method this publication of the resolutions would go way further than »barely beyond the book«[13].

From this overview of the previous partial editions of the resolutions of the States General, it becomes clear that providing access to the resolutions was always a matter of making choices. In the Old Series, the editors chose to make a selection of the resolutions and transcribed many of these verbatim, while in the New Series and the XML edition, the editors summarised the resolutions in modern Dutch, both for reasons of space and accessibility for modern readers. An implicit choice in at least the Old and the New Book Series, was also that the pace of publishing was low, resulting in the publication of just one volume every few years. Consequently, over a period of about a century, only about a quarter of the resolutions were published. This meant that the editions were only beneficial to students of the sixteenth and the first quarter of the seventeenth century. The idea at the time was that digital publishing would speed up the process, but producing the XML edition turned out to be very time-consuming as well.

The way of editing the resolutions in the REPUBLIC project diverges rather radically from the previous edition efforts. Unlike the previous editors, who approached the corpus sequentially and chronologically, making the information in

---

11 *Gijsbers/Hell/Schooneveld*, Geweld, gewin en geweten; the idea that full-text search would replace indexes was widespread. See for example *Eijnatten/Pieters/Verheul*, Big Data for Global History, or *Van Zundert*, Scholarship, esp. chapter 4; *id.*, Barely Beyond the Book, p. 103: »gradually the use of full text search as a replacement for the index became accepted, even appreciated …«.
12 Extrapolated from a count of the XML edition; also see *Hoekstra/Nijenhuis/Dreijer*, Rapport.
13 Phrase by *Van Zundert* in his Scholarship, chapter 4, p. 95–115, and a previous version in *id.*, Barely Beyond the Book.

the resolutions available for users page by page and year by year, in the REPUBLIC project we approach the corpus as a whole. We work our way from the outside in, so to speak, iteratively making more and more fine-grained information available for the corpus as a whole.[14] The consequence of this formal approach is that the granularity of access is different from human-made decisions, as human decisions depend much more on interpretation. Automated processes will make all information accessible that is available to them, but depend on the information modelling they exploit and the encoded knowledge that is connected with them. There are no ruptures in a chronological sense, so that the same level of encoded information will be made available for the whole corpus, as long as its structure is consistent enough. As we have seen, manually produced editions may change policies in response to changes in scientific views. Digital editions are never finished or final in the sense that manual editions are. If significantly improved versions of the software become available, these could be rerun on the corpus. More detailed processing or interpretations can be added at a later stage (for instance if new funds are raised) and alternative views or classifications could be added, even if in practice this is rare.

II. Edition and Users

When we set up the REPUBLIC project, there was a lot of resolution publishing history to consider. Like the previous editors, we wanted to serve a wide range of users. But different research questions require different models for the editions. Therefore, we made an inventory of the types of analysis that scholars might want to conduct with the publication of the resolutions:

- *Narrative analysis*: a narrative analysis is conducted to offer an explanation of the temporal sequence of events[15]. For instance, the role of the States General in developments and shifts, both internationally and within Dutch society, and the causes and effects of these developments. For example, what was the relative position and wealth of the province of Zeeland; how did the competition between navy and army develop; how important were the different colonies; how did the States General deal with different religious groups; and what caused these developments?
- *Thematic analysis*: thematic analyses trace the development of certain themes/topics over time. For instance, do the resolutions over time reflect an increasing possibility for citizens to put forward their concerns to the States General? Do we see changes in the treatment of petitions and can they be used to analyse the States General's accessibility?

---

14 Even if for practical reasons we divided the resolutions into the printed and the handwritten section, the methods we developed on the printed resolutions were always designed to work also for the handwritten resolutions.
15 *Bryman*, Social Research Methods.

- *Content analysis*: content analysis is a quantitative analysis with regard to what or who was discussed, when and how often. For instance, how many resolutions deal with financial and economic policy, nominations for officeholders or army positions, or with petitions by citizens?
- *Network analysis*: network analyses focus on the relationships between actors and how they interact and influence each other. Performing serial research on the attendance at meetings and in committees can address questions such as: Can we identify where formal politics turns into informal politics and politics behind the scenes? Who worked together? Who were involved in decisions around specific topics and in larger policy issues and how were these persons related?
- *Linguistic analysis*: analysis of the (development of the) language used in the States General. How did the language of decision-making develop and is it possible to link transformation of the States General's language with its growing administrative competence? Were formulaic phrases used consistently over time or did new ones appear and did old ones disappear or change?

Except for the most trivial cases, none of these questions can be answered directly using queries. Addressing them requires operationalising several elements from the logical structure of the written and printed texts into multiple layers of metadata. The purpose of this is to organise and classify the resolutions and make useful selections. For instance, to study changes in how petitions of citizens were treated (the example under thematic analysis above), a researcher needs to select resolutions related to petitions, categorise them according to what group a petitioner belonged to, and order them temporally. In order to study the network of actors who attended the meetings and those who were involved in committees, it is necessary to operationalise these attendance lists and identify which committees were set up following a decision by the States General, and who submitted reports that were the subject of later resolutions. Next, we need to consider how these questions can be related to the structure of the archive and subsequently, how this can be translated to queries to the information system. Citizens of the Dutch Republic could put forward their concerns via petitions (referred to as »requesten« in the resolutions). Each resolution triggered by a petition states who submitted the petition, on what date, from which location, and what it was about. Petitions that were discussed in the States General appear in the resolutions with one of two opening formulas, examples of which are shown in Figure 1. The one on the left contains the formula »IS ter Vergaderinge gelesen de Requeste van ...« (English: »Was read in the assembly the petition of ...«), followed by the name of the person who submitted the petition, Frederik Batavodorus Taats van Amerongen, and a qualification or attribute, such as a title, occupation or legal status. In this case, the proposer states he is »Commandeur der Stadt Maastricht« (English: »commander of the city of Maastricht«). The petition on the right uses the other formula, »OP de Requeste van ...« (English: »Upon the petition of ...«), followed again by the name of the person submitting the petition, »Pieter le Cointe«, and a qualification, namely »Koopman« (English: »merchant«) and the city where he operates, »Leyden«. There are tens of thousands of resolutions that use one of these two formulas, with some spelling variation and spelling changes over time. For example, from the second half of the eighteenth century »geleesen« is used instead of »gelesen«.

> OP de Requeste van *Pieter le Cointe*, Koopman te Leyden, IS na voorgaande deliberatie goedtgevonden ende verstaan, dat ten behoeve van den Suppliant een Pasport sal werden gedepescheert, om de Goederen breeder in de voorschreve Requeste gespecificeert, tot monteeringe van het Regiment van den Generaal-Major de Viçouze, naar Doornick te mogen uytvoeren, vry ende sonder betaalinge van 's Landts gerechtigheydt; ende sal het voorschreve Pasport goedt wesen voor den tydt van een maandt, naar dat de laatste attache daar op sal wesen gestelt. Ende sal Extract van dese haar Hoogh Mogende Resolutie gesonden werden aan het Collegie ter Admiraliteyt in Zeelandt, en het selve aangeschreven, soodanige ordre te stellen en voorsieninge te doen, dat de voorschreve Monteeringe op der selver Comptoiren, vry, onverhindert, en sonder eenige molestatie mogen passeren.

> OP de Requeste van *Johan François Lemmens*, Leverancier alhier, IS naar voorgaande deliberatie goedtgevonden ende verstaan, dat ten behoeve van den Suppliant een Pasport sal werden gedepescheert, om de Goederen breeder in de voorschreve Requeste gespecificeert, tot monteringe van het Regiment van den Colonel Volckershoven, naar Namen te mogen uytvoeren, vry ende sonder betalinge van 's Landts gerechtigheydt; ende sal het voorschreve Pasport goedt wesen voor den tydt van een maandt, naar dat de laatste attache daar op sal wesen gestelt. Ende sal Extract van dese haar Hoogh Mogende Resolutie gesonden werden aan het Collegie ter Admiraliteyt in Zeelandt, ende het selve aangeschreven, soodanige ordre te stellen en die voorsieninge te doen, dat de voorschreve Monteeringe op der selver Comptoiren, vry, onverhindert ende sonder eenige molestatie mogen passeren.

Fig. 1: two resolutions in response to petitions submitted to the States General on 8 and 9 February 1725 respectively, with different opening formulas. Images courtesy of Nationaal Archief – The Hague.

Adding metadata for these different aspects requires extracting the relevant information from an estimated one million resolutions. This requires an information extraction process that is automated where possible, but which needs to be informed by expert knowledge and a human in the loop. On top of that, each selection or reorganisation made by users creates a different view on the data, the interpretation of which is influenced by our decision in creating the metadata layers. Therefore, it is important that our processing choices are transparent and visible to the user.

III. Incrementally Modelling Resolutions

The process with which we transform the scans to information that is queryable in a structured way can best be described as incremental modelling. It makes heavy use of the structure of the resolution corpus itself. As explained above, the resolutions are very structured and extremely repetitive, both in their reporting format and in the formulaic language they used for recording the decisions.

In order to make it possible to understand the process of incremental modelling, we first give a short description of the structure of the resolutions. As said above, the volumes of the resolutions constitute a continuous series summarising and recording the decisions made during the daily meetings of the States General. The core elements are sessions and resolutions. Each session starts with a date, the president of the day and an attendance list ordered by province, followed by a varying number of resolutions.

There are proposals and petitions (see Figure 2) about a wide variety of subjects. All summarised issues consist of at least the following two parts: a proposition and a conclusion or decision. The proposition refers to both the actual proposal submitted to the States General in oral or written form, and the written summary of it in the resolution[16]. The conclusion contains a decision (resolution) of acceptance, rejection or deferral, pending further investigation or requests for information[17]. Both unresolved and resolved issues led to trails of resolutions. All resolutions had to be traceable for the States General and other governing bodies, as the decisions had the force of law. Sometimes the States General wanted to know what had been decided previously in the same case or a similar case, and had the clerks refer to the archived decisions, called »retroacta«.[18] In addition, some resolutions contain copies of letters or other important incoming documents as insertions.

The resolutions were drafted and archived by the griffier (English: greffier, i.e. chief clerk) and partially read aloud for approval at the beginning of the next day's session[19]. The griffier also indexed the resolutions, to facilitate access to them at a later date. Over the years, a fairly fixed set of index terms was used. For each year, an index was created with references to that year's resolutions. In this way, resolutions that were again relevant to decision-making could be retrieved.

Incremental modelling works from the outside in, that is to say, we begin with the largest structures and work towards smaller structures. The already identified structures then act as both context and constraints for the new elements we are trying to identify. For example, once we have identified the names of delegates for the sessions of a given year from the attendance lists, all references to delegates in the text of the resolutions of that year necessarily have to be to one of the identified names. This greatly reduces the number of possibilities.

Below, we describe the elements we want to harvest from the resolutions. In order not to elaborate too much, we limit ourselves to showing the principles of our method. All our methods yield data from the text, that are stored as annotations on parts of the text. As the machine-readable text itself is generated (using text recognition) from the scans, it is an interpretation of the image data, which in turn is a digital interpretation of the original pages and volumes. The annotations together constitute a model of the resolutions corpus. At the current stage of the research project, the model is still evolving.

---

16   *Thomassen*, Onderzoeksgids, p. 188.
17   *Riemsdijk*, De griffie van Hare Hoog Mogenden; *Thomassen*, Onderzoeksgids.
18   *Hoekstra*, Griffiers.
19   See *Thomassen*, Onderzoeksgids, p. 204.

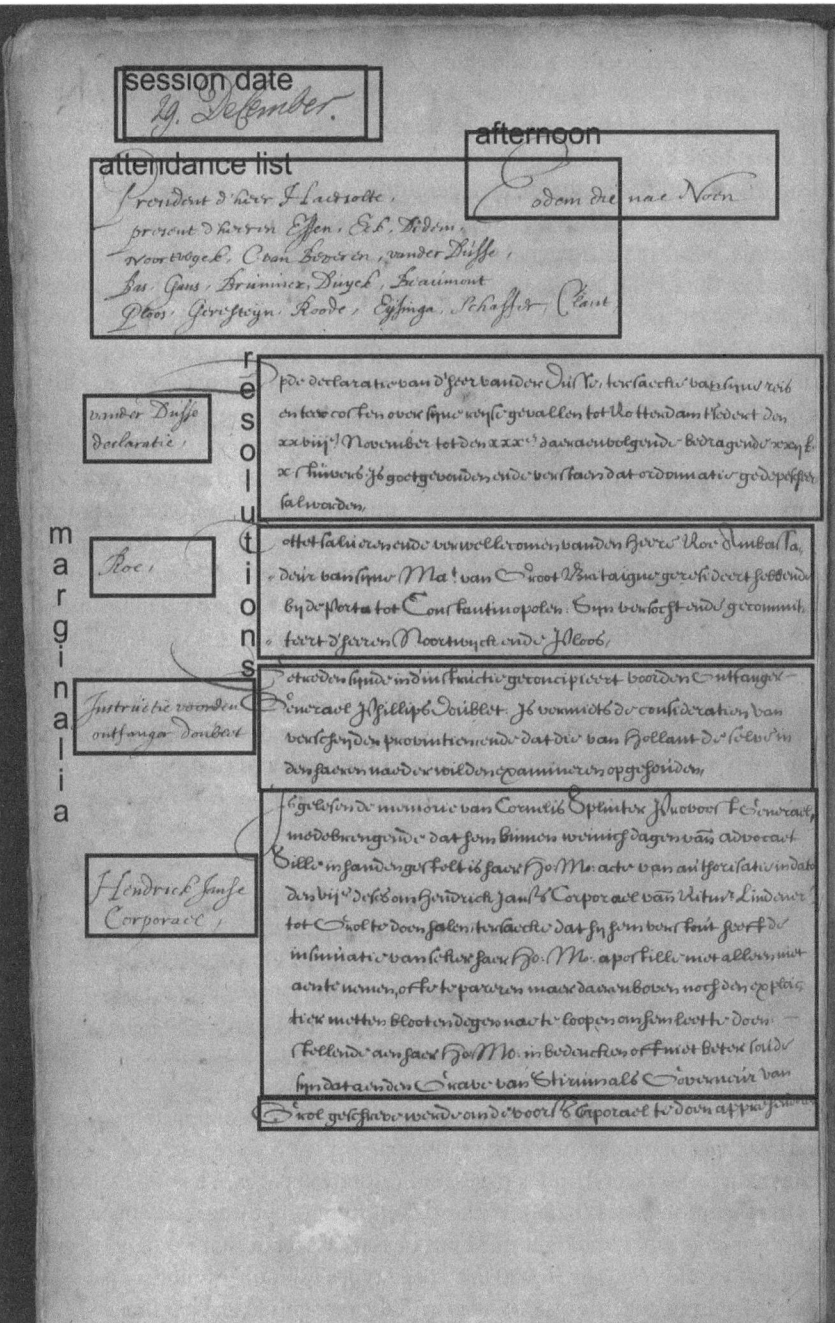

Fig. 2: structure of the handwritten resolutions. Image courtesy of Nationaal Archief.

Our edition is based on the scans of the official version of the resolutions. All resolutions were recorded in handwritten registers. From the beginning of the eighteenth century the States General started to print the official version of the resolutions, the text of which was supposed to be identical to the official handwritten version. The scans have been converted to machine readable text using Optical Character Recognition (OCR) for the printed resolutions, and Handwritten Text Recognition (HTR) for the handwritten resolutions. We decided to start with the printed resolutions because we expected OCR results on printed text to be better and available faster than HTR results on handwritten resolutions. At the time, it was still unknown what the performance of HTR would be. Fortunately, it soon became clear that with appropriate »ground truth« preparation, a set of near-perfect manual transcriptions, the quality of our HTR could match that of the OCR. Although the quality of OCR and HTR is more than satisfactory, recognition errors of two to five per 100 characters remain, depending on damage to or possible ink weakness of the original and, in the case of HTR, the hand in which they were written. The errors usually occur in names, as they are unknown to the automatic error detection algorithms that always run in a text recognition process. Text recognition errors are complicated because of the unstable orthographic characteristics of the resolution corpus that dates from a time when there was no fixed spelling, and when there were many shifts in language and writing. To tackle this challenge, we have developed a fuzzy search tool that can search for words, phrases and their (orthographic) variants[20]. We have deliberately chosen not to use standard Natural Language Processing (NLP) tools for Dutch, as they were developed for modern text and have not been optimised for this type of language and writing.

IV. Identifying Page Types

The first step was to convert the physical structure of the corpus to a logical structure containing the meeting sessions and the resolutions. Before we could identify the meeting sessions and the resolutions, we had to establish which pages contain the text of the sessions. Here we elaborate on this step to illustrate how the method in general makes use of structural elements. In this case it is mainly about elements of the layout, while in other cases we also use context and content. The corpus contains five types of pages: empty pages, title pages, pages of »respecten« (i. e. listings of the main index terms), index pages and resolution pages. The vast majority consists of resolution pages (82 %). Without identifying anything, guessing a page is a resolution page would be right in 82 out of 100 cases, but that is not good enough because it would result in 36,000 false page types (all non-resolution pages). The PageXML output consists of XML files with the recognised text per line and (many)

---

20 Available at https://github.com/marijnkoolen/fuzzy-search (13.09.2023).

pixel coordinates on the image of the scan indicating the location of the text blocks and lines on the page (see Figure 3 for an example).[21]

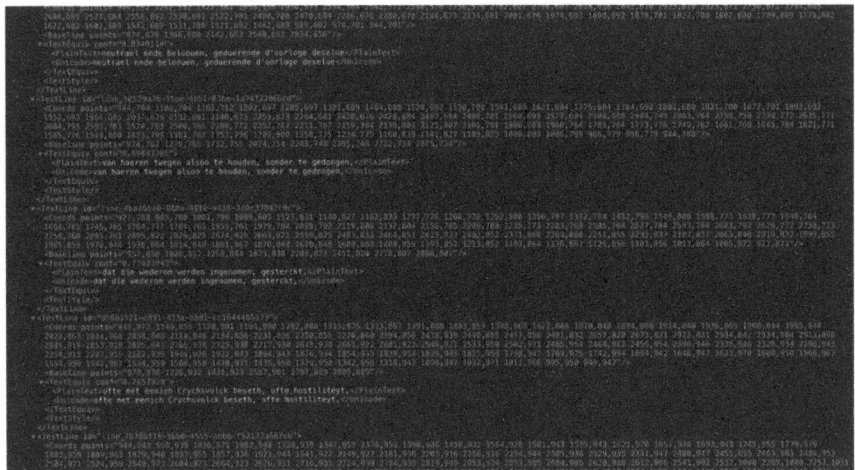

Fig. 3: example PageXML output.

Based on individual page layout, the number of correctly identified page types rises to 91 %. But the resolution volumes are divided into sections. Though there is some variation, a typical volume starts with a title page, then contains an index section followed by another title page and a section with the resolution text. For example, an index page in the middle of the resolution section is certainly wrongly classified. In this (simple) way, the context contributes to the accuracy of the identification. In Table 2 we have summarised the results of the respective identification refinements. The last three columns indicate the accuracy in the three different steps explained above.

Tab. 2: progressive accuracy of page type identification.

Page Type	# Pages	Accuracy		
		Always Resolution	Individual Page Analysis	Section-Based Correction
Total	3,376	0.82	0.91	0.99
Empty	47	0.00	0.98	0.98
Title	30	0.00	1.00	1
Respect	27	0.00	0.89	0.89
Index	525	0.00	0.87	0.96
Resolution	2,754	1.00	0.92	0.9993

---

21 *Pletschacher/Antonacopoulos*, PAGE.

Using comparable methods, we identify the following structural elements:

Meetings and meeting dates: the specific date on which a proposition was discussed and a decision taken, including the day of the week.

Attendance lists and president: the persons who were present and involved in the decision-making process of each resolution, as well as the person presiding over the meeting. The latter is especially important since the president set the agenda together with the griffier, and thereby determined which propositions were discussed.

Resolutions: the text that belongs to a single resolution, as well as metadata[22] on the proposition and decision, including the type of proposition that was submitted, e.g. a petition, report or missive, who submitted the proposition, whether it was accepted, rejected or postponed for later discussion, and what action was decided on.

Insertions: extracts of earlier resolutions or of resolutions by one of the Provincial States, or of memorandums by foreign envoys submitted to the States General[23]. Identifying previous resolutions of the States General offers a way to link trails of related resolutions. Insertions of resolutions by other organisations and other documents provide a starting point for linking the resolutions to other archives. At the moment we have no concrete plans to do this, as many of these documents are not digitised yet. We do aim to identify and categorise these references so they can be easily selected for analysis.

Extracting these structural information elements required combining information about their layout, their context in the corpus and textual clues such as formulaic phrases. An evaluation of the accuracy of a number of elements can be found in Table 4[24].

Tab. 3: evaluation of accuracy of identification of structural elements.

Task	Test Set Size	Precision/Recall
Meeting Start	300 meetings	1.00/0.97
Meeting Date	300 meetings	0.99/0.93
Resolution Start	312 resolutions	0.99/0.93
Delegates Attending	20 attendance lists	1.00/0.89

---

22 For want of a better term we use the term metadata in a technical sense here, that is a structural representation of the information in the text. In a more common library and information science context metadata refers to data about an object (e.g. a book or article). These metadata are conceptually apart from the object itself. In the republic infrastructure the metadata are (eventually) stored as annotations, but in other frameworks they would end up as the tag, attributes and content in a marked-up file. These should be seen as technically different but conceptually equivalent though often not entirely interchangeable ways of representing the information.

23 *Van Riemsdijk*, De griffie van Hare Hoog Mogenden, p. 91.

24 The evaluations are based on a random test set from the eighteenth-century printed resolutions. Precision: the accuracy of the type of found element (e.g. is a found meeting day really a meeting day) in percent. Recall: the percentage of found elements out of all the total population of these elements in the test set.

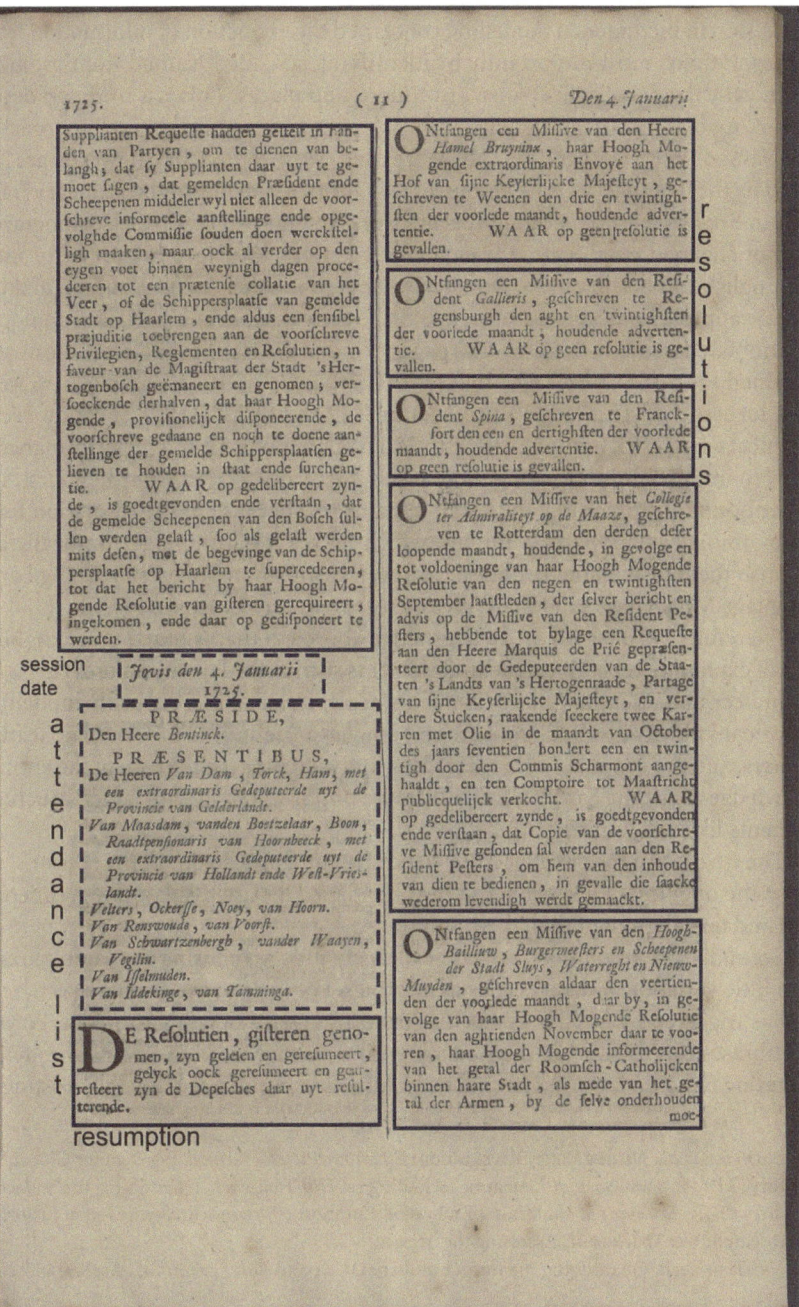

Fig. 4: elements in the printed resolutions of 1755: a meeting starts with a date and attendance list, followed by individual resolutions with opening propositions and decision formulas. Original image courtesy of Nationaal Archief.

A next step in incremental modelling concerned the extraction of information from the resolutions, most importantly by identifying so-called Named Entities, more specifically the names of persons, institutions and places. This is a common desire in making historical text digitally accessible, for which often general approaches like Named Entity Recognition (NER) are used. Such approaches, however, are hindered by the lack of good NLP resources for historical spelling and vocabulary[25]. For texts in English these generic approaches work to some extent. English orthography has not changed much since the eighteenth century, therefore resources for modern English can be effective[26]. Dutch has undergone much larger changes, making generic approaches less useful. To investigate the value of generic NER techniques, we annotated named entities in 200 pages of manually transcribed resolutions and retrained the Spacy NER tagger with 90 % of the pages; the remaining 10 % were used for testing[27]. This led to a precision of 0.49 and recall of 0.19. Such low recall is typical when NER is applied to historical documents[28]. Although performance is likely to improve by annotating more pages, there are two large hurdles. First, the upper bound for precision and recall remains low because in the resolution texts, many nouns have uppercase initials, which makes it hard to algorithmically distinguish them from named entities. However, vastly improving results using Large Language Model based methods, give us reason to further explore NER.

Therefore, we decided on an alternative approach that is based on a combination of exploiting repetitive structural elements such as the layout and ordering used for indices and attendance lists (similar to Colavizza et al.[29]), explicitly modelling historical knowledge about content and language use in lists of formulaic textual phrases, and approximate string searching and matching. In the case of the entities, knowledge about the content is slightly more important than with larger structural elements like resolutions.

The first feature we exploit is the fixed structure and layout of the sessions, because the opening of a session and the attendance list are displayed in a different font and text alignment than the resolutions.

Secondly, the resolution texts are extremely repetitive, using the same phrases with little variation across decades of meetings. For instance, as we have seen, resolutions triggered by petitions made use of two standard opening formulas. Formulaic phrases can be short or long, ranging from a single word to an entire sentence including punctuation. We search the resolutions using phrase models consisting of

---

25 *Ehrmann et al.*, Named Entity Recognition; *Eijnatten/Pieters/Verheul*, Big Data for Global History; *Meroño-Peñuela et al.*, Semantic technologies; *Hill/Hengchen*, Quantifying the impact of dirty OCR; *Leemans et al.*, Mining Embodied Emotions; *Piersma/Ribbens*, Digital historical research; *Van Strien et al.*, Assessing the impact.
26 *Hill/Hengchen*, Quantifying the impact of dirty OCR; and *Van Strien et al.*, Assessing the impact.
27 https://spacy.io/models/nl (13.09.2023).
28 *Borin et al.*, Naming the past; *Díez Platas et al.*, Medieval Spanish; *Ehrmann et al.*, Named Entity Recognition; *Kepa Joseba et al.*, Comparison.
29 *Colavizza/Ehrmann/Bortoluzzi*, Index-driven digitization.

lists we compiled of these fixed formulas and assign each phrase to a metadata category and one or more labels, in such a way that an approximate match in the text can be tied to a metadata layer. For instance, phrases for the opening sentence of a proposition have been assigned the label *proposition opening*, and the phrase »OP de Requeste van« (English: »Upon the petition of ...«) has the additional label of *proposition_type:request*. Phrases can also have known variants, e. g. alternative phrasings that we have encountered. The phrase models represent knowledge of the domain and the corpus, what information we expect to find, where, and in what order.

Third, our approach exploits the fact that, even with a relatively high word error rate, the majority of characters in frequently occurring phrases and names are correct and in the right order, such that the string distance between the recognised text and its corresponding phrase in our model is small. We have developed a fuzzy searching algorithm that accepts one or more phrase models to find approximate matches, and uses configurable string distance thresholds to control how much textual variation is accepted. The phrase model for opening formulas contains 32 different formulas, each with a list of variant phrasings and a label for the type of proposition. For instance, the opening formula »Is ter vergaderinge gelesen de Requeste van ...« (English: »Was read in the assembly the petition of ...«) indicates that the proposition is a petition. For the resolutions of 1705–1796, 56,713 matches are found with 3,242 different OCR strings (Table 4).

Tab. 4: OCR text string matches found for the opening formula »Is ter Vergadering gelesen de Requeste van« in the resolutions for the years 1705–1796.

Text String Found	Frequency	Fraction
IS ter Vergaderinge geleesen de Requeste van	13,767	0.24
IS ter Vergaderinge gelesen de Requeste van	10,854	0.19
Is ter Vergaderinge gelesen de Requeste van	5,942	0.10
IS ter Vergaderinge geleezen de Requeste van	2,956	0.05
ls ter Vergaderinge gelesen de Requeste van	2,396	0.04
15 ter Vergaderinge gelesen de Requeste van	1,299	0.02
18 ter Vergaderinge gelesen de Requeste van	1,273	0.02
IS ter Vergaderinge geleesen de Requestevan	1,177	0.02
15 ter Vergaderinge geleesen de Requeste van	1,171	0.02
3,333 other variations	15,878	0.28
Total	56,713	1.00

The most frequent OCR string occurs 13,767 times, and corresponds only 24 % of the resolutions with that formula found through fuzzy searching. Other proposition types include missives, reports, memos (diplomatic notes), and (previous) resolutions. We exploit historical knowledge about the context of the resolutions differently over multiple iterations of information extraction. In the first iteration we focus on extracting information with very high precision, by using high thresholds for approximate string searching, to build lists of, for example, the starting point of meeting sessions and names of attendants. In later iterations, we use additional knowledge. For instance, if we have found the starting points of the meeting sessions for 12 and 15 January 1725 in the first iteration, we exploit our knowledge that sessions are chronologically ordered. This means that we know that the sessions for 13 and 14 January should be in between these starting points. In the second iteration, we can search specifically for 13 and 14 January in a much smaller amount of text, using lower fuzzy matching thresholds, with a much higher chance of success. For individual resolutions, we use the textual formulas for the start of a proposition and of a decision (see Figure 4). For all elements which we extract, we store them with the fuzzy matches of phrases as evidence to explain how our metadata was created. Together with the explicit phrase models that we publish in our GitHub repository, it makes the process of generating metadata transparent and repeatable.

Using formulaic phrases for modelling the resolutions is promising, but the challenge is to find all relevant formulaic phrases and their variations. The corpus of eighteenth-century resolutions has 286,871 resolutions and over 58 million words, but we have no reliable estimates of the total number of formulaic expressions that are used and how often they occur. To identify the start of proposition paragraphs of resolutions, we use a list of 32 formulas, most of which are between 5 and 10 words long[30]. But we do not know if these are all the formulas used for openings of proposition and decision paragraphs. We also do not know which other elements of a resolution are expressed in formulas and how much variation there is within formulas[31]. The methods for identifying and operationalising formulas for finding finer-grained structures will be further developed in the REPUBLIC project. We think our method may find further use for other large text corpora where documents are structured with repetitive formulaic phrases.

The essence of this process of incremental modelling is that we continuously build upon previous results to make increasingly fine-grained layers of information from the resolutions corpus available for research. In principle, this iterative process of using internal corpus structures and growing knowledge about the corpus and its structures could be refined over time as more of the information becomes available in more detailed form. In practice, however, time and capacity are limited by the parameters of the REPUBLIC project.

---

30 Koolen et al., Modelling resolutions, and Koolen et al., The Value of Preexisting Structures.
31 Variation was larger until circa 1637 when it was decided to make a *resumption* of the resolutions in the next sessions. This contributed to consistent redaction *Van Riemsdijk*, De griffie van Hare Hoog Mogenden, p. 90.

V. Conclusion

The aim to publish the resolutions of the States General has a long history. Subsequent editors tried to accommodate the needs of their intended users as best as possible. Their choices were influenced both by scholarly and methodological preferences and the possibilities of the medium. Manual editing of the resolutions resulted in partial editions that because of various limitations resorted to providing selections or summaries of the resolutions corpus. The XML edition also offered summaries, but now primarily for reasons of readability. Another limitation was that a century of chronological editing led to a combined edited corpus that just covered about a quarter of all resolutions. Like the previous editions, the digital edition that is built by the REPUBLIC project takes into account different types of users, each with their own research questions. The edition is created through a process of incremental modelling, an approach in which the corpus as a whole is modelled in an increasingly fine-grained way, building upon previously-gained results. This process exploits structural elements within the highly structured and repetitive resolution corpus, using elements of layout and recurring formulaic language. This results in consistent access to many elements. However, automatic extraction targets structural elements of resolutions but skips less structured aspects and exceptions. Limitations in time and correction capacity prevent manually correcting these omissions. As the REPUBLIC project is still underway, many of the more fine-grained results are not yet available, but evaluations of previous stages of the incremental modelling process have yielded reliable results.

Bibliography

Sources

Japikse, Nicolaas (ed.): Resolutiën der Staten-Generaal, van 1576 tot 1609, vol. 1: 1576–1577, Den Haag 1915 (= Rijk Geschiedkundige Publicatiën, Grote Serie, vol. 26), all volumes of the Resolutions are available online at http://resources.huygens.knaw.nl/retroboeken/statengeneraal (13.09.2023).

Id. (ed.): Resolutiën der Staten-Generaal, van 1576 tot 1609, vol. 2: 1578–1579, Den Haag 1917 (= Rijk Geschiedkundige Publicatiën, Grote Serie, vol. 33).

Id. (ed.): Resolutiën der Staten-Generaal, van 1576 tot 1609, vol. 3: 1580–1582, Den Haag 1918 (= Rijk Geschiedkundige Publicatiën, Grote Serie, vol. 41).

Id. (ed.): Resolutiën der Staten-Generaal, van 1576 tot 1609, vol. 4: 1583–1584, Den Haag 1919 (= Rijk Geschiedkundige Publicatiën, Grote Serie, vol. 43).

Id. (ed.): Resolutiën der Staten-Generaal, van 1576 tot 1609, vol. 5: 1585–1587, Den Haag 1921 (= Rijk Geschiedkundige Publicatiën, Grote Serie, vol. 47).

Id. (ed.): Resolutiën der Staten-Generaal, van 1576 tot 1609, vol. 6: 1588–1589, Den Haag 1922 (= Rijk Geschiedkundige Publicatiën, Grote Serie, vol. 51).

Id. (ed.): Resolutiën der Staten-Generaal, van 1576 tot 1609, vol. 7: 1590–1592, Den Haag 1923 (= Rijk Geschiedkundige Publicatiën, Grote Serie, vol. 55).

Id. (ed.): Resolutiën der Staten-Generaal, van 1576 tot 1609, vol. 8: 1593–1595, Den Haag 1925 (= Rijk Geschiedkundige Publicatiën, Grote Serie, vol. 57).

Id. (ed.): Resolutiën der Staten-Generaal, van 1576 tot 1609, vol. 9: 1596–1597, Den Haag 1926 (= Rijk Geschiedkundige Publicatiën, Grote Serie, vol. 62).

Id. (ed.): Resolutiën der Staten-Generaal, van 1576 tot 1609, vol. 10: 1598–1599, Den Haag 1930 (= Rijk Geschiedkundige Publicatiën, Grote Serie, vol. 71).

Id. (ed.): Resolutiën der Staten-Generaal, van 1576 tot 1609, vol. 11: 1600–1601, Den Haag 1941 (= Rijk Geschiedkundige Publicatiën, Grote Serie, vol. 85).

Rijperman, H. H. P. (ed.): Resolutiën der Staten-Generaal, van 1576 tot 1609, vol. 12: 1602–1603, Den Haag 1950 (= Rijk Geschiedkundige Publicatiën, Grote Serie, vol. 92).

Id. (ed.): Resolutiën der Staten-Generaal, van 1576 tot 1609, vol. 13: 1604–1606, Den Haag 1957 (= Rijk Geschiedkundige Publicatiën, Grote Serie, vol. 101).

Id. (ed.): Resolutiën der Staten-Generaal, van 1576 tot 1609, vol. 14: 1607–1609, Den Haag 1970 (= Rijk Geschiedkundige Publicatiën, Grote Serie, vol. 131).

Roelevink, Joke (ed.): Resolutiën der Staten-Generaal, Nieuwe Serie, vol. 5: 1621–1622, Den Haag 1983 (= Rijk Geschiedkundige Publicatiën, Grote Serie, vol. 187).

Id. (ed.): Resolutiën der Staten-Generaal, Nieuwe Serie, vol. 6: 1623–Juni 1624, Den Haag 1989 (= Rijk Geschiedkundige Publicatiën, Grote Serie, vol. 208).

Id. (ed.): Resolutiën der Staten-Generaal, Nieuwe Serie, vol. 7: Juli 1624–1625, Den Haag 1994 (= Rijk Geschiedkundige Publicatiën, Grote Serie, vol. 223).

Smit, J. G. (ed.): Resolutiën der Staten-Generaal, Nieuwe Serie, vol. 3: 1617–1618, Den Haag 1975 (= Rijk Geschiedkundige Publicatiën, Grote Serie, vol. 152).

Id. (ed.): Resolutiën der Staten-Generaal, Nieuwe Serie, vol. 4: 1619–1620, Den Haag 1981 (= Rijk Geschiedkundige Publicatiën, Grote Serie, vol. 176).

Van Deursen, Arie Theodorus (ed.): Resolutiën der Staten-Generaal, Nieuwe Serie, vol. 1: 1610–1612, Den Haag 1971 (= Rijk Geschiedkundige Publicatiën, Grote Serie, vol. 135).

Id. (ed.): Resolutiën der Staten-Generaal, Nieuwe Serie, vol. 2: 1613–1616, Den Haag 1974 (= Rijk Geschiedkundige Publicatiën, Grote Serie, vol. 151).

Literature

Borin, Lars et al.: Naming the past: Named entity and animacy recognition in 19th century Swedish literature, in: Proceedings of the Workshop on Language Technology for Cultural Heritage Data (LaTeCH 2007), Prag 2007, p. 1–8.

Bryman, Alan: Social Research Methods, Oxford 2016.

Colavizza, Giovanni/Ehrmann, Maud/Bortoluzzi, Fabio: Index-driven digitization and indexation of historical archives, in: Frontiers in Digital Humanities 6 (2019).

Díez Platas, Luisa et al.: Medieval Spanish (12th–15th centuries) named entity recognition and attribute annotation system based on contextual information, in: Journal of the Association for Information Science and Technology 72/2 (2021), p. 224–38.

Ehrmann, Maud et al.: Named Entity Recognition and Classification on Historical Documents: A Survey, in: arXiv 2021, http://arxiv.org/abs/2109.11406 (13.09.2023).

Eijnatten, Joris van/Pieters, Toine/Verheul, Jaap: Big Data for Global History: The Transformative Promise of Digital Humanities, in: BMGN – Low Countries Historical Review, 128/4 (2013), p. 55–77, https://doi.org/10.18352/bmgn-lchr.9350 (13.09.2023).

Gijsbers, Wilma/Hell, Maarten/Schooneveld, Judith: Geweld, gewin en geweten. Besluiten van de Staten-Generaal (1626–1630), https://resources.huygens.knaw.nl/besluitenstatengeneraal1576-1630/BesluitenStaten-generaal1626-1651/BesluitenStaten-generaal1626-1651/Webartikel (13.09.2023).

Hill, Mark J./Hengchen, Simon: Quantifying the impact of dirty OCR on historical text analysis: Eighteenth Century Collections Online as a case study, in: Digital Scholarship in the Humanities 34/4 (2019), p. 825–43, https://doi.org/10.1093/llc/fqz024 (13.09.2023).

Hoekstra, Rik: The griffiers and the keeping of information in the Resolutions of the States General of the United Dutch Provinces, 1576–1796, Paper given at the Information and Power in History Conference, 16–17 March, 2017, Amsterdam, https://www.researchgate.net/publication/352679752 (13.09.2023).

Id./Nijenhuis, Ida/Dreijer, Gijs: Rapport ontsluiting staten general, 2016, https://doi.org/10.13140/RG.2.2.28184.80645 (13.09.2023).

Koolen, Marijn et al.: Modelling resolutions of the dutch states general for digital historical research, in: COLCO 2020: Proceedings of the International Conference Collect and Connect: Archives and Collections in a Digital Age, 2021, p. 37–50 (= CEUR Workshop Proceedings, vol. 2810), http://ceur-ws.org/Vol-2810 (13.09.2023).

Koolen, Marijn et al.: The Value of Preexisting Structures for Digital Access: Modelling the Resolutions of the Dutch States General, in: *ACM Journal of Computation and Cultural Heritage*, in press 2022.

Leemans, Inger et al.: Mining Embodied Emotions: A Comparative Analysis of Sentiment and Emotion in Dutch Texts, 1600–1800, in: Digital Humanities Quarterly 11/4 (2017), n.pag.

Meroño-Peñuela, Albert et al.: Semantic technologies for historical research: A survey, in: Semantic Web 6/6 (2015), p. 539–564.

Nijenhuis, Ida: Besluiten ontsloten. Resolutiën Staten-Generaal (1626–1630), in: De Zeventiende Eeuw. Cultuur in de Nederlanden in interdisciplinair perspectief 22/2 (2006), p. 272–282, https://www.dbnl.org/tekst/_zev001200601_01/_zev001200601_01_0020.php (13.09.2023).

Piersma, Hinke/Ribbens, Kees: Digital historical research: Context, concepts and the need for reflection, in: BMGN-Low Countries Historical Review 128/4 (2013), p. 78–102.

Pletschacher, Stefan/Antonacopoulos, Apostolos: The PAGE (Page Analysis and Ground-Truth Elements) Format Framework, in: Proceedings of the 20th International Conference on Pattern Recognition (ICPR2010), Istanbul, August 23–26, 2010, p. 257–260, http://dx.doi.org/10.1109/ICPR.2010.72, https://github.com/PRImA-Research-Lab/PAGE-XML (13.09.2023).

Rodriquez Kepa Joseba et al.: Comparison of named entity recognition tools for raw OCR text, in: Konvens (2012), p. 410–14.

Sluijter, Ronald et al.: Opening the Gates to the Dutch Republic: A Comparison between Analogue and Digital Editions of the Resolutions of the States General, in: *DiPaDA@DHNB*. 2022 (= CEUR Workshop Proceedings, vol. 3133), http://ceur-ws.org/Vol-3133/paper11.pdf (13.09.2023).

Thomassen, Theo: Onderzoeksgids: Instrumenten van de macht: de Staten-Generaal en hun archieven 1576–1796, vol. 1, Leiden 2019.

Van Riemsdijk, T. H. F.: De griffie van Hare Hoog Mogenden: bijdrage tot de kennis van het archief van de Staten-Generaal der Vereenigde Nederlanden, Den Haag 1885.

Van Strien et al.: Assessing the impact of OCR quality on downstream NLP tasks, in: ICAART 1 (2020), p. 484–496, https://doi.org/10.5220/0009169004840496 (13.09.2023).

Van Zundert, Joris: Barely Beyond the Book, in: *Matthew James Driscoll/Elena Pierazzo (ed.)*, Digital Scholarly Editing. Theories and Practices, Cambridge 2016, p. 83–106 (= Digital Humanities Series).

Id.: Scholarship in Interaction. Case Studies at the Intersection of Codework and Textual Scholarship, Leiden 2022.

Praxisbeispiele II:
Digitale Editionen frühneuzeitlicher Quellen

Ronald G. Asch (Freiburg im Breisgau)

Die Tagebücher Christians II. von Anhalt und ihre digitale Edition

I. Zur Edition

Die Diarien Christian II. (1599–1656) stellen eine in ihrer Weise einzigartige Quelle für die Geschichte des Dreißigjährigen Krieges und der unmittelbaren Nachkriegszeit dar[1]. In insgesamt 23 handschriftlichen Bänden – die Aufzeichnungen dokumentieren, wenn auch mit Lücken, die Jahre 1621 bis 1656 – führt Anhalt Buch nicht nur über seine eigenen Kriegserfahrungen, sondern auch über seine Reisen, seine Träume und seine sehr persönlichen Ängste und Hoffnungen. Der besondere Wert der Aufzeichnungen liegt dabei nicht nur in der Vielfalt der Perspektiven, die andere Selbstzeugnisse so oft nicht zu bieten vermögen, sondern auch in den besonderen Voraussetzungen, die ihr Autor als Schreiber eines Tagebuches mitbrachte. Zum einen hatte er als Reichsfürst – auch wenn Anhalt-Bernburg natürlich zu den mindermächtigen Ständen im Reich gehörte – privilegierten Zugang zum kaiserlichen und zu anderen Höfen und war zugleich Teil eines Netzwerkes von Kontakten, das sich bis an den Rand des Reiches und darüber hinaus etwa in die Niederlande erstreckte. Zum anderen war Christian in der Tat ein ausgezeichneter Beobachter, dessen Interesse weit über das rein Politische oder das Schicksal seiner Stammlande hinaus reichte.

Die Existenz der im Landesarchiv Dessau-Roßlau verwahrten Tagebücher ist seit langem bekannt, aber vor dem Zeitalter digitaler Editionen galt die Aufgabe, sie zu publizieren, als eine kaum zu bewältigende Herausforderung. Die jetzige Edition (http://diglib.hab.de/edoc/ed000228/start.htm) beruht auf einer Kooperation der Universität Freiburg (Lehrstuhl für Geschichte der frühen Neuzeit) mit der HAB Wolfenbüttel, die nicht zuletzt auch wichtige technische Expertise, die in anderen digitalen Editionsprojekten über die Jahre gewonnen werden konnte, in das Projekt einbringt. Finanziert wird die Edition von der DFG im Rahmen eines Langfristvorhabens, das soeben in seine vierte abschließende Phase gegangen ist. Das Interesse an dieser in ihrer Weise einmaligen Quelle ging auf der Freiburger Seite nicht zuletzt auf die langjährige Beschäftigung des Projektleiters (Prof. Dr. R. G. Asch) und

---

[1] Siehe die Projektbeschreibung http://www.tagebuch-christian-ii-anhalt.de/index.php?article_id=14 (13.09.2023) – Digitale Edition und Kommentierung der Tagebücher des Fürsten CHRISTIAN II. von Anhalt-Bernburg (1599–1656) (künftig: Tagebuch bzw. Tagebucheintrag). Dieser Beitrag stellt die modifizierte und erweiterte Fassung meines Kommentars zu Anhalts politisch-konfessioneller Haltung dar: *Asch*, Loyalitätskonflikte eines reformierten Reichsfürsten. Weitere Beiträge: http://www.tagebuch-christian-ii-anhalt.de/index.php?article_id=40 (13.09.2023).

des leitenden Freiburger Bearbeiters (Dr. Arndt Schreiber) mit der Geschichte des Adels zurück – Dr. Schreiber hat eine Dissertation über den protestantischen Adel in den österreichischen Erblanden nach 1620 publiziert[2], während das Interesse des Projektleiters eher den europäischen Adelslandschaften galt und gilt[3]. In dieser vergleichenden europäischen Perspektive sind die Diarien Anhalts von besonderem Wert, denn bislang konnte man leicht den Eindruck gewinnen, dass der deutsche Sprachraum für das 16. und frühe 17. Jahrhundert kaum Adelsmemoiren oder sonstige adlige Selbstzeugnisse zu bieten hat, die etwa mit den entsprechenden Quellen für Frankreich konkurrieren könnten. Dort wurden einschlägige Ego-Dokumente freilich schon im 19. Jahrhundert etwa in der Reihe der »Nouvelle collection des mémoires pour servir à l'histoire de France: depuis le XIIIe siècle jusqu'à la fin du XVIIIe« einem weiteren Publikum zugänglich gemacht[4]. Jedenfalls entstand selbst für Kenner der Materie der Eindruck, dass französische Adlige ihren deutschen Standesgenossen vor 1700 nicht nur in ihrer Fähigkeit, sich sprachlich zu artikulieren, überlegen waren, sondern auch zu einem höheren Grad von Selbstreflexion neigten. Mit Blick auf die Diarien Christians von Anhalt muss dieses Urteil revidiert werden. Dabei ist freilich zu berücksichtigen, dass Anhalt durch sein Studium in Genf und durch einschlägige Reisen mit der Adelskultur Frankreichs und Westeuropas gut vertraut war – ein nicht unwichtiger Umstand.

Anhalt kann dabei als fast schon obsessiver Tagebuchschreiber gelten. Offenbar ging es ihm auch darum, sich vor seinen Nachkommen und vor seinen Verwandten zu rechtfertigen und je mehr er sich als Verlierer des Zeitgeschehens sah, desto stärker wurde dieser Wunsch nach Selbstrechtfertigung offenbar. So notierte er im Juli 1634 während eines Aufenthaltes in Italien:

»Jch muß nur alles aufzeichnen, ob es schon eines theils inutilia scheinen zu sein, damit man sehe heütte oder morgen, wie ich meine sachen mitt mühe Vndt sorgen geführet vndt wie ich darneben, (wiewol vnbekandter weyse) seye tractirt worden. Es gehöret ejne große gedultt, zu solchen tractaten vndt beginnen, vndt wer es nur von außen ansiehet, vndt nicht selber in der heißen brühe steckt, findet leichtlich etwas zu tadeln dran, kan es aber schwehrlich beßer machen.«[5]

Jenseits der Adelsgeschichte kommt den Diarien eine zentrale Bedeutung für die Geschichte des Dreißigjährigen Krieges zu. Der Freiburger Projektleiter hat sich schon vor Jahren in einer englischsprachigen Monographie mit dem Dreißigjährigen Krieg auseinandergesetzt[6], und sich auch deshalb diesem Editionsprojekt zugewandt. Auf

---

2 *Schreiber*, Adeliger Habitus und konfessionelle Identität.
3 *Asch*, Europäischer Adel in der frühen Neuzeit; siehe auch *ders.*, European Nobilities and the Reformation.
4 *Michaud/Poujoulat (Hg.)*, Nouvelle collection des mémoires. Zu den Adelsmemoiren in Frankreich siehe *Deguin*, L'Écriture familiale des mémoires. Vgl. auch als prominente Beispiele adliger Memoiren: *Blaise de Monluc*, Commentaires (1521–1576), und *Jean-François Paul de Gondi*, Oeuvres.
5 Tagebucheintrag für den 7./17. Juli 1634, Fol. 77r.
6 *Asch*, The Thirty Years War, und jetzt auch *ders.*, Vor dem Großen Krieg.

der Seite der HAB Wolfenbüttel stellte hingegen die Edition der Briefe und sonstigen Quellen aus der Geschichte der Fruchtbringenden Gesellschaft (ein Projekt der Sächsischen Akademie der Wissenschaften in Zusammenarbeit mit der HAB)[7], ein wesentliches Fundament der Bearbeitung der Diarien Christians II. von Anhalt dar. Christian II. gehörte ihr wie alle anderen regierenden Fürsten von Anhalt in der Epoche des Dreißigjährigen Krieges selbst als Mitglied an und teilte auch den Reichspatriotismus, der viele Fruchtbringer auszeichnete.

Die Entscheidung für eine digitale Publikation fiel rasch und schon vor der Antragstellung. Im Vergleich zu einer gedruckten Edition bietet die Digitalisierung, die natürlich auch preisgünstiger ist, eine ganze Reihe von Vorteilen: dazu gehört z. B. die Möglichkeit, das Sach- und Personenregister im Lichte späterer Erkenntnisse auch für die bereits publizierten Passagen zu ergänzen. Auch stellten anfänglich die fremdsprachlichen Passagen des Tagebuches eine erhebliche Herausforderung dar. Immerhin rund 11 % der Aufzeichnungen schrieb Christian II. in Französisch nieder, dazu kommen Passagen in Italienisch und Latein, sowie gelegentlich auch kürzere Bemerkungen in Spanisch oder Niederländisch. Das Französische Christians, das er besonders dann benutzt, wenn er über eher vertrauliche Angelegenheiten schreibt, ist oft recht idiosynkratisch und erschließt sich an einigen Stellen nur nach wiederholter Lektüre. Hier war es wichtig, dass die Übersetzungen aus der Pilotphase des Projektes später noch korrigiert werden konnten. Die Übersetzungen sind im Übrigen unmittelbar dem Originaltext hinterlegt und können durch Anklicken der blau markierten Textpassagen aufgerufen werden.

Auf aufwendige Sachkommentare haben wir hingegen verzichtet, weil das Projekt dann nicht innerhalb der dafür vorgesehenen zwölf Jahre abzuschließen wäre. Dafür wird jedoch jedes Jahr des Tagebuches durch eine längere Einleitung erschlossen, die die wichtigsten Passagen hervorhebt und historisch einordnet. Im Übrigen bietet die digitale Edition auch erweiterte Suchfunktionen, die in einer gedruckten Publikation so nicht zur Verfügung stehen würden. Alle vom Autor erwähnten Personen, Orte und Körperschaften werden durch eigene Register erfasst, die im Text vorkommenden oder zitierten Dokumente und Werke nach Möglichkeit identifiziert. Außerdem bietet die Edition tabellarische und kartographische Itinerare des Fürsten zur Illustration der europäischen Dimension seiner Aufzeichnungen. Eine solche Erschließung der Handschrift ist zu ihrer wissenschaftlichen Verwendung unabweisbar, denn nicht ohne Grund hat sich dieses einmalige Selbstzeugnis bis heute jeder »spontanen« Auswertungsbemühung verschlossen, die auf keine verlässliche Kenntnis der geographischen, personellen und historischen Zusammenhänge zurückgreifen kann.

---

7   *Conermann (Hg.)*, Fruchtbringende Gesellschaft.

II. Ein Leben im Schatten des Vaters

Christian war natürlich, das wurde bereits betont, keiner der dominanten Akteure der Reichspolitik seiner Zeit, am Ende war er eher Opfer als Akteur und sah sich selbst auch so, wie im Tagebuch immer wieder deutlich wird. Sein Vater Christian I. von Anhalt (1569–1630) war mit seinen Bemühungen, eine große protestantische Allianz gegen das Haus Habsburg zustande zu bringen, zwar am Ende gescheitert – ja hatte die pfälzischen Wittelsbacher durch die böhmische Thronkandidatur in eine katastrophale Situation manövriert – aber er hatte durchaus historische Spuren hinterlassen und die Geschichte seiner Zeit mitgeprägt, wenn auch am Ende eher auf der Seite der Verlierer[8]. Seinem Sohn blieb eine solche führende Rolle verwehrt, was ihm nur allzu schmerzlich bewusst war. Nicht selten erscheint ihm sein Vater im Traum, als unerreichtes Vorbild, aber auch als tadelnder Mahner[9]. Allerdings versuchte Christian II. immer wieder zumindest eine Bestallung als Obrist zu erhalten; vorzugweise vom Kaiser, denn seit seiner endgültigen Begnadigung im Jahr 1622 sah sich Christian, der noch 1620 in der Schlacht am Weißen Berg gegen das Haus Habsburg gekämpft hatte und gefangen genommen worden war[10], als treuer Gefolgsmann des Kaisers. Das galt trotz seiner reformierten Konfession, der er im Übrigen durchaus treu blieb, auch wenn man am Kaiserhof zeitweilig auf eine Konversion gehofft haben mag und selbst im Ausland bereits Gerüchte umliefen, der Fürst sei tatsächlich Katholik geworden. Für Anhalt wäre eine mögliche Konversion aber im wahrsten Sinne des Wortes bei aller Kaisertreue ein Albtraum gewesen: So notierte er im Februar 1637:

»Seltzame somnia de peccato in Spiritum Sanctum so ich begangen, in dem ich mich auch noch durch die päbstischen vndt Jesuiten zur Meße wieder meinen willen zu gehen, vndt mitt gar schwehrem gewißen, durch Sophistische vnwiedertreibliche argumenten (dem schein nach) bereden laßen, darüber der Kayser sich so hoch erfreüet hette, daß er gesagt, Nun wollte er gern vndt frölich sterben, daß er dieses glück an mir erlebet hette. Jch war aber darnach froh, daß es nur ein Trawm gewesen, vndt daß ich auß solcher erschrecklichen gewißensangst, in etwas erlediget wardt.«[11]

---

8 *Deinet*, Christian I.
9 Zu den Träumen Anhalt siehe *Herz*, Traum und Traumdiskurs in den Tagebüchern Fürst Christians II.
10 Zur endgültigen Begnadigung siehe Tagebucheintrag 30. Dezember 1622/9. Januar 1623, Fol. 35v–36v, mit der abschließenden Bemerkung: »Darauf rief mich der Kayser zu sich mit vermelden, Sie wolten mich numehr für einen freyen Reichsfürsten erkennen, verhoften ich würde numehr auch Jhrer Mayestät treü verbleiben, vndt nicht allein, vor meine person, meinen gehorsam erzeigen, sondern auch andere fürsten helfen zu Jhrer Mayestät devotion bringen.«
11 Tagebucheintrag für den 24. Februar 1637, Fol. 367r. Zu den Gerüchten über eine Konversion siehe Tagebucheintrag für den 4./14. Juli 1634, Fol. 70v. Unterhaltung mit dem Kardinal von Savoyen in Turin.

Die Tagebücher Christians II. von Anhalt und ihre digitale Edition 149

III. Ein kaisertreuer Protestant

Ein besonderer Wert des Tagebuches liegt darin, den Krieg aus der Sicht eines protestantischen, aber weitgehend kaisertreuen Reichsfürsten zu zeigen. Diese Haltung war natürlich gar so selten nicht, man denke an Kursachsen oder Hessen-Darmstadt, aber sie ist sonst nicht so stark aus der persönlichen Sicht eines Zeitgenossen dokumentiert wie hier, bis hin zu persönlichen Gewissenskonflikten, die Anhalt mehr als einmal anspricht. Solche Gewissenskonflikte traten auch in Momenten auf, in denen Anhalts Kaisertreue auf eine harte Probe gestellt wurde, etwa nach Erlass des Restitutionsediktes und in den Jahren, in denen Schweden in weiten Regionen des Reiches militärisch dominant war; darauf wird zurückzukommen sein.

Freilich war Christians Kaisertreue auch ein Zeichen politischer Vorsicht, und er war im Haus Anhalt nicht der Einzige, der nach 1621 zu einer solchen Vorsicht neigte. Schon 1623 hatte sein Onkel, Fürst August, folgt man den Diarien, bemerkt, man solle sich als Gesamthaus darauf festlegen, nie wieder gegen den Kaiser zu kämpfen: »Es wehre gut man machte eine sazung im hause Anhaltt, Nota Bene daß sich nimmermehr kein fürst sollte wieder den Römischen Kayser gebrauchen laßen, denn alle Historien gäbenß, daß wir nie kein glück wieder den Kayser gehabt.«[12]

Das Prinzip, dass man ohne Rücksicht auf die Konfession ›dem Kaiser geben müsse, was des Kaisers sei‹, und der gottgegebenen Obrigkeit gegenüber gehorsam sein müsse, findet sich in Anhalts Überlegungen entsprechend immer wieder, so auch viele Jahre später nach Abschluss des Prager Friedens[13]. Seine diesbezüglichen Gedanken über den Fall der Mächtigen durch Gottes Ratschluss könnten, wie er meinte, den allzu Ehrgeizigen unter den Mächtigen dieser Welt zur Mahnung dienen[14]. Besonders verwies er dabei auf Fälle wie den Friedrichs V. von der Pfalz und Albrechts von Wallenstein. Beide hätten sich gegen ihren kaiserlichen Herren aufgelehnt, weil sie mit ihrem erreichten Status und ihren Privilegien nicht zufrieden gewesen waren. Der Protest gegen die gottgegebene Obrigkeit könne am Ende nur in die Katastrophe führen, diese Lehre scheint Christian aus dem Schicksal seines Vaters und aus seinem eigenen gezogen zu haben.

---

12 Tagebucheintrag für den 11. April 1623, Fol. 87r.
13 Tagebucheintrag für den 1. Juni 1635, Fol. 289v, der ein Gespräch mit dem Hofkriegsratspräsidenten Graf Heinrich Schlick wiedergibt: »Ob ich schon der reformirten Religion zugethan, so hielte ich nichts von denen, die nicht glauben hielten, vndt dem Kayser nicht geben, waß des Kaysers wehre, noch der Obrigkeitt, die gewallt vber Sie hette vndterthenig sein wollten, das lehrete auch das wortt Gottes.« Vgl. auch die Bemerkung über Wallenstein und die Hinrichtung seiner Anhänger im Tagebucheintrag für den 27. Juni 1635, Fol. 320r: »Voyla, ce que c'est, de s'opposer au Magistrat, & aux puissances superieures. Faut bien observer la reigle de Saint Paul; Romains 18 13. caput.«.
14 Tagebucheintrag für den 13. Juni 1635, Fol. 304r–306r, vgl. Fol. 306r, über Wallenstein: »devroyent avoir au moins horreur de l'exemple tout seul arrivé l'année passée, du Duc de Fridlande, lequel ne se contentant pas, de tant d'inesperèe fortune, qu'il avoit obtenuë par la grace de Dieu, & de son bon maistre Sa Majestè Jmperiale nostre Sire, avec tant de benignitè«.

Deutlich wurde die Kaisertreue Christian II. vor allem nach den ersten großen Erfolgen der schwedischen Waffen in Deutschland, als die Stände des obersächsischen Kreises unter Druck gerieten, sich den Schweden anzuschließen und ein Bündnis gegen den Kaiser einzugehen. Die regierenden Fürsten von Anhalt, mit denen Christian II. sich im September 1631 in Halle beriet, wohin sie Gustav Adolf hatte kommen lassen, befürworteten am Ende mehrheitlich eine Allianz mit dem siegreichen Schwedenkönig, aber Christian II. beharrte auf seinen Vorbehalten. Das Evangelium hebe die irdischen Gesetze und Verfassungen nicht auf, und man müsse dem Kaiser geben, was des Kaisers sei, schließlich sei Ferdinand II. ja nicht von den Kurfürsten abgesetzt worden. Und außerdem habe auch der böhmische Ständeaufstand, »als man dem Kayser in die Fenster zu Wien geschoßen« (Ferdinand war in der Tat zeitweilig von den aufständischen österreichischen Ständen in der Hofburg bedrängt worden, während vor Wien böhmische Truppen aufmarschierten), nicht viel gefruchtet[15]. All dies habe nur in den Abgrund geführt.

Christian II. wusste, wovon er sprach, denn er war, wie schon erwähnt, in der Schlacht am Weißen Berg in Gefangenschaft geraten. Und es ist interessant zu sehen, wie in seinen Aufzeichnungen Versatzstücke der lutherischen Lehre von der gottgegebenen Autorität der Obrigkeit rezipiert werden; um eine reine Theorie handelte es sich also nicht.

Allerdings setzte er sich im konkreten Fall nicht durch. Seine Verwandten, angeführt von den Fürsten Ludwig und Johann Kasimir, argumentierten, die Reichsfürsten seien doch keine »Sklaven« des Kaisers und das Reich keine Monarchie, sondern eine Aristokratie. Der Lehenseid verpflichte einen nicht nur zur Treue gegenüber dem Kaiser, sondern gegenüber dem Reich als Rechtsgemeinschaft, und wenn der Kaiser diese Rechtsgemeinschaft zerstöre, dann höre die Gehorsamspflicht ihm gegenüber auf. Und am Ende führe man diesen Krieg ja nicht gegen den Kaiser, sondern für ihn, denn die Katholische Liga habe ihm das Heft des Handelns aus der Hand genommen und folge seinen Anweisungen nicht mehr. Letzteres war ein klassisches Argument, das wir bei Revolten in der Frühen Neuzeit oft genug finden, so auch im Englischen Bürgerkrieg, in dem die Führer des Parlamentes zumindest anfänglich dem Anspruch nach für die Rechtsperson des Königs gegen seine natürliche Person, die zum Gefangenen böser Ratgeber geworden sei, kämpften[16].

---

15 Tagebucheintrag für den 15. September 1631, Fol. 91vf.: »vndt alß man dem Kayser in die fenster zu Wien geschoßen, auch wie die Vnion, vndt confœderation der Erbländer sich dem Kaiser potenter wiedersezt vndt dennoch nichts außrichten können. Verhüte den Verlust des Landes und der Köpfe, einen schändlichen Tod.« Vgl. *Reißner*, Kämpfe vor Wien.
16 Tagebucheintrag für den 15. September 1631, Fol. 92v: »Que les Princes libres de l'Empire n'estoyent pas esclaves, & ne devoyent se laisser gourmander contre la capitulation de l'Emp*er*eur l'Empire n'estant pas Monarchique ains Aristocratique & electif, Que l'Emp*er*eur avoit enfraint les constitutions de l'Empire, en plusi*eur*s façons, Que sur tout il falloit donner a Dieu le sien, & a la religion la vie & les biens.«

Schließlich führte der Bernburger Regierungspräsident Heinrich von Börstel noch an[17], man dürfe die wahre Religion zwar nicht mit dem Schwert ausbreiten – den Gedanken eines »Heiligen Krieges« für den wahren Glauben lehnte er also wie die meisten Protestanten ab –, dürfe sie aber, wo sie einmal etabliert sei, durchaus mit Waffengewalt verteidigen[18]. Börstel war anders als Anhalt generell geneigt, spätestens seit 1629/30 den Konflikt als Religionskrieg zu betrachten, in dem es für aufrechte Protestanten keine Neutralität geben könne[19]. Auch hier haben wir also einen bemerkenswerten Einblick in ständische Argumentationsmuster vor dem Hintergrund der komplexen Verfassung des Reiches; Argumentationsmuster, die gar nicht so viel anders angelegt waren als bei Ständekonflikten und -revolten außerhalb des Reiches wie etwa in England in den 1640er Jahren.

Anhalt selbst freilich akzeptierte dieses Plädoyer für ein Widerstandsrecht im Herbst 1631 nicht. Dennoch musste er sich am Ende dem Druck beugen und den Allianzvertrag mit Schweden, wenn auch sehr widerwillig, unterschreiben. Christian berief sich ausdrücklich auf diesen Zwang, in der Hoffnung, dass ihn Gott für diese Tat, die er eigentlich mit seinem Gewissen nicht vereinbaren konnte, nicht bestrafen werde[20].

Gewiss wird er auch befürchtet haben, dass er, da Ferdinand II. ihn 1622 begnadigt hatte – im Gegenzug für das Versprechen, nie wieder gegen ihn zu kämpfen –, im Falle des Scheiterns härter bestraft werden würde als andere, die ein solches Versprechen nicht gegeben hatten. Seine Kaisertreue scheint dennoch aufrichtig genug gewesen zu sein. Den Prager Frieden sah Christian II. freilich einige Jahre später durchaus kritisch; er befürchtete ein kaiserliches »Dominat«, also eine Einschränkung der deutschen Libertät und der Privilegien der Reichsstände, für deren Erhalt doch ursprünglich die protestantische Union begründet worden war[21]. Trotz alledem muss er froh gewesen sein, dass er sich nun wieder als loyaler Untertan des Kaisers betrachten konnte.

17 Heinrich von Börstel (1581–1647), Sohn des Bernburger Oberhauptmanns Curt von Börstel (1549–1618); Erbherr auf Güsten, Plötzkau und Ilbersedt; ab 1623 Regierungspräsident sowie Amtshauptmann und Kammerrat in Bernburg; 1639 Rücktritt, danach Tätigkeit als unbestallter fürstlicher Berater.
18 Ebd., Fol. 94v.
19 *Schreiber*, Handlungsmöglichkeiten und Selbstbehauptung des Fürsten Christian II., bes. S. 120.
20 Tagebucheintrag für den 15. September 1631, Fol. 94rf.: »Je le fis donc avec une main Tremulant, en protestant a l'encontre.«
21 Tagebucheintrag 31. Januar 1635, Fol. 207v; vgl. *Zirr*, Eine enttäuschte Hoffnung, und *Schmidt*, Die Reiter der Apokalypse, S. 467–505.

IV. Höfische Präsenz und Lavieren zwischen den politisch-konfessionellen Fronten

Grundsätzlich kaisertreu gesinnt legte Christian Wert darauf, auch bei wichtigen zeremoniellen Anlässen am kaiserlichen Hof präsent zu sein. Er ließ sich nach dem Tode seines Vaters persönlich vom Kaiser belehnen – eine Form der symbolischen Loyalitätsbekundung, die im 17. Jahrhundert bei weltlichen Fürsten schon recht ungewöhnlich geworden war[22], und nahm Ende 1636/Anfang 1637 auch an den Feierlichkeiten zur Wahl und Krönung Ferdinands III. zum römischen König und an der Krönung seiner Gattin in Regensburg teil. Da die mächtigen weltlichen Reichsfürsten – für die geistlichen galt das freilich noch nicht in gleicher Weise –, auch wenn sie wichtige Erzämter innehatten, ihre Funktionen beim Krönungszeremoniell und ähnlichen Anlässen kaum noch persönlich wahrnahmen, war die Anwesenheit Anhalts dem Kaiser offenbar durchaus willkommen, auch wenn er natürlich nicht zu den Mächtigen im Reich gehörte. Aber er stammte aus einer alten Fürstenfamilie, die im Mittelalter noch zu den führenden Dynastien des obersächsischen Raumes gehört hatte. Allerdings war es nicht immer leicht für Anhalt, seinen Rang bei Hofe zu behaupten. Zwar gelang es ihm z. B. die Leuchtenberger in die Schranken zu verweisen[23], aber als er in Regensburg einmal einen Platz oberhalb der Gesandten der Kurfürsten von Bayern und Brandenburg in Anspruch nahm, ließ man ihm ausrichten, dass er auf solche Anmaßungen in Zukunft verzichten solle, »weil die Churfürstlichen gesandten, vber alle Fürsten giengen, ohne contradiction, es auch in der güldenen bulla außdrücklich stünde, [...] daß die churfürstlichen gesandten vber alle Fürsten gehen sollten.«[24] Diese Auskunft mag Christian nicht gefallen haben, aber er musste sich damit abfinden.

Im Übrigen ist freilich auffällig, wie vertraut Christian auch mit führenden Geistlichen am Hof Ferdinands II. umging. So führte er 1629 ein langes Gespräch mit Kardinal Melchior Khlesl (1552–1630), der freilich nicht mehr lange zu leben hatte und politisch zu diesem Zeitpunkt schon lange marginalisiert worden war. Aber immerhin war Khlesl bis 1619 der wichtigste Minister und Berater des Kaisers gewesen und damit eigentlich auch ein entscheidender Gegenspieler Christians I. von Anhalt. Man sollte meinen, dass auch zehn Jahre nach der Absetzung Ferdinands II. als König von Böhmen und der Königswahl des Pfälzer Kurfürsten die Beziehungen zwischen einem reformierten Reichsfürsten und Khlesl eher von Spannungen belastet sein würden. Vor allem hatte Anhalts Vater zu den militanten Reformierten gehört, die die Machtstellung des Hauses Habsburg im Reich hatten zerschlagen wollen. Aber nichts dergleichen war der Fall, das Gespräch fand in über-

---

22 Tagebucheintrag für den 29. Juni 1635, Fol. 321vf.: »Man macht sich lustig vber mich, wenn ich selber sollte wollen die lehn entpfangen, vndt nichts beßers verrichten, als was ein agent köndte, wie Löben vndt seines gleichen.« Vgl. *Stollberg-Rilinger*, Des Kaisers alte Kleider, S. 210–217, 123–131.
23 Tagebucheintrag für den 24. Januar 1637, Fol. 343r: »Preseance obtenuë sur Leüchtembergk, au couronnement, aux festins, & en toutes occasions«.
24 Tagebucheintrag für den 20./30 November 1636, Fol. 246r.

aus freundlicher Atmosphäre statt und Khlesl beschwerte sich nur darüber, dass Anhalt ihn bei seinem Besuch in Rom 1623 nicht aufgesucht habe. Für die Zukunft legte er ihm nahe, falls er noch einmal nach Rom komme, auch mit dem Papst Kontakt aufzunehmen, denn dieser »Wehre ein frischer Munterer herr, ein sehr guter Græcus, vndt eloquentissimus jn ljngua Latina. Er der Cardinal hette dem Pabst offtermalß viel guts von Meinem herrenvatter gesagt, vndt der Pabst hette gewüntschett, das er ihn kennen, vndt mitt ihm tractiren möchte.«[25]

Über die Calvinisten hatte Khlesl fast nur Positives zu sagen, vor allem seien sie theologisch seiner Ansicht nach gebildeter und argumentationsstärker als die Lutheraner[26]. Offenbar versuchte Khlesl, Christian II. hier zu schmeicheln; er mag vielleicht auch ein wenig gehofft haben, ihn irgendwann zu einer Konversion bewegen zu können, eine Hoffnung, die andere Gesprächspartner am Hof geteilt haben mögen. Aber bemerkenswert bleibt dennoch, dass mitten auf dem Höhepunkt des Krieges, als das Restitutionsedikt die schiere Existenz des Protestantismus im Reich bedrohte, solche Gespräche überhaupt möglich waren. Das ist ein Indiz dafür, dass im Dreißigjährigen Krieg der Gesprächsfaden zwischen den verfeindeten Konfessionsparteien nie wirklich abriss. Zum Teil waren die Konflikte auch situativ. Es gab Situationen, im Streit etwa um säkularisiertes Kirchengut, in denen die gegnerischen Rechtsauffassungen, die ihrerseits in konfessionellen Weltanschauungen verwurzelt waren, unmittelbar aufeinanderstießen und Kompromisse nahezu unmöglich machten. Es gab aber auch andere Situationen, die es den Beteiligten gestatteten, ihre religiösen Differenzen auszuklammern, wie es Khlesl ja schon vor dem Ausbruch des Krieges mit seiner Kompositionspolitik gegenüber den Protestanten versucht hatte[27]. Hier griffen Verhaltenskonventionen, auf die sich beide Seiten einigen konnten, etwa die höfischen Gesellschaft oder der *res publica litteraria*. Das unterschied den Dreißigjährigen Krieg auch von den Französischen Religionskriegen, die zu einer Vergiftung aller politischen und sozialen Beziehungen geführt hatten, auch wegen des abgrundtiefen Misstrauens und offenen Hasses, mit dem sich die verfeindeten Seiten begegneten.

In Deutschland, das machen auch die Diarien Christians deutlich, gab es hingegen auch auf dem Höhepunkt des Konflikts immer noch Themen, die eine Annäherung der beiden Seiten zumindest denkbar erscheinen ließen. Kann man daraus folgern, dass Konfession und religiöse Überzeugungen in dem Krieg, der 1618 ausbrach, ohnehin nur ein Vorwand waren, dass es von Anfang an nur um die reine politische Macht ging[28]? Das wäre sicher ein Fehler. Dass eine mögliche Kon-

---

25 Tagebucheintrag für den 9. Dezember 1629, Fol. 281rf. Gemeint war Urban VIII. Barberini, der von 1623–1644 den Stuhl Petri innehatte.
26 Ebd., Fol. 285r: »Die lutrischen wehren gar grobe leütte, hetten keine solche fundamenta vndt rationes wie die reformirten, die er zimlich lobete, vndt vber zwey mal nicht Calvinisten, sondern wol 12 mal reformirte hieß.«
27 Ebd., Fol. 284v–285r: »Er hielte es vor kein gut Politisch stücklein, wann man bey Evangelischen leütten von der Religion disputirte. Er hette sichs allezeit endthalten, wann man ihm nicht sonderbahre vrsach gegeben.« – Zu Khlesl siehe u. a. *Johnston*, Melchior Khlesl.
28 So etwa *Schmidt*, Reiter, S. 155.

version für Christian Albtraum war, wurde bereits angesprochen. In manchen seiner Träume sah er sich umgekehrt gar als Retter des Evangeliums:

»Somnium diesen Morgen gehabt: [...] vndt alle leütte auf den gaßen, altt vndt iung, hetten vnß im vorüber ziehen, mitt Threnen gesegenet, vndt sich höchlich vber meiner ankunft erfreẅet, bevorab darüber, daß Sie noch durch mich, bey Nota Bene der reinen warheitt des Evangelij sollten erhalten, Nota Bene vndt geschützt werden.«[29]

Gleichgültig gegenüber konfessionellen Fragen war Christian also in keiner Weise, aber das schloss die Bereitschaft zum Gespräch mit Vertretern der Gegenseite eben nicht aus, wie etwa mit dem Pater Wilhelm Lamormaini, dem kaiserlichen Beichtvater. Mit ihm hatte Anhalt im August 1635 eine lange Diskussion über Glaubensfragen. Der Jesuit betonte, dass die Differenz zwischen den Lutheranern und den Katholiken in der Abendmahlslehre doch gar nicht so groß sei und man wohl auch mit den Calvinisten einig werden könne. Allerdings trenne die Konfessionsparteien die Ekklesiologie und auch die Prinzipien der Bibelexegese seien andere, denn für Katholiken könne nur die Amtskirche mit dem päpstlichen Lehramt im Lichte der Tradition die vielen Mysterien in der Bibel richtig interpretieren, nicht der einfache Gläubige. Das sah Christian II. ganz anders, aber eigentlicher Streitpunkt im Gespräch war doch eine andere Frage[30]. Der Reichsfürst hielt Lamormaini vor, es sei doch die Maxime der Jesuiten oder gar der Katholiken allgemein, »haereticis fides non servanda est« und dass sie gegebenenfalls auch bereit seien, Gift und das Messer des Attentäters gegen konfessionelle Gegner einzusetzen. Daraufhin reagierte der Beichtvater empört:

»Il le desavoua, & dit, qu'on en calomnie les Jesuites, & que Jacques Clement estoit un perfide, un Regicida, un homicida, un meschant & pervers, quj tua le Roy Henrj III de France. [...] Que la societè humaine, devoit estre reiglèe par bonnes loix & Polices, qu'il ne convenoit pas de transgredier. [...] Quod essent bellj sicut et pacis jura, quæ inviolata servanda.«[31]

Lamormaini distanzierte sich also nicht nur vehement vom Königsmörder Jacques Clement, der 1589 Heinrich III. von Frankreich, den die Sorbonne zuvor für exkommuniziert erklärte hatte, umgebracht hatte, sondern betonte auch, es gebe eben klare Gesetze des Friedens und des Krieges, die man in jedem Fall beachten müsse. Im weiteren Gespräch musste der Beichtvater freilich einräumen, dass ein Eid, den man unter Druck geleistet habe und welcher den christlichen Prinzipien fundamental widerspreche oder die Grundlagen der Kirche in Frage stelle, natürlich nicht verbindlich sei, was Christian von Anhalt nicht unbedingt beruhigte[32]. Am Ende

29 Tagebucheintrag für den 8. August 1637, Fol. 464v.
30 Tagebucheintrag für den 3. August 1635, Fol. 378v–380v. Zu Lamormaini vgl. *Bireley*, Religion and Politics.
31 Tagebucheintrag für den 3. August 1635, Fol. 379rf.
32 Tagebucheintrag für den 4. August 1635, Fol. 380v: »Ich hatte ihm aber nicht dieses, sondern ein anders proponirt, das Sie statuiren: Juramentum, contra Ecclesiastjcam utilitatem præstitum, non tenet, darauf gedachte er, es wehre die utilitas animae darmitt gemeinet.«

zeigte sich hier das Grundproblem aller Friedensbemühungen vor 1618, aber auch während des Krieges: das gegenseitige Misstrauen[33]. Wie konnte man einem Gegner vertrauen, von dem man annehmen musste, dass er einen für verdammt hielt, den man aber auch selber als Ketzer oder als Anhänger der Idolatrie betrachtete?

V. Das Selbstzeugnis eines Gescheiterten und eines Grenzgängers

Es bleibt die Erkenntnis, dass Christians Haltung und sein Handeln widersprüchlich blieben. Einerseits war er sich durchaus bewusst, wie stark Maßnahmen wie das Restitutionsedikt den Protestantismus im Allgemeinen und ganz besonders die Position der Reformierten im Reich bedrohten. Andererseits sah er im Kaiser die gottgegebene Obrigkeit, der man sich nicht widersetzen dürfe. Ein gewisses persönliches Kalkül spielte dabei natürlich auch eine Rolle. Eine militärische Karriere schien am ehesten noch in Diensten des Kaisers möglich zu sein, zumal Anhalt weder für die Schweden, deren König er als allzu herrisch und arrogant ansah, noch für Kursachsen sonderliche Sympathien hegte. Hinzu kam der Faktor, dass man am Kaiserhof wusste, wie man mit Reichsfürsten wie Anhalt umgehen musste, um ihnen das Gefühl zu geben, sie würden geschätzt. Niemand war dankbarer für Zeichen der Anerkennung als Anhalt, der offenbar Zeit seines Lebens unter dem Gefühl litt, eigentlich ein Versager zu sein. Es war aber vielleicht doch bezeichnend, dass Christians Träume von einer militärischen Karriere am Ende nicht in Erfüllung gingen. Am Hof des Kaisers mochte man ihm gelegentlich schmeicheln, aber man zögerte offenbar doch, dem ältesten Sohn und Erben des Mannes, der 1618/19 den Krieg ausgelöst hatte – zumindest aus kaiserlicher Sicht –, ein höheres Kommando zu übertragen, obwohl sein jüngerer Bruder Ernst tatsächlich als kaiserlicher Obrist zwischen 1628 und 1631 in Italien focht. Christians faktischer Mangel an fundierter militärischer Erfahrung mag auch ein Hindernis gewesen sein. Dennoch entwickelte er in den Jahren 1626–1628 einen ambitionierten Plan, wie er sich unterstützt von Spanien und dem Kaiser neben dem Herzog von Rohan an die Spitze der französischen Hugenotten setzen könne, um so zugleich dem Hause Habsburg und der Sache des Protestantismus zu dienen. Noch im Januar 1629, als die protestantische Festung La Rochelle bereits von den königlichen Truppen zur Kapitulation gezwungen worden war, plädierte er für eine Intervention in Frankreich. Er versprach sich von einem solchen Feldzug offenbar auch persönlichen Ruhm. Untätig im heimischen Fürstentum, »diesem langwieligem ortt«, zu verharren, erschien ihm

---

33 Dazu auch *Ziegler*, Trauen und Glauben; vgl. jetzt auch *Asch*, Dissimulation and Lack of Trust.

unerträglich und eine Art Sterben bei lebendigem Leibe, obwohl sein Vater seine Pläne offenbar missbilligte und für ein Zeichen von Selbstüberschätzung hielt[34].

Sehr realistisch waren Christians Vorstellungen freilich nicht; Anfang 1629 war der protestantische Widerstand in Frankreich ja schon weitgehend zusammengebrochen, und für Wallenstein besaß der Konflikt zwischen Ludwig XIII. und Spanien keine sonderliche Priorität. In Spanien wiederum dürfte man gezögert haben, sich offen mit Ketzern, noch dazu mit Calvinisten, zu verbünden. Christians Pläne ließen sich daher nicht umsetzen. Sie zeigen aber, wie komplex der Verlauf der politisch-konfessionellen Fronten im Dreißigjährigen Krieg sein konnte.

Im Übrigen gab Christian II. Anhalt seine Träume von einer militärischen Karriere nach diesen Rückschlägen nicht auf. 1632 reiste er sogar nach Polen, um dort eine Bestallung als Kommandant deutscher Söldner im Kampf gegen die Moskowiter zu erhalten. In der Tat plante der polnische Kronprinz Ladislaus (Władysław) Wasa einen Feldzug gegen die Russen, bei dem es auch um die Durchsetzung seiner Ansprüche auf den russischen Thron – einige Bojaren hatten ihn schon 1610 als Zaren ausgerufen – gehen sollte. Allerdings besaß er nicht wirklich die Unterstützung seines Vaters Sigismund, dem er nach dessen Tod (Ende April 1632) im November des Jahres 1632 als König folgen sollte[35]. Von daher war Christian eher zu früh nach Polen gereist, wo seine Pläne mit Zurückhaltung aufgenommen wurden. Seine eigenen Eindrücke vom polnischen oder genauer genommen masowischen Adel – ob nun durch übliche Vorurteile oder persönliche Erfahrungen geprägt, sei dahingestellt – war freilich auch kein sehr günstiger. Am 9. März 1632 notierte er:

»Sie seindt gar sehr grobe Barbarische leütte die Masawer oder Masuren, (die Masaw, jst ein landt vor sich, darinnen Warschow ligt, ob es zwar mitt dem Königreich Polen incorporirt ist) wollen alle Schlachtitz oder edelleütte sein, wann sie nur einen Sebel vndt pferdt haben. Achten wenig geseze. Schätzen einen Todtschlag gar gering.«[36]

---

34 Tagebucheintrag für den 9. Januar 1629, Schreiben an den kaiserlichen Obristen Pecker, Fol. 202r–209r. Offenbar kam es über diese Pläne zum Konflikt zwischen Vater und Sohn (Fol. 208v–209r): »Dieweil aber Jhre Gnaden die sache improbirt, sonderlich die weil ich sie nicht eher derselben gesagtt, vndt geloso auf mich worden, das ich eben der iehnige wehre, der einen General agiren wollte, mich auch immerfortt basso gehalten, vndt mir alle media abgeschnitten, auß diesem langweiligem ortt, weg zukommen, so bin ich abgeschreckt worden, etwas weiter in der sache zu gedencken. Drüber ist die gewaltige stadt Rochelle verlohren worden. Der herr hat mir aber nun anlaß selber gegeben, das ich mich abermals habe selbsten gleichsamb auß dem schlaff, vndt Todt, ermuntern müßen, vndt mein hertz gegen ihme außschütten. Weil mir niemandt alhier helfen will, muß ich mir selbst helfen, vndt raht suchen, wo ich kan. Der herr wolle dieses schreiben recht maneggiiren.«
35 Vgl. *Frost*, The Northern Wars, S. 46f. und S. 142–147 zum polnisch-russischen Krieg um Smolensk, 1632–1634; vgl. zur Politik Ladislaus IV.: *Tricoire*, Mit Gott rechnen, S. 259–266, und *Dybas*, Schwedischer Druck, S. 318f.
36 Tagebucheintrag für den 9./19. März 1632, Fol. 252vf.

Christians Urteil über die besonderen Privilegien und Freiheitsrechte des Adels – auch das *liberum veto* erwähnte er – fiel ebenfalls entsprechend ambivalent aus[37], auch wenn er mit Interesse die Verhandlungen der polnischen Stände in Gegenwart des Königs beobachtete[38] und sich von seinen Gesprächspartnern, darunter der Fürst Christoph Radziwill, über die Rechte der Stände in Polen instruieren ließ[39].

Seine Pläne für eine Feldzug gegen die Moskowiter lösten sich ohnehin rasch in Luft auf; sie wären in jedem Fall recht riskant gewesen, da die Schweden, die indirekt Moskau gegen Polen unterstützten und damals den sächsisch-anhaltischen Raum militärisch dominierten, den Kampf eines anhaltischen Fürsten für eine gegnerische Macht wohl als Provokation gesehen und mit entsprechenden Repressalien beantwortet hätten. Darauf wiesen jedenfalls Christians Räte und Verwandte nach seiner Rückkehr ins Reich hin[40].

Immerhin, in einem seiner zahlreichen Träume gelangte der Fürst dann doch nach Moskau, allerdings nicht als Eroberer, sondern als Gast, wenn nicht gar als Gefangener des russischen Großfürsten respektive Zaren, der ihn zwang, ihn als seinen Herren anzuerkennen[41]. Bei solchen Träumen blieb es dann freilich und Christian sollte noch Jahre später bedauern, dass er seine polnischen Pläne nicht energischer verfolgt hatte[42].

Christian von Anhalt blieb aber letzten Endes ein Grenzgänger zwischen den verfeindeten Lagern – das macht seine Diarien für uns als Quelle so wertvoll, weil er Zugang zu unterschiedlichen Entscheidungszentren hatte und als aktiv nicht beteiligter, bloßer Beobachter manches klarer sah als die Handelnden selbst. Aber eben dieses Grenzgängertum war kein Erfolgsrezept in den Wirren des Krieges, da man am Ende von keiner der kriegführenden Parteien wirklich Schutz, Förderung und Unterstützung erfuhr, sondern bestenfalls Schonung. Und so hatte es Christian vermutlich auch sich selbst zu verdanken, dass er ein Verlierer blieb und sein Traum von einem Generalat genau dies blieb: ein bloßer Traum, den er freilich noch 1636 in seinem Tagebuch festhielt, als er von einer nächtlichen Vision berichtete, in der ihm träumend die Jungfrau Maria (sic) erschienen war und er seine geheimen

---

37 Siehe etwa den Eintrag für den 18./28. März, Fol. 259v: »Die Pollnischen herren vndt vom adel haben ihre Ober vndt vndtergerichte, iagten vndt andere jura vndt waß der edelmann gläubet, müß<en> seine vndterthanen auch gläuben, es seye Päbstisch, lutrisch, Reformirt, Schwenckfeldisch, Arrianisch, Photinianisch, Griechisch, Armenisch, oder was es wolle, oder man zwinget sje oft mitt prügeln darzu, vndt gibt dannenhero vielerley secten«.
38 Tagebucheintrag für den 20./30. März 1632, Fol. 265r–266r. Vgl. 25. März/4. April, Fol. 274v–275v.
39 Tagebucheintrag für den 25. März/4. April 1632, Fol. 275rf.
40 Siehe die Tagebucheinträge für den 18. April 1632, Fol. 293r, und den 14. Juli desselben Jahres, Fol. 53r. Hier bringt der Regierungspräsident von Börstel vor: »1. Que le Roy de Swede a dit voyant la lettre de Madame ha ha, da haben wir wieder einen neẅen General in Polen bekommen: Wir müßen ihm zur werbung helfen. 2. Que Fürst Ernst a dit avoir entendu du Palatin Auguste, daß der König gesagt hette, wo ich würde vor Polen werben, so wollte der König das Fürstenthumb Anhalt, eben so kahl machen, wie er Bayern gemacht hette.«
41 Tagebucheintrag für den 29. März/8. April 1632 (Gründonnerstag), Fol. 279r–280r.
42 Tagebucheintrag für den 16. Februar 1635, Fol. 221r.

Wünsche äußerte: »Als die reye an mich gekommen, vndt ich meine Meynung bey Meiner herzlieb(st)en gemahlin bette also stehende, sagen sollen, hette ich zwar gesagt, Jch wüntzschte mir ejn regiment zu roß, eines zu fuß vndt ein generalat darneben.« Im Traum gab es freilich für Anhalt dann doch noch ein höheres Ziel als militärischen Ruhm: die ewige Seligkeit, oder, wie er es ausdrückte, »die höchste vergnüglichkeitt.«[43] Diesem Ziel konnte Anhalt immerhin ganz unabhängig von den wechselnden Konstellationen des Krieges und von der Gunst des Kaisers oder anderer Potentaten nachstreben.

Literaturverzeichnis

Asch, Ronald G.: The Thirty Years War. The Holy Roman Empire and Europe 1618–1648, Basingstoke 1997.

Ders.: Europäischer Adel in der frühen Neuzeit. Eine Einführung, Köln 2008 (= UTB Taschenbuch, Bd. 3086).

Ders.: European Nobilities and the Reformation, in: *Ulrike Rublack (Hg.)*, The Oxford Handbook of the European Reformations, Oxford 2017, S. 565–583.

Ders.: Vor dem Großen Krieg. Europa im Zeitalter der spanischen Friedensordnung 1598–1618, Darmstadt 2020.

Ders.: Dissimulation and Lack of Trust. A Central Problem in Politics and Interconfessional Relations at the Turn of the Seventeenth-Century, in: *Monika Fludernik/Stephan Packard (Hg.)*, Being Untruthful. Lying, Fiction and the Non-Factual, Baden-Baden 2021, S. 187–212.

Ders.: Digitale Edition und Kommentierung der Tagebücher des Fürsten Christian II. von Anhalt-Bernburg (1599–1656), http://diglib.hab.de/edoc/ed000228/start.htm (13.09.2023).

Ders. : Loyalitätskonflikte eines reformierten Reichsfürsten. Christian II. von Anhalt-Bernburg zwischen Kaisertreue und protestantischem Bekenntnis, http://www.tagebuch-christian-ii-anhalt.de/index.php?article_id=14 (13.09.2023).

Bireley, Robert: Religion and Politics in the Age of the Counterreformation. Emperor Ferdinand II, William Lamormaini, S. J. and the Formation of Imperial Policy, Chapel Hill 1981.

Conermann, Klaus (Hg.): Fruchtbringende Gesellschaft – Die deutsche Akademie des 17. Jahrhunderts. Kritische Ausgabe der Briefe, Beilagen und Akademiearbeiten (Reihe I), Dokumente und Darstellungen (Reihe II), https://www.hab.de/fruchtbringende-gesellschaft-die-deutsche-akademie-des-17-jahrhunderts/ (13.09.2023).

Deguin, Yohann: L'Écriture familiale des mémoires. Noblesse 1570–1750, Paris 2020.

Deinet, Klaus: Christian I. von Anhalt-Bernburg (1568–1630), Stuttgart 2020.

Dybas, Boguslaw: Schwedischer Druck und offensive Politik im Osten: Außenpolitik 1609–1648, in: *Michael Müller u. a. (Hg.)*, Polen in der europäischen Geschichte, Bd. II: Frühe Neuzeit, 16. bis 18. Jahrhundert, hg. in Verbindung mit Hans-Jürgen Bömelburg, Stuttgart 2017, S. 315–348.

Frost, Robert: The Northern Wars, 1558–1721, Harlow 2000.

Gondi, Jean-François Paul de, Cardinal de Retz: Oeuvres, hg. v. *Marie-Thérese Hipp* und *Michel Pernot*, Paris 1984.

Herz, Andreas: Traum und Traumdiskurs in den Tagebüchern Fürst Christians II., http://www.tagebuch-christian-ii-anhalt.de/index.php?article_id=41 (13.09.2023).

---

43 Tagebucheintrag für den 28. Februar 1636, Fol. 70v.

Johnston, Rona: Melchior Khlesl und der konfessionelle Hintergrund der kaiserlichen Politik im Reich nach 1610, in: *Friedrich Beiderbeck u. a. (Hg.)*, Dimensionen der europäischen Außenpolitik zur Zeit der Wende vom 16. zum 17. Jahrhundert, Berlin 2003, S. 199–222.

Michaud, Joseph-François/Poujoulat, Jean-Joseph-François (Hg.): Nouvelle collection des mémoires pour servir à l'histoire de France depuis le XIIIe siècle jusqu'à la fin du XVIIIe siècle, 32 Bde., Paris 1836–1839.

Monluc, Blaise de: Commentaires (1521–1576), hg. v. *Paul Courteault* und *Jean Giono*, Paris 1964.

Reißner, Sonja: »Aber auch wie voriges tags außer Scharmüzieren anders nichts verricht …«. Die Kämpfe vor Wien im Oktober 1619 im Spiegel zeitgenössischer Quellen, in: *Andreas Weigl (Hg.)*, Wien im Dreißigjährigen Krieg. Bevölkerung, Gesellschaft, Kultur, Konfession, Wien 2001, S. 446–481.

Schmidt, Georg: Die Reiter der Apokalypse. Geschichte des Dreißigjährigen Krieges, München 2018.

Schreiber, Arndt: Adeliger Habitus und konfessionelle Identität: die protestantischen Herren und Ritter in den österreichischen Erblanden nach 1620, Wien 2013.

Ders.: »Nicht nach dem Winde schnappen«. Handlungsmöglichkeiten und Selbstbehauptung des Fürsten Christian II. von Anhalt-Bernburg im Dreißigjährigen Krieg nach seinen Tagebüchern, in: *Andreas Erb/Andreas Pečar (Hg.)*, Der Dreißigjährige Krieg und die mitteldeutschen Reichsfürsten. Politische Handlungsstrategien und Überlebensmuster, Halle (Saale) 2020, S. 109–132.

Stollberg-Rilinger, Barbara: Des Kaisers alte Kleider. Verfassungsgeschichte und Symbolsprache des Alten Reiches, München 2008.

Tricoire, Damien: Mit Gott rechnen. Katholische Reform und politisches Kalkül in Frankreich, Bayern, und Polen-Litauen, Göttingen 2013.

Ziegler, Hannes: Trauen und Glauben. Vertrauen in der politischen Kultur des Alten Reiches im Konfessionellen Zeitalter, Affalterbach 2017.

Zirr, Alexander: Eine enttäuschte Hoffnung. Der Prager Frieden in den Tagebüchern des Fürsten Christian II. von Anhalt-Bernburg, in: *Katrin Keller/Martin Scheutz (Hg.)*, Die Habsburgermonarchie und der Dreißigjährige Krieg, Wien 2020, S. 311–330.

Andreas Zecherle (Mainz), Kevin Wunsch (Darmstadt)

Das Projekt »Europäische Religionsfrieden Digital – EuReD«

Projektvorstellung und exemplarische Analyse des Augsburger Interims (1548)[1]

I. Projektvorstellung

1. Organisatorische Rahmenbedingungen

Das Projekt »Europäische Religionsfrieden Digital«, abgekürzt »EuReD«, wird seit April 2020 an der Akademie der Wissenschaften und Literatur (Mainz) und der Universitäts- und Landesbibliothek Darmstadt bearbeitet. Die Projektleitung liegt bei Prof. Dr. Irene Dingel und Prof. Dr. Thomas Stäcker. Gefördert wird das auf 21 Jahre angelegte Vorhaben im Rahmen des Akademienprogramms der Union der deutschen Akademien der Wissenschaften. Die Website des Projekts ist unter https://www.eured.de/ zu erreichen. Von dort gelangt man auch zu der im Aufbau befindlichen digitalen Edition.

2. Zielsetzung

Ziel des Projekts ist es, die europäischen Religionsfriedensregelungen im Zeitraum von 1485 (Kuttenberger Landtagsabschied) bis 1791 (Constitution Française) zu edieren und digital im Open Access für die Forschung zugänglich zu machen. Unter dem Begriff »Religionsfriedensregelungen« werden dabei politisch-rechtliche Regelungen verstanden, die ein friedliches Zusammenleben konfessionsverschiedener Gruppen zum Ziel hatten[2]. Sie bezogen sich in erster Linie auf innerchristliche Differenzen[3] und konnten in unterschiedlichen juristischen Formen erlassen werden, etwa als Verträge, Abschiede, (Wahl-)Kapitulationen, Edikte, Mandate, Privilegien und Majestätsbriefe[4]. Sie konnten alleiniger Inhalt von in sich abgeschlossenen Tex-

---

1   Die Abschnitte I.5 und II.2.b wurden von Kevin Wunsch verfasst, der übrige Text von Andreas Zecherle.
2   *Dingel*, Religionsfrieden, S. 267 f.
3   *Dies.*, Einleitung, S. xiif.; *dies.*, Religionsfrieden, S. 268 f.
4   *Brockmann*, Religionsfrieden, S. 588 f.; *Dingel*, Religionsfrieden, S. 275 f.

ten, aber auch Bestandteile von anderen rechtsrelevanten Dokumenten sein, wie zum Beispiel von Reichstagsabschieden, zwischenstaatlichen Friedensschlüssen, Handels- und Bündnisverträgen oder von Eheverträgen zwischen konfessionsverschiedenen Partnern des Adels[5]. »Es existierte also im frühneuzeitlichen Europa eine unübersichtliche Fülle unterschiedlicher juristischer Textgattungen und Rechtsformen, derer man sich zur Regulierung religiöser Koexistenz bediente.«[6] Auch der Geltungsbereich der Regelungen differierte stark: Manche galten für mehrere Herrschaftsgebiete, andere auf föderaler, territorialer oder nur lokaler Ebene[7]. Das Editionsprojekt möchte all diese Religionsfriedensregelungen in ihrer Vielfalt zu einem umfangreichen digitalen Korpus zusammenführen und auf diese Weise insbesondere vergleichende Untersuchungen ermöglichen. Als hintere zeitliche Grenze bei der Korpusbildung dient dabei die im späten 18. Jahrhundert einsetzende Entwicklung hin zu einer systematischen Religionsgesetzgebung der europäischen Staaten. Solche Religionsgesetze lösten die anlassbezogenen vielgestaltigen Religionsfriedensregelungen ab und rezipierten über diese hinausgehend zum Teil die von der Aufklärung propagierten Vorstellungen von Persönlichkeitsrechten und individueller Religionsfreiheit[8].

Das zu erstellende umfassende digitale Korpus von europäischen Religionsfrieden soll es ermöglichen, die Entwicklung von Religionsfriedensregelungen im »Kommunikationsraum Europa«, ihre textlichen Abhängigkeiten sowie ihre Rezeption und Wirkung über Kulturräume hinweg vergleichend zu analysieren. Solche Untersuchungen können dazu beitragen, die Entwicklung des Toleranzgedankens und die Konstituierung des modernen europäischen Staatswesens besser zu verstehen.

3. Arbeitsprogramm

Insgesamt sollen im Rahmen unseres Projekts 234 Texte mit Religionsfriedensregelungen ediert werden. Ihre Bearbeitung erfolgt in 12 Modulen, die jeweils Texte vereinen, die geographisch, chronologisch oder inhaltlich eng zusammengehören. Die einzelnen Module sind:
1) Regelungen für das gesamte Heilige Römische Reich Deutscher Nation
2) Regelungen für einzelne Territorien des Heiligen Römischen Reichs Deutscher Nation bis 1648
3) Böhmen, Schlesien, Siebenbürgen, Österreichische Erblande
4) Niederlande, Eidgenossenschaft, Italien
5) Frankreich
6) Osteuropa, Baltikum, Skandinavien

---

5 *Dingel*, Religionsfrieden, S. 274 f.
6 Ebd., S. 275.
7 Vgl. auch ebd., S. 276.
8 Ebd., S. 276; vgl. auch *Brockmann*, Religionsfrieden, S. 587 f.

7) Regelungen für einzelne Territorien des Heiligen Römischen Reichs Deutscher Nation 1648 bis 1788
8) England und die englischen Kolonien in Nordamerika
9) Das europäische Refuge
10) Interkonfessionelle Heiratsverträge
11) Bündnis-, Handels- und Friedensverträge
12) Verfassungsdokumente am Ende des 18. Jahrhunderts

4. Editionsprinzipien

Die Überlieferung der einzelnen edierten Texte wird in den Einleitungen erschlossen. Die Handschriften und zeitgenössischen Drucke werden aufgelistet und, soweit vorhanden, mit elektronischen Katalogeinträgen und Digitalisaten verlinkt. Da die Druckgeschichte vieler Religionsfriedensregelungen bisher kaum oder gar nicht untersucht worden ist, wird dabei oft Pionierarbeit geleistet.

Als Editionsgrundlage dient der Erstdruck (editio princeps), da die Frieden in dieser Gestalt öffentlichkeitswirksam wurden. In den Fällen, in denen kein zeitgenössischer Druck existiert, werden Handschriften als Editionsgrundlage herangezogen. Ansonsten wird die handschriftliche Überlieferung berücksichtigt, indem eine auf den Handschriften beruhende Edition kollationiert wird, sofern sie vorhanden ist.

Ediert werden jeweils nur die rechtskräftigen Religionsfrieden selbst, keine weiteren Quellen zur Entstehungs- und Wirkungsgeschichte, weil dies den Rahmen des Projekts sprengen würde. Die Entstehungs- und Wirkungsgeschichte der Religionsfrieden wird in den ausführlichen Einleitungen dargestellt, die in Deutsch und künftig auch in Englisch veröffentlicht werden. In den Anmerkungen der Einleitungen wird dabei auf edierte Quellen zur Entstehungs- und Wirkungsgeschichte verwiesen. Sofern diese digital verfügbar sind, werden sie verlinkt. Auch im Stellenkommentar zum Editionstext werden Hinweise zur Entstehungs- und Wirkungsgeschichte einzelner Regelungen gegeben. Die zum Verständnis der Texte notwendige Einbettung in den Mikrokontext soll auf diese Weise trotz des weit ausgreifenden komparatistischen Ansatzes gewährleistet werden.

Um den Zugang zum Inhalt der Religionsfrieden zu erleichtern, bieten die Einleitungen Inhaltsangaben. Da im Rahmen unserer Edition Texte in den verschiedensten europäischen Sprachen ediert werden, werden zeitgenössische deutsche Übersetzungen beigegeben, sofern sie existieren. Fehlen zeitgenössische deutsche Übersetzungen, werden bei Religionsfriedensregelungen, die in Sprachen verfasst wurden, welche nur wenige Nicht-Muttersprachler beherrschen, moderne Übersetzungen ins Deutsche angefertigt.

Bereits kritisch edierte Texte werden erneut ediert, um ein umfassendes, einheitliches digitales Korpus zu schaffen.

In den Texten vorkommende Personen, Orte, Organisationen und Ereignisse werden mit XML-Tags ausgezeichnet und mit Normdaten verknüpft.

5. Die digitale Edition

Die digitale Edition basiert auf Exist-DB und dem darauf aufbauenden quelloffenen Framework wdbplus, das bereits in mehreren Projekten zum Einsatz kommt, wie dem github-Repository entnommen werden kann (vgl. https://github.com/dariok/wdbplus). Bei der technischen Umsetzung folgt das Projekt gängigen Standards, die Texte werden etwa anhand der Richtlinien der Text Encoding Initiative transkribiert, kommentiert und korrigiert, sowie mittels spezifischer XSLT-Skripte dynamisch in HTML umgewandelt und so zitierfähig mit persistenten Identifiern bereitgestellt. Ein großer Vorteil einer digitalen Edition ist die Möglichkeit, Ergebnisse im laufenden Betrieb zu veröffentlichen und nicht auf Printbände warten zu müssen. Diesem Paradigma folgend werden edierte Texte sukzessive veröffentlicht. Generell können Texte auch im Entwurfsstadium für Forschung und Lehre genutzt werden, ein entsprechender Vermerk weist in diesem Falle auf den Entwurfscharakter des Textes hin. Forschung und Lehre können also ständig auf aktuellste Forschungsergebnisse zu den hier edierten Religionsfriedensregelungen zurückgreifen.

Dabei entwickelt die Universitäts- und Landesbibliothek Darmstadt ein Basisformat, das auf dem Basisformat des Deutschen Textarchivs[9] basiert und die Besonderheiten der Darmstädter Projekte berücksichtigt[10]. Das Projekt wird von einer Webseite (www.eured.de) flankiert, auf der Interessierte neben den Editionsrichtlinien weiteres Zusatzmaterial finden, etwa einen Überblick über bisher edierte und veröffentlichte Texte, oder eine Dokumentation bisher bestehender Schnittstellen. Zukünftig sollen die Projektwebseite und die Edition (https://purl.ulb.tu-darmstadt.de/vp/a000008-0000) näher zusammenrücken, etwa über eingebundene Suchfunktionen oder Register, die Nutzerinnen und Nutzern eine Übersicht über Entitäten und ihr Vorkommen liefern. In unregelmäßigen Abständen informiert das Team auf der Website zudem über Aktivitäten jenseits der Edition, etwa Vorträge und Veröffentlichungen oder Erweiterungen des Editionsframeworks.

Für die digitale Edition sind die Entwicklung gängiger Funktionen sowohl geplant als auch in Teilen bereits umgesetzt: Verschiedene Ansichten, etwa eine reduzierte Ansicht für Mobilgeräte, wie Smartphones oder Tablets, sind bereits implementiert, sollen aber sukzessive erweitert werden, etwa um eine reine Leseansicht, in der weder Hervorhebungen noch kritische Anmerkungen die Leserinnen und Leser vom Text ablenken. Erweitert werden soll das beinahe klassische Angebot einer digitalen Edition um verschiedene Auswertungsmöglichkeiten, die in enger Kooperation zwischen Fachwissenschaft und digitaler Geisteswissenschaft konzipiert werden. Eine solche Auswertungsmöglichkeit wird im zweiten Kapitel des vorliegenden Beitrags exemplarisch vorgestellt.

---

9 Siehe den Beitrag von Marius Hug und Linda Kristen in diesem Band.
10 https://www.deutschestextarchiv.de/doku/basisformat/ (22.11.2022).

II. Das Augsburger Interim (1548) als Solitär im digitalen Editionskorpus

Im Folgenden soll am Beispiel eines Textes aus unserem Korpus ein Einblick in unsere Arbeit gegeben werden. Ich greife dazu das Augsburger Interim von 1548 heraus. Betrachtet man dieses im Kontext unseres Korpus, so wird deutlich, dass es sich um einen atypischen Religionsfrieden handelt. Die Sonderstellung des Interims zeigt sich zum einen im Umfang der gewährten religiösen Toleranz, zum anderen in der Begründung der getroffenen Regelungen.

1. Der Umfang der gewährten religiösen Toleranz

Das Interim ist ein ungewöhnlich restriktiver Religionsfrieden, da es die Religionsausübung der Evangelischen inhaltlich einschränkt. Alle anderen uns bisher bekannten Religionsfrieden klammern die theologischen Streitfragen aus und wollen den Religionskonflikt stattdessen mit juristischen Regelungen einhegen[11]. Die Lehren der in den jeweiligen Religionsfrieden eingeschlossenen Glaubensrichtungen bleiben dabei unangetastet, die Religionsausübung wird aber mehr oder weniger stark auf bestimmte Orte oder Personengruppen beschränkt. Das Interim versucht hingegen, auf einem politisch-juristischen Verfahrensweg einen theologischen Kompromiss zu finden, der allerdings nur übergangsweise bis zur endgültigen Entscheidung durch das Konzil gelten soll. Dementsprechend bietet das Interim einen Abriss der Dogmatik und wurde im Auftrag des Kaisers von einer Theologenkommission ausgearbeitet[12]. Die Bestimmungen des Interims schränken die evangelische Lehre massiv ein: Von den spezifisch evangelischen Lehren bleiben im Wesentlichen nur die Priesterehe und der Laienkelch erlaubt, wobei auch diese beiden Zugeständnisse bis zu einer definitiven Entscheidung des Konzils befristet sind[13]. In der Rechtfertigungslehre hebt das Interim zwar die Bedeutung des Glaubens nachdrücklich hervor, unterstreicht aber auch die Notwendigkeit der caritas, die als eingegossene Liebe den Menschen zum Tun guter Werke instand setzt[14]. In vielen anderen Streitpunkten wurde von den Evangelischen die Rückkehr zu altgläubigen Lehren verlangt, auch wenn diese Forderungen oft relativ versöhnlich formuliert waren[15]. So

---

11 *Wolgast*, Religionsfrieden, S. 60; *Dingel*, Religionsfrieden, S. 277, 283; *dies.*, Einleitung, S. xvii.
12 *Rabe*, Entstehung, S. 53–63.
13 *Mehlhausen (Hg.)*, Interim, Art. 26, S. 142 f.; *Zecherle (Bearb.)*, Interim deutsch, Art. 26, Z. 2180–2211; *ders. (Bearb.)*, Interim lateinisch, Art. 26, Z. 1771–1796.
14 *Mehlhausen (Hg.)*, Interim, Art. 4–8, S. 42–59; *Zecherle (Bearb.)*, Interim deutsch, Art. 4–8, Z. 304–567; *ders. (Bearb.)*, Interim lateinisch, Art. 4–8, Z. 250–453. Zur Rechtfertigungslehre des Interims vgl. *Lohse*, Dogma, S. 107; *Mehlhausen*, Interim, S. 232; *Moritz*, Interim, S. 122–124.
15 Vgl. auch *Rabe*, Entstehung, S. 62.

sollte unter anderem der päpstliche Primat anerkannt werden[16]. Die Siebenzahl der Sakramente[17], die Messopferlehre[18], der Messkanon[19], die Anrufung der Heiligen[20], zahlreiche Heiligenfeste[21] und die Fastengebote[22] sollten verbindlich sein.

Dass das Interim sehr restriktive Regelungen enthielt, wird vor dem Hintergrund seines geschichtlichen Entstehungskontextes verständlich. Im Vorfeld des Interims waren die politischen Machtverhältnisse zwischen den Altgläubigen und den Evangelischen für einen Religionsfrieden außergewöhnlich asymmetrisch. In den im Reich vorausgehenden Religionsfrieden, dem Nürnberger Anstand von 1532 und dem Frankfurter Anstand von 1539, war der Kaiser zu Zugeständnissen an die evangelischen Stände gezwungen, weil er deren Hilfe im Kampf gegen die Osmanen benötigte[23]. Im Schmalkaldischen Krieg 1546/47 hatte Karl V. aber dann gegen die im Schmalkaldischen Bund organisierten evangelischen Stände einen triumphalen Sieg errungen[24]. Während der Reichstag 1547/48 in Augsburg beriet, demonstrierte der Kaiser seine Macht, indem er die Stadt militärisch besetzt hielt[25]. Dennoch wollte Karl V. den protestantischen Ständen nicht einfach die Rückkehr zum alten Glauben befehlen, sondern ihnen mit dem Interim etwas, wenn auch nicht weit, entgegenkommen. Anfang Januar 1547 hatte der Kaiser in einem Brief an seinen Bruder Ferdinand noch die Handlungsoption zur Diskussion gestellt, die Besiegten sofort zur vollständigen Rückkehr zum alten Glauben zu zwingen[26]. Er war dann aber dem Rat seines Bruders gefolgt, die religionspolitischen Entscheidungen erst später auf einem Reichstag zu treffen[27]. Wahrscheinlich schon zu Beginn des Augsburger Reichstags von 1547/48 setzte Karl V. eine Theologenkommission ein,

---

16 *Mehlhausen (Hg.)*, Interim, Art. 13, S. 70–73; *Zecherle (Bearb.)*, Interim deutsch, Art. 13, Z. 809–840; *ders. (Bearb.)*, Interim lateinisch, Art. 13, Z. 658–682.

17 *Mehlhausen (Hg.)*, Interim, Art. 14–22, S. 72–123; *Zecherle (Bearb.)*, Interim deutsch, Art. 14–22, Z. 841–1792; *ders. (Bearb.)*, Interim lateinisch, Art. 14–22, Z. 683–1464.

18 *Mehlhausen (Hg.)*, Interim, Art. 22, S. 102–123; *Zecherle (Bearb.)*, Interim deutsch, Art. 22, Z. 1379–1792; *ders. (Bearb.)*, Interim lateinisch, Art. 22, Z. 1119–1464.

19 *Mehlhausen (Hg.)*, Interim, Art. 26, S. 136 f.; *Zecherle (Bearb.)*, Interim deutsch, Art. 26, Z. 2074–2077; *ders. (Bearb.)*, Interim lateinisch, Art. 26, Z. 1695–1698.

20 *Mehlhausen (Hg.)*, Interim, Art. 23, S. 124–129; *Zecherle (Bearb.)*, Interim deutsch, Art. 23, Z. 1793–1899; *ders. (Bearb.)*, Interim lateinisch, Art. 23, Z. 1465–1553.

21 *Mehlhausen (Hg.)*, Interim, Art. 26, S. 138 f.; *Zecherle (Bearb.)*, Interim deutsch, Art. 26, Z. 2104–2130; *ders. (Bearb.)*, Interim lateinisch, Art. 26, Z. 1719–1731.

22 *Mehlhausen (Hg.)*, Interim, Art. 26, S. 140 f.; *Zecherle (Bearb.)*, Interim deutsch, Art. 26, Z. 2141–2172; *ders. (Bearb.)*, Interim lateinisch, Art. 26, Z. 1739–1764.

23 Vgl. die Einleitungen und Editionen der beiden Religionsfrieden in *Dingel (Hg.)*, Religionsfrieden 1, S. 131–180.

24 Zusammenfassend *Held*, Schlacht.

25 *Rabe*, Reichsbund, S. 181 f.

26 Vgl. den Brief Karls V. an König Ferdinand vom 9. Januar 1547 in *Pfeilschifter (Hg.)*, Acta 5, Nr. 7, S. 11, Z. 6–15, deutsche Übersetzung in *Kohler (Hg.)*, Quellen, Nr. 93, S. 364; vgl. dazu auch *Rabe*, Reichsbund, S. 125 f.

27 Vgl. den Brief König Ferdinands an Karl V. vom 18. Januar 1547 in *Pfeilschifter (Hg.)*, Acta 5, Nr. 9, S. 16, Z. 21–S. 18, Z. 8; *Machoczek (Bearb.)*, Reichstagsakten 18,1, Nr. 5, S. 118–120; vgl. dazu auch *Rabe*, Reichsbund, S. 127 f.

die für ihn unter strenger Geheimhaltung einen Entwurf für eine vorläufige Regelung der religiösen Verhältnisse im Reich ausarbeiten sollte. Sie bestand ausschließlich aus altgläubigen Mitgliedern, von denen fast alle Zugeständnisse an die Protestanten ablehnten[28]. Spätestens im Dezember 1547 legte die Kommission dem Kaiser einen schroff antiprotestantischen Interimsentwurf vor, der letztlich die Rückkehr zur altgläubigen Lehre verlangte[29]. Ein anonym überliefertes Gutachten, das wahrscheinlich von dem Naumburger Bischof Julius Pflug stammt, kritisierte den Interimsentwurf und forderte eine den Protestanten gegenüber versöhnlichere Darstellung der Lehre[30]. Wohl in Kenntnis dieses Gutachtens griff der Kaiser den ersten Interimsentwurf nicht auf und setzte stattdessen eine neue Kommission zur Ausarbeitung eines weiteren Interimsentwurfs ein[31], der die den Protestanten gegenüber relativ verständigungsbereiten altgläubigen Theologen Julius Pflug und Michael Helding sowie mit Johannes Agricola auch ein protestantischer Theologe angehörten[32]. Diese zweite Kommission übergab dann im März 1548 dem Kaiser einen Interimsentwurf[33], der mit kleineren Änderungen[34] die Grundlage für die endgültige Fassung des Interims bildete. Da diese wie oben dargestellt ein paar Zugeständnisse an die Evangelischen enthielt, lässt sich das Interim gerade noch als Religionsfrieden im Sinne einer konfessionellen Koexistenzordnung kategorisieren, es handelt sich aber um einen ungewöhnlich restriktiven Religionsfrieden, um einen Religionsfrieden hart an der Grenze zum Unfrieden, der das damalige sehr ungleiche politische Kräfteverhältnis widerspiegelt.

2. Die Begründung der Regelungen

a) Theologische Argumentation

Die Sonderstellung des Interims im Vergleich zu anderen Religionsfrieden zeigt sich nicht nur in den ungewöhnlich restriktiven Regelungen, sondern auch in deren Begründung. Wie die neuere Forschung am Beispiel Frankreichs herausgearbeitet hat, waren die Diskurse über Religionsfriedensregelungen von theologischen Argumentationsmustern geprägt. Eine wichtige Rolle spielte dabei der Gedanke, dass falsche Religionsausübung den Zorn Gottes hervorrufe und dadurch auch das Fortbestehen des politischen Gemeinwesens gefährde[35]. Die Texte der Religionsfrieden selbst enthalten aber nur selten theologische Begründungen.

---

28 *Rabe*, Entstehung, S. 36–38.
29 *Pfeilschifter (Hg.)*, Acta 6, Nr. 17, S. 258–301; vgl. auch *Rabe*, Entstehung, S. 41 f.
30 *Pfeilschifter (Hg.)*, Acta 6, Nr. 18, S. 301–308; vgl. auch *Rabe*, Entstehung, S. 41 f.
31 *Rabe*, Entstehung, S. 42.
32 Ebd., S. 54 f.
33 *Pfeilschifter (Hg.)*, Acta 6, Nr. 19, S. 308–348.
34 Zusammenfassend *Rabe*, Entstehung, S. 82–84.
35 *Niggemann/Wenzel*, Seelenheil; *Wenzel*, Ruine. Für Hinweise danke ich Prof. Dr. Christoph Kampmann, Marburg.

Diese haben dann zum Ziel, die Gewährung religiöser Toleranz zu rechtfertigen[36]. Im Unterschied dazu bietet das Interim zahlreiche theologische Argumente, die die Festlegung bestimmter dogmatischer Lehren untermauern sollen. Der schroff antiprotestantische Interimsentwurf, den die erste, ausschließlich altgläubig besetzte Theologenkommission dem Kaiser spätestens im Dezember 1547 vorlegte, bemühte sich allerdings noch nicht um eine theologische Begründung[37]. Das wahrscheinlich von Julius Pflug stammende anonym überlieferte Gutachten zum ersten Interimsentwurf, das eine den Protestanten gegenüber versöhnlichere Darstellung der Lehre forderte, hielt es für notwendig, Belege aus der Bibel und den Schriften der Kirchenväter anzuführen, damit diejenigen, die vom katholischen Glauben abgefallen seien, leicht zum Bekenntnis und zur Einheit der Kirche zurückgerufen werden könnten[38]. Wie von Pflug in seinem Gutachten vorgeschlagen enthielten dann der zweite Interimsentwurf und schließlich auch die auf ihm beruhende endgültige Fassung zahlreiche Verweise auf Bibelstellen und Kirchenväterschriften. Zum Teil handelt es sich dabei um wörtliche Zitate, zum Teil um indirekte. Viele der Zitate, allerdings bei Weitem nicht alle, werden in den Erstdrucken des Interims am Rand nachgewiesen.

Im Stellenkommentar unserer digitalen Edition bemühen wir uns um einen Nachweis sämtlicher ermittelbaren Zitate[39]. Die Kirchenväterzitate und die biblischen Zitate wurden im XML-Text des Kommentars jeweils spezifisch getaggt und können daher leicht computergestützt gesucht und ausgewertet werden. Eine solche Auswertung der biblischen Zitate soll im Folgenden vorgenommen werden, um die Möglichkeiten zu veranschaulichen, die unsere digitale Edition bietet. Das durch quantitative Analyse gewonnene Datenmaterial soll dabei in einem zweiten Schritt inhaltlich interpretiert werden.

b) Die computergestützte Auswertung der zitierten Bibelstellen

Bei der computergestützten Auswertung der Bibelstellen im Augsburger Interim stellten wir uns vier Fragen: (1) In welchem Umfang wird die Bibel zitiert? (2) Welche Stellen werden zitiert? (3) Wie groß ist der Anteil an wörtlichen Zitaten? (4) Gibt es Kapitel, in denen die Bibel überdurchschnittlich häufig wörtlich zitiert wird?

---

36 Theologische Begründungen finden sich im Thorenburger Landtagsabschied von 1568 (*Armgart [Bearb.]*, Kirchenordnungen 24, Nr. 14, S. 84) und im Edikt von Nantes von 1598 (*Walder [Hg.]*, Religionsvergleiche 2, S. 15 f.; vgl. dazu auch *Seresse*, Sicherheit, S. 244 f.). Nur angedeutet ist eine solche Begründung im Zweiten Kappeler Landfrieden von 1531 (*Dingel [Hg.]*, Religionsfrieden 1, S. 119, Z. 4).
37 *Pfeilschifter (Hg.)*, Acta 6, Nr. 17, S. 258–301.
38 Ebd., Nr. 18, S. 301,24.32–37: »[...] articuli [...] auctoritate ac ratione scripturae et sanctorum patrum testimoniis illustrandi atque explicandi videntur. Sed praecipue ii, qui in controversiam adduci facile et solent et possunt, ut non solum peritis, doctis atque catholicis satisfieri, sed hi etiam, qui a catholica religione nostra dissentiunt, ad confessionem et unitatem ecclesiae revocari facilius queant.«
39 *Zecherle (Bearb.)*, Interim deutsch.

Wie in den Editionsrichtlinien des Projektes vorgesehen, werden Bibelstellen mittels des TEI-Tags *ref* mit einem zugewiesenen type *biblical* und dem Attribut *cRef* angereichert, wie das nachfolgende Beispiel zeigt.

<note type="annotation">Vgl. <ref type="biblical" cRef="Rm_8,32">Röm 8,32</ref>.</note>

Um nun also alle derart ausgezeichneten Bibelstellen zu finden, wird mittels BeautifulSoup nach dieser Struktur im heruntergeladenen XML-Dokument gesucht[40]. Zur Auswertung wird die Data-Science Bibliothek »Pandas« genutzt[41]. Im Folgenden werden die Analyse-Schritte »Vom Text zu den Daten« exemplarisch am gesamten Text des Augsburger Interims vorgestellt. Analog zu diesen Schritten wurden die Informationen für die einzelnen Kapitel gewonnen[42].

Zunächst wird die Datei geöffnet und mittels BeautifulSoup die Datengrundlage erstellt:

	kuerzel	atnt	stelle	zitat
0	Gn_1,26-27	at	Gen 1,26f.	not a direct quote
1	Sir_15,14	at	Sir 15,14	hat in Gott gelassen inn der hand seines eig -...
2	Rm_5,12	nt	Röm 5,12	not a direct quote
3	Rm_5,15-19	nt	15-19	not a direct quote
4	Eph_2,1-3	nt	Eph 2,1-3	not a direct quote

```
def analyse(filename):
    '''Opens a file specified by the filename, including the directory and creates dataframe for the respective f
    this function analyses the chapter with regard to our criteria: 1) Length of the text 2) direct bible quote 3
    #Öffnen der Datei "filename"
    file_title = filename.split(".")[0]
    with open(filename, 'r') as f:
        file = f.read()
    soup = bs.BeautifulSoup(file, 'lxml')
    
    #Wählen aller ref-Elemente, die das Attribut cRef haben
    Refs = soup.select('ref[cRef]')
    # Konvertierung der Daten in data. Dies ist die Grundlage für die Auswertungen
    data = []
```

Abb. 1 und 2: BeautifulSoup-Abfragecode und -ergebnis zum Auffinden der Bibelzitate im Augsburger Interim (1548). BeautifulSoup erfasst alle <ref cRef="{bible">.

---

40 BeautifulSoup ist die Webscraping Bibliothek in Python; https://www.crummy.com/software/BeautifulSoup/ (20.11.2022). Sobald die Edition des Augsburger Interims abgeschlossen ist, wird die Edition selbstverständlich über eine Dateischnittstelle zum Download bereitstehen. Informationen dazu finden sich auf der Projektwebseite eured.de. Die XML-Datei steht unter https://github.com/WunschK/Graz_Bibelstellen (20.11.2022) zum Download bereit.
41 https://pandas.pydata.org/ (20.11.2022)
42 Artikelweise Visualisierungen und Fakten sind auf dem Github-Repository zu finden: https://github.com/WunschK/Graz_Bibelstellen/tree/master/Visualisierungen (22.11.2022).

Diese werden nun als in Quadrupel-Form in eine Liste überführt, deren einzelne Einträge dem Muster (cRef, ›at/nt‹, Kürzel, Zitat) folgen. Ein Eintrag für das Buch Sirach, Kapitel 15, Vers 14, der wörtlich zitiert wurde, steht also wie folgt in der Liste der Bibelstellen:

(›Sir_15,14‹, ›at‹, ›Sir 15,14‹, ›hat in Gott gelassen inn der hand seines eig-nen Raths‹).

Diese Liste wird nun in einen Pandas-Dataframe konvertiert, der die üblichen Analysemöglichkeiten liefert. Die ersten vier Einträge in diesen Dataframe werden mittels head() ausgegeben:

Dieser Dataframe liefert nun die Grundlage für weitere Analysen: Der Gesamttext umfasst 98.764 Zeichen ohne Leerzeichen oder Zeilenumbrüche. Es werden 283 Bibelstellen zitiert:

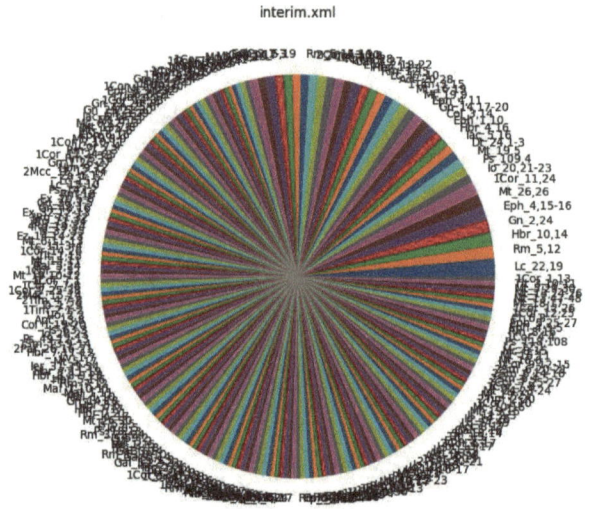

Abb. 3: Visualisierung aller 283 Bibelzitate im Augsburger Interim (1548).

Betrachtet man diese etwas genauer, so fällt ein starkes Übergewicht der Stellen aus dem Neuen Testament auf: 57 Stellen aus dem Alten Testament stehen 226 Stellen aus dem Neuen Testament gegenüber.

Von den 283 erfassten Bibelstellen werden 114 wörtlich zitiert. Zur Ermittlung der wörtlichen Zitate wurde zunächst eine leere Liste erstellt, in der im nächsten Schritt die entsprechenden Zitate eingefügt wurden. Aus den in der fünften Zeile der Funktion analyse() erstellten Refs wurden hierfür alle tei:ref-Elemente extrahiert, deren Eltern-Element, tei:note, ein sibling-Element tei:q hat. Nur wörtliche Zitate werden mittels tei:q erfasst, sodass Vollständigkeit garantiert ist. Anschließend wurde die Länge dieser Liste gezählt. len(qs) liefert als Länge 114 – die Anzahl an wörtlichen Zitaten. Der Text umfasst in seiner Gesamtheit eine Länge von 98.764 Zeichen, ohne Leerzeichen und Zeilenumbrüche. Von diesen 98.764 Zeichen sind 9,84 % wörtlich

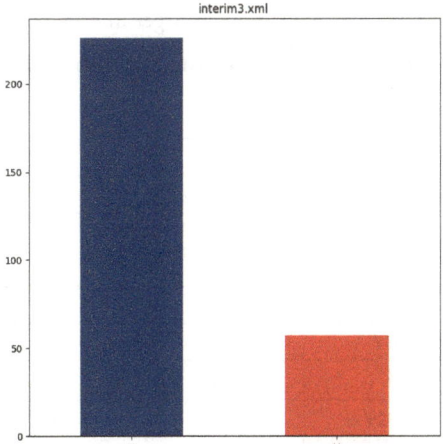

Abb. 4: 226 Stellen aus dem Neuen Testament stehen 57 Stellen aus dem Alten Testament gegenüber.

zitiert: 9.720 Zeichen stehen in wörtlichen Zitaten[43]. Diesen wörtlich zitierten Stellen stehen 169 mehr oder weniger frei zitierte Stellen gegenüber.

c) Inhaltliche Interpretation der Ergebnisse der computergestützten Auswertung

Für eine inhaltliche Interpretation ist es zweckmäßig, aus den Ergebnissen der computergestützten Auswertung zunächst noch die biblischen Parallelüberlieferungen herauszurechnen. Jedes wörtliche Bibelzitat im Text des Interims wird nur einmal gezählt, auch wenn es in der Bibel mehrfach vorkommt und deshalb in unserem Sachkommentar mit mehreren Stellenangaben verzeichnet wurde. Die einschlägigen Anmerkungen lassen sich im XML-Text des Interims mithilfe eines regulären Ausdrucks finden[44]. Bei den indirekten Zitaten ist ein sinnvolles Herausrechnen biblischer Parallelüberlieferungen etwas komplizierter. Nicht mitgezählt werden nur Parallelüberlieferungen im strengen Sinne, die in unserem Kommentar mit »par.« vermerkt wurden. Auch diese Stellen können mit einem regulären Ausdruck gesucht werden[45]. Nach der Bereinigung um die biblischen Parallelstellen ergibt sich die folgende Tabelle:

---

43 Visualisierungen und harte Fakten für jedes Kapitel finden sich im zuvor erwähnten github-Repository unter https://github.com/WunschK/Graz_Bibelstellen/tree/master/Visualisierungen (22.11.2022).

44 Verwendet wurde der folgende reguläre Ausdruck: (?!\Q<note type="annotation"><ref type="biblical"\E(.*?note.*?)(\Q<ref type="biblical"\E).*?\Q</note>\E)\Q<note type="annotation"><ref type="biblical"\E.*?(\Q<ref type="biblical"\E).*?\Q</note>\E.

45 Verwendet wurde der folgende reguläre Ausdruck: (?!\Q<note type="annotation">Vgl. <ref type="biblical"\E(.*?note.*?)(\Q<ref type="biblical"\E).*?\Q</note>\E)\Q<note type="annotation">Vgl. <ref type="biblical"\E.*?(\Qpar. <ref type="biblical"\E).*?\Q</note>\E.

Tab. 1: Bibelzitate im Augsburger Interim (1548).

Artikel	Zeichenzahl (ohne Leerzeichen)	Bibelzitate	davon wörtlich	Anteil der wörtlichen Zitate am Text
Vorrede	8.022	0	0	0 %
1	1.087	2	1	4,14 %
2	2.464	14	1	3,04 %
3	1.823	8	1	9,49 %
4	3.752	13	7	25,16 %
5	591	3	0	0 %
6	2.471	11	2	6,03 %
7	3.829	32	6	8,15 %
8	977	2	0	0 %
9	5.205	18	7	16,83 %
10	2.175	10	6	36,0 %
11	2.049	9	3	8,93 %
12	1.252	2	2	21,73 %
13	1.305	7	2	5,44 %
14	986	0	0	0 %
15	3.251	7	3	4,21 %
16	2.755	6	2	5,12 %
17	3.275	5	4	8,40 %
18	2.406	8	7	16,0 %
19	2.772	4	2	8,77 %
20	2.038	6	6	23,01 %
21	5.977	27	11	24,31 %
22	18.559	42	20	9,86 %
23	4.810	19	8	17,28 %
24	5.009	2	0	0 %
25	957	0	0	0 %
26	8.188	11	2	0,89 %
Schluss	779	0	0	0 %
Gesamt	98.764	268	103	9,84 %

Unter Abzug der biblischen Parallelüberlieferungen enthält das Interim somit insgesamt 268 direkt oder indirekt zitierte Bibelstellen. Die im anonymen Gutachten erhobene Forderung nach einer biblischen Begründung der festgesetzten Lehren wurde also ziemlich umfassend erfüllt. Mit der recht beachtlichen Zahl von 103 wörtlichen Zitaten sollte offenbar, wie in dem anonymen Gutachten verlangt[46], insbesondere auch den Bedürfnissen ungelehrter und unerfahrener Leser Rechnung getragen werden, die auch ohne umfassende Bibelkenntnisse und ohne Heranziehung einer Bibel die Möglichkeit bekommen sollten, sich von der Richtigkeit der im Interim vorgeschriebenen Lehren überzeugen zu lassen.

Die zahlreichen Bibelstellen sind in unserem Korpus von Religionsfrieden ein Spezifikum des Interims. Ansonsten findet sich in den von uns bisher erschlossenen Religionsfriedensregelungen nur noch ein einziges biblisches Zitat, nämlich im Thorenburger Landtagsabschied von 1568. Dort wird die Gewährung religiöser Toleranz in Siebenbürgen in Anlehnung an den Brief des Paulus an die Römer (Röm 10,17) damit begründet, dass der Glaube ein Geschenk Gottes sei und durch das Hören des Wortes Gottes entstehe[47]. Das biblische Zitat dient in diesem Fall also der Begründung der Toleranz, nicht wie im Interim als Beleg für die Festlegung einer bestimmten Lehre.

Betrachtet man im Interim die Zahl der Bibelzitate pro Artikel, so fällt die große Schwankungsbreite auf. Zum Teil ist sie darauf zurückzuführen, dass die Länge der einzelnen Artikel stark variiert. Setzt man die Zahl der Bibelzitate in Relation zur Zeichenzahl der jeweiligen Artikel, zeigen sich aber doch markante Unterschiede. Mit 8,35 Bibelzitaten pro 1.000 Zeichen findet sich im siebten Artikel, der die Bedeutung der Liebe und der guten Werke hervorhebt, die höchste Zitatdichte. Ebenfalls hohe Werte weisen mit 5,68 beziehungsweise 5,08 Bibelzitaten pro 1.000 Zeichen die Artikel zwei und fünf auf. Der erstgenannte Artikel unterstreicht die durch die Erbsünde bedingte Verdorbenheit des Menschen, der zweitgenannte behandelt die Früchte und den Nutzen der Rechtfertigung. Insgesamt lässt sich somit feststellen, dass zur Untermauerung der im Interim enthaltenen Rechtfertigungslehre besonders viele Bibelstellen angeführt werden. Mit 5,36 Bibelzitaten pro 1.000 Zeichen ist die Zitatdichte auch im relativ kurzen 13. Artikel ziemlich hoch, in dem die Unterordnung unter den Primat des Papstes und unter die Autorität der Bischöfe verlangt wird. Überhaupt keine Bibelzitate enthalten hingegen die kurzen Artikel 14 und 25. Artikel 14 bietet allgemeine Ausführungen über die Funktion der Sakramente, Artikel 25 fordert zum häufigen Kommunionempfang auf. Mit 0,40 beziehungsweise 1,34 Bibelzitaten pro 1.000 Zeichen finden sich auch in den Artikeln 24 und 26 vergleichsweise wenige Zitate. Artikel 24 rechtfertigt die Fürbitte für die Verstorbenen bei der Eucharistie und führt zur Begründung zahlreiche Kirchenväterzitate, aber kaum Bibelzitate an. Artikel 26 schreibt die Beibehaltung der herkömmlichen Zeremonien vor, gesteht aber den Laienkelch und die Priester-

---

46 Vgl. oben Anm. 38.
47 Vgl. die auszugsweise Edition des Abschieds in *Armgart (Bearb.)*, Kirchenordnungen 24, Nr. 14, S. 84.

ehe bis zu einer Entscheidung des Konzils zu. Bemerkenswert ist, dass diese zwei bedeutendsten Zugeständnisse des Interims an die Evangelischen gerade nicht biblisch, sondern nur pragmatisch begründet werden[48]. In beiden Fällen wird darauf verwiesen, dass eine Abkehr von der bei den Protestanten üblichen Praxis bei diesen auf starken Widerstand stoßen würde[49]. Änderungen seien daher momentan »one schwere zerrüttung« (»sine gravi rerum perturbatione«) beziehungsweise »one schwere bewegung« (»sine gravi rerum motu«[50]) nicht möglich. Das Interim argumentiert hier also ähnlich wie andere Religionsfrieden, die Zugeständnisse an andere Konfessionen mit der Notwendigkeit der Wahrung des Friedens rechtfertigen[51].

Vergleicht man den prozentualen Anteil der wörtlichen Bibelzitate am Text der einzelnen Artikel des Interims, so lässt sich ebenfalls eine große Schwankungsbreite feststellen. Im zehnten Artikel, der Merkmale der wahren Kirche aufzählt, ist der Anteil wörtlicher Zitate mit 36,0 % besonders hoch. Auch der vierte Artikel, der die Rechtfertigung thematisiert, sowie der 21. Artikel, der das Ehesakrament behandelt, weisen mit 25,16 % beziehungsweise 24,31 % einen hohen Anteil wörtlicher Zitate auf. Der vierthöchste Anteil findet sich mit 23,01 % im 20. Artikel, der sich mit dem Sakrament der Priesterweihe befasst. In fünf Artikeln werden dagegen gar keine wörtlichen Zitate angeführt. Neben den bereits oben erwähnten kurzen Artikeln 14 und 25, die überhaupt keine Bibelzitate enthalten, handelt es sich dabei um die ebenfalls ziemlich kurzen Artikel 5 und 8 sowie um Artikel 24. Der fünfte Artikel, der auf die Früchte und den Nutzen der Rechtfertigung eingeht, bietet allerdings im Verhältnis zu seiner Länge recht viele indirekte Bibelzitate, so dass er, wie oben dargelegt, eine hohe Zitatdichte aufweist. Eine deutlich geringere Dichte indirekter Bibelzitate findet sich im achten Artikel, dem zufolge man das Vertrauen auf die Vergebung der Sünden nicht auf sich selbst, sondern auf das Blut Christi gründen soll. Am signifikantesten ist das Fehlen wörtlicher Bibelzitate im relativ umfangreichen Artikel 24, der die Fürbitte für die Verstorbenen bei der Eucharistie rechtfertigt und dabei auch nur sehr wenige indirekte Bibelzitate verwendet. Mit 0,89 % auffällig gering ist schließlich der Anteil wörtlicher Zitate im 26. Artikel über die Zeremonien.

Zusammenfassend lässt sich feststellen, dass das Interim viele der in ihm vorgeschriebenen Lehren recht ausführlich biblisch zu begründen versucht. Dies gilt insbesondere für die Rechtfertigungslehre, aber unter anderem auch für die Ekklesiologie und Teile der Sakramentenlehre. Das Interim macht sich jedoch das reformatorische Schriftprinzip nicht zu eigen. In ihm werden auch zahlreiche Festlegungen getroffen, besonders im Bereich der Zeremonien, die nicht biblisch be-

48 Vgl. auch *Mehlhausen*, Interim, S. 232.
49 *Ders. (Hg.)*, Interim, Art. 26, S. 142 f.; *Zecherle (Bearb.)*, Interim deutsch, Art. 26, Z. 2184–2191, 2195–2203; *ders. (Bearb.)*, Interim lateinisch, Art. 26, Z. 1774–1779, 1784–1790.
50 *Mehlhausen (Hg.)*, Interim, Art. 26, S. 142 f.; *Zecherle (Bearb.)*, Interim deutsch, Art. 26, Z. 2190, 2198; *ders. (Bearb.)*, Interim lateinisch, Art. 26, Z. 1778, 1785 f.
51 Vgl. etwa den Ersten Kappeler Landfrieden vom 26. Juni 1529 in *Dingel (Hg.)*, Religionsfrieden 1, S. 68, Z. 7–S. 70, Z. 10 und das Mandat Karls V. für einen allgemeinen Frieden im Reich vom 3. August 1532 in ebd., S. 151, Z. 8–S. 152, Z. 1.

gründet werden und sich auch nicht biblisch begründen lassen. Im 11. Artikel wird dementsprechend ausdrücklich festgehalten, dass es neben der Bibel von Christus und den Aposteln stammende verbindliche Traditionen gebe, die durch die Bischöfe überliefert worden seien[52].

III. Resümee

Der letztlich erfolglose Versuch des Interims, mit biblischer Argumentation auf politisch-juristischem Verfahrensweg einen Lehrkonsens herbeizuführen, wurde offenbar nicht nochmals unternommen. Wahrzunehmen, dass es diesen Versuch gab, ist aber für das Verständnis der Geschichte der Religionsfriedensregelungen von großer Bedeutung. Die Einbeziehung des Interims in ein umfassendes digitales Korpus von Religionsfrieden ist dafür ein wichtiger Schritt.

Quellen- und Literaturverzeichnis

Quellen

Armgart, Martin (Bearb.): Die evangelischen Kirchenordnungen des XVI. Jahrhunderts, Bd. 24: Das Fürstentum Siebenbürgen. Das Rechtsgebiet und die Kirche der Siebenbürger Sachsen, bearb. unter Mitwirkung von Karin Meese, Tübingen 2012.
Dingel, Irene (Hg.): Europäische Religionsfrieden der Frühen Neuzeit. Quellen, Bd. 1: Religionsfrieden 1485–1555, Gütersloh 2021 (= Quellen und Forschungen zur Reformationsgeschichte, Bd. 98).
Kohler, Alfred (Hg.): Quellen zur Geschichte Karls V., Darmstadt 1990 (= Ausgewählte Quellen zur deutschen Geschichte der Neuzeit, Bd. 15).
Mehlhausen, Joachim (Hg.): Das Augsburger Interim. Nach den Reichstagsakten deutsch und lateinisch, Neukirchen-Vluyn ²1996 (= Texte zur Geschichte der evangelischen Theologie, Heft 3).
Pfeilschifter, Georg (Hg.): Acta reformationis catholicae ecclesiam Germaniae concernentia saeculi XVI. Die Reformverhandlungen des deutschen Episkopats von 1520 bis 1570, Bd. 5: 1538 bis 1548. 3. Teil erste Hälfte, Regensburg 1973.
Ders. (Hg.): Acta reformationis catholicae ecclesiam Germaniae concernentia saeculi XVI. Die Reformverhandlungen des deutschen Episkopats von 1520 bis 1570, Bd. 6: 1538 bis 1548. 3. Teil zweite Hälfte, Regensburg 1974.
Walder, Ernst (Hg.): Religionsvergleiche des 16. Jahrhunderts, Bd. 2: Januaredikt 1562. Edikt von Nantes 1598, Bern 1946 (= Quellen zur neueren Geschichte, Bd. 8).
Zecherle, Andreas (Bearb.): Augsburger Interim. Deutscher Text, in: *Irene Dingel (Hg.)*, Europäische Religionsfrieden Digital. Eine digitale Edition der politisch-rechtlichen Ordnungen konfessioneller Koexistenz in der Frühen Neuzeit, https://tueditions.ulb.tu-darmstadt.de/v/pa000008-0129 (06.07.2024).

---

52 *Mehlhausen (Hg.)*, Interim, Art. 11, S. 68 f.; *Zecherle (Bearb.)*, Interim deutsch, Art. 11, Z. 755–759; *ders. (Bearb.)*, Interim lateinisch, Art. 11, Z. 609–613.

Zecherle, Andreas (Bearb.): Augsburger Interim. Lateinischer Text, in: *Irene Dingel (Hg.)*, Europäische Religionsfrieden Digital. Eine digitale Edition der politisch-rechtlichen Ordnungen konfessioneller Koexistenz in der Frühen Neuzeit, https://tueditions.ulb.tu-darmstadt.de/v/pa000008-0128 (06.07.2024).

Literatur

Brockmann, Thomas: Die frühneuzeitlichen Religionsfrieden – Normhorizont, Instrumentarium und Probleme in vergleichender Perspektive, in: *Christoph Kampmann u. a. (Hg.)*, L'art de la paix. Kongresswesen und Friedensstiftung im Zeitalter des Westfälischen Friedens, Münster 2011, S. 575–611 (= Schriftenreihe der Vereinigung zur Erforschung der Neueren Geschichte, Bd. 34).

Dingel, Irene: Einleitung, in: dies. (Hg.), Europäische Religionsfrieden der Frühen Neuzeit. Quellen, Bd. 1: Religionsfrieden 1485–1555, Gütersloh 2021, S. xi–xxvii (= Quellen und Forschungen zur Reformationsgeschichte, Bd. 98).

Dingel, Irene: Religionsfrieden, in: dies. u. a. (Hg.), Handbuch Frieden im Europa der Frühen Neuzeit, Berlin/Boston 2021, S. 267–290.

Held, Wieland: 1547. Die Schlacht bei Mühlberg/Elbe. Entscheidung auf dem Wege zum albertinischen Kurfürstentum Sachsen, Beucha 1997.

Lohse, Bernhard: Dogma und Bekenntnis in der Reformation: Von Luther bis zum Konkordienbuch, in: *Carl Andresen/Adolf Martin Ritter (Hg.)*, Handbuch der Dogmen- und Theologie-Geschichte, Bd. 2: Die Lehrentwicklung im Rahmen der Konfessionalität, Göttingen ²1998, S. 1–164 (= UTB für Wissenschaft. Uni-Taschenbücher, Bd. 8161).

Mehlhausen, Joachim: Interim, in: *Gerhard Müller u. a. (Hg.)*, Theologische Realenzyklopädie, Bd. 16, Berlin/New York 1987, S. 230–237.

Moritz, Anja: Interim und Apokalypse. Die religiösen Vereinheitlichungsversuche Karls V. im Spiegel der magdeburgischen Publizistik 1548–1551/52, Tübingen 2009 (= Spätmittelalter, Humanismus, Reformation, Bd. 47).

Niggemann, Ulrich/Wenzel, Christian: Seelenheil und Sicherheit. Einleitende Überlegungen zur Rolle des Religiösen im Sicherheitsdenken der Frühen Neuzeit am Beispiel der französischen Bürgerkriege, in: Historisches Jahrbuch 139 (2019), S. 199–235.

Rabe, Horst: Zur Entstehung des Augsburger Interims 1547/48, in: Archiv für Reformationsgeschichte 94 (2003), S. 6–104.

Rabe, Horst: Reichsbund und Interim. Die Verfassungs- und Religionspolitik Karls V. und der Reichstag von Augsburg 1547/1548, Köln/Wien 1971.

Seresse, Volker: Sicherheit und Seelenheil in der politischen Sprache Heinrichs IV. (ca. 1589–1600), in: Historisches Jahrbuch 139 (2019), S. 236–249.

Wenzel, Christian: »Ruine d'estat«. Sicherheit in den Debatten der französischen Religionskriege 1557–1589, Heidelberg 2020 (= Pariser Historische Studien, Bd. 116), https://doi.org/10.17885/heiup.513 (22.11.2022).

Wolgast, Eike: Religionsfrieden als politisches Problem der frühen Neuzeit, in: Historische Zeitschrift 282 (2006), S. 59–96.

ANDREAS WAGNER (FRANKFURT AM MAIN)

Die Integration von Editionen frühmoderner Rechtstexte in eine Linked-Open-Data-Landschaft

Dieser Beitrag gibt einen Überblick über verschiedene Arbeitsperspektiven der Anreicherung von Quelleneditionen mit semantischen Daten und ihrer Auswertung. Im Zuge eines Durchgangs durch konkrete Beispiele soll dabei auch deutlich werden, welches Gewicht pragmatische Erwägungen und Community Building in der Projektentwicklung haben. Vor diesem Hintergrund werden einige Best Practices von Projekten skizziert, die sich explizit in einen trans-institutionellen Forschungszusammenhang, wie er in gängigen Linked-Open-Data-Szenarien angedacht wird, einzuschreiben suchen.

Der Beitrag ist wie folgt gegliedert: Zuerst erfolgt eine allgemeine Einführung in Prinzipien von Linked Open Data (LOD) (I), danach wird beschrieben, wie entsprechende, semantische Informationen in digitalen Editionen hinterlegt und dort auch wieder extrahiert werden können (II). In der Diskussion einiger mit Rechtstexten befasster Projekte werden zwei idealtypische Arbeitsperspektiven der semantischen Anreicherung digitaler Editionen beschrieben (III). Anschließend werden die damit verbundenen Bedarfe der Organisation von Arbeitsformen und Infrastrukturen verdeutlicht (IV), um schließlich anhand dreier beispielhafter kollaborativer Initiativen zu entwickeln, inwiefern der Gedanke von Linked Open *Usable* Data die Verschränkung projektinterner Organisationsaufgaben mit über den einzelnen Projektkontext hinausreichenden, virtuellen oder tatsächlichen Rezeptions- und Nachnutzungszusammenhängen erfordert (V).

I. Linked Open Data

Anfang der 2000er Jahre hatten Tim Berners-Lee, James Hendler und Ora Lassila mit dem Begriff des *Semantic Web* eine grundlegende Neuerung im Verständnis von über das Internet verfügbaren Ressourcen eingeführt, indem sie auf die Maschinenlesbarkeit der Ressourcen und ihrer Verknüpfungen abstellten. Sie entwickelten ein allgemeines Modell zur Darstellung von Wissen in der Form von dreistelligen Subjekt-Prädikat-Objekt-Aussagen und eine Methode, die Verwendung von Begrifflichkeiten in solchen Darstellungen in der Form maschinenlesbarer Ontologien zu dokumentieren und zwischen verschiedenen Prozessen global zu teilen. Außerhalb akademischer Diskussionen wurde dieses Verständnis jedoch nur zurückhaltend in Datenpublikationen im Internet übernommen. Mit »Linked Data« entwickelte Berners-Lee vor diesem Hintergrund von 2006 bis 2010 eine Handreichung, die in einfacher Weise verschiedene »Qualitätsstufen« von Internet-Datenpublikationen unterschied und für die Berücksichtigung des genannten Verständnisses durch die Befolgung einfacher Empfehlungen warb. Diese Qualitätsstufen und Empfehlungen werden heute zumeist im sogenannten 5-Sterne-Schema wiedergegeben[1]:

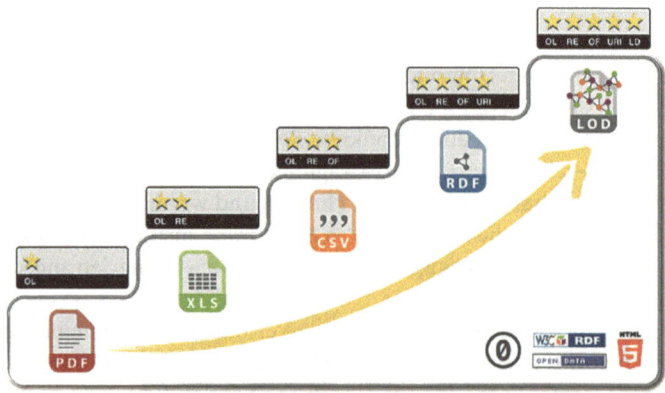

Abb. 1: Stufen des Linked-Open-Data-Modells.

1) Der einfachste Schritt besteht in der Veröffentlichung unter einer Lizenz, die die Nachnutzung der Daten durch andere erlaubt.
2) Dann folgt die Verwendung eines strukturierten Datenformats, so dass die publizierten Inhalte prozessiert (zusammengefasst, visualisiert, analysiert) werden können.
3) Die nächste Stufe ist erreicht, wenn das verwendet Datenformat offen dokumentiert und standardisiert ist, so dass auch die Wahl der Hilfsmittel für die Prozessierung nicht von vornherein eingeschränkt ist.
4) Auf der vierten Stufe werden alle Datenpunkte, Begriffe und Aussagen mit Internet-URIs bezeichnet und die Publikation folgt den Regeln des Semantic Web.
5) Schließlich werden Datenpunkte und Begriffe mit anderen Publikationen zu demselben Gegenstand verknüpft. So sollen Netzwerkeffekte wie reichere Informationen zu den Gegenständen und höhere Auffindbarkeit der Angebote erzielt werden.

In der Publikation wissenschaftlicher Editionen ergibt sich in dieser Perspektive die Aufgabe, die in den eigenen Texten auftretenden Entitäten mit den Informationen anderer Datenanbieter zu verknüpfen – zum Beispiel mit nationalen oder internationalen Normdatenbanken, mit von einer globalen Öffentlichkeit gepflegten Datenbank wie Wikidata oder einfach mit Publikationen verwandter oder gar ko-

---

1 https://5stardata.info/de/ (22.10.2022).

operierender Forschungsprojekte. Insbesondere für bibliographische, biographische oder geographische Daten liegen die Möglichkeiten solcher Verknüpfungen auf der Hand. Allerdings ist diese Aufgabe ja kein Selbstzweck, sondern eröffnet der eigenen Forschung wie der Fachgemeinschaft die Möglichkeit, die Informationen verschiedener Datenbanken zum selben Gegenstand zusammenzutragen und in forschungsrelevanten Abfragen zu kombinieren. Die Möglichkeit, (Ab-)Fragen zu stellen und zu beantworten – etwa nach den wichtigsten Schlagworten zu Publikationen einer bestimmten Zeitperiode von Personen, die an einer Universität lehrten, deren Landesherr einer bestimmten Konfession angehörte –, ist für ideengeschichtliche Forschung verschiedener Disziplinen eine faszinierende Aussicht[2].

II. Semantische Daten als Annotationen in digitalen Editionen

Zur Frage, wie solche Informationen in digitalen Editionen hinterlegt werden können, haben sich durchaus bereits Standards und Best Practices etabliert: Zunächst implizieren die verwendeten TEI-Elemente ja selbst semantische Informationen (durch ihren Elementtyp, das @*type*-Attribut usw.) wie etwa, dass der durch sie markierte Text eine Überschrift, eine Marginalnote, ein Name oder ein Werktitel ist. Textelemente, die eine Entität außerhalb des Textes bezeichnen, wie eine Person oder Organisation, einen Ort, ein Ereignis oder einen Werktitel, können mittels des @*ref*-Attributs auf Ressourcen verweisen, die für die jeweilige Entität Definitionen oder weitere Informationen vorhalten[3]. Diese Informationen lassen sich durch das sogenannte *Semantic Lifting*, also durch Mapping und Extraktion in das für Semantic Web und Linked (Open) Data erforderliche Resource-Description-Framework-Format (RDF) exportieren, wofür ebenfalls geeignete und nutzerfreundliche Werkzeuge zur Verfügung stehen[4]. Anschließend können die Daten in geeigneten Datenbanken (Triple Stores) im Web publiziert werden, wofür zahlreiche Produkte, zum Teil unter freier Lizenz, verfügbar sind[5].

---

2   Das Suchformular der Seite enslaved.org bietet einen Einblick in die Reichhaltigkeit eines Informationsangebots, das derzeit 24 Datenbanken verschiedener Projekte – zu Sklavenschiffen und -auktionen, zu Aufständen, Bestattungen, Militärdiensten und lokale Prosopographien von Sklaven, ehemaligen Sklaven oder Nachkommen von Sklaven – unter einer gemeinsamen Abfrageoberfläche zugänglich macht: https://enslaved.org/advancedSearch (25.10.2022).

3   Vgl. Abschnitt »13.1.1 Linking Names and Their Referents« der P5: Guidelines for Electronic Text Encoding and Interchange, Version 4.4.0, https://tei-c.org/release/doc/tei-p5-doc/en/html/ND.html (25.10.2022).

4   Zwar ist die Entwicklung eigener Extraktionsprozesse mit XSLT oder XQuery auch nicht allzu kompliziert, es haben sich jedoch Tools wie vor allem der XTriples-Webdienst (*Grüntgens/Schrade*, Data repositories in the Humanities and the Semantic Web) oder das X3ML Toolkit (*Theodoridou u. a.*, X3ML Toolkit) bewährt.

5   Eine Übersicht etwa unter https://en.wikipedia.org/wiki/Comparison_of_triplestores (25.10.2022). Zum Prozess insgesamt vgl. *Wettlaufer*, Der nächste Schritt?, und *Vogeler*, The ›assertive edition‹. Auch die Bemühungen, die markierten Textpassagen selbst mit individuellen URIs zu versehen

Anders als in vielen anderen Forschungsfeldern ist man in historischen Editionen jedoch mit der Schwierigkeit konfrontiert, dass etablierte Werkzeuge zur automatischen Erstellung von Annotationen kaum befriedigende Ergebnisse erzielen. Zum einen machen historische Texte mit variierender Orthographie, zahlreichen und unregelmäßigen Abkürzungen und grundsätzlich spärlicher verfügbaren Trainingsdaten die Extraktion von Personen, Organisationen, Orten, Ereignissen usw. schwieriger[6]. Zum anderen sind historische Fachdisziplinen wie Rechts-, Ideen-, Sozial- und Wirtschaftsgeschichte und andere oftmals in erster Linie an anderen Informationsgehalten interessiert. Für die automatische Erkennung und Identifikation von Aktivitäten und Kommunikationen, Ideen und Vorstellungen, Referenzen und Argumenten, Beziehungen und Rollen usw. sind die Werkzeuge noch keineswegs so ausgereift wie die für die Erkennung von Personen, Organisationen, Orten und Ereignissen. So müssen Editionsprojekte, die sich in einer historischen Forschungsperspektive verorten, ihre Annotationskategorien zumeist allererst klären und die Annotationen oftmals aufwändig von Hand in die edierten Texte einbringen.

Der Aufwand manueller Annotationen ist allerdings so hoch, dass in der Regel für eine umfassende Annotation die zeitlichen und personellen Ressourcen nicht zur Verfügung stehen und stattdessen gut abgewogen werden muss, welche(n) Themenbereich(e) die Editionsbemühungen primär erschließen sollen. Weitere Aspekte ausdrücklich zu kodieren, muss dann der Nachnutzung oder Anschlussprojekten überlassen werden. Diese Abwägungsprozesse und wie sich die entsprechenden Entscheidungen in der Projektarbeit sowie im Ergebnis digitaler Edition widerspiegeln, soll im Folgenden beispielhaft vorgestellt werden.

III. Beispielszenarien

1. Text-Editionen und Referenzen zwischen Texten

Das Max-Planck-Institut für Rechtsgeschichte und Rechtstheorie ist in eine ganze Reihe von Projekten involviert, die frühmoderne Rechtstexte (im weiteren Sinne) betreffen und editorische Aspekte aufweisen. Eine erste Gruppe von Projekten lässt sich dadurch charakterisieren, dass »doktrinäre« oder pragmatische Texte

---

und so zum Gegenstand (oder Subjekt) von RDF-Aussagen machen zu können – diskutiert in *Wagner*, What's in a URI?; und zuletzt in *Cayless/Romanello*, Towards Resolution Services for Text URIs –, ist in dieser Perspektive zu sehen und für historische Forschung essenziell, da diese grundsätzlich die Quellen aller Einsichten und Aussagen nachzuweisen hat.

6 Dies gilt umso mehr für die *Identifikation* der erwähnten Entitäten: viele Mechanismen zur Verknüpfung von Erwähnungen mit Einträgen in Normdatenbanken sind darauf angewiesen, dass ein entsprechender Eintrag bei Wikipedia o. ä. vorhanden ist. Für aktuelle Entwicklungen auf dem Feld der Erkennung und Identifikation von sogenannten *Named Entities* in historischen Texten vgl. *Ehrmann u. a.*, Extended Overview of HIPE-2022.

behandelt werden: Hier wird nicht verbindliches Recht untersucht, sondern Texte der Rechtstheorie, der Kommentierung und der Ratgeberliteratur (für Kaufleute oder Beichtväter zum Beispiel). Das Projekt »Die Schule von Salamanca. Eine digitale Quellensammlung und ein Wörterbuch ihrer juristisch-politischen Sprache«[7] ediert 116, zum Teil mehrbändige und sehr umfangreiche, lateinische und spanischsprachige, gedruckte Werke mit politischem oder juristischem Charakter aus dem Umfeld der sogenannten Schule von Salamanca des 16. und 17. Jahrhunderts. Die Textedition und das diese begleitende Wörterbuch sind als Beitrag zur Erforschung der Frage zu verstehen, welchergestalt der mit »Schule von Salamanca« bezeichnete Diskussionszusammenhang war und wie er – nicht zuletzt unter dem Eindruck und in Auseinandersetzung mit den Kräften und Entwicklungen der Kolonien – den abendländischen Rechtsdiskurs geprägt hat. Das Projekt »HyperAzpilcueta«[8] erfasst verschiedene gedruckte Auflagen eines Beichthandbuches aus diesem Zusammenhang – Martín de Azpilcuetas »Manual de Confessores« –, die vom Autor selbst übersetzte und gleichzeitig zum Teil weitgehend überarbeitete und an verschiedene Bedarfe angepasste Versionen desselben Textes darstellen. Das Projekt zielt darauf ab, die verschiedenen Ziele, die mit den unterschiedlichen Editionen verfolgt wurden, und die dafür in Anspruch genommenen Mittel herauszuarbeiten, um Prozesse der Bildung und Weiterbildung normativen Wissens in der Frühmoderne zu veranschaulichen.

Die Erwähnung von Personen ist in beiden Projekten von zentralem Interesse, insbesondere, insofern sie mit Referenzen auf andere Werke verbunden sind: Im einen Fall stellt sich die Frage, ob sich die ›Schule‹ über bestimmte Muster in den Literaturreferenzen bildet. Im anderen Fall ist zu untersuchen, ob sich für die Anpassung an ein bestimmtes – z. B. akademisches – Zielpublikum oder für die Reaktion auf Diskussionen in der Literatur oder auf neue Normen – z. B. die Beschlüsse des Konzils von Trient – charakteristische Muster von Referenzen abzeichnen. Beide Projekte investieren daher erhebliche Ressourcen in die manuelle Annotation von Autoren und Referenzen und loten kontinuierlich Möglichkeiten aus, mit solchen selbst angelegten Trainingsdaten weitere Annotationen desselben Typs ab irgendeinem Zeitpunkt (halb-)automatisch erstellen zu können. Abstrakte Konzepte und Argumente, aber auch Orte, Ereignisse und Organisationen wären gewiss ebenfalls faszinierende Gegenstände von Annotationen in diesen Textsammlungen – die Texte spiegeln ja auch in vielfältiger Weise die geographische Dimension der kolonialen und ökonomischen Entwicklung wieder und eröffnen Einblicke in die Rolle, die kirchliche und politische administrative Einheiten und Funktionen wie die Casa de Contratación, die Protectoría de indios, Ostindien-Kompanien oder religiöse Orden gespielt haben. Aus den genannten Gründen kann der Aufwand, diese Annotationen in der digitalen Edition ebenfalls anzulegen, jedoch nicht betrieben werden.

---

7   https://salamanca.school/ (25.10.2022).
8   https://www.lhlt.mpg.de/forschungsprojekt/hyperazpilcueta (25.10.2022).

Für das Semantic Lifting kommen in diesen Projekten mithin also folgende Informationen und Vokabulare in Frage:
- Metadaten wie Drucker, Veröffentlichungsdatum usw., die im *teiHeader* kodiert sind und in Vokabularen wie Dublin Core[9] oder SPAR/FaBiO[10] ausgedrückt werden
- Strukturdaten wie die Verschachtelung, Typ, Umfang und Titel von Werkteilen wie Kapiteln, Unterkapiteln, Disputationen usw., die im verwendeten TEI-Markup explizit z. B. durch @*type*-Attribute, aber auch implizit, durch die hierarchische Struktur der Elemente, enthalten sind und etwa in der »Document Component Ontology«[11] ausgedrückt werden können
- ausdrücklich hinterlegte Personen und Werktitel und andere Verweise, die im Rahmen von Literaturreferenzen vorkommen und als *persName*-, *title*- oder *ref*-Elemente kodiert sind, deren @*ref*-Attribut auf bibliographische Normdatenbanken wie den Thesaurus des Consortium of European Research Libraries (CERL)[12], die »Gemeinsame Normdatei« (GND) der Deutschen Nationalbibliothek[13], den Online Computer Library Center (OCLC) Worldcat[14] oder das »Virtual International Authority File« (VIAF)[15] verweisen. Wir verwenden aktuell zwei verschiedene Prädikate, je nachdem, ob die Verweise in unseren Texten innerhalb von ausdrücklichen Zitaten (*cit*-Elementen) stehen oder nicht: im einen Fall verwenden wir *includesQuotationFrom*, im anderen Fall *citesAsRelated*, beide aus dem SPAR/CiTO-Vokabular[16].
- möglicherweise einige nicht systematisch erfasste ausdrücklich hinterlegte Ortsangaben, die in *placeName*-Elementen kodiert sind, deren @*ref*-Attribute auf die Einträge in Normdatenbanken wie den »Getty Thesaurus of Geographic Names« (TGN)[17] verweisen, und die etwa als Gegenstand des *mentions*-Prädikat des schema.org/Books-Vokabulars[18] von Werken oder Passagen prädiziert werden können

```
@prefix rdf:    <http://www.w3.org/1999/02/22-rdf-syntax-ns#> .
@prefix rdfs:   <http://www.w3.org/2000/01/rdf-schema#> .
@prefix fabio:  <http://purl.org/spar/fabio/> .
@prefix po:     <http://www.essepuntato.it/2008/12/pattern#> .
@prefix book:   <http://schema.org/Book/> .
@prefix cito:   <http://purl.org/spar/cito/> .
@prefix doco:   <http://purl.org/spar/doco/> .
```

9 https://www.dublincore.org/specifications/dublin-core/dcmi-terms/ (25.10.2022).
10 http://www.sparontologies.net/ontologies/fabio (25.10.2022).
11 http://www.sparontologies.net/ontologies/doco (25.10.2022).
12 http://thesaurus.cerl.org/ (25.10.2022).
13 https://gnd.network/Webs/gnd/EN/Home/home_node.html (25.10.2022).
14 https://www.worldcat.org/ (25.10.2022).
15 https://viaf.org/ (25.10.2022).
16 http://www.sparontologies.net/ontologies/cito (25.10.2022).
17 http://www.getty.edu/research/tools/vocabularies/tgn/index.html (25.10.2022).
18 https://schema.org/Book (25.10.2022).

```
@prefix sal:      <https://id.salamanca.school/texts/>.
@prefix cerl:     <http://thesaurus.cerl.org/record/>.
@prefix viaf:     <http://viaf.org/viaf/>.
@prefix tgn:      <http://vocab.getty.edu/tgn/>.

sal:W0004 rdf:type          fabio:work;
fabio:hasShortTitle         »Tratado de Cuentas«;
fabio:hasCreator            viaf:110309881;
fabio:hasPublisher          cerl:cni00098583;
fabio:hasPublicationYear    "1552";
fabio:hasLanguage           "Latin";
rdfs:seeAlso                <https://www.salamanca.school/work.html?wid=W0004>.

sal:W0004:1 rdf:type    doco:section;
rdfs:label              "Pars ›Primera Parte‹";
po:isContainedBy        sal:W0004;
book:mentions           tgn:7024097.
```

Abb. 2: Meta-, Struktur-, Zitationsdaten (1).

Interessant zu bemerken ist hierbei, dass Zitationen, da sie mehr Informationen involvieren, als in dreistelligen Aussagen ausgedrückt werden können – Welcher Text zitiert? Welcher Text wird zitiert? Um welche Art der Zitation handelt es sich? –, in der Weise der sog. *Reifizierung* ausgedrückt werden, d.h. es wird ein Zitations-»Ereignis« postuliert, das selbst zum Subjekt dreistelliger Aussagen wird:

```
@prefix rdf:   <http://www.w3.org/1999/02/22-rdf-syntax-ns#>.
@prefix cito:  <http://purl.org/spar/cito/>.
@prefix sal:   <https://id.salamanca.school/texts/>.
@prefix cerl:  <http://thesaurus.cerl.org/record/>.

blankNode rdf:type                  cito:Citation;
cito:hasCitationCharacterization    cito:citesAsRelated;
cito:hasCitingEntity                sal:W0004:1;
cito:hasCitedEntity                 cerl:cni00098583.
```

Abb. 3: Zitationsdaten (2).

Die Projekte sind in ihrer Umsetzung dieser Vorgaben mit kleinen wie mit großen Herausforderungen konfrontiert, die nur zum Teil technisch bedingt sind: Ein Beispiel für ein minder dramatisches Problem ist, dass alle Erwähnungen von Personen in dieses Schema der Referenz-Relationen gepresst werden: Wenn also politische Akteure wie Könige und Fürsten, biblische Figuren wie Noah und Salomon oder auch nur fiktive Personen in juristischen Fallbeispielen wie »Max Mustermann« (in diesen Texten zumeist »Petrus« und »Paulus«) erwähnt werden, werden diese Erwähnungen etwas irreführend als »Zitationen«, nicht als »Erwähnungen« registriert. Ein gewichtigeres Problem ist, dass auch diese reduzierte Anreicherung mit Daten von Literaturreferenzen immer noch beträchtliche manuelle Arbeit verlangt und – jenseits einiger Experimente zu automatischer Erkennung von Personennamen – nur langsam voranschreitet. Die eigentlich angezielte analytische Arbeit der Extraktion von Zitationsnetzwerken und der Identifikation von Zitationsmustern konnte so noch gar nicht begonnen werden.

2. Datenbanken normativer Regelungen und ihrer Gegenstände

Eine ganz andere Gruppe von Projekten beschäftigt sich mit Texten, die tatsächlich rechtsverbindliche Inhalte dokumentieren. Wenn solche Texte auf andere Texte referieren, dann oft weniger in der Form der Referenz auf Argumente, sondern in einer technischen oder »performativen«, die Rechtsgeltung direkt betreffenden Weise, etwa als Konkretisierung, Ausnahme oder Änderung einer früheren oder allgemeineren Norm, oder als Ausweis der Rechtsgrundlage bzw. der Legitimation der vorliegenden Norm. Mehr als die textuelle Gestalt und Verfassung solcher Dokumente ist die im Text ausgedrückte normative Dimension einer sozialen Praxis von Interesse. Das Projekt »Repertorium der Policeyordnungen«[19] hat zu einer Zeit, als an die Digitalisierung der Quellen selbst noch nicht zu denken war, mit ungeheurem personellem Aufwand in zahlreichen Archiven Daten aus den Dokumenten extrahiert und in einer mittlerweile zwölfbändigen Buchreihe publiziert und stellt diese aktuell nach und nach in einer online durchsuchbaren Datenbank zur Verfügung[20]. Es erlaubt – obwohl kein Editionsprojekt – Rückschlüsse auf einige der wichtigsten Informationen, die für historische und rechtshistorische Erforschung von Rechtstexten von Interesse sind. Ein weiteres Projekt am Max-Planck-Institut für Rechtsgeschichte und Rechtstheorie hat sich allerdings tatsächlich die digitale Publikation von Rechtstexten im engeren Sinne zum Ziel gesetzt: Das Projekt »Nichtstaatliches Recht der Wirtschaft«[21] erfasst rechtlich verbindliche Verhaltensregulierungen im Kontext industrieller Arbeitsverhältnisse: Tarifverträge, Haus- und Fabrikordnungen, Musterarbeitsverträge für Auszubildende, Satzungen betrieblicher Vorsorge- und Sozialeinrichtungen usw. Allerdings steht hier nicht die philologische Genauigkeit einer klassischen digitalen Edition im Fokus – OCR-Fehler werden so weit als möglich korrigiert, aber auch die Emendation von Schreibfehlern in den Originalen wird in der Regel stillschweigend vorgenommen.

Obwohl nun die Form, in der die als relevant angesehenen Daten hinterlegt werden, sich unterscheidet – im letztgenannten Fall als Textannotationen, im »Policeyordnungs«-Projekt als Datenfelder einer relationalen Datenbank – sind beide genannten Projekte vor allem daran interessiert, die Regulierungstätigkeit als sol-

---

19 https://www.lhlt.mpg.de/forschungsprojekt/repertorium-der-policeyordnungen (25.10.2022).
20 https://policey.lhlt.mpg.de/ (25.10.2022).
21 https://www.lhlt.mpg.de/forschungsprojekt/nichtstaatliches-recht-der-wirtschaft (25.10.2022).

che zu erschließen. Wer beschließt und verkündet eine Verhaltensnormierung aufgrund welcher Autorität? Welche Jurisdiktion bzw. Reichweite hat die Norm und wer ist als Adressat angesprochen? Wird eher ein Verbots- oder ein Berechtigungs-»Mechanismus« verwendet? Mit welchen Normen interagiert die vorliegende Norm auf welche Weise (als Ausnahme, Rechtsgrundlage o. ä.)? Und natürlich: welcher Bereich des individuellen oder sozialen Verhaltens wird reguliert, welche Rollen werden thematisiert und definiert? Im Falle des Projekts »Nichtstaatliches Recht« haben wir einen Katalog für diese Informationskategorien angelegt, der sich in sechs Bereiche aufteilt: Definitionen und Regelungsbegriffe, Aktivitäten, Rollen, Objekte und Räume, präskriptive Aspekte und Meta- bzw. reflexive Angaben. Gewiss ist neben diesen »norm-internen« Informationen auch die Verortung der Normen in einem historischen, geographischen und kulturellen Kontext unabdingbar, diese geschieht in erster Linie durch die Metadaten der Normtexte wie Entstehungsdatum, Firma und Firmensitz, Typ der Norm (Fabrikordnung, Satzung eines Sozialwerks, Tarifvertrag usw.). Im »Policeyordnungen«-Projekt werden Angaben zum Gesetzgeber und zum Territorium, zum Datum und zum Typ oder zur Form des Gesetzes (Mandat, Marktordnung, Befehl usw.), zur Reichweite und zu Bezügen zu anderen Gesetzen, aber vor allem zu Regelungsmaterien erfasst, die in einem umfangreichen, in einem aufwändigen und langwierigen Prozess erstellten Katalog systematisch geordnet sind[22].

Da hier vor allem die Anreicherung von digitalen Editionen im Zentrum der Aufmerksamkeit steht, sei kurz erwähnt, wie im Projekt »Nichtstaatliches Recht der Wirtschaft« die entsprechenden Annotationen in unserem TEI/XML aussehen:
- Begriffe werden mit *term* annotiert und im jeweiligen @*ana*-Attribut wird eine (Kurzform der) URI des Normdatensatzes des Begriffs hinterlegt.
- Geplant ist eine Flexibilisierung der annotierbaren Textpassagen: außer einzelnen Wörtern oder Wortkombinationen auch ganze Absätze oder längere Textpassagen. Das @*ana*-Attribut wird dann auch in *p*- und *anchor*-Elementen Verwendung finden, das ist in unserer Annotationsumgebung aber aktuell noch nicht möglich.
- Was die Normdatensätze für unsere Klassifikationsbegriffe angeht, so haben wir für das Klassifikationsschema ein eigenes, LOD-fähiges SKOS-Vokabular publiziert, so dass das Begriffsschema ebenso wie jeder einzelne Begriff als persistente URI angesprochen werden kann[23].

Dieses Verfahren wurde auch vor dem Hintergrund der zu erwartenden Auswertungsszenarien und ihrer Alternativen gewählt. Als eine solche Alternative seien vor allem Ansätze genannt, die rechtliche Regeln – Gebote, Verbote, Rechte usw. – als solche formal zu beschreiben und aus Rechtstexten zu extrahieren suchen[24]. Dies

---

22 https://w3id.org/rhonda/polmat/scheme (25.10.2022).
23 Z. B. https://w3id.org/mpilhlt/worktime/a1.7 (25.10.2022).
24 Als Datenmodell und Beschreibungssprache kann hier zum Beispiel LegalRuleML (*Palmirani u. a.*, LegalRuleML) dienen, welches genau für diesen Bedarf entwickelt wurde.

würde gezielte Abfragen danach erlauben, welche Strafen zum Beispiel zur Sanktionierung bestimmter Vergehen vorgesehen waren oder welche Ausnahmen für eine bestimmte Rechtsregel galten. Es würde jedoch eine sehr komplexe Erfassung nicht nur der in den Texten vorkommenden Komponenten, sondern auch deren Relationen zueinander erfordern, ob z. B. bestimmte Räumlichkeiten den Gegenstand oder eine Qualifikation eines Verbots, bestimmte Rollen die Adressaten oder die mit der Durchsetzung der Norm beauftragten Instanzen beschreiben usw. Das schien uns im Projektrahmen nicht leistbar und auch eigentlich nicht den uns vorschwebenden Forschungsfragen entsprechend[25]. So zielt unser Projekt auf einfache Suchen nach dem bloßen Vorkommen bestimmter Schlagwörter oder Schlagwort-Kombinationen ab, und die Ergebnisliste ist eine Reihe von relevanten Absätzen aus Normtexten, die sich nach Meta- und Kontext-Daten wie Datum, Region oder Dokumenttyp sortieren oder filtern lassen. Auch hier hat sich gezeigt, dass die begrenzten Kapazitäten für manuelle Annotationen nur Raum für ein Proof of Concept lassen: Wir konnten manuelle Annotationen vornehmen, die die grundsätzliche technische Realisierung und die sich durch die Annotationen eröffnenden neuen Abfragemöglichkeiten demonstrieren, mussten uns dabei aber auf ein spezielles Phänomen und eine Teilmenge der Texte konzentrieren und weit hinter dem Ideal einer vollumfänglichen Nutzung unseres Begriffsschemas und der Anreicherung des gesamten Korpus zurückbleiben[26].

IV. Workflow, Tooling und Infrastruktur

1. Konkretisierung der Projektausrichtung

Neben den Unterschieden in der Natur der edierten Texte sind pragmatische Entscheidungen während des Projektverlaufs ganz entscheidend für die Entwicklung der Arbeitsperspektiven, die Konkretisierung der Forschungsfragen und -methoden und schließlich für das wissenschaftliche Profil der Projektergebnisse. Gerade bei Strategien der Anreicherung von digital edierten Texten mit semantischen Daten kann die Reichhaltigkeit der Texte, und damit die Konkretisierung von Art und Umfang der »zu hebenden« Informationen oft erst abgeschätzt werden, nachdem eine Weile intensiv mit und in den Texten gearbeitet wurde. Diese »Lernkurve« wird auch dadurch erweitert, dass Mitarbeitende während der Projektlaufzeit zum Projekt hinzustoßen und Forschungsinteressen und -fragen, Kompetenzen und

---

25 Vgl. jedoch *Martín-Chozas/Revenko*, Thesaurus Enhanced Extraction of Hohfeld's Relations, und zuletzt *Liga*, Hybrid Artificial Intelligence to Extract Patterns and Rules. Für ein historisches Projekt, das sich einer vergleichbaren Aufgabe auf manuelle Weise annimmt – und dabei Ansprüche an die Edition der Quellen ermäßigt –, vgl. *Zbíral u. a.*, Model the source first.
26 Vgl. dazu *Ebbertz u. a.*, New Approaches in Labor Law History.

Methoden und zum Teil wissenschaftliche Planungen eigenen Rechts einbringen. So ist etwa an studentische und wissenschaftliche Hilfskräfte zu denken, die oft genug digitale oder andere Kompetenzen mitbringen und so der Gruppe bestimmte Fragestellungen oder auch technische Erleichterungen für diese, oder eben für jene, Arbeitsschritte eröffnen. Mit den Planungen eigenen Rechts sind hingegen vor allem Doktorandinnen und Doktoranden angesprochen, die sich im Projektrahmen ein eigenständiges Thema suchen und deren besondere Interessen einen großen Einfluss auf die Arbeitsmethoden des Gesamtprojekts haben können.

Insbesondere, wenn sich bei der Konkretisierung der Anreicherungsbedarfe, der genaueren Einschätzung des Aufwands für die »technische« Textaufbereitung und der ggf. anwachsenden Menge an Texten, herausstellt, dass Abstriche bei den Projektzielen gemacht werden müssen – entweder gegenüber der ursprünglichen Planung oder auch *zugunsten* der ursprünglichen Planung, bei der Nicht-Verfolgung wichtiger neuer Einsichten – sind diese pragmatischen Faktoren und die Revision der Projektziele Themen, die regelmäßig mit Projektbeiräten, -förderern u. ä. diskutiert werden (sollten), da es aus strukturellen Gründen nie möglich sein wird, sie zum Zeitpunkt der Projektplanung und des Projektstarts zu berücksichtigen.

Ich habe oben beschrieben, welche Schwerpunkte in unseren Projekten gewählt wurden und wie sich das auf die von den Mitarbeitenden durchzuführenden Aufgaben der manuellen Textannotation oder des Research Software Engineering (RSE) auswirkt. Mit RSE ist neben der Entwicklung technischer Alternativen für eine automatische Anreicherung von Texten übrigens auch die Entwicklung von Arbeitsmitteln für die manuelle Annotation gemeint, und auch dies ist ein beträchtliches Arbeitspaket.

2. Tooling und Infrastruktur

Angesichts des in den meisten Fällen erforderlichen manuellen Annotationsaufwands ist die Integration leicht und effizient nutzbarer Funktionen in komfortable Arbeitsumgebungen ein wichtiges Element der LOD-Strategie der Projekte. Die in III.1. genannten Projekte realisieren dies mit einem eigens entwickelten Framework für den oXygen XML-Editor[27]. Dort lassen sich Kommandos zum Auszeichnen einer markierten Passage als Personenname oder Werktitel leicht aus dem Kontextmenü, der Symbolleiste oder per Tastenkürzel aufrufen. Noch nicht abgeschlossen ist hier die Verbindung zu relevanten Normdatenbanken ebenso wie die (von der Annotationsumgebung auch unabhängige) Entwicklung automatischer Auszeichnungsmechanismen.

Für die Entwicklung oder Anpassung einer Software für die unter III.2. genannten Projekte waren hingegen keine vergleichbaren Kapazitäten eingeplant. Dort greifen wir daher stärker auf Lösungen ›von der Stange‹ zurück und bedienen uns

---

27 https://www.oxygenxml.com/xml_editor.html (25.10.2022), bzw. für die angepassten Frameworks https://www.oxygenxml.com/xml_editor/extensible_xml_editor_frameworks.html (25.10.2022).

für Annotation und Publikation der Quellen der freien Software TEI Publisher[28], die für die häufigsten Bedarfe von digitalen Editionen fertige Zusammenstellungen von Webseitenelementen bietet und so ohne oder mit nur geringem Anpassungsaufwand die Publikation von TEI-basierten digitalen Editionen erlaubt. Seit der Version 7.10, die im August 2021 erschienen ist, verfügt der TEI Publisher auch über eine Annotationsfunktion, eine automatische Annotation von Entitäten ist in Vorbereitung für die Version 8[29]. Da die Annotationsfunktionalität zwar auf externe Normdatenbanken zurückgreifen konnte, diese aber nur über je individuell programmierte spezifische APIs ansprechen konnte, haben wir eine Schnittstelle für das generische Reconciliation-API-Protokoll entwickelt[30], die unterdessen in den TEI Publisher integriert wurde. Wir nutzen die skohub.io- und github-pages-Plattformen, um unser Vokabular als Webseite, LOD-Angebot und in einer Reconciliation API anzubieten und im TEI Publisher als Annotations-Vokabular zu verwenden[31].

Wenn in TEI Publisher eine Textpassage markiert und der entsprechend konfigurierte Abgleich mit einem so publizierten SKOS-Schema aufgerufen wird, wird der entsprechende Katalog – je nach Konfiguration des Servers – nach Vorkommnissen des markierten Textes oder ähnlicher Textstrings in den vorgehaltenen Begriffen, ihren Synonymen, Beschreibungen, Definitionen und Beispielen der verschiedenen Sprachen durchsucht, eine Liste von Kandidaten präsentiert und bei der Auswahl eines Begriffs die entsprechende ID in das @ana-Attribut eines neu erstellten *term*-Elements, das den markierten Text umgibt, eingetragen. So können sehr flüssig Annotationen vorgenommen werden, die direkt mit Normdatensätzen verbunden sind und leicht zu entsprechenden semantischen Daten extrahiert werden können.

Die beiden Ansätze (oXygen XML Editor mit einem angepassten Framework und TEI Publisher mit Normdatenbanken)[32] machen deutlich, dass für projektspezifische Annotationstasks der Aufbau einer Arbeitsumgebung oder Infrastruktur eine nicht zu vernachlässigende Größe ist, insbesondere wenn projektspezifische Annotationen und Annotationsschemata als Ressourcen in Linked-Data-Szena-

28 https://teipublisher.com/ (25.10.2022).
29 https://teipublisher.com/exist/apps/tei-publisher/doc/blog/tei-publisher-710.xml (25.10.2022), bzw. https://www.e-editiones.org/posts/names-sell-named-entity-recognition-in-tei-publisher/ (25.10.2022).
30 https://reconciliation-api.github.io/specs/latest/ (25.10.2022).
31 https://w3id.org/rhonda/polmat/scheme (25.10.2022), bzw. https://w3id.org/mpilhlt/worktime/scheme (25.10.2022). Es handelt sich um persistente Identifier für Begriffe, Begriffsschemata und Dienste. Vgl. *Romein/Wagner/Van Zundert*, Classifaction Schema.
32 Weitere Alternativen sind Annotationsplattformen wie CaTMA (http://catma.de/ [25.10.2022]), oder INCEpTION (https://inception-project.github.io/ [17.06.2024]), KI-Trainingsumgebungen wie Doccano (https://doccano.github.io/doccano/ [25.10.2022]) oder das kommerzielle TagTog (https://www.tagtog.com/ [25.10.2022]), aber auch QDA-Systeme wie Taguette (https://www.taguette.org/ [25.10.2022]) oder die kommerziellen Angebote MaxQDA (https://www.maxqda.com/ [25.10.2022]) bzw. Atlas.TI (https://atlasti.com/ [25.10.2022]). Diese entfernen sich aber zum Teil deutlich von TEI/XML und dem Arbeits- und Datenfluss der Vorbereitung einer digitalen Edition, weshalb sie für uns nicht in Frage kamen.

rien eingebunden und ausgespielt werden sollen. Außerdem können die durchwachsenen Erfahrungen mit manuellen Annotationen selbst bei reduzierten Zielen Anlass geben, über die Rolle automatischer Annotationen nachzudenken. Das Beschreiten dieses Weges sollte jedoch einerseits die nötigen Kapazitäten zum Aufbau komplexer automatischer Mechanismen in der Projektstruktur vorsehen, andererseits aber mit der frühzeitigen, transparenten Diskussion der Frage einhergehen, ob und wie weit von Qualitätsanforderungen, wie sie durch manuelle Annotation (idealerweise) erzielt werden können, Abstand genommen werden kann.

V. Community und Ausblick

Die oben angesprochenen Themen der Infrastruktur, der Bezugnahme auf Normdaten und der Föderation von Daten in Linked-Data-Szenarien brechen das Feld der Projektorganisation oft über die lediglich inneren Abläufe, Regeln und Begrifflichkeiten hinaus auf zur Entwicklung einer projekt-, institutionen- und ggf. disziplinübergreifenden Forschungsgemeinschaft. Diese drei Aspekte sollen abschließend beleuchtet und anhand von Beispielen guter Praxis illustriert werden, bevor ein resümierender Ausblick versucht wird.

In technischer und infrastruktureller Hinsicht wird seit 2018 unter dem Stichwort LOUD (Linked Open *Usable* Data) eine stärkere Berücksichtigung der Rezeptions- und Weiterverarbeitungsbedingungen des je eigenen Datenangebots empfohlen[33]. Die in diesem Rahmen einschlägigen Prinzipien betreffen die Dokumentation und Selbstdokumentation der ausgelieferten Daten ebenso wie die Einfachheit der Protokolle und Schnittstellen, und beziehen sich explizit auf die Ausrichtung an Use Cases[34]. Für deren Modellierung ist der Austausch mit einem offenen Kreis prospektiv interessierter Kolleginnen und Kollegen und deren technischen und fachwissenschaftlichen Bedarfen entscheidend, was die zunächst technische und konzeptionelle Herausforderung um eine soziale Komponente erweitert.

Im Hinblick auf die Etablierung von projektübergreifend nachnutzbaren Normvokabularen und -daten liegt auf der Hand, dass ein solches Normangebot sich nicht allein aus der Sammlung von Daten bzw. Begriffen und stabilen und eindeutigen Identifiern, sondern auch aus deren guten Zugänglichkeit und Integrierbarkeit in vielseitige Verwendungskontexte und vor allem aus dem Konsens einer Nutzendengemeinschaft speist. Jede Normdatenbank ist in eine soziale Praxis eingebettet, in der die Anbieterinnen und Anbieter glaubhaft, oft auch institutionell abgesichert, Gewähr für die Konsistenz, Persistenz und wissenschaftliche Fundiertheit der angebotenen Daten übernehmen, und in der eine Gemeinschaft von Nutzenden sich einig ist, dieses Angebot zu einem zentralen Orientierungs- und Vernetzungspunkt ihrer ansonsten ganz unabhängigen und unterschiedlichen Datenpraxis zu machen.

---

33 Vgl. *Sanderson*, Shout it Out: LOUD.
34 https://linked.art/loud/ (25.10.2022).

Was schließlich die (faktische Nutzung der) Möglichkeiten angeht, die Daten projekt-, institutionen- und disziplinübergreifend zu vernetzen, zu kombinieren, abzufragen und auszuwerten, wird dies umso eher gelingen, als gemeinsame Interessen und Schnittmengen auf unterschiedlichen Abstraktionsebenen ebenso wie partikulare Herausforderungen bei der Datenmodellierung und Begriffsbildung thematisiert werden und sich so eine wenigstens ephemere Diskursgemeinschaft um den Gegenstandsbereich bildet.

Wie die beschriebenen Dimensionen der gemeinschaftlichen Entwicklung wissenschaftlicher Auseinandersetzung mit einem Gegenstandsbereich veranschaulichen, sind ganz unterschiedliche konkrete Aktivitäten und Angebote von Projekten vorstellbar, um eine solche Entwicklung zu fördern. Diese reichen von der technischen Frage der Bereitstellung barrierearmer und flexibler Datenangebote in der Form von gut dokumentierten Datenabzügen einzelner Datensätze oder kompletter Bestände[35] oder in der Form von Abfragemöglichkeiten, die von Muster-Abfragen oder Abfrage-Assistenten begleitet werden, bis zur aktiven Einrichtung von Gelegenheiten zu einem offenen Dialog über Datenmodelle, Begrifflichkeiten und Daten-Verwendungsszenarien, etwa im Rahmen von Workshops oder durch die Erhebung von User Stories über Fragebögen o. ä. Solche Bemühungen sind keineswegs als bloß nachgeordnete »Outreach«-Aktivitäten zu verstehen, die die eigenen Ergebnisse nurmehr verbreiten helfen sollen, sondern sind – gemeinsam mit den oben beschriebenen »projektinternen« pragmatischen Einflüssen – integraler Faktor der Ausrichtung der wissenschaftlichen Strategie und als solche, so gut es geht, einzuplanen.

Zur Illustration sollen drei wissenschaftliche Initiativen genannt werden, deren Bemühungen einer Integration von Daten in eine Linked-Open-Data-Landschaft besonders erfolgreich sind[36]:

- »Linked.art«[37] ist eine Initiative, die sich um die Entwicklung und Anwendung der LOUD-Prinzipien für den Bereich des Kulturerbes bemüht. Diese Bemühungen umfassen die Entwicklung eines Datenmodells ebenso wie die eines Protokolls, über das Kulturerbe-Ressourcen einheitlich angesprochen werden können. Weitere Angebote umfassen ein »Kochbuch« mit Kurzanleitungen zum Umgang mit typischen Phänomenen oder eine an Datenmodell und Protokoll angepasste Software-Bibliothek, mit der Ressourcen besser in eigenen Programmen verarbeitet werden können. Wesentlich ist aber ein Spektrum regelmäßiger Veranstaltungen sowie Kommunikationskanäle wie Online-Diskussionsgruppen oder sog. *Issue tracker.*

---

35 Idealerweise enthalten die Daten ihre eigene Dokumentation oder wenigstens Verweise darauf, wie das beispielsweise bei TEI/XML oder JSON-LD-Formaten etablierte Praxis ist.
36 Alle drei Initiativen versammeln die relevanten Informationen auf je einer zentralen Webseite, die zu konsultieren sehr empfehlenswert ist, um die angebotenen Ressourcen, aber auch die organisatorische Struktur der Initiativen besser zu verstehen.
37 https://linked.art/community/ (25.10.2022).

- »Enslaved: Peoples of the Historical Slave Trade«[38] führt Informationen verschiedenster Projekte über den historischen Sklavenhandel zu einem Angebot für Wissenschaft und allgemeine Öffentlichkeit zusammen. Die zentrale Webseite bietet eine gemeinsame Abfrageoberfläche, Visualisierungen und Datendumps für die gesammelten Daten der verschiedenen teilnehmenden Einzelprojekte an und dokumentiert Datenmodell, Normdaten und Best Practices. Von besonderer Relevanz für den Gegenstandsbereich der Sklaverei-Forschung sind eine Stellungnahme zu den ethischen Aspekten von Forschung und Forschungsdatenmanagement und die Präsentation von »Featured Stories« für die breite Öffentlichkeit. Auch diese Initiative weist institutionalisierte Kommunikationskanäle wie Konferenzen und eine eigene Zeitschrift, das »Journal of Slavery and Data Preservation«[39], auf.
- »Monasterium.net«[40] bietet eine zentrale, kollaborative Datenbank historischer europäischer Urkunden seit dem Mittelalter. Neben der Publikationsplattform für Faksimiles, Metadaten und Transkriptionen bietet es für registrierte Nutzer auch Möglichkeiten zum Erfassen und Editieren dieser Informationen ebenso wie der verwendeten Normvokabulare an. Die Instrumente und Vokabulare sind eng verschränkt mit Entwicklungen der »Charters Encoding Initiative«[41] einer Arbeitsgruppe innerhalb der Text Encoding Initiative. »Monasterium« wird als Arbeitsgruppe von ICARUS unterstützt und getragen, einem als Verein verfassten Konsortium von Archiven und internationalen Forschungseinrichtungen. Neben der gemeinsamen Pflege und Weiterentwicklung der Datenbank (die über GitHub Wiki und Issue Tracker koordiniert werden), finden sich unter den Aktivitäten dieser Initiative auch Veranstaltungen wie die sog. *MOMAthons*[42], Online-Diskussionsforen und eine kollaborative Bibliographie mit Forschungspublikationen zum Gegenstandsbereich.

Alle drei Initiativen vereinen zahlreiche Einzelprojekte und sind eher als Scientific Communities denn als Infrastrukturen, Projekte oder Institutionen zu verstehen, und es ist dieses Motiv, das letztlich dazu führt, dass sie die Idee von Linked Open Data als eine Landschaft von Ressourcen, deren Vernetzung untereinander substanziell erweiterte Abfragen und Analysen möglich macht, erfolgreich realisieren können[43]. Sie veranschaulichen so, dass die Integration auch von Editionen früh-

---

38 https://enslaved.org/ (25.10.2022).
39 https://jsdp.enslaved.org/ (25.10.2022).
40 https://www.monasterium.net/mom/home (25.10.2022).
41 http://www.cei.lmu.de/ (25.10.2022).
42 https://www.icar-us.eu/de/cooperation/online-portals/monasterium-net/momathon/ (25.10.2022).
43 Ein weiteres eindrucksvolles Beispiel stellen die finnischen Sampo-Portals dar, wenngleich es sich hier tatsächlich doch um ein stärker institutionell integriertes Angebot handelt. Dies scheint mir aber eher die Ausnahme denn die Regel zu sein. Vgl. https://seco.cs.aalto.fi/applications/sampo/ (25.10.2022).

moderner Rechtstexte in eine Linked-Open-Data-Landschaft nicht zuletzt als eine Aufgabe des Community Building zu verstehen ist.

Literaturverzeichnis

Berners-Lee, Tim/Hendler, James/Lassila, Ora: The Semantic Web: a new form of Web content that is meaningful to computers will unleash a revolution of new possibilities, in: Scientific American 284/5 (2001), S. 34–43, http://www.jstor.org/stable/26059207 (19.10.2022).

Berners-Lee, Tim: Linked Data. July 2006, https://www.w3.org/DesignIssues/LinkedData.html (19.10.2022).

Cayless, Hugh A./Romanello, Matteo: Towards Resolution Services for Text URIs, in: Graph Data-Models and Semantic Web Technologies in Scholarly Digital Editing. Norderstedt 2021, S. 31–44, http://nbn-resolving.de/urn:nbn:de:hbz:38-552234, http://kups.ub.uni-koeln.de/id/eprint/55223 (19.10.2022).

Ebbertz, Matthias u.a.: Neue Ansätze in der Arbeitsrechtsgsechichte. Ein digitales Quellenedititionsprojekt am Max-Planck-Institut für Rechtsgeschichte und Rechtstheorie, in: Rechtsgeschichte – Legal History 30 (2022), S. 199–213, https://doi.org/10.12946/rg30/199-213 (17.06.2024).

Ehrmann, Maud u.a.: Extended Overview of HIPE-2022: Named Entity Recognition and Linking in Multilingual Historical Documents, in: *Guglielmo Faggioli u.a. (Hg.)*, Proceedings of the Working Notes of CLEF 2022, o.S. (= CEUR-WS, Bd. 3180), https://doi.org/10.5281/zenodo.6979577 (19.10.2022).

Grüntgens, Max/Schrade, Torsten: Data repositories in the Humanities and the Semantic Web: modelling, linking, visualising, in: *Alessandro Adamou/Enrico Daga/Leif Isaksen (Hg.)*, Proceedings of the 1st Workshop on Humanities in the Semantic Web co-located with 13th ESWC Conference 2016 (ESWC 2016), Anissaras 2016, S. 53–64 (= CEUR-WS, Bd. 1608), http://ceur-ws.org/Vol-1608/paper-07.pdf (19.10.2022).

Liga, Davide: Hybrid Artificial Intelligence to Extract Patterns and Rules from Argumentative and Legal Texts. Dissertation thesis, Bologna 2022, https://doi.org/10.48676/unibo/amsdottorato/9996 (19.10.2022).

Martín-Chozas, Patricia/Revenko, Artem: Thesaurus Enhanced Extraction of Hohfeld's Relations from Spanish Labour Law, in: *Sarra Ben Abbès/Rim Hantach/Philippe Calvez (Hg.)*, DeepOntoNLP & X-SENTIMENT 2021. Advances in Semantics and Explainability for NLP: Joint proceedings of the DeepOntoNLP and X-SENTIMENT Workshops 2021, S. 30–38 (= CEUR-WS, Bd. 2918), http://ceur-ws.org/Vol-2918/paper4.pdf (19.10.2022).

Palmirani, Monica u.a.: LegalRuleML: XML-Based Rules and Norms, in: *Frank Olken/dies./Davide Sottara (Hg.)*, Rule-Based Modeling and Computing on the Semantic Web. RuleML 2011. Berlin 2011, o.S. (= LNCS, Bd. 7018), https://doi.org/10.1007/978-3-642-24908-2_30 (19.10.2022).

Romein, C. Annemieke/Wagner, Andreas/van Zundert, Joris: Building and Deploying a Classification Schema Using Open Standards and Technology, in: Journal for Digital Legal History 2/1 (2023), o.S., https://doi.org/10.21825/dlh.85751 (17.06.2024).

Sanderson, Robert: Shout it Out: LOUD. EuropeanaTech 2018 Keynote am 15. Mai 2018. Rotterdam, 2018, Video: https://youtu.be/r4afi8mGVAY (19.10.2022), Folien: https://de.slideshare.net/azaroth42/europeanatech-keynote-shout-it-out-loud (19.10.2022).

Theodoridou, Maria u.a.: X3ML Toolkit. 2015, https://www.ics.forth.gr/isl/x3ml-toolkit (19.10.2022).

Vogeler, Georg: The ›assertive edition‹. On the consequences of digital methods in scholarly editing for historians, in: International Journal of Digital Humanities 1 (2019), S. 309–322, https://doi.org/10.1007/s42803-019-00025-5 (19.10.2022).

Wagner, Andreas: What's in a URI? Part I: The School of Salamanca, the Semantic Web and Scholarly Referencing, in: The School of Salamanca Blog. Eintrag vom 15. November 2016, o.S., https://blog.salamanca.school/de/2016/11/15/whats-in-a-uri-part-1/ (19.10.2022).

Wettlaufer, Jörg: Der nächste Schritt? Semantic Web und digitale Editionen, in: *Roland S. Kamzelak/Timo Steyer (Hg.)*, Digitale Metamorphose: Digital Humanities und Editionswissenschaft. Wolfenbüttel 2018, o.S. (= Sonderband der Zeitschrift für digitale Geisteswissenschaften, Bd. 2), https://doi.org/10.17175/sb002_007 (19.10.2022).

Zbíral, David u. a., Model the source first! Towards Computer-Assisted Semantic Text Modelling and source criticism 2.0., in: Zenodo (2022), https://doi.org/10.5281/zenodo.6963579 (22.10.2024).

MARTIN DE LA IGLESIA (WOLFENBÜTTEL)

Besondere Herausforderungen des digitalen Edierens frühneuzeitlicher Texte am Beispiel der Reiserelationen Philipp Hainhofers

I. Einleitung

Dieser Beitrag zeigt die drei womöglich größten Herausforderungen auf, die sich beim Anfertigen einer digitalen Edition stellen, und zwar speziell bei Editionen von Werken, die aus der Frühen Neuzeit stammen, im Unterschied vor allem zu späteren Texten. Obwohl es dabei unter anderem um Probleme bezüglich der frühneuhochdeutschen Sprachstufe gehen wird, ist die Perspektive dieses Beitrags keine germanistische, sondern eine kunsthistorische und bibliothekarische und somit gewissermaßen eine fachfremde, was aber dennoch bzw. vielleicht gerade deshalb bereichernd sein kann. Die Beispiele werden dabei nämlich einem kunsthistorisch ausgerichteten Editionsprojekt entnommen sein: dem der kommentierten digitalen Edition der Reise- und Sammlungsbeschreibungen Philipp Hainhofers (https://hainhofer.hab.de/), welches an der Herzog August Bibliothek Wolfenbüttel angesiedelt ist.

Der Augsburger Kaufmann Philipp Hainhofer unternahm zwischen 1594 und 1636 zahlreiche Reisen in Städte innerhalb des heutigen Deutschlands und auch darüber hinaus. Zu diesen Reisen fertigte er für seine überwiegend adligen Auftraggeber 20 Berichte an, die in mehrfachen handschriftlichen Ausfertigungen überliefert sind. Diese Texte sind überwiegend auf Deutsch verfasst, so dass sich die folgenden Anmerkungen über Schrift und Sprache auf das Frühneuhochdeutsche beziehen, aber mit Einschränkungen sicherlich auch für das Latein der Frühen Neuzeit und andere Sprachen gelten. Im Rahmen des auf zwölf Jahre angelegten Editionsprojekts sind in den ersten knapp sechs Jahren bereits acht Reiserelationen ediert und auf der Webseite hainhofer.hab.de veröffentlicht[1]. Aufgrund der in diesen Reiseberichten enthaltenen zahlreichen Beschreibungen sowie gelegentlichen Abbildungen von Bauwerken, Artefakten und Kunstsammlungen sind diese Texte auch und vor allem für die Kunstgeschichte interessant. Aus dieser disziplinären Ausrichtung des Editionsprojekts ergibt sich die Anforderung, dass man die betreffenden edierten Texte auch ohne Germanistikstudium verstehen können soll.

---

1 *Hainhofer*, Reiseberichte.

II. Schrift

Die Schwierigkeiten fangen dabei bereits beim grundlegendsten Schritt des digitalen Edierens an, nämlich dem Transkribieren, also dem Übertragen der in diesem Fall überwiegend handgeschriebenen Schriftzeichen aus der Vorlage in digitale Zeichen, welche von einem Computer gespeichert und weiterverarbeitet werden können. Bei den meisten Zeichen ist dies unproblematisch, da die 26 Groß- und Kleinbuchstaben des lateinischen Alphabets bereits damals verwendet wurden und auch heute im ASCII-Zeichensatz enthalten sind, so dass sie von praktisch allen Computersystemen verstanden werden. Nicht mehr ganz so einfach wird es jedoch bei denjenigen Schriftzeichen, die ebenfalls in frühneuhochdeutschen Texten verwendet werden, jedoch nicht durch die 128 ASCII-Zeichen oder gar den über eine Million Zeichen umfassenden Unicode-Standard abgedeckt sind.

Genauer gesagt müssen mehrere verschiedene Transkriptionsprobleme unterschieden werden. Erstens kann ein Zeichen aus der Vorlage mit einem falschen Unicode-Zeichen transkribiert werden. ›Falsch‹ bedeutet hier, dass die in Unicode intendierte Bedeutung des Zeichens eine andere ist als die in der Vorlage. Die Verwechselung beruht dabei meist auf der rein äußeren Ähnlichkeit der Glyphen. Diese sind jedoch in der Regel gar nicht Gegenstand des Unicode-Standards, welcher das abstrakte Zeichen, weitgehend unabhängig von seiner Erscheinungsform, definiert. Als Beispiel sei eine Verwechslung genannt, die auch während der Arbeit an der Hainhofer-Edition anfänglich vorkam: Anstelle des in der Vorlage verwendeten Buchstaben ÿ (der lateinische Buchstabe y mit Trema) wurde das Zeichen ӱ in den Computer eingegeben, also der kyrillische Buchstabe u mit Trema. Im Unicode-Standard belegen diese beiden Zeichen unterschiedliche Codepoints, U+00FF LATIN SMALL LETTER Y WITH DIAERESIS bzw. U+04F1 CYRILLIC SMALL LETTER U WITH DIAERESIS. Letzterer Buchstabe wird vor allem in den Alphabeten einiger Uralischer und Turksprachen verwendet. Es ist äußerst unwahrscheinlich, dass dieser Buchstabe vom Schreiber eines ansonsten frühneuhochdeutschen Textes gemeint worden sein könnte, so dass die Verwendung dieses Zeichens in der Transkription semantisch falsch ist. Verschärft wird dieses Problem natürlich dann, wenn in derselben Transkription einmal das eine und einmal das andere Zeichen verwendet wird, was oft dann der Fall ist, wenn mehrere Personen denselben Text bearbeiten. Konkrete Auswirkungen solcher Verwechslungen können sein, dass beispielsweise die Volltextsuche unvollständige Ergebnisse liefert, oder dass die betreffenden Zeichen auf der Editionswebseite nicht korrekt angezeigt werden.

Eine zweite Art von Transkriptionsproblem ist das bewusste oder unbewusste Ersetzen eines Sonderzeichens durch ein geläufigeres Zeichen. Das bekannteste Beispiel dürfte das lange s oder Schaft-s sein, das in einigen Editionen, wie auch in der Hainhofer-Edition, durch dasselbe Zeichen repräsentiert wird wie das ebenfalls in der Vorlage vorkommende runde s, obwohl es für das lange s ein eigenes Unicode-Zeichen gäbe: ſ (U+017F LATIN SMALL LETTER LONG S). Bei diesem Vorgehen handelt es sich nicht um ein Versehen, sondern es beruht auf einer bewussten Entscheidung, die einige Vorteile mit sich bringt: Für die transkribierenden Projektmitarbeiterinnen und -mitarbeiter ist es gerade bei einem so häufig vorkommenden Zeichen eine Erleichterung, das s einfach direkt mit der Tastatur eintippen zu können. Wenn das primäre Ausgabeformat eine HTML-Webseite oder ein PDF-Dokument ist, kann man sicher sein, dass das reguläre s-Zeichen durch die verwendeten Schriften gut lesbar dargestellt wird. Und auch für die meisten Nutzerinnen und Nutzer der Edition dürfte es von Vorteil sein, bei der Volltextsuche – auch direkt durch die Suchfunktion des Web-Browsers, oder durch Suchmaschinen, die die Editionswebseite indexiert haben – nicht zwischen den beiden s-Zeichen unterscheiden zu müssen, das s-Zeichen durch die Tastatur eingeben zu können und dadurch alle Wörter, egal mit welchem der beiden s-Zeichen, zu finden.

Grundsätzlich ist jedoch ein deutlicher Nachteil solcher Nivellierungen, dass dadurch diejenigen Nutzerinnen und Nutzer enttäuscht werden, die sich für genau solche Ausprägungen der frühneuhochdeutschen Schrift interessieren. So schrieb Franz Simmler 1992, also noch im weitgehend vor-digitalen Editionszeitalter, zu einem ganz ähnlichen Problem, nämlich dem der editorischen Auflösung von Abkürzungen:

»[...] das Nebeneinander von [durch Abkürzungsstrich über dem Wort] abgekürzten und nicht abgekürzten Wortformen [gehört] zur historischen Realität der handgeschriebenen und gedruckten Textexemplare. Werden die Abkürzungen einfach aufgelöst, ohne dies explizit zu kennzeichnen, wird eine Schreib- oder Druckrealität geschaffen, die so nicht existiert hat. Die Editionen von Texten der Frühen Neuzeit müssen diese Realität wiedergeben [...].«[2]

Übertragen auf die Problematik der zeichengenauen Transkription hieße das, das Nebeneinander von z. B. langem s und rundem s gehöre ebenfalls zur historischen Realität der Texte, welche von den Editionen wiedergegeben werden müsse. Könnten digitale Editionen die Lösung dieses Problems darstellen? In einem Aufsatz von 2018 zeigte sich Norbert Ankenbauer diesbezüglich optimistisch:

»Heutzutage ist die linguistische Analyse großer Textmengen zwar vergleichsweise einfach zu leisten, es mangelt jedoch oft an ausreichend originalgetreu edierten Texten, um verlässliche Ergebnisse sicherstellen zu können. Mit der Digitalisierung gedruckter Texteditionen kann zwar die verfügbare Datenbasis erheblich erweitert werden, das Problem der sprachlich nivellierenden Abweichungen im Vergleich zum Original bleibt dabei jedoch weiterhin bestehen. Jüngere digitale Editionen schaffen hier Abhilfe: Da Restriktionen im Hinblick auf den Umfang und mögliche Annotationen im Vergleich zu gedruckten Editionen entfallen, kann durch entsprechende Gestaltung der Transkriptionen gewährleistet werden, dass beliebig viele mehr oder weniger originalgetreue Versionen des Textes nebeneinander gestellt werden können.«[3]

---

2 *Simmler*, Prinzipien.
3 *Ankenbauer*, Newe landte.

Im Prinzip ist dies nicht falsch: Anstatt sich zwischen abgekürzten und aufgelösten Wortformen, oder zwischen langem s und regulärem s, entscheiden zu müssen, kann man in einer digitalen Edition beides anbieten. Allerdings werden dadurch nicht alle Probleme gelöst, denn Dateneingabe, -ausgabe und -weiterverarbeitung werden dadurch erheblich aufwändiger.

Eine dritte, eher selten vorkommende Kategorie von Transkriptionsproblemen ist das Gegenteil der zweiten, nämlich dass ganz gewöhnliche Zeichen in der Vorlage durch exotische oder sogar irreführende Sonderzeichen repräsentiert werden. Ein Beispiel dafür finden wir abermals bei Franz Simmler in einem Auszug aus einer gedruckten Edition, in der er das runde s durch das Zeichen σ (den griechischen Buchstaben Sigma) darstellt[4]. Genauer gesagt verwendet Simmler vier verschiedene s-Zeichen, das ß nicht mitgerechnet: das lange s, das vermeintliche Sigma, das heutige, also schlangenförmige S als Großbuchstabe sowie zweimal als Kleinbuchstabe, wobei Letzteres ein Versehen zu sein scheint. Diese Vielfalt mag durch die didaktische Motivation begründet sein, dass schriftgeschichtlich das heutige, schlangenförmige s weder mit dem langen s noch mit dem frühneuzeitlichen runden s gleichzusetzen sei. Allerdings wäre die Verwirrung kaum auszudenken, wenn ein solcher Editionstext nicht nur frühneuhochdeutsche sondern auch griechische Passagen enthielte.

Als ein weiteres Beispiel für diese Problematik sei eine von Stefan Gippert vorgeschlagene Computerschrift für frühneuhochdeutsche Editionen genannt, die ein eigenes Zeichen für die Abkürzung »et cetera« enthielt[5]. Dabei lässt sich diese Abkürzung eigentlich leicht zerlegen in ein Tironisches Et (U+204A TIRONIAN

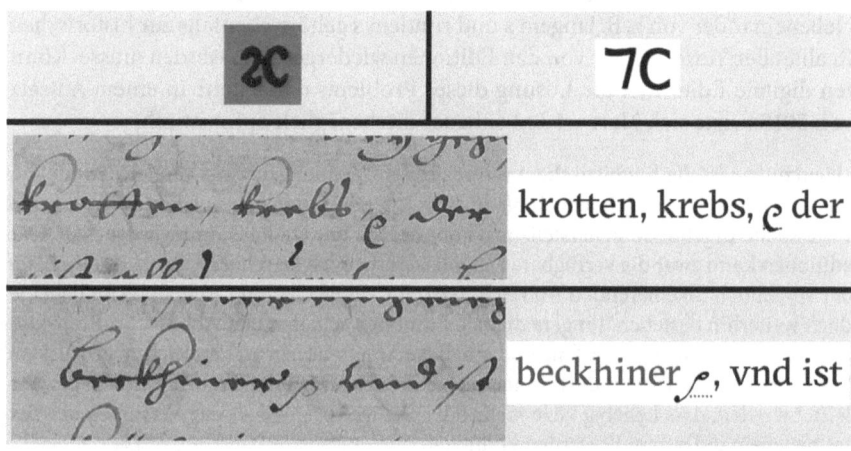

Abb. 1: verschiedene »Et cetera«-Darstellungsformen und -Zeichen. Links oben: aus *Gippert*, Frühneuhochdeutsch. Rechts oben: Kombination aus den Unicode-Zeichen U+204A und U+0063. Mitte und unten: Screenshots von *Hainhofer*, Reiseberichte.

4   *Simmler*, Prinzipien.
5   *Gippert*, Frühneuhochdeutsch.

SIGN ET) und den lateinischen Kleinbuchstaben c, so dass kein spezielles Zeichen für die Kombination aus beiden nötig wäre. Stattdessen müsste man sich eher fragen, wie mit einigen anderen Erscheinungsformen der Wendung »et cetera« umgegangen werden soll, die sich nicht ohne weiteres auf einzelne herkömmliche Buchstaben zurückführen lassen. Die Hainhofer-Edition beispielsweise definiert für zumindest zwei dieser Et-cetera-Abkürzungen (die eine ähnelt dem Buchstaben c, die andere einem p) eigene Zeichen (vgl. Abb. 1). Entscheidender ist jedoch, dass bei allen Et-cetera-Abkürzungen die entsprechende Auflösung hinterlegt ist, so dass sie durch eine Volltextsuche gefunden werden können.

III. Sprache

Unabhängig von der Transkription der Schriftzeichen besteht beim Lesen, und folglich auch beim Edieren, das Problem der frühneuhochdeutschen Sprachstufe im Allgemeinen und ihrer Verständlichkeit für heutige Leserinnen und Leser. Auch wenn es einem nicht ganz so fremd ist wie Mittelhochdeutsch, so stellt das Frühneuhochdeutsche so manche Hürde in den Weg zum Textverständnis. Wörter folgen einer anderen Orthographie, die sich oft, aber nicht immer durch Lautverschiebungen erklären lässt, manche Wörter sind vollkommen aus dem Gebrauch und somit in Vergessenheit geraten, und der ungewohnte Satzbau sowie zeitgebundene Inhalte tun ihr Übriges, um die Bedeutung des Textes geradezu zu verschleiern. Daher kann diese Sprachproblematik als die zweite große Herausforderung beim Edieren frühneuzeitlicher Texte angesehen werden.

Zum Umgang mit dieser Problematik scheint es zwei gegensätzliche Positionen zu geben. Zum einen gibt es die Ansicht, wie sie beispielsweise Hans-Gert Roloff[6] und die Kommission für die Edition von Texten der Frühen Neuzeit[7] vertreten, den Leserinnen und Lesern diesbezüglich nur wenige Hilfestellungen anzubieten. Demzufolge sollten in der Edition eines frühneuzeitlichen Textes allenfalls »althochdeutsche und mittelhochdeutsche Stellen von besonderem Schwierigkeitsgrad«, darüber hinaus »seltene, nicht geläufige Wörter und Begriffe«, »Mundartliches«, »semantische Verschiebungen«, »syntaktische Schwierigkeiten« sowie »unklare und ggf. zu Mißverständnissen führende Wörter und Formulierungen« durch den Kommentar erläutert werden. Zu übersetzen sind nur Fremdsprachen. Ausnahmen gelten lediglich für den gesonderten Editionstypus der Studienausgabe, in der auch sprachliche Besonderheiten des Frühneuhochdeutschen erläutert werden dürfen.

Zum anderen gibt es den entgegengesetzten Ansatz, den Text vollständig vom Frühneuhochdeutschen ins heutige Neuhochdeutsch zu ›übersetzen‹, also sozusa-

---

6 *Roloff*, Fragen.
7 *Kommission für die Edition von Texten der Frühen Neuzeit*, Kommentar-Empfehlungen.

gen ›nachzudichten‹ oder, wie man bisweilen liest, zu ›modernisieren‹[8]. Gerade bei digitalen Editionen ließe sich eine solche Lesefassung zusätzlich zur Transkription anbieten, so dass eine solche Edition immer noch wissenschaftlichen Zwecken dienen, zugleich aber der Stellenkommentar entlastet und der Lesefluss verbessert werden könnte. Jedoch entbindet eine solche Übersetzung die Editorinnen und Editoren nicht von der Aufgabe, Textpassagen zu erläutern, die vielleicht sprachlich verständlich, aber inhaltlich schwierig sind.

Die übliche Editionspraxis bewegt sich zwischen diesen beiden Extremen, indem sie den Großteil des frühneuhochdeutschen Textes als verständlich voraussetzt, aber die Transkription mit punktuellen sprachlichen Erläuterungen anreichert. Dieses Verfahren wird auch bei der Hainhofer-Edition angewandt. Um die Herausforderungen dieser Herangehensweise zu illustrieren, sei der Anfang des ersten Satzes aus dem innerhalb der Edition zuerst veröffentlichten Reisebericht Hainhofers zitiert, der Münchener Reise von 1603:

»Adj 13. Julij. 1603 mit meim schwager Daniel
Rem, Martin Horndacher, Doktor Jeorg
Miller nach München geraist, dan
sie wegen Anzenhoffen lehen alda
zuempfangen gehabt, haben ihr
aigne Pferdt vnd gutschen genomen
vnd ain Ainspenniger haist Hans
Wachter, [...].«[9]

In diesen Zeilen fügt die Edition lediglich eine Fußnote ein, welche das Wort »Ainspenniger« als »Fuhrknecht« erläutert. Der ungefähre Sinn dieses Satzes lässt sich sicherlich leicht erfassen. Anders sieht es jedoch aus, wenn man seinen genauen und vollständigen Sinn verstehen möchte, also wenn man beispielsweise den Satz mit eigenen Worten formulieren müsste. Neben vielen kleineren Hürden wie der aus heutiger Sicht ungewohnten Orthographie und Zeichensetzung spielen sich die wahrscheinlich größten Probleme auf drei verschiedenen Ebenen ab: Dies wäre erstens das Funktionswort »dan« in der dritten Zeile, welches wohl ein ›Falscher Freund‹ ist, da es an das Wort ›dann‹ im heutigen Deutsch denken lässt, aber nicht dessen Bedeutung einer zeitlichen Abfolge haben kann, denn das Ziel der Reise wird vor ihrem Beginn genannt. Kniffligerweise kennt auch das Frühneuhochdeutsche

---

8   Als Beispiel sei *Friedrich Lucaes* Schrift »Das edle Kleinod an der hessischen Landeskrone« aus den Jahren 1700–1701 genannt. Dort heißt es z. B. im Wortlaut des handschriftlichen Originals: »Kaysers Ludovici Pii regierung wehrete biß ins 840 iahr« (zitiert nach *Ortmüller*, Geschichte, S. 11). In der von *Hans-Günther Kittelmann* bearbeiteten »modernisierten« Fassung aus dem Jahr 1996 wurde daraus: »Kaiser Ludwig des Frommen Regierung währte bis ins 840. Jahr« (*Lucae*, Kleinod, S. 31).

9   *Hainhofer*, Reiseberichte, Fol. 127v, https://hainhofer.hab.de/reiseberichte/muenchen1603#fol127v (10.08.2022).

das Wort ›dan‹ in derselben Schreibweise in dieser Funktion im temporalen Sinn[10]. Vielmehr ist hier jedoch wahrscheinlich die kausale Konjunktion ›denn‹ gemeint; es scheint also eine Lautverschiebung zwischen e und a vorzuliegen. Zweitens ist der Satzbau anspruchsvoll, da anscheinend das Prädikat verkürzt ist; es fehlt das Hilfsverb ›haben‹, also: ›denn sie haben zu empfangen gehabt‹. Drittens liegt die Schwierigkeit auch auf der inhaltlichen Ebene, da der Vorgang des ›Empfangens von Lehen‹ mit der arg verkürzten Begründung »wegen Anzenhoffen« erst einmal verstanden werden muss. Später in diesem Reisebericht wird geschildert, dass die besagten Personen in München eine Gebühr entrichten, um gewissermaßen den Nutzungsvertrag für die bei Anzenhof gelegenen Ländereien zu verlängern. Man könnte also durchaus diesen Satz mit mindestens drei weiteren erläuternden Kommentaren versehen.

Zwar wäre im Gegensatz zu gedruckten Editionen ausreichend Platz vorhanden, um weitere Worterklärungen, auch von häufigen Wörtern, unterzubringen, doch muss man sich fragen, wie diese Informationen den Nutzerinnen und Nutzern der digitalen Edition dargeboten würden. Ein derart ›aufgeblähter‹ Stellenkommentar würde sicherlich den Lesefluss durch die Häufung von Fußnoten oder Ähnlichem stören. Zudem könnte man in Bezug auf dieses Beispiel sagen: Es ist ja auch nicht so wichtig, diese Textstelle im Detail zu verstehen; das Interessante an diesem Reisebericht fängt erst mit dem Eintreffen Hainhofers an seinem Zielort München an, und auf welchem Wege und in wessen Begleitung er dort hinreist, ist nebensächlich. Eine solche Sichtweise verengt allerdings unweigerlich das Zielpublikum und schließt etwaige Leserinnen und Leser aus, die sich womöglich für genau solche scheinbar unwichtigen Einzelheiten interessieren. Grundsätzlich ist es für Editorinnen und Editoren ratsam, den Text der eigenen Edition nicht als alleinigen Mittelpunkt des Interesses aller etwaigen Leserinnen und Leser anzusehen. Stattdessen sollte man den Text als einen kleinen Teil eines großen Korpus begreifen, der vielleicht nur am Rande und auszugsweise von Forscherinnen und Forschern aus ganz anderen Fachgebieten und vor allem auch aus anderen Sprachräumen konsultiert wird.

IV. Linked Open Data

An die Forderung nach der Möglichkeit der sprachunabhängigen Nutzung einer Edition schließt sich die dritte und letzte besondere Herausforderung des digitalen Edierens frühneuzeitlicher Texte an, obwohl diese strenggenommen gar nicht spezifisch für die Frühe Neuzeit ist. Es geht nämlich um das Semantic Web beziehungsweise Linked Open Data (LOD), die in Bezug auf Texte aller möglichen Epochen sinnvoll sind. Deren Potential entfaltet sich jedoch erst, wenn diese Daten, wie der

---

10 Frühneuhochdeutsches Wörterbuch, s.v. »dan«, http://fwb-online.de/go/dan.h1.4adv_1646432883 (10.08.2022).

Name sagt, auch tatsächlich verlinkt werden, und das geschieht natürlich am leichtesten mit anderen Daten aus derselben Domäne. Diese Domäne kann etwa dieselbe Epoche sein, und insofern ist diese Herausforderung, also das Bereitstellen von LOD, doch wieder spezifisch für die Frühe Neuzeit, da es für diese Daten und ihre Datenquellen besondere Gegebenheiten und Möglichkeiten der Modellierung, der Vernetzung, dem Schaffen von Synergien und auch hinsichtlich der technischen Infrastruktur gibt.

Prinzipiell geht es bei Linked Data um das Formulieren von Aussagen in einer bestimmten Form, in der Subjekte, Prädikate und Objekte vorzugsweise aus Internetadressen bestehen, die auf Normdateien bzw. kontrollierte Vokabulare verweisen. Dadurch werden diese Informationen sprachunabhängig und maschinenlesbar gemacht[11]. Viele verschiedene Aspekte einer digitalen Edition, ja sogar der gesamte Text, ließen sich auf diese Weise ausdrücken. Am sinnvollsten scheint es jedoch, diejenigen Informationen als Linked Data bereitzustellen, die man in der Regel ohnehin bereits als editorial erzeugte Faktenaussagen vorliegen hat, nämlich Registereinträge. In seiner einfachsten Form besteht ein Register, beispielsweise ein Personenregister, aus einer Liste von Namen, denen die jeweiligen Textstellen zugeordnet sind. Allein diese Information – Person X ist erwähnt auf Seite Y – lässt sich bereits im beschriebenen Format des Resource Description Framework (RDF) formulieren.

Derartige Daten sind interoperabel, so dass man Daten aus verschiedenen Quellen zueinander in Beziehung setzen kann. Im Folgenden sei ein einfaches Beispiel dafür beschrieben: Zur Edition »Quellen zur habsburgisch-osmanischen Diplomatie in der Neuzeit – Die Internuntiatur des Johann Rudolf Schmid zum Schwarzenhorn (1649): Reisebericht, Instruktionen, Korrespondenz, Berichte« gibt es ein Personenregister, welches auch im RDF-Format veröffentlicht wurde[12]. Die zeitliche Nähe und die gleiche Textgattung (Reisebericht) lassen vermuten, dass es auch eine inhaltliche Nähe dieser edierten Texte zu den Reiseberichten Philipp Hainhofers gibt. Es ist nun auf technisch sehr einfache Weise möglich, die personenbezogenen RDF-Daten aus beiden Editionen miteinander zu vergleichen. Ein solcher Abgleich offenbart immerhin vier Personen, die in beiden Reiseberichtskonvoluten erwähnt werden, nämlich die drei römisch-deutschen Kaiser Matthias, Ferdinand II. und Ferdinand III., sowie Kaiserin Eleonora.

Ein derartiger Abgleich wäre jedoch auch mit anderen Datenformaten möglich. Wirklich interessant werden LOD erst dann, wenn sie weiterverarbeitet und Anwendungen darauf aufgebaut werden. Beispielsweise könnte man sich Folgendes vorstellen: Die Herzog August Bibliothek Wolfenbüttel beherbergt eine digitalisierte Porträtsammlung mit mehreren zehntausend Druckgraphiken aus der Frühen Neuzeit[13]. Demnächst sollen auch die Personendaten aus diesem Kontext als LOD veröffentlicht werden. Nun könnte man diese Daten abgleichen mit dem Personenregister der besagten Schwarzenhorn-Edition und dessen Web-Ansicht automatisch

---

11 Vgl. den Beitrag von Andreas Wagner in diesem Band.
12 *Strohmeyer/Vogeler*, Internuntiatur, https://gams.uni-graz.at/o:dipko.persons/RDF (10.08.2022).
13 *Mortzfeld*, Porträtsammlung.

anreichern mit den Wolfenbütteler Porträts, die die jeweilige Person im Register zeigen, um dadurch der Nutzerin oder dem Nutzer direkt einen visuellen Eindruck der betreffenden Person zu geben (vgl. Abb. 2). Dies mag vielleicht wie eine reine Spielerei erscheinen, doch lassen sich sicherlich nach demselben Prinzip der Synergie aus verschiedenen LOD-Quellen beliebige andere, sinnvollere Anwendungen denken, sofern der entsprechende Bedarf seitens der Fachwissenschaft geäußert wird.

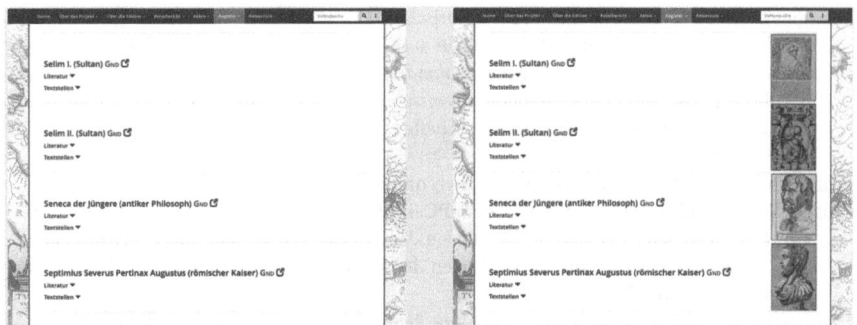

Abb. 2: links: Screenshot von *Strohmeyer/Vogeler*, Internuntiatur, https://gams.uni-graz.at/o:dipko.persons (10.08.2022); rechts: Dieselbe Ansicht mit eingeblendeten Porträts aus *Mortzfeld*, Porträtsammlung (Mockup).

V. Fazit

Wenn es einen roten Faden gibt, der die drei in diesem Beitrag behandelten Problemfelder der Schrift, der Sprache und der Linked Data miteinander verbindet, so ist es das Ziel der Anschlussfähigkeit. Digitale Editionen frühneuzeitlicher Texte sollten von möglichst vielen Forscherinnen und Forschern gelesen und auch anderweitig genutzt werden können.

»Digitale Editionen stehen wegen der vielfältigen Anschluss- und Nutzungsmöglichkeiten der Daten nicht nur für sich, sondern sind interoperabel und in weitere Nutzungsszenarien eingebunden. Digitale Editionen werden dadurch nicht nur als Publikationen, sondern gerade durch ihre algorithmisch verwendbaren Daten zu Treibern der weiteren Forschung. [Die Verfügbarkeit dieser Daten] ist nach den FAIR-Prinzipien zu organisieren: auffindbar, zugänglich, interoperabel und nachnutzbar. Die benötigten personellen, institutionellen und finanziellen Ressourcen sind auch für die Langzeitarchivierung und Langzeitverfügbarkeit ausreichend zu bemessen.«[14]

Diese vier letzten Sätze stammen aus dem kürzlich veröffentlichten »Manifest für digitale Editionen«, welches in kürzester Zeit zahlreiche Unterzeichnerinnen und Unterzeichner fand. Es bleibt abzuwarten, ob es sich bei den dort formulierten

---

14 *Institut für Dokumentologie und Editorik (Hg.)*, Manifest für digitale Editionen, Abs. 9, Abs. 14.

Zielen nur um fromme Wünsche handelt, die eine Utopie beschreiben. Doch was wir bereits heute tun können, ist, uns diese Ziele als Leitlinien für unsere tägliche Arbeit mit digitalen Editionen zu setzen.

Literaturverzeichnis

Ankenbauer, Norbert: »Newe landte« in der historischen Sprachwissenschaft. Ein Beitrag zur Druckersprache der Nürnberger Offizin Georg Stüchs auf Grundlage der Digitaledition Paesi novamente retrovati – Newe unbekanthe landte, in: *Roland S. Kamzelak/Timo Steyer (Hg.),* Digitale Metamorphose. Digital Humanities und Editionswissenschaft, Wolfenbüttel 2018, o. S. (= Sonderband der Zeitschrift für digitale Geisteswissenschaften, Bd. 2), https://doi.org/10.17175/sb002_009 (10.08.2022).

Frühneuhochdeutsches Wörterbuch, https://fwb-online.de (10.08.2022).

Gippert, Stefan: Frühneuhochdeutsch auf dem PC, in: *Lothar Mundt/Hans-Gert Roloff/Ulrich Seelbach (Hg.),* Probleme der Edition von Texten der Frühen Neuzeit. Beiträge zur Arbeitstagung der Kommission für die Edition von Texten der Frühen Neuzeit, Tübingen 1992, S. 178–181 (= Beiheft zu Editio, Bd. 3).

Hainhofer, Philipp: Reiseberichte und Sammlungsbeschreibungen 1594–1636. Edition und Datensammlung zur Kunst- und Kulturgeschichte der ersten Hälfte des 17. Jahrhunderts, hg. v. Michael Wenzel, Transkription und Kommentar von Ursula Timann und Michael Wenzel, Wolfenbüttel 2020 ff. (= Wolfenbütteler Digitale Editionen, Bd. 4), https://hainhofer.hab.de/ (10.08.2022).

Kommission für die Edition von Texten der Frühen Neuzeit: Kommentar-Empfehlungen für Editionen von Texten der Frühen Neuzeit, in: *Lothar Mundt/Hans-Gert Roloff/Ulrich Seelbach (Hg.),* Probleme der Edition von Texten der Frühen Neuzeit. Beiträge zur Arbeitstagung der Kommission für die Edition von Texten der Frühen Neuzeit, Tübingen 1992, S. 160–166 (= Beiheft zu Editio, Bd. 3).

Lucae, Friedrich: Das edle Kleinod an der hessischen Landeskrone. Geschichte der Stadt und des Amtes Rotenburg. Rotenburger Chronik, Bd. 1: Von den Anfängen bis 1700, bearb. v. *Hans-Günther Kittelmann,* Kassel 1996 (= Hessische Forschungen zur geschichtlichen Landes- und Volkskunde, Bd. 29).

Institut für Dokumentologie und Editorik (Hg.): Manifest für digitale Editionen, 2022, https://dhdblog.org/?p=17563 (10.08.2022).

Mortzfeld, Peter (Bearb.): Die Porträtsammlung der Herzog August Bibliothek Wolfenbüttel, Wolfenbüttel 2015, http://portraits.hab.de (10.08.2022).

Ortmüller, Hans: Kurze Geschichte des landgräflichen Schlosses in Rotenburg a. d. Fulda, in: Zeitschrift des Vereins für Hessische Geschichte und Landeskunde 81 (1970), S. 9–63.

Roloff, Hans-Gert: Fragen zur Gestaltung von Kommentaren zu Textausgaben der Frühen Neuzeit, in: *Lothar Mundt/Hans-Gert Roloff/Ulrich Seelbach (Hg.),* Probleme der Edition von Texten der Frühen Neuzeit. Beiträge zur Arbeitstagung der Kommission für die Edition von Texten der Frühen Neuzeit, Tübingen 1992, S. 130–139 (= Beiheft zu Editio, Bd. 3).

Simmler, Franz: Prinzipien der Edition von Texten der Frühen Neuzeit aus sprachwissenschaftlicher Sicht, in: *Lothar Mundt/Hans-Gert Roloff/Ulrich Seelbach (Hg.),* Probleme der Edition von Texten der Frühen Neuzeit. Beiträge zur Arbeitstagung der Kommission für die Edition von Texten der Frühen Neuzeit, Tübingen 1992, S. 36–127 (= Beiheft zu Editio, Bd. 3).

Strohmeyer, Arno/Vogeler, Georg (Hg.): Die Internuntiatur des Johann Rudolf Schmid zum Schwarzenhorn (1649), Salzburg 2019 (= Digitale Edition von Quellen zur habsburgisch-osmanischen Diplomatie 1500–1918, Projekt 2), https://hdl.handle.net/11471/1020.20.1 (hdl:11471/1020.20.1) (10.08.2022).

Marius Hug, Linda Kirsten (Berlin)

Historische Texte der neuhochdeutschen Sprachstufe als Forschungsdaten

Das »Deutsche Textarchiv« im Kontext der Nationalen Forschungsdateninfrastruktur (NFDI)

I. Das »Deutsche Textarchiv«

1. Die Geschichte des »Deutschen Textarchivs«. Korpus und Standard

Die Geschichte des »Deutschen Textarchivs« (DTA) reicht mittlerweile gut 15 Jahre zurück. Das in drei Phasen von der Deutschen Forschungsgemeinschaft (DFG) geförderte Projekt startete 2007 mit dem Ziel der Erstellung eines Korpus von digitalisierten Texten, die einen Zeitraum von ca. 1.600 bis 1.900 umfassen. Das sogenannte DTA-Kernkorpus war als Grundlage für ein Referenzkorpus der neuhochdeutschen Sprache konzipiert.

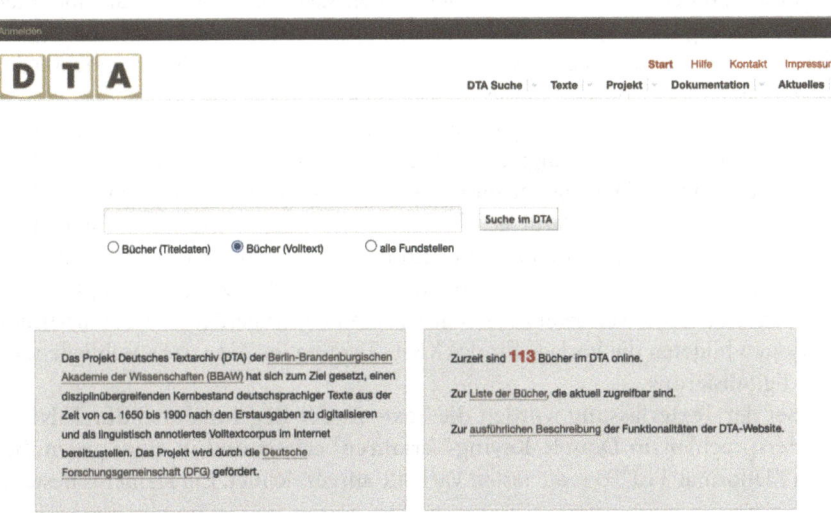

Abb. 1: Startseite des DTA mit 113 digitalisierten Büchern, September 2009.

Auf der Basis einer umfangreichen Bibliographie, die von Akademiemitgliedern erstellt und ausführlich kommentiert wurde, erfolgte die Auswahl der zu digitalisierenden Texte[1]. Ergänzt wurde diese Auswahl durch eine Auswertung von einschlägigen Literaturgeschichten und Fachbibliographien. Anschließend stellte die DTA-Projektgruppe mithilfe dieser Vorauswahl ein hinsichtlich der repräsentierten Textsorten und Disziplinen ausgewogenes Korpus zusammen, wobei für die Digitalisierung in der Regel auf die Erstausgaben der Werke zurückgegriffen wurde. So sollte gewährleistet werden, dass der historische Sprachstand möglichst genau abgebildet wird. Die Texte des DTA-Kernkorpus dokumentieren die Entwicklung einer überregionalen Umgangssprache im hochdeutschen Sprachraum seit dem Ende der frühneuhochdeutschen Sprachperiode.

Das DFG-Projekt war als sprachwissenschaftlich orientiertes Korpusprojekt mit einer starken literatur- und bibliothekswissenschaftlichen Komponente konzipiert. Die ursprünglichen Projektziele (für die ersten drei Jahre) waren:
- Digitalisierung von ca. 750 Texten (ca. 200.000–250.000 Druckseiten) aus dem Zeitraum 1780–1900[2]
- Bereitstellung der Bilddigitalisate und der Volltexte (XML/TEI-P5)
- Verknüpfung von Volltext und Bild für die Leseansicht
- Eine linguistische Grundannotation

Da die Werke mehrheitlich aus den Beständen von größeren Bibliotheken (z. B. aus der Staatsbibliothek zu Berlin – Stiftung Preußischer Kulturbesitz, der Zentral- und Landesbibliothek Berlin, der Niedersächsischen Staats- und Universitätsbibliothek (SUB) Göttingen oder dem Max-Planck-Institut für Rechtsgeschichte und Rechtstheorie) stammten, erfolgte die *Bilddigitalisierung* nach der Klärung rechtlicher Fragen in der Regel durch externe Dienstleister.

Für die *Volltextdigitalisierung* wurde ebenfalls ein Dienstleister beauftragt, wobei die Vorbereitung der Textdigitalisierung – die Makrostrukturierung der Bilddigitalisate – vom DTA-Projektteam vorgenommen wurde. Mithilfe eines einfach zu bedienenden, eigens dafür geschaffenen Werkzeuges wurden auf jedem Digitalisat – d. h. auf jedem einzelnen Bild der jeweiligen Druckseiten – die verschiedenen Textzonen wie z. B. Kapitelüberschrift, Absatz, Seitenzahl, Fußnote etc. definiert. Diese von Hand auf dem Faksimile hinzugefügten (Struktur-)Informationen bildeten die Vorlage für das XML-Tagging im Zuge der anschließenden Textdigitalisierung.

Bei der Texterfassung wurden die Texte in der Regel manuell durch Nicht-Muttersprachler im Double-Keying-Verfahren[3] erfasst und in einer gegenüber dem Zielformat TEI-P5 reduzierten Variante ausgezeichnet. Ein kleinerer Bestand

---

1   *Geyken/Haaf*, Integration heterogener historischer Textkorpora.
2   In der zweiten Förderphase erfolgte eine Erweiterung des Korpus bis ca. 1600/1650.
3   Von *Double Keying* ist die Rede, wenn ein vorliegender Text von zwei Personen erfasst/transkribiert wird und die beiden Fassungen nachträglich hinsichtlich eventueller Abweichungen voneinander verglichen werden.

wurde ebenfalls im Double-Keying-Verfahren durch Muttersprachler erfasst. Und auch die Texterfassung durch eine Texterkennungssoftware (OCR) mit manueller Nachkorrektur wurde für einen festen Bestand jüngerer Werke (19. Jh.) erprobt. Während in den letzten Jahren im Bereich der automatischen Zeichenerkennung v. a. im Kontext von Entwicklungen im Bereich der KI einige erfreuliche Fortschritte erzielt werden konnten, stellte sich der Sachverhalt zu Beginn des DFG-Projekts gänzlich anders dar: Eine sehr hohe Erfassungsgenauigkeit auf der Zeichenebene konnte für historische Schriften – v. a. wenn es sich dabei um in Fraktur gedruckte Texte handelte – nur im Double-Keying-Verfahren erreicht werden.

Nach der manuellen Erfassung wurden die Texte in der Regel automatisch mithilfe von eigens erstellten Skripten in das TEI-P5-Format[4] konvertiert und in einer projektinternen Qualitätskontrolle geprüft und korrigiert. Dafür wurde im Projektverlauf die Webanwendung *DTAQ* entwickelt, in der Nutzerinnen und Nutzer über personalisierte Accounts gemeinsam an Texten arbeiten konnten und die auch externen Personen und Forschungsprojekten für communitybasierte Kollaboration zur Verfügung stand.

Im Anschluss an die Konvertierung nach TEI-P5 wurden die Volltexte linguistisch erschlossen, d.h. mit computerlinguistischen Hilfsmitteln aufbereitet. Nach der Verwendung von automatischen Verfahren zur Tokenisierung, Lemmatisierung und zum Part-of-Speech (POS)-Tagging[5] erfolgte eine Indizierung durch die linguistische Suchmaschine DDC[6], die für das Projekt »Digitales Wörterbuch der Deutschen Sprache« (DWDS)[7] entwickelt worden war[8]. Schließlich wurden die publizierten Volltexte über das Internet frei zugänglich gemacht und sind damit sowohl für die Forschung als auch für die interessierte Öffentlichkeit vielfältig nutzbar.

Für die zweite Förderphase ab 2010 wurde dann – neben einer Erweiterung des Kernkorpus um ca. 650 Texte aus der Zeit von ca. 1650 bis 1780 – eine weitere Öffnung hin zur Community mit dem Ziel des »Aufbaus eines Aktiven Archivs« vorgesehen. Dabei sollte der Kernbestand »in Kooperation mit anderen Wissenschaftlern und Forschungsstätten ständig ausgebaut werden, und zwar nach Umfang wie nach Tiefe der Aufbereitung.«[9] Neben dem Kernkorpus und den verschiedenen im sogenannten Modul DTAE (DTA-Erweiterungen) aggregierten Korpuserweiterungen war v. a. die Entwicklung des zunächst projektspezifischen

---

4 Das für die XML-Auszeichnung gewählte TEI-P5-Format ist der De-facto-Standard zur Auszeichnung geisteswissenschaftlicher Texte. Die Text Encoding Initiative (heute TEI-Konsortium, https://tei-c.org/ [13.09.2023]) entwickelt seit 1988 ein gleichnamiges Format (TEI) zur Kodierung natürlichsprachlicher Texte, das in seiner aktuellen P5-Version auf der Auszeichnungssprache XML basiert.
5 Gemeint sind damit vollautomatische Verfahren für die Zuordnung der in einem Text vorkommenden Wörter und Satzzeichen zu einer festen Auswahl von Wortarten (Adjektive, Nomen, Pronomen, Verben etc.).
6 https://www.dwds.de/d/korpussuche (13.09.2023).
7 https://www.dwds.de/ (13.09.2023).
8 *Jurish/Thomas/Wiegand*, Querying the Deutsches Textarchiv.
9 *Klein*, Deutsches Textarchiv (DTA).

Auszeichnungsstandards DTA-Basisformat (DTABf) mitentscheidend für den Erfolg des Projekts. Das DTABf ist ein vom Projekt festgelegtes Subset des von der Text Encoding Initiative entwickelten TEI-P5-Standards.

Da die P5-Richtlinien der TEI den Anspruch haben, für sämtliche Bedürfnisse bei der Textaufbereitung eine Lösung anzubieten, sind sie entsprechend umfangreich und vielfältig. Im konkreten Fall bedeutet das, dass es mehrere valide Möglichkeiten geben kann, ein bestimmtes Phänomen zu beschreiben. Ein einfaches Beispiel wäre die Auszeichnung von Personen, wofür die TEI-Richtlinien verschiedene Möglichkeiten bereitstellen. So ist es gleichbedeutend, ob die Person per <name type="person"> oder mittels <persName> ausgezeichnet wird. Derartige Variationsspielräume bei der Textauszeichnung schränkt das DTABf ein und ermöglicht somit die Interoperabilität der entsprechend annotierten Texte untereinander.

Das DTABf ist im Rahmen der DTA-Annotationsrichtlinien[10] ausführlich dokumentiert. Die Pflege und Weiterentwicklung erfolgt durch die DTABf-Steuerungsgruppe, die sich aus Expertinnen und Experten für die TEI-Auszeichnung und -Anpassung mit Verankerung in verschiedenen Communities zusammensetzt. Nachdem das DTABf von der DFG und CLARIN-D[11] zur Nachnutzung empfohlen wurde, setzen mehr und mehr externe Projekte auf die Verwendung des ursprünglich im Projektkontext des DTA entwickelten Standards mit dem Ziel, Ambiguitäten und folglich Fehlinterpretationen der Auszeichnungsmöglichkeiten zu minimieren.

Zwischen 2014 und 2016 wurde der Aufbau des DTA-Kernkorpus im Rahmen einer dritten Förderphase abgeschlossen. Parallel dazu ermöglichte ein Beitritt in den CLARIN-Verbund und die dortige Förderung bis 2019 umfangreiche Kurationsarbeiten. Statt selbst zu digitalisieren, erfolgte die Korpuserweiterung hier unter Einbezug der Community. Außerdem brachte sich das DTA mit seiner Expertise zum Basisformat in verschiedene Standardisierungsgremien ein. Schließlich erfolgte zwischen 2019 und 2021 im Kontext des Projekts CLARIAH-DE – dem Zusammenschluss der beiden Forschungsdateninfrastrukturen CLARIN-D und DARIAH-DE – mit der Einbindung von Texten aus der Digitalen Bibliothek ein weiterer wesentlicher Korpusaufbau.

Mit dem DTA entstand somit nicht nur ein Referenzkorpus für eine bisher nicht digital erschlossene Epoche der deutschen (Sprach-)Geschichte, sondern auch ein Goldstandard und Werkzeugkasten für zukünftige korpusbasierte Projekte der Digital Humanities. Das DTA konnte bis dato in vielfältiger Weise von der wissenschaftlichen Community nachgenutzt werden und ist bereits Bestandteil geplanter und sich im Aufbau befindlicher größerer Forschungsdateninfrastrukturen.

---

10 https://www.deutschestextarchiv.de/doku/basisformat/ (13.09.2023).
11 CLARIN-D ist der deutsche Partner des europäischen Forschungsinfrastrukturverbunds Common Language Resources and Technology Infrastructure.

2. (Nach-)Nutzungen des »Deutschen Textarchivs«

Das DTA macht im Grunde ein Angebot für zwei unterschiedliche Aspekte der Digital Humanities: Zum einen findet sich die bereits länger etablierte, traditionelle Computerlinguistik und Korpuslinguistik in den linguistischen Annotationen, Lemmatisierung, Tokenisierung, Suchwerkzeugen usw. wieder. Zum anderen wird durch die parallele Darstellung von Faksimile und Volltext, eine HTML-Lesefassung, die einfache Benutzbarkeit sowie die Verwendung des sehr gut dokumentierten Kodierungsstandards DTABf ein Angebot für Forscherinnen und Forscher geisteswissenschaftlicher Disziplinen wie Geschichts-, Kultur- und Literaturwissenschaften gemacht, für welche die Nutzung und Vermittlung computergestützter Methoden noch immer eher die Ausnahme als die Regel darstellt. Das DTA bietet eine Benutzeroberfläche inkl. Suchfunktion, die ohne die Installation zusätzlicher Software frei genutzt werden kann und für die die Kenntnis korpuslinguistischer Abfragesprachen nicht zwingend notwendig ist.

Das DTABf ist, wie oben bereits erwähnt, inzwischen in zahlreichen digitalen Editionen verwendet worden. Im Bereich der Wissenschaftsgeschichte wurde es in den Online-Editionen »schleiermacher digital«[12], der »edition humboldt digital«[13], der Berner Ausgabe der unselbständigen Schriften Alexander von Humboldts[14] und dem »Hidden Kosmos«-Projekt[15] zur Auszeichnung von Manuskripten und Drucken eingesetzt. Mit der Quellenedition von Schlüsseldokumenten zur jüdischen Geschichte in Hamburg[16] und der digitalen Edition der Briefe Erdmuthe Benignas von Reuß-Ebersdorf[17] orientierten sich zwei geschichts-, kultur- und religionswissenschaftliche Projekte bei der Texterstellung am DTABf. Die Online-Editionen »Jean Paul – Sämtliche Briefe digital«[18] und »Narragonien digital«[19] seien als Beispiele aus der Literaturwissenschaft zu nennen. Alle genannten digitalen Editionen haben das DTABf mehr oder weniger umfänglich an eigene projektspezifische Richtlinien angepasst. Im Rahmen des Projektes »Hidden Kosmos« zur Rekonstruktion von Alexander von Humboldts Kosmos-Vorlesungen aus Nachschriften wurde die eigens entwickelte DTABf-Variante »DTABf-M«[20] für die Auszeichnung von Manuskripten dokumentiert. Die Verwendung in so vielfältigen Fachbereichen wird durch die Anpassungsfähigkeit des DTA an unterschiedliche Textformen und Forschungsbedarfe erst ermöglicht.

12 https://schleiermacher-digital.de/ (13.09.2023).
13 https://edition-humboldt.de/ (13.09.2023).
14 https://humboldt.unibe.ch/text (13.09.2023).
15 https://www.culture.hu-berlin.de/de/forschung/projekte/hidden-kosmos (13.09.2023).
16 https://juedische-geschichte-online.net/ (13.09.2023).
17 https://erdmuthe.thulb.uni-jena.de/start.html (13.09.2023).
18 https://www.jeanpaul-edition.de/start.html (13.09.2023).
19 https://kallimachos.de/kallimachos/index.php/Narragonien (13.09.2023).
20 *Haaf/Thomas*, Historische Korpora des Deutschen Textarchivs.

Viele der auf Grundlage des DTABf edierten und annotierten Dokumente wurden schließlich auch als Volltexte in das DTA übertragen. Durch die Integration in das DTA können Editions- und Digitalisierungsprojekte zum einen eine größere Reichweite erzielen und die erstellten Forschungsdaten interdisziplinär nachnutzbar machen. Zum anderen werden die Forschungsdaten nachhaltig gesichert, was wissenschaftliche Institutionen und vor allem kleinere Projekte nicht immer aus eigenen Ressourcen gewährleisten können. Diese Möglichkeit stand und steht bisher im Rahmen der Förderung des DTA auch digitalen Editionen und Korpora offen, die ursprünglich nicht nach DTABf erstellt wurden, und dessen Forschungsdaten erst konvertiert und aufbereitet werden müssen. Für die »Texte der ersten Frauenbewegung«[21] ist die Integration ins DTA von nach DTABf erstellten Volltexten beschrieben, für die Stuttgarter digitalen Editionen »Das Himmlische Gastmahl« und »Meerwunder«[22] die Anpassung an das DTABf und Übertragung in das DTA.

Da das DTA in einer Vielzahl von Kooperationen den Workflow und die Hilfsmittel zur Erstellung eigener Textdigitalisate und die anschließende Integration in das Archiv optimieren konnte, entstanden in der Folge mehrere Projekte, die bereits in der Antragstellung die Zusammenarbeit mit dem DTA einplanten, so etwa die Volltextdigitalisierung der »Staats- und Gelehrte[n] Zeitung des Hamburgischen Unpartheyischen Correspondenten« und ihrer Vorläufer (1712–1848)[23] und »Die Evolution von komplexen Textmustern« (t.evo)[24] in Kooperation mit der Universität Paderborn sowie die »Archiv-, Editions- und Distributionsplattform für Werke der Frühen Neuzeit«[25] in Kooperation mit der Herzog August Bibliothek Wolfenbüttel. Einen weiteren Fall der Nachnutzung stellt die Integration von im DTA enthaltenen Volltexten in neu entwickelte Korpora bzw. Angebote dar, oftmals zum Zwecke spezifischer Forschungsfragen, die zusätzliche Verarbeitungsschritte, Annotationen oder die Anbindung an besondere Tools verlangen, wie bspw. das deutschsprachige Subkorpus des Dramenkorpus »Dracor«[26] oder das »GiesKaNe«-Korpus des DFG-Langzeitvorhabens »Syntaktische Grundstrukturen des Neuhochdeutschen«[27].

Aufgrund der linguistischen Aufbereitung und Annotation der Volltexte mit Tokenisierung, Lemmatisierung und POS-Tagging wurde das DTA insbesondere in den (historischen) Sprachwissenschaften stark rezipiert und verwendet. Es findet sich als Belegquelle und Analysetool in zahlreichen Veröffentlichungen, die grammatischen Wandel – allen voran morphologische, syntaktische und morphosyntaktische Phänomene – behandeln.

---

21 *Pfundt/Grumt Suárez/Gloning*, Word Usage.
22 *Kirchhoff/Ketschik*, Online durch die Elemente.
23 *Schuster/Wille*, Volltextdigitalisierung.
24 https://www.uni-paderborn.de/forschungsprojekte/tevo/ (13.09.2023).
25 https://www.hab.de/aedit-fruehe-neuzeit-archiv-editions-und-distributionsplattform-fuer-werke-der-fruehen-neuzeit/ (13.09.2023).
26 https://dracor.org/ger (13.09.2023).
27 https://gieskane.com/ (13.09.2023).

Über systemlinguistische und im engeren Sinne grammatische Phänomene hinaus konnten mithilfe des DTA auch für textlinguistische und literaturwissenschaftliche Forschungsfragen korpuslinguistische Methoden eingesetzt werden. Hervorzuheben sei hier das textlinguistische Projekt t.evo, in dem der Wandel textsortenspezifischer Merkmale und Strukturen in Zeitungen und Erbauungsliteratur anhand von bereits im DTA vorhandenen und neu in jenes zu integrierenden Volltexten untersucht wurde.

3. Aktueller Status des DTA

Zum jetzigen Zeitpunkt verfügt das DTA über 6.482 Volltexte und 370 Mio. Token. Während die letzte Projektphase 2016 endete, wurden das Korpus und die dazugehörigen Services und Funktionen im Rahmen sich anschließender projektbezogener Förderungen weiterhin betreut. Bis heute wird das DTA für den Aufbau des Arbeitsbereiches der historischen Korpora des Zentrums für digitale Lexikographie der deutschen Sprache (ZDL) mit neuen Volltexten erweitert. Außerdem dient es im Cluster »Historische Texte« des NFDI-Konsortiums Text+ als Archiv für historische, deutschsprachige Korpora (s. Kap. 4). Mit der Einbindung in diese Strukturen wird auch weiterhin eine möglichst große Zugänglichkeit und Reichweite der Forschungsdaten gewährleistet.

II. Die NFDI und ihr Konsortium Text+

Am 16. November 2018 beschlossen die Bundesregierung und die Regierungen der Länder der Bundesrepublik Deutschland in einer sogenannten Bund-Länder-Vereinbarung den Aufbau und die Förderung einer Nationalen Forschungsdateninfrastruktur (NFDI). Die Ausgangsstellung wird folgendermaßen problematisiert: Datenbestände von Wissenschaft und Forschung sind »heute oft dezentral, projektförmig und temporär gelagert«.[28] Obwohl in digitaler Form vorliegend, ist ein Zugang zu diesen Daten in systematischer, nachhaltiger Form nicht möglich. Das Ziel besteht demnach darin, die Bestände so verfügbar zu machen, »dass sie auch für Dritte leicht und geordnet auffindbar sind und über die Grenzen einzelner Datenbanken, Fachdisziplinen und Länder hinweg analysiert und verknüpft werden können.«[29] Dabei werden besonders zwei Mittel zur Erreichung dieser Ziele genannt: Einhaltung und gegebenenfalls Entwicklung von Standards und in diesem Zusammenhang auch die Befolgung der sogenannten FAIR-Prinzipien[30].

---

28 *BMBF*, Nationale Forschungsdateninfrastruktur.
29 Ebd.
30 *GWK*, Bund-Länder-Vereinbarung.

Um einen »langfristigen Mehrwert für das gesamte Wissenschaftssystem«[31] zu sichern, wurde am 12. Oktober 2020 der Verein »Nationale Forschungsdateninfrastruktur« (NFDI) e. V. gegründet. Da der Aufbau der NFDI von bis zu 30 Konsortien aus unterschiedlichen wissenschaftlichen Disziplinen mitgestaltet wird, ist die konsortienübergreifende Zusammenarbeit ein wichtiger Baustein der Initiative. Das gilt besonders für Themen, die für die sehr unterschiedlich geprägten Konsortien von gemeinsamem Interesse sind, bspw. »rechtliche Fragen rund um das Teilen von Forschungsdaten oder auch die technische Umsetzung der Zitierbarkeit von veröffentlichten Forschungsdaten.«[32]

Ein zentrales Anliegen aller NFDI-Konsortien ist die (Weiter-)Entwicklung derjenigen Infrastruktur, die den Zugang und die Arbeit mit (Forschungs-)Daten erst ermöglicht. Mit den Worten der damaligen Bundesforschungsministerin und GWK-Vorsitzenden, Anja Karliczek:

»Wenn wir von Daten als dem Rohstoff der Zukunft sprechen, dann ist die NFDI quasi eine Raffinerie, in der Daten aufbereitet, für alle zugänglich und damit nutzbar werden. Dabei hat die NFDI einen entscheidenden Vorteil: Die Daten werden nicht verbraucht – sie sind auch weiterhin in ihrem Rohzustand vorhanden, können von anderen Wissenschaftlern nachgenutzt und für eigene, auch völlig andere Forschungsfragen herangezogen werden. Der Datenschatz in der NFDI wird durch seinen Gebrauch nicht verringert, er wächst dadurch vielmehr immer weiter.«[33]

Am nationalen Vorhaben der NFDI sind vier Konsortien aus dem Bereich der Geisteswissenschaften beteiligt. *NFDI4Culture*[34] ist ein Konsortium für Forschungsdaten zu materiellen und immateriellen Kulturgütern. Die Interessengemeinschaft reicht von Architektur-, Kunst- und Musik- bis hin zu Theater-, Tanz-, Film- und Medienwissenschaften. Der Schwerpunkt von *NFDI4Objects*[35] liegt auf dem materiellen Erbe von rund drei Millionen Jahren Menschheits- und Umweltgeschichte. Zu den angesprochenen Disziplinen gehören nicht nur verschiedene Archäologien, sondern bspw. auch Anthropologie, Bauforschung, Geoarchäologie und nicht zuletzt Einrichtungen des Kulturerhalts und Provenienzforschung. *NFDI4Memory*[36] umfasst die Geschichtswissenschaft, aber auch andere Disziplinen, die historische Daten als Teil ihrer Methodik nutzen, wie z. B. die Wirtschafts- und Sozialwissenschaften, die Geographie und Regionalstudien. Schließlich komplettiert das Konsortium *Text+*[37] das geisteswissenschaftliche Kleeblatt.

---

31 *Kraft*, NFDI, S. 2.
32 Ebd., S. 8.
33 *GWK*, Bund-Länder-Vereinbarung.
34 https://nfdi4culture.de/de/index.html (13.09.2023).
35 https://www.nfdi4objects.net/ (13.09.2023).
36 https://4memory.de/ (13.09.2023).
37 https://www.text-plus.org/ (13.09.2023). Die vorliegende Publikation wurde im Rahmen des Konsortiums Text+ im Kontext der Arbeit des Vereins »Nationale Forschungsdateninfrastruktur« (NFDI) e. V. verfasst. NFDI wird von der Bundesrepublik Deutschland und den 16 Bundesländern finanziert. Das Konsortium Text+ wird gefördert durch die Deutsche Forschungsgemeinschaft (DFG) – Projektnummer 460033370.

Abb. 2: Visualisierung der Struktur des NFDI-Konsortiums Text+ inkl. der Aufteilung in verschiedene Datendomänen und Cluster.

Im Zentrum des seit Herbst 2021 im Kontext der NFDI geförderten Verbunds Text+ stehen digitale Forschungsdaten, die bzgl. Sprachräumen und Modalitäten von Sprache und Schriftsystemen sehr heterogen sind. Text+ konzentriert sich initial auf drei Datendomänen und ist im Aufbau entsprechend gegliedert: (1) sprach- und textbasierte Sammlungen, (2) lexikalische Ressourcen und (3) Editionen. In der geisteswissenschaftlichen Forschung haben digitale Sammlungen, Editionen und lexikalische Ressourcen eine lange Tradition und sind mit ausgereiften methodologischen Paradigmen verknüpft. Als Forschungsdaten sind die drei Datendomänen für eine breite Palette von Fachdisziplinen zentral, bspw. für die Linguistik, Literaturwissenschaft, Philologie, Philosophie, Sozial- und Politikwissenschaften. Außerdem sind sie grundlegend für interdisziplinäre Forschungspraktiken der Hermeneutik, Paläographie, Genealogie, Editionsphilologie, Lexikographie und Computerphilologie sowie Computerlinguistik.

Die einzelnen Datendomänen sind selbst nochmals in sogenannte Cluster unterteilt. Die Domäne der »sprach- und textbasierten Sammlungen« bspw. gliedert sich in die drei Cluster »Gegenwartssprachliche Daten«, »Historische Texte« sowie »Unstrukturierte Texte«, wobei das Cluster »Historische Texte« von der Berlin-Brandenburgischen Akademie der Wissenschaften (BBAW) koordiniert wird[38].

---

38 Zur Rolle des DTA im Cluster »Historische Texte« s. Kap. IV.

III. (Historische) Forschungsdaten

Forschungsdaten, so wurde die Initiative zur NFDI oben begründet, werden häufig »dezentral, projektförmig und temporär« gespeichert. Aus diesem Desiderat leitet sich der Auftrag ab, diese besser zugänglich und langfristig nachnutzbar zu machen. Was aber, wenn der oder die Forschende gar kein Interesse daran hat, die Forschungsdaten für die Nachnutzung bereitzustellen? »Ein offensichtliches Haupthindernis liegt sicher im [...] deutlichen Missverhältnis von Aufwand und Nutzen.«[39] Viel Arbeit also für wenig Reputation? Es kommt sogar noch schlimmer: »Die zweite große Herausforderung liegt in einer unklaren Rechtslage in Bezug auf Forschungsdaten.«[40]

Diesen beiden Einwänden zum Trotz sind Angaben zum Forschungsdatenmanagement oder formale Datenmanagementpläne für Fördereinrichtungen wie das Bundesministerium für Bildung und Forschung (BMBF) oder die Deutsche Forschungsgemeinschaft (DFG) in den letzten Jahren zu einem obligatorischen Beiwerk geworden. Dabei wurde man auf ein Desiderat aufmerksam, das dem gerade angedeuteten »I would prefer not to« eigentlich gar noch vorgelagert war. Um nämlich Forschungsdaten für die Nachnutzung bereitstellen zu können, muss erst einmal Konsens darüber bestehen, was Forschungsdaten überhaupt sind. Dass es hier große disziplinäre Unterschiede gibt, darauf weist Susanne Blumesberger in einer ihrer Publikationen hin[41]. Im Frühjahr 2021 veranstaltete die »Deutsche Initiative für Netzwerkinformation e.V.« (DINI) unter Beteiligung der DFG eigens eine Workshop-Reihe zum Thema »Datenmanagementpläne zwischen Vorgaben der Förderer und Forschungspraxis«. Einer DFG-Checkliste »für Antragstellende zur Planung und zur Beschreibung des Umgangs mit Forschungsdaten in Forschungsvorhaben« vom 21. Dezember 2021 ist schließlich zu entnehmen:

»Zu Forschungsdaten zählen u.a. Messdaten, Laborwerte, audiovisuelle Informationen, Texte, Surveydaten oder Beobachtungsdaten, methodische Testverfahren sowie Fragebögen. Korpora, Software und Simulationen können ebenfalls zentrale Ergebnisse wissenschaftlicher Forschung darstellen und werden daher ebenfalls unter den Begriff Forschungsdaten gefasst. Da Forschungsdaten in einigen Fachbereichen auf der Analyse von Objekten basieren (z.B. Gewebe-, Material-, Gesteins-, Wasser- und Bodenproben, Prüfkörper, Installationen, Artefakte und Kunstgegenstände), muss der Umgang mit diesen ebenso sorgfältig sein [...].«[42]

Die Zukunft Deutschlands als Technologienation hängt davon ab, »dass Daten in hoher Qualität dauerhaft und in immer größerem Umfang zur Verfügung stehen«[43]. In diesem Kontext obliegt es der NFDI, »die Datensouveränität für die Forschung

---

39 *Kaden*, Forschungsdaten, S. 6.
40 Ebd.
41 *Blumesberger*, Forschungsdaten, S. 2.
42 *DFG*, Forschungsdaten.
43 *Wiarda*, Keine Innovation.

in Deutschland sicher[zu]stellen und langfristig aus[zu]bauen.«[44] Was hat es aber mit den oben bereits erwähnten FAIR-Prinzipien auf sich? Oder anders: Was macht Forschungsdaten zu »fairen« Forschungsdaten?

Die FAIR-Prinzipien[45] wurden erstmals im März 2016 – und damit in den letzten Monaten der DTA-Projektförderung – vorgestellt. Können die Forschungsdaten im DTA also überhaupt FAIR sein? Für die von einem Konsortium aus Wissenschaftlerinnen und Wissenschaftlern und Organisationen 2016 im Journal »Scientific Data« veröffentlichen Prinzipien gibt es Vorläufer. Und einer dieser ist eine Publikation der Organisation for Economic Cooperation and Development (OECD) aus dem Jahr 2007 – »OECD Principles and Guidelines for Access to Research Data from Public Funding« – also genau im Jahr des DTA-Projektstarts. Insofern verwundert es nicht, dass das, was später mit dem erfolgreichen Akronym FAIR bezeichnet wurde, die Entwicklungen des DTA von Beginn an begleitete. Die Antwort lautet also ja, das DTA ist FAIR: Die Daten sind

- Findable, z. B. auch durch die im Kontext des Infrastrukturprojekts CLARIN-D entwickelte Metasuche VLO[46]
- Accessible, auf der Seite des DTA: www.deutschestextarchiv.de
- Interoperable, u. a. durch die strikte Anwendung des Kodierungsstandards TEI/DTABf
- Re-Usable, durch die Verwendung standardisierter Metadaten und die Vergabe der Lizenz CC BY-SA

Dabei kann im Kontext der FAIR-Prinzipien die Bedeutung von Metadaten kaum hoch genug eingeschätzt werden. Im Grunde ist die Verwendung von standardisierten Metadaten für alle vier Kriterien ein zentraler Punkt.

IV. Das »Deutsche Textarchiv« (DTA) in Text+

Das »Deutsche Textarchiv« (DTA) an der BBAW hat langjährige Expertise im Umgang mit historischen Texten. Neben textuellen Daten bringt das DTA mit dem Basisformat (DTABf) v. a. Kompetenzen im Bereich der Standardisierung von Text-, Annotations- und Metadaten mit. Im Zusammenspiel mit Software-Entwicklungen aus dem Akademienvorhaben »Digitales Wörterbuch der deutschen Sprache« (DWDS) bündelt das Zentrum Sprache der BBAW ausgewiesenes Fachwissen auf dem Gebiet der Bereitstellung von nachnutzbaren Forschungsdaten sowie von Such- und Analysemöglichkeiten.

---

44 Ebd.
45 https://www.go-fair.org/fair-principles/ (13.09.2023).
46 https://vlo.clarin.eu/ (13.09.2023).

1. Korpusbereitstellung

Im Kontext des NFDI-Konsortiums Text+ fungiert das DTA im Cluster »Historische Texte« der Datendomäne »text- und sprachbasierte Textsammlungen« als Archiv für strukturierte, historische, v. a. deutschsprachige Textkorpora. Dabei enthalten die Korpora des DTA – im Gegensatz zu manch anderen (linguistischen) Repositorien – keine automatisch generierten Referenzkorpora aus Textstücken, sondern vollständige Werke. Das DTA deckt den Zeitraum des Neuhochdeutschen, also die Zeitspanne von ca. 1600 bis 1920 ab.

Für jeden (neuen) Datensatz wird zuallererst eine maschinenlesbare Sammlungsbeschreibung[47] angelegt. Auf Objektebene werden dann die Metadaten in den Blick genommen: In welchem Format liegen diese vor? Wie vollständig/korrekt sind sie? Welches Potential gibt es bspw. durch die Anreicherung unter Verwendung von Authority Files (GND)? Nach der Transformation der eigentlichen Texte – diese können in verschiedenen Eingangsformaten vorliegen – in das Zielformat TEI-P5/DTABf wird der vollständige Datensatz in der DTA-Infrastruktur veröffentlicht. In der Regel fallen für die Korpora des DTA keine urheberrechtlichen Beschränkungen an, sie werden dann unter der Lizenz CC-BY SA 4.0 veröffentlicht. Außerdem werden die Forschungsdaten als Teilsammlung des Metakorpus »Historische Korpora« (dtaxl)[48] bereitgestellt.

Im ersten Jahr der Projektförderung wurden verschiedene Korpora unterschiedlicher Provenienz in das Spezialkorpus »Historische Texte« aufgenommen[49]. Die Kuration und Integration von Forschungsdaten, die im Rahmen einer Dissertation entstanden sind, zeigt bspw. ganz konkret den Mehrwert für die Nachnutzbarkeit. Das Korpus »Soldatenbriefe«[50] wurde im Bereich der Metadaten angereichert, linguistisch aufbereitet und kann jetzt – durch die korpusübergreifende Suche – mit anderen Ressourcen verglichen und analysiert werden. Die Forschungsdaten stehen unter der Creative-Commons-Lizenz CC BY-SA 4.0[51] zur weiteren Nachnutzung bereit. Die Sichtbarkeit wurde dadurch bereits erheblich verbessert. Durch die Möglichkeit der Integration in die konsortienweite Infrastruktur von Text+ werden die Forschungsdaten Teil der NFDI.

---

47 Diese schema-orientierte Sammlungsbeschreibung dient nicht zuletzt als Grundlage für die Integration in das Text+-Nachweissystem.
48 https://www.dwds.de/d/korpora/dtaxl (13.09.2023).
49 Eine Übersicht über alle Korpora des Spezialkorpus findet sich auf der Seite des DWDS: https://www.dwds.de/d/korpora/dtaxl (13.09.2023). Für Text+ wurden bislang folgende Sammlungen integriert: Briefe von Jean Paul (1781–1825), Nachrichten aus der Brüdergemeine (1819–1894), Der Neue Pitaval (1842–1890), Soldatenbriefe (1745–1872).
50 https://www.dwds.de/d/korpora/soldatenbriefe (13.09.2023).
51 https://creativecommons.org/licenses/by-sa/4.0/ (13.09.2023).

2. Korpusanalyse historischer Texte im Zusammenspiel aus Daten und Diensten am Zentrum Sprache

Ein Alleinstellungsmerkmal der Infrastruktur des Zentrums Sprache an der BBAW besteht in der Aufbereitung der Texte durch (computer-)linguistische Methoden. Diese sind bspw. die Voraussetzung für eine schreibweisentolerante Suche, welche im Kontext von historischen Texten – die mitunter orthographisch nicht einheitlich sind – eine besondere Bedeutung hat. So kann man sich durchaus vorstellen, dass Texte aus einem bestimmten Korpus ganz unterschiedliche graphematische Varianten des Wortes »Kleid« enthalten, bspw. »Kleidt«, »Kleydt«, »Cleyd«, »Cleit« etc. Nach der automatischen, linguistischen Aufbereitung der Texte würde eine Suche nach »Kleid« alle diese Varianten finden.

Neben der Bereitstellung von Derivatformaten wie das im Kontext von CLARIN-D entwickelte CMDI[52] und der Möglichkeit, Daten maschinell über Schnittstellen wie OAI-PMH abzufragen, beinhaltet das Zusammenspiel aus Daten und Diensten am Zentrum Sprache v. a. die Bereitstellung einer (auch korpusübergreifenden) Suche (inkl. Anbindung an Thesauri) sowie Tools zur Korpusanalyse (bspw. zur diachronen Analyse von Kollokationen mittels DiaCollo[53]).

V. Ausblick

Die bisherige Geschichte des »Deutschen Textarchivs« spiegelt eine rasante Entwicklung der Rahmenbedingungen für Digitalisierungsprojekte wider. Während Förderanträge um 2005 noch mit dem Ziel antreten konnten, das Ergebnis auf einer Compact Disc (CD) zu publizieren, wurden wenige Jahre später schon komplette virtuelle Forschungsumgebungen versprochen. Zweifellos ist die Vorstellung einer solchen Infrastruktur reizvoll: Eine allumfassende Lösung für »(a) die Gewinnung und Analyse von Primärdaten, (b) die Interpretation, Annotation oder Bearbeitung dieser Daten und damit die Erstellung von Sekundärdaten, (c) die Synthese und Erstellung einer Publikation oder (d) die Präsentation von Daten und Ergebnissen […]«[54]. Die damit verbundenen Herausforderungen sind allerdings nicht zu unterschätzen, denn eines ist klar geworden: Jede Disziplin hat eine eigene Vorstellung davon, was Forschungsdaten sind und nimmt damit für sich in Anspruch, eine auf diese Bedarfe angepasste Infrastruktur zu benötigen.

Auch das »Deutsche Textarchiv« hat zwischenzeitlich diesen Weg eingeschlagen. Als »Aktives Archiv« wurde es ausgebaut zu einer »Plattform zur Produktion, Kuration, Publikation, Analyse und Nachnutzung umfangreicher historischer Korpus-

---

52 https://www.clarin.eu/content/component-metadata (13.09.2023).
53 https://www.clarin-d.net/de/kollokationsanalyse-in-diachroner-perspektive (13.09.2023).
54 *Kindling*, Forschungsumgebungen, S. 8.

daten«[55]. Die Archivierung der Daten erfolgte im CTS-zertifizierten Clarin-Service-Center. Aktuell sieht das DTA im Kontext der NFDI seine Rolle weniger in einer virtuellen Forschungsumgebung oder einem Virtual Lab, sondern als Archiv für die Aufnahme neuer, hochqualitativer Forschungsdaten und deren Bereitstellung gemäß der FAIR-Prinzipien. Das DTA leistet somit einen wertvollen Beitrag dafür, mit einer standardkonformen und transparenten Datenaufbereitung für möglichst hohe Interoperabilität und maximale Nachnutzbarkeit von Forschungsdaten zu sorgen.

Literaturverzeichnis

Blumesberger, Susanne: Forschungsdaten in den Geisteswissenschaften. Bereits selbstverständlich oder doch noch etwas exotisch?, in: o-bib. Das offene Bibliotheksjournal Bd. 8, Nr. 4 (2021), S. 1–8, https://doi.org/10.5282/o-bib/5739 (13.09.2023).

Bundesministerium für Bildung und Forschung (BMBF): Nationale Forschungsdateninfrastruktur, 22. April 2021, https://www.bmbf.de/bmbf/de/forschung/das-wissenschaftssystem/nationale-forschungsdateninfrastruktur/nationale-forschungsdateninfrastruktur_node.html (13.09.2023).

Deutsche Forschungsgemeinschaft (DFG): Umgang mit Forschungsdaten Checkliste für Antragstellende zur Planung und zur Beschreibung des Umgangs mit Forschungsdaten in Forschungsvorhaben, 2021, https://www.dfg.de/download/pdf/foerderung/grundlagen_dfg_foerderung/forschungsdaten/forschungsdaten_checkliste_de.pdf (13.09.2023).

Fischer, Frank u. a.: Programmable Corpora: Introducing DraCor, an Infrastructure for the Research on European Drama, in: Proceedings of DH2019, Utrecht 2019, o.S.

Geyken, Alexander u. a.: Das Deutsche Textarchiv als Forschungsplattform für historische Daten in CLARIN, in: *Henning Lobin/Roman Schneider/Andreas Witt (Hg.)*, Digitale Infrastrukturen für die germanistische Forschung, Berlin/Boston 2018, S. 219–248 (= Germanistische Sprachwissenschaft um 2020, Bd. 6), Online-Version, https://doi.org/10.1515/9783110538663-011 (13.09.2023).

Geyken, Alexander/Haaf, Susanne: Integration heterogener historischer Textkorpora in das Deutsche Textarchiv. Strategien der Anlagerung und Perspektiven der Nachnutzung, in: *Joachim Gessinger/Angelika Redder/Ulrich Schmitz*: Korpuslinguistik, Duisburg 2018, S. 175–192 (= Osnabrücker Beiträge zur Sprachtheorie, Bd. 92).

Geyken, Alexander u. a.: Das Deutsche Textarchiv: Vom historischen Korpus zum aktiven Archiv, in: *Silke Schomburg u. a. (Hg.)*, Digitale Wissenschaft. Stand und Entwicklung digital vernetzter Forschung in Deutschland, 20./21. September 2010. Beiträge der Tagung, 2., ergänzte Fassung, Köln 2011, S. 157–161.

Gemeinsame Wissenschaftskonferenz (GWK): Pressemitteilung: Forschungsdaten nachhaltig sichern und nutzbar machen – Startschuss für eine Nationale Forschungsdateninfrastruktur, 16. November 2018, https://www.gwk-bonn.de/fileadmin/Redaktion/Dokumente/Pressemitteilungen/pm2018-13.pdf (13.09.2023).

Dies.: Bund-Länder-Vereinbarung zum Aufbau und Förderung einer Nationalen Forschungsdateninfrastruktur (NFDI) vom 26. November 2018, https://www.gwk-bonn.de/fileadmin/Redaktion/Dokumente/Papers/NFDI.pdf (13.09.2023).

Haaf, Susanne/Boenig, Matthias/Hug, Marius: Das Deutsche Textarchiv gestern und heute, in: Mitteilungsheft des Deutschen Germanistenverbandes 69/2 (2022), S. 127–134.

---

55 *Klein*, Deutsches Textarchiv (DTA). Vgl. auch *Geyken u. a.*, Das Deutsche Textarchiv.

Haaf, Susanne/Thomas, Christian: Die Historischen Korpora des Deutschen Textarchivs als Grundlage für sprachgeschichtliche Forschungen, in: *Holger Runow/Volker Harm/Levke Schiwek (Hg.)*, Sprachgeschichte des Deutschen: Positionierungen in Forschung, Studium, Schule, Stuttgart 2016, S. 217–234.
Dies./ders.: Enabling the Encoding of Manuscripts within the DTABf. Extension and Modularization of the Format, in: Journal of the Text Encoding Initiative [online] Issue 10 (2017), https://doi.org/10.4000/jtei.1650 (13.09.2023).
Hinrichs, Erhard u. a.: Text+: Language- and text-based Research Data Infrastructure, in: Zenodo, 2022, https://doi.org/10.5281/zenodo.6452002 (13.09.2023).
Jurish, Bryan/Geyken, Alexander/Werneke, Thomas: DiaCollo. diachronen Kollokationen auf der Spur, in: *Digital Humanities im deutschprachigen Raum e. V. (Hg.)*, http://dhd2016.de/ (Leipzig, 7.–12. März, 2016), Leipzig 2016, S. 172–175.
Jurish, Bryan/Thomas, Christian/Wiegand, Frank: Querying the Deutsches Textarchiv, in: *Udo Kruschwitz/Frank Hopfgartner/Cathal Gurrin (Hg.)*, Proceedings of the Workshop MindTheGap 2014: Beyond Single-Shot Text Queries: Bridging the Gap(s) between Research Communities (co-located with iConference 2014, Berlin, 4. März, 2014), 2014, S. 25–30.
Kaden, Ben: Warum Forschungsdaten Nicht Publiziert Werden, in: LIBREAS. Library Ideas 33 (2018), o.S., https://edoc.hu-berlin.de/bitstream/handle/18452/20046/kaden-fd.pdf?sequence=1 (13.09.2023).
Klein, Wolfgang: Deutsches Textarchiv (DTA) – Aufbau eines Aktiven Archivs deutscher Texte und Entwicklung entsprechender Werkzeuge, 2018, https://gepris.dfg.de/gepris/projekt/37149321/ (13.09.2023).
Kindling, Maxi: Virtuelle Forschungsumgebungen zur wissenschaftlichen Zusammenarbeit, in: cms-journal 35 (2012), S. 8.
Kirchhoff, Matthias/Ketschik, Nora: Online durch die Elemente. Die Stuttgarter digitalen Editionen »Das Himmlische Gastmahl« und »Meerwunder« und ihre nachhaltige Sicherung im Netz, in: Zeitschrift Für Deutsches Altertum Und Deutsche Literatur 149 (2020), S. 78–89, https://doi.org/10.3813/zfda-2020-0006 (13.09.2023).
Kraft, Sophie u. a.: Aufbau und Ziele von Nationale Forschungsdateninfrastruktur (NFDI) e. V., in: Bausteine Forschungsdatenmanagement 2 (2021), S. 1–9, https://doi.org/10.17192/bfdm.2021.2.8332 (13.09.2023).
OECD: OECD Principles and Guidelines for Access to Research Data from Public Funding, OECD Publishing, Paris, https://doi.org/10.1787/9789264034020-en-fr (13.09.2023).
Pfundt, Anna/Grumt Suárez, Melanie/Gloning, Thomas: Word Usage in German Texts on Women's Suffrage around 1900. Corpus Building, Lexical Documentation and the CLARIN-D Infrastructure, in: Selected Papers from the CLARIN Annual Conference 2019 (2020), S. 108–118, https://doi.org/10.3384/ecp2020172013 (13.09.2023).
Rißler-Pipka, Nanette u. a.: Community Involvement in Research Infrastructures: The User Story Call for Text+ (1.0.0), in: Zenodo, 2021, https://doi.org/10.5281/zenodo.5384085 (13.09.2023).
Schuster, Britt-Marie/Wille, Manuel: Die Volltextdigitalisierung der »Staats- und Gelehrten Zeitung des Hamburgischen Unpartheyischen Correspondenten« und ihrer Vorgänger (1712–1848) und ihr Nutzen. Befunde zur Genese und zum Wandel von Textmustern', in: *Oliver Pfefferkorn/Jörg Riecke/Britt-Marie Schuster (Hg.)*, Die Zeitung als Medium in der neueren Sprachgeschichte, Berlin/Boston 2017, S. 99–120, https://doi.org/10.1515/9783110517132-007 (13.09.2023).
Wiarda, Jan-Martin: Keine Innovation ohne Daten, in: Wiarda-Blog, 28. Juli 2022, http://www.jmwiarda.de/2022/07/28/keine-innovation-ohne-daten/ (13.09.2023).
Wiegand, Frank u. a.: Recherchieren, Arbeiten und Publizieren im Deutschen Textarchiv: ein Praxisbericht, in: Zeitschrift für Germanistische Linguistik 46.1 (2018), S. 147–161, https://doi.org/10.1515/zgl-2018-0009 (13.09.2023).

Organisationenverzeichnis

Akademie der Wissenschaften und der Literatur Mainz
Berlin-Brandenburgische Akademie der Wissenschaften (BBAW)
Bundesministerium für Bildung und Forschung (BMBF)
Deutsche Forschungsgemeinschaft (DFG)
Deutsche Initiative für Netzwerkinformation e.V. (DINI)
Deutsches Archäologisches Institut
Gemeinsame Wissenschaftskonferenz (GWK)
Göttinger Digitalisierungszentrum
Leibniz-Institut für Deutsche Sprache Mannheim
Leibniz-Institut für Europäische Geschichte
Max-Planck-Institut für Rechtsgeschichte und Rechtstheorie
Nationale Forschungsdateninfrastruktur e.V. (NFDI)
Staatsbibliothek zu Berlin – Stiftung Preußischer Kulturbesitz
Zentral- und Landesbibliothek Berlin
Zentrum Sprache BBAW

Roman Bleier (Graz), Elisabeth Brantner (Graz),
Josef Leeb (Oberpöring/München),
Eva Ortlieb (München/Bonn),
Constanze Rammer (Graz), Florian Zeilinger (Graz)

Der Reichstag zu Regensburg 1576

Eine digitale Edition

Der Reichstag gilt als eines der wenigen zentralen Foren, die das Heilige Römische Reich Teutscher Nation als Gemeinwesen hervorgebracht hat. Bis zu seiner Verstetigung ab 1663 arbeitete er in Gestalt von unregelmäßig durch den Kaiser einberufenen Versammlungen eines sich im 16. Jahrhundert verfestigenden Kreises von Herrschaftsträgerinnen und Herrschaftsträgern, den sogenannten Reichsständen, die für mehrere Wochen oder Monate in einer Reichsstadt zusammenkamen. In einer seit dem Beginn der Neuzeit zunehmend formalisierten Weise berieten sie gemeinsam mit dem Reichsoberhaupt über aktuelle und strukturelle Fragen der Reichspolitik und kamen dabei in der Regel auch zu Entscheidungen, die in einem als Reichsabschied bezeichneten Schlussdokument mit Gesetzescharakter zusammengefasst wurden. Der Reichstag war Teil einer gemeineuropäischen Kultur von Ständeversammlungen, in denen Ansprüche auf politische Teilhabe verhandelt und verwirklicht wurden[1].

Dies gilt auch für den Reichstag, der am 25. Juni 1576 von Kaiser Maximilian II. in Regensburg eröffnet wurde und am 12. Oktober desselben Jahres mit einem Reichsabschied zu Ende ging. In Regensburg persönlich anwesend oder durch Bevollmächtigte vertreten waren rund 200 Herrschaftsträger, Gesandte mehrerer europäischer Mächte – etwa Frankreichs, Spaniens oder des russischen Zarenreichs – sowie zahlreiche Supplikantinnen und Supplikanten, die im Reichstag eine Gelegenheit sahen, ihre Bitten und Beschwerden vorzubringen[2].

Die historische Bedeutung der Reichstage veranlasste die Historische Kommission bei der Bayerischen Akademie der Wissenschaften schon in der Mitte des 19. Jahrhunderts, die Edition ihrer Akten in Angriff zu nehmen. Als jüngste Abteilung dieses Unternehmens sind die »Reichsversammlungen 1556–1662« für die Reichstage und weitere Reichsversammlungen nach 1555 zuständig. Während diese Editionen bisher in Buchform erschienen und zum Teil retrodigitalisiert wurden,

---

1 *Liebmann*, Reichstag; *Haug-Moritz*, Reichstag; *dies.*, Historische Einführung.
2 *Leeb*, Der Reichstag 1576: Verhandlungsthemen und -ergebnisse.

stellt die Edition zum Reichstag von 1576 die erste vollständig digitale Edition von Reichstagsakten dar[3].

Der vorliegende Beitrag bietet einen Überblick über diese Edition. Neben den edierten Texten als Kernstück jeder Edition (Kap. II) werden andere, nur digital mögliche Dokumentationsformen vorgestellt (Kap. I und III). Weitere Abschnitte sind der Anreicherung der Daten, Suchfunktionen und Visualisierungen gewidmet (Kap. IV–VI). Die Edition schlägt darüber hinaus eine bestimmte Deutung des Reichstags vor, die sich in einem exemplarisch umgesetzten Datenmodell niederschlägt (Kap. VII). Am Schluss stehen einige Beobachtungen aus der Praxis des digitalen Edierens (Kap. VIII).

I. Die Archivdokumentation: Ein virtuelles Reichstagsarchiv?

Wie die meisten Editionen stand auch die digitale Edition zum Reichstag von 1576 vor der Aufgabe, aus einer großen Menge an potentiell relevantem Material in zahlreichen Archiven auszuwählen, welche Quellen als Grundlage für die Edition im engeren Sinn sowie deren Kommentierung durchgesehen werden sollten. Die Wahl fiel auf Bestände von insgesamt 34 deutschen und österreichischen Archiven und Bibliotheken, in denen die Überlieferung von rund 100 Reichsständen verwahrt wird – das ist etwa die Hälfte derer, die den Reichstag besuchten. Ziel der Auswahl war, die geographische, ständische und konfessionelle Vielfalt des Reichs so gut wie möglich abzubilden und dabei auch besonders reichhaltige Archive zu berücksichtigen[4].

Das digitale Edieren bietet die Möglichkeit, diesen von allen Editorinnen und Editoren in der einen oder anderen Form zu leistenden Arbeitsschritt nicht nur in Gestalt eines Quellenverzeichnisses zu dokumentieren, sondern die erhobenen Informationen systematisch festzuhalten und zur Verfügung zu stellen. Die Nennung einer archivalischen Einheit kann durch Angaben zu ihrem Inhalt bis hin zu Stückverzeichnungen ergänzt werden; Archivalien, die entgegen den Erwartungen kein relevantes Material enthielten, lassen sich mit einem entsprechenden Hinweis kennzeichnen. Damit wird eine Fülle von zusätzlichen Datumsangaben sowie Informationen zu Personen (z. B. Korrespondenzpartner), Orten (z. B. Ausstellungsorte) und Sachzusammenhängen (z. B. in Dorsalvermerken) zugänglich, selbst wenn die Angaben nicht für das Sachregister verwertet werden konnten. Alle diese zusätzlichen Informationen sind recherchierbar und können mit anderen Daten verknüpft werden.

Die digitale Edition zum Reichstag 1576 präsentiert diese Informationen in ihrer »Archivdokumentation«[5]. Alphabetisch nach den betreffenden Archiven geordnet sind dort alle eingesehenen archivalischen Einheiten gemäß der jeweiligen Archivtektonik mit mehr oder weniger zusätzlichen Informationen nachgewiesen.

---

3   Ders., Editorische Einführung 1576.
4   Ausgewählte Archive und Bibliotheken, https://gams.uni-graz.at/o:rta1576.bt496a1a2 (01.02.2024).
5   https://gams.uni-graz.at/context:rta1576.ad (01.02.2024).

Wie viele Informationen Berücksichtigung finden, hängt von der anzunehmenden Relevanz der Materialien für die Thematik der Edition ab. Das Spektrum reicht von summarischen Beschreibungen des Inhalts einer Einheit über unterschiedlich detaillierte Hinweise auf interessante Teile darin bis hin zu Stückverzeichnungen, Letztere im Wesentlichen für alle Archivalien, die bereits zeitgenössisch oder durch die verwahrenden Archive ausdrücklich als Akten des Reichstags 1576 ausgewiesen wurden. Die »Archivdokumentation« erhebt ihre Informationen gemäß einer festgelegten Liste von Kategorien und verwendet dabei ein kontrolliertes Vokabular[6]. Bietet ein Archiv online Findbücher oder Bilder der betreffenden Archivalien an, führen Links an die entsprechenden Stellen. Unabhängig von der Auswahl bestimmter Stücke für die Edition stehen in der »Archivdokumentation« Informationen zu über 10.000 Stücken in mehr als 1.000 archivalischen Einheiten zur Verfügung.

Die »Archivdokumentation« erfüllt im Rahmen der digitalen Edition drei Hauptaufgaben. Zum einen erhöht sie die Menge an Informationen, die angeboten werden, und macht die Edition damit – so die Hoffnung – auch für Fragen jenseits des in Texten edierten Reichstagsgeschehens im engeren Sinn nutzbar. Zum anderen dient die Dokumentation als Einstieg auch in andere Teile der Edition und Erschließungsinstrument: Ist ein aufgelistetes Stück als edierter Text oder als Bild zugänglich, ermöglichen Links den direkten Zugriff auf diese Ressourcen. Für zentrale Stücke wird in Gestalt einer Link-Liste angegeben, in welchen weiteren Überlieferungen sie enthalten sind, womit vorsichtige Rückschlüsse auf ihre Verbreitung bzw. Bedeutung für bestimmte Reichsstände möglich werden. Indem die relevante Überlieferung so detailliert wie möglich beschrieben wird, lässt sich drittens nachvollziehen, auf welcher Grundlage die Editorinnen und Editoren die von ihnen edierten oder erschlossenen Stücke ausgewählt haben.

Zum virtuellen Reichstagsarchiv wird die »Archivdokumentation« natürlich nur insofern, als sie das eingesehene Archivmaterial in der Ordnung der besuchten Archive erschließt. Dem Ziel, diese Überlieferung auch online einsehbar zu machen, dient ein eigener Abschnitt der Edition, der mit »Archivalien in Bildern«[7] überschrieben ist.

II. Die Edition

1. Aufbau und Gliederung der Edition

Um bei der digitalen Edition die Vergleichbarkeit mit den in Buchform publizierten Bänden[8] zu wahren, wurden die bislang geltenden Richtlinien der Abteilung »Deut-

---

6 Dokumentation Archivdokumentation, https://gams.uni-graz.at/o:rta1576.docu.ad (01.02.2024).
7 https://gams.uni-graz.at/context:rta1576.facs (01.02.2024).
8 Vgl. deren Zusammenstellung: https://www.historischekommission-muenchen.de/abteilungen/deutsche-reichstagsakten-reichsversammlungen-1556-1662#c171 (01.02.2024).

sche Reichstagsakten, Reichsversammlungen 1556–1662« hinsichtlich der Auswahl der edierten Texte[9] und ihrer Anordnung in Form von Kapiteln beibehalten. Die Edition gliedert sich demnach, orientiert am zeitlichen Ablauf und thematischen Kriterien, in neun Abschnitte, die von den Vorakten bis zum Reichsabschied das Verhandlungsgeschehen abdecken. Vorangestellt ist eine Einleitung, die die Beratungspunkte erläutert, den Reichstag historisch verortet und die beteiligten Akteurinnen und Akteure auflistet.

Grundsätzlich ist festzuhalten, dass trotz der gegenüber den gedruckten Bänden erweiterten Möglichkeiten auch bei der digitalen Edition eine umfassende Darbietung aller in den Archiven aufgefundenen Akten nicht möglich ist. Vielmehr bedingen der Überlieferungsumfang und zeitliche Limitierungen bei der Bearbeitung eine selektive Präsentation, die sich überwiegend an Relevanzkriterien orientiert: Ediert werden neben singulären Vorakten die beiden Eckpunkte des Reichstags, die Proposition und der Reichabschied, sodann Protokolle und Reichstagsberichte, die den Verhandlungsgang wiedergeben, sowie Dokumente, die die Ergebnisse der Beratungen auf den verschiedenen Verhandlungsebenen enthalten. Dabei treten neben die im Volltext edierten Quellen zum einen weitere, inhaltlich über Schlagworte erschlossene Aktenstücke als Bestandteil der edierten Texte. Zum anderen ist es in der digitalen Edition möglich, viele Quellen im Bild (»Archivalien in Bildern«) zu präsentieren, deren Erschließung über die »Archivdokumentation« erfolgt.

Insgesamt umfasst die Edition damit 314 Einzelstücke (178 im Volltext – gemäß der Zählweise der analogen Editionspraxis in der Reihe der »Reichsversammlungen« entspräche dies 632 Stücken[10] – sowie 136 in inhaltlich erschlossener Form). Wenngleich dieses Programm nicht alle Quellen einbezieht, so gewährleistet doch die »Archivdokumentation« deren vollumfängliche Erfassung. Dies bedeutet auch, dass die »edierten Texte« nur einen Bestandteil der digitalen Edition darstellen, den komplementierend die »Archivdokumentation« und die »Archivalien in Bildern« als weitere Elemente ergänzen.

2. Die edierten und erschlossenen Texte im Einzelnen

Im ersten Abschnitt werden die vor der Eröffnung des Reichstags angefallenen Akten ediert[11], beginnend mit dem Ausschreiben Kaiser Maximilians II. und der zugehörigen Adressatenliste der geladenen Stände, die eine wichtige Quelle für den formaljuristisch-reichsrechtlichen Korpus aller Reichsstände darstellt, der freilich von der realpolitischen Wirklichkeit erheblich abwich. Es folgen Bekanntgaben zum

---

9 Vgl. dazu *Lanzinner (Bearb.)*, Der Reichstag zu Speyer 1570, S. 75–113.
10 In den gedruckten Bänden der Editionsreihe »Reichsversammlungen 1556–1662« werden einzelne Protokolltage als jeweils eigene Stücknummer erfasst. Im Gegensatz dazu zählen wir in der digitalen Edition jeweils ein ganzes Protokoll als ein Stück.
11 Vgl. Kap. A, https://gams.uni-graz.at/context:rta1576.ed (01.02.2024).

Aufschub der Versammlung[12] und eine Reichstagswerbung, mit welcher der Kaiser vorrangig die persönliche Teilnahme der Kurfürsten anstrebte. Zu diesen im Volltext edierten Quellen kommen als inhaltlich durch Schlagworte erschlossene Vorakten die Instruktionen der führenden Reichsstände für ihre Gesandten nach Regensburg[13].

Ein zentrales Dokument auf jedem Reichstag stellte die Proposition dar, mit der der Kaiser die Programmatik festlegte und zugleich die Verhandlungen offiziell eröffnete[14].

Der Verhandlungsgang zu diesem Reichstagsprogramm, aber ebenso zu weiteren Gegenständen, die daneben zur Sprache kamen, wird anhand von 17 Protokollen oder Protokollauszügen dokumentiert. Diese umfassen das gesamte institutionelle Gefüge, das den Reichstag konstituierte: die kaiserliche Seite mit dem Protokoll des Geheimen Rats[15], die Beratungen in den drei Reichstagskurien, dem Kurfürstenrat[16], Fürstenrat[17] und Städterat[18], die Verhandlungen im Supplikationsausschuss[19] zu den Bittschriften an den Kaiser und die Reichsstände sowie, als weiteres prägendes Element der Reichstage in der zweiten Hälfte des 16. Jahrhunderts, die Religionsdebatten, die im Gegensatz zu den strikt nach Kurien getrennten Hauptverhandlungen in den interkurialen Versammlungen beider Konfessionsparteien geführt wurden[20]. Ergänzend wird in inhaltlich erschlossener Form das Resolutionsprotokoll des kaiserlichen Reichshofrats[21] präsentiert, das wichtige Aufschlüsse zu den während der Reichsversammlung an den Kaiser gerichteten Supplikationen und Anträgen aus der Bevölkerung des Reichs gibt. Es verdeutlicht damit die über das Verhandlungsspektrum in den Kurien hinausgehende Funktion des Reichstags als bedeutendes Forum für die intensivierte Kommunikation zwischen dem Kaiser und nicht nur den Reichsständen, sondern überdies mit weiteren Reichsgliedern.

Neben den Protokollen gehen auch die Berichte der Reichstagsgesandten an ihre Herrschaften auf das Verhandlungsgeschehen ein und bieten kommentierende oder erläuternde Aspekte aus dem spezifischen Blickwinkel der jeweiligen Ständevertreter, die im Duktus der offiziösen Mitschriften oftmals fehlen. Während in den gedruckten Editionen die Berichte und ebenso die Weisungen an die Gesandten aus

---

12 Zur Vorgeschichte des Reichstags und dessen Verzögerung vgl. die Einleitung zur Edition, Kap. 1, https://gams.uni-graz.at/o:rta1576.bt34fgr#d1e25 (01.02.2024).
13 Instruktionen, https://gams.uni-graz.at/o:rta1576.et443 (01.02.2024).
14 Proposition, https://gams.uni-graz.at/o:rta1576.edd1e12w110525 (01.02.2024).
15 https://gams.uni-graz.at/o:rta1576.edd1e7w15223 (01.02.2024).
16 Kurmainzer Protokoll, https://gams.uni-graz.at/o:rta1576.edd1e11W110511 (01.02.2024); kursächsisches Protokoll, https://gams.uni-graz.at/o:rta1576.edd1e10d24421 (01.02.2024).
17 Österreichisches Protokoll, https://gams.uni-graz.at/o:rta1576.edd1e7w152270 (01.02.2024); dazu drei kleinere Protokollauszüge, Kap. C.I.c, https://gams.uni-graz.at/context:rta1576.ed (01.02.2024).
18 Ulmer Protokoll, https://gams.uni-graz.at/o:rta1576.edd1e10u1591 (01.02.2024).
19 https://gams.uni-graz.at/o:rta1576.edd1e7W1109116 (01.02.2024).
20 Verhandlungen der protestantischen Stände, https://gams.uni-graz.at/o:rta1576.edd1e11 m515221 (01.02.2024); der katholischen Stände, https://gams.uni-graz.at/o:rta1576.edd1e10 m5152274 (01.02.2024); dazu weitere Protokollauszüge, Kap. C.I.g, https://gams.uni-graz.at/context:rta1576.ed (01.02.2024).
21 https://gams.uni-graz.at/o:rta1576.et1987 (01.02.2024).

Platzgründen nur im Kommentar ausgewertet werden können[22], ist in der digitalen Edition eine integrale Berücksichtigung möglich: Für den Reichstag 1576 werden 60 Berichte der kursächsischen Delegation im Volltext ediert[23], die zugehörigen Weisungen Kurfürst Augusts von Sachsen sind als Einzeldokumente durch Schlagworte erschlossen[24]; Gleiches gilt für die Kurmainzer Reichstagskorrespondenz[25]. Auf diese Weise erfasst die Edition 158 Berichte und Weisungen.

Das Resultat der protokollierten und in Berichtsform geschilderten Beratungen geben die Verhandlungsakten wieder, die in der Edition in die drei Unterbereiche Haupt-, Neben- und Religionsverhandlungen aufgeteilt werden.

Erstere finden sich im Kapitel »Proponierte Themen«, das die Akten der Themen beinhaltet, die der Kaiser in der Proposition festlegte, die sogenannten Hauptartikel[26]. Sie betrafen auch 1576 die Standardthemen der Reichstage in der zweiten Hälfte des 16. Jahrhunderts[27]: die kaiserliche Forderung einer Reichssteuer für die Abwehr der osmanischen Bedrohung in Ungarn und Kroatien, zeitgenössisch bezeichnet als »Türkenhilfe«, sowie die reichsinternen Belange Sicherung des Landfriedens, Verbesserung des Reichsjustizwesens und des Reichswährungssystems (Reichsmünzordnung), die Rektifizierung der Reichsmatrikel als Grundlage des Reichssteuersystems, die Bemühungen um die Rückgewinnung verlorener Reichsterritorien und die Frage des Vorrangs beim Reichstag, also die strittige Sessionsfolge bei offiziellen Anlässen und in den Kurien. Innerhalb der einzelnen Hauptartikel ist das Ordnungsprinzip die chronologische Abfolge der Interaktion zwischen Kaiser und Reichsständen: Als erstes Aktenstück jeweils die Antwort der Reichsstände auf die Vorgaben in der Proposition, sodann die Replik des Kaisers, die Duplik der Stände usw. Diesen zentralen Schriften werden zugehörige Beilagen oder Resolutionen zugeordnet. Daneben werden hier Eingaben und Werbungen im thematischen Kontext ediert, am Beispiel der »Türkenhilfe« etwa die Debatte um die Einrichtung eines Ritterordens in Ungarn oder die Supplikationen der innerösterreichischen Landstände um eine separate Reichshilfe.

Als Nebenverhandlungen werden alle Gegenstände eingestuft, die nicht in der Proposition enthalten waren, sondern von anderer Seite an den Reichstag gebracht wurden oder sich während des Verhandlungsverlaufs ergaben. Die Berücksichtigung für die Edition und die Auswahl der edierten Dokumente[28] orientieren sich zum

---

22 Vgl. *Lanzinner*, Der Reichstag zu Speyer 1570, S. 77–80.
23 Erster Bericht, https://gams.uni-graz.at/o:rta1576.edd1e7d24431 (01.02.2024).
24 https://gams.uni-graz.at/o:rta1576.et234 (01.02.2024).
25 Berichte, https://gams.uni-graz.at/o:rta1576.et439 (01.02.2024); Weisungen, https://gams.uni-graz.at/o:rta1576.et863 (01.02.2024).
26 Vgl. Kap. E, https://gams.uni-graz.at/context:rta1576.ed (01.02.2024).
27 Zu den proponierten Themen, deren Hintergründen und Beratung vgl. die Einleitung zu den edierten Texten, Kap. 2 (mit Literaturangaben): https://gams.uni-graz.at/o:rta1576.bt34fgr#d1e344 (01.02.2024).
28 Vgl. Kap. F, https://gams.uni-graz.at/context:rta1576.ed (01.02.2024). Zu den Nebenthemen und deren Beratung vgl. die Einleitung zu den edierten Texten, Kap. 3 (mit Literaturangaben), https://gams.uni-graz.at/o:rta1576.bt34fgr#d1e2255 (01.02.2024).

einen daran, ob sie mit der Aufnahme in den Reichsabschied reichsgesetzliche Relevanz erhielten (Reichspoliceyordnung und Zollangelegenheiten), und zum anderen an ihrer politischen Bedeutung. Dies betrifft als außenpolitische Belange die von Maximilian II. den Reichsständen vorgebrachte Problematik der Doppelwahl eines Königs in Polen mit seiner eigenen Nominierung, die moskowitische Gesandtschaft an den Kaiser sowie eine Werbung an die Reichsstände für die aufständischen niederländischen Provinzen in deren Krieg gegen Spanien.

Ein gesondertes Kapitel beinhaltet die in den erwähnten Religionsprotokollen angesprochenen Religionsgravamina und den kontroversen Aktenwechsel der Konfessionsparteien mit dem Kaiser[29]. Die beträchtliche Anzahl von 23 präsentierten Aktenstücken verweist auf die erhebliche Relevanz und Brisanz dieser Problematik auch beim Reichstag 1576.

Angesichts ihres Umfangs ist die Edition der während des Reichstags vorgebrachten Supplikationen nicht möglich, auch nicht beschränkt auf diejenigen Bittschriften, die der Kanzlei des Kurfürsten von Mainz als Reichstagskanzlei vorgelegt wurden[30]. An ihre Stelle tritt die Stückverzeichnung der drei umfangreichen Bände des sogenannten »Liber supplicationum« in der »Archivdokumentation«. In diesen Aktenbänden sammelte die Mainzer Kanzlei die dort eingegangenen Bittschriften samt ihren Beilagen und etwaiger weiterer Korrespondenz[31]. Die Bände sind auch als Bilder verfügbar und können direkt aus der »Archivdokumentation« oder – über ihre Signatur – über die »Archivalien in Bildern« angesteuert werden[32]. Im letzten Abschnitt der »edierten Texte« folgt der Reichsabschied[33], der die greifbaren Resultate der Reichsversammlung rechtsverbindlich festhielt und mit dem diese Ergebnisse in gedruckter Form im gesamten Reich publiziert wurden. Zugleich markierte dessen Verlesung den Abschluss des Reichstags.

3. Die Gestaltung der Stücke – Editionsgrundsätze

Die Editionsgrundsätze und die Gestaltung der edierten Stücke weichen bei der digitalen Edition von den Regeln für die gedruckten Bände der »Reichsversammlungen 1556–1662«[34] insofern ab, als der Zwang zur Reduktion des Umfangs im Gegen-

---

29 Vgl. Kap. G, https://gams.uni-graz.at/context/rta1576.ed (01.02.2024). Vgl. dazu Kap. 4 der Einleitung, https://gams.uni-graz.at/o:rta1576.bt34fgr#d1e3269 (01.02.2024).
30 Zu diesem Thema: https://gams.uni-graz.at/o:rta1576.bt2353es1 (01.02.2024).
31 Bd. 1, https://gams.uni-graz.at/o:rta1576.adwn1#W1.10.7 (01.02.2024); Bd. 2, https://gams.uni-graz.at/o:rta1576.adwn1#W1.10.8 (01.02.2024); Bd. 3, https://gams.uni-graz.at/o:rta1576.adwn1#W1.10.9 (01.02.2024).
32 https://gams.uni-graz.at/o:rta1576.imgw1107b83 (01.02.2024); https://gams.uni-graz.at/o:rta1576.imgw1108b104 (01.02.2024); https://gams.uni-graz.at/o:rta1576.imgw1109b103 (01.02.2024).
33 https://gams.uni-graz.at/o:rta1576.edd1e10w13411 (01.02.2024).
34 Vgl. *Lanzinner*, Der Reichstag zu Speyer 1570, S. 85–89, 98–102, 113.

satz zur Buchform entfällt. Deshalb können unter Verzicht auf Regesten oder Textreferate viele Stücke im Volltext dargeboten werden.

Aufbau und Strukturierung der edierten Texte nutzen die variablen Möglichkeiten der digitalen Form: Bei den Protokollen[35] erscheint zunächst der Stückkopf mit der Angabe der Textgrundlage und des zeitgenössischen Titels sowie mit zusätzlichen Informationen aus der »Archivdokumentation«. Mit dem zweiten Reiter sind das Verzeichnis aller protokollierten Tage und nachgeordnet die Tageseinträge aufrufbar. Für den eigentlichen Protokolltext sind wahlweise die Leseansicht oder die textkritische Ansicht möglich. In Verbindung mit der Leseansicht erscheint der Sachkommentar mit Querverweisen auf andere edierte Stücke oder die »Archivdokumentation« sowie mit der Erläuterung historischer Rückbezüge und unklarer Formulierungen. Jeder einzelne Tageseintrag wird mit einer vorangestellten Liste von Schlagworten (»Sachbegriffe«) erschlossen. Diese dienen nicht nur dazu, die Sachverhalte zu erfassen, sondern ihre Auswahl berücksichtigt auch das Reichstags- und Beratungsverfahren; zudem stellen sie die Verbindung zum Sachregister her. Die textkritische Ansicht ermöglicht Aufschlüsse zur Textgenese, indem Hervorhebungen, Streichungen, Einfügungen und Marginalien des Quellentexts farblich markierbar sind. Weitere Reiter führen zur Ansicht des Aktenstücks in TEI/XML[36] bzw. zur RDF[37]-Ansicht.

Die editorische Gestaltung der Haupt- und Nebenverhandlungsakten[38] gleicht jener der Protokolle. Der Stückkopf wird hier zusätzlich um den Nachweis der beiden Kollationierungsexemplare (B und C) ergänzt, die Ansicht als Lesetext entspricht jener der Protokolle mit dem Volltext der Quelle und dem Sachkommentar. Die textkritische Ansicht enthält bei den Verhandlungsakten neben der Veranschaulichung der Textgenese in einer gesonderten Spalte alle Abweichungen, Zusätze oder Streichungen gegenüber der Textgrundlage in zwei kollationierten Textzeugen.

Die im Gegensatz zur Volltextdarbietung durch Schlagworte erschlossenen Quellen[39] geben jeweils das Datum, die erwähnten Personen und Orte sowie Sachbegriffe an, um auf diese Weise den thematischen Kontext zu veranschaulichen. Die erschlossenen Texte werden mit der »Archivdokumentation« verlinkt, von wo aus vielfach der Schritt zum zugehörigen Aktenstück im Bild (»Archivalien in Bildern«) und damit zum Volltext der originären Quelle möglich ist.

Die Optionen der digitalen Edition werden zudem erweitert um in die Texte eingebrachte Anreicherungen.

---

35 Vgl. am Beispiel des Mainzer Kurfürstenratsprotokolls, https://gams.uni-graz.at/o:rta1576. ed1e11W110511 (01.02.2024).
36 Vgl. unten Kap. IV.
37 Vgl. unten Kap. VII.
38 Vgl. am Beispiel der Antwort der Reichsstände zum 1. Hauptartikel, https://gams.uni-graz.at/o:rta1576.ed1e24w15224 (01.02.2024).
39 Vgl. am Beispiel der Weisungen Kf. Augusts von Sachsen, https://gams.uni-graz.at/o:rta1576.et234 (01.02.2024).

III. Archivalien in Bildern

Dank der Kooperationsbereitschaft der besuchten Archive[40] kann die digitale Edition der Akten des Regensburger Reichstags 1576 als erste Edition innerhalb der »Deutschen Reichstagsakten« nicht nur edierte bzw. erschlossene Texte und Verzeichnisse anbieten, sondern ermöglicht unter dem Menüpunkt »Archivalien in Bildern«[41] auch den Zugriff auf digitale Repräsentationen von Teilen des gesichteten Archivguts. Benutzerinnen und Benutzer erhalten damit Zugriff auf ein Vielfaches des Materials, das im Rahmen des Projekts transkribiert und kommentiert bzw. durch Schlagworte erschlossen werden konnte. Damit soll, ebenso wie im Fall der »Archivdokumentation«, der Wert der Edition für diejenigen erhöht werden, die nicht oder nicht in erster Linie an dem Ausschnitt des Reichstagsgeschehens interessiert sind, der im Mittelpunkt der »edierten Texte« steht.

Für die als Bilder zur Verfügung stehenden Archivalien wurden vor allem die im Hinblick auf Material für den Reichstag 1576 größten Archive herangezogen. Am umfassendsten sind die Akten im Haus-, Hof- und Staatsarchiv in Wien präsentiert, das die kaiserliche bzw. österreichische sowie die Kurmainzer Überlieferung verwahrt. Damit soll zugleich der Bedeutung des Kaisers Rechnung getragen werden, die aus den klassischerweise für die Edition ausgewählten Texten nicht deutlich genug hervortritt. So stehen beispielsweise in Gestalt des »Liber supplicationum« aus dem Mainzer Erzkanzlerarchiv nicht nur die der Reichstagskanzlei übergebenen Supplikationen in Bildern zur Verfügung[42], sondern auch das Resolutionsprotokoll des den Kaiser nach Regensburg begleitenden Reichshofrats[43]. Die Überlieferung im Dresdener Hauptstaatsarchiv ist wegen der Schlüsselrolle des sächsischen Kurfürsten im Reichstagsgeschehen von 1576 zentral; hier liegt der Schwerpunkt der Bilder auf dessen Korrespondenzen. Ebenfalls von großer Wichtigkeit war der Kurfürst von der Pfalz; die »Archivalien in Bildern« berücksichtigen aus dem Bayerischen Hauptstaatsarchiv in München insbesondere die Religionsakten sowie ein Protokoll des Kurfürstenrats Kurpfälzer Provenienz. Württembergische Reichstagsakten aus dem Hauptstaatsarchiv Stuttgart runden das Angebot ab.

Alle Bilder sind mit den Daten zu den präsentierten archivalischen Einheiten bzw. Stücken aus der »Archivdokumentation« als Metadaten verknüpft. Für die Ansicht stehen der METS- sowie der Mirador-Viewer zur Verfügung. Insgesamt werden über 26.000 Bilder bereitgestellt.

---

40 Kooperationspartner, https://gams.uni-graz.at/o:rta1576.bt432kp2 (01.02.2024).
41 https://gams.uni-graz.at/context:rta1576.facs (01.02.2024).
42 Oben Anm. 31.
43 https://gams.uni-graz.at/o:rta1576.imgw111b41 (01.02.2024).

IV. Anreicherung und Register: Namen, Orte, Sachbegriffe

Alle Texte und Daten der digitalen Edition wurden von Beginn an händisch in einem maschinenlesbaren Format erfasst. Versuche mit automatisierten Workflows wurden unternommen, jedoch erwies sich die manuelle Auszeichnung als effizienter[44]. Die Verwendung von XML (Extensible Markup Language) gemäß den Richtlinien der TEI (Text Encoding Initiative) ermöglicht die Anreicherung der »Archivdokumentation« und der edierten bzw. erschlossenen Texte durch zusätzliche Informationen sowie die Zusammenführung und Verknüpfung von Daten, die anschließend auf verschiedene Weise dargestellt werden können.

Im vorliegenden Fall ging es darum, Einzelpersonen, Orte und geographische Bezeichnungen, Gruppen/Körperschaften sowie Sachbegriffe in den Texten als solche auszuzeichnen und über Identifikatoren (IDs) je einem Register zuzuordnen. Über die vergebenen IDs lassen sich unterschiedliche Schreibweisen, beispielsweise »Toggey« und »Tokaj« für einen Ort in Ungarn, sowie variierende Bezeichnungen für ein und dieselbe Person, als Beispiel sei hier der unter seinem Namen oder in seiner Funktion als »meinzischer cantzler«[45] genannte Dr. Christoph Faber erwähnt, zusammenführen und mit entsprechenden Registereinträgen verbinden. Die Registereinträge enthalten weitere Informationen, die in der Edition auf verschiedene Weise sichtbar gemacht werden. Für die »Archivdokumentation« sowie die Lesefassung eines Texts beispielsweise gilt, dass bei Bewegung des Mauszeigers über einen Personennamen (Mouseover) in einem Pop-up eine Verknüpfung zum Eintrag zu dieser Person in der Gemeinsamen Normdatendatei (GND) sowie Informationen über ihre Zugehörigkeit zu einer Herrschaft (z. B. dem Kurfürstentum Mainz), ihre Funktion (z. B. Kanzler) sowie ihr Titel (z. B. Doktor) erscheinen. Folgt man der ebenfalls angegebenen Verlinkung zum Personenregister, sieht man im entsprechenden Eintrag, ob die Person bei diesem Reichstag persönlich anwesend war, ob sie auch in den Editionen der Akten der Reichstage 1570 und 1582 sowie des Kurfürstentags 1575 genannt wurde, ob ein konkreter Anmeldetag bekannt ist, ob sie im Reichsabschied genannt wird, außerdem ihren Rang (sofern es sich um eine im Abschied genannte Herrschaftsträgerin oder einen solchen Herrschaftsträger handelt) oder ob die Person als bevollmächtigter Vertreter einer Herrschaftsträgerin oder eines Herrschaftsträgers fungierte. Die Register enthalten Angaben zur Anzahl der Fundstellen und, in Form von filter- und sortierbaren Data-Tables, diese Fundstellen selbst, von denen man direkt an die betreffenden Stellen der »Archivdokumentation« oder der »edierten Texte« springen kann[46].

---

44 Es wurde im Projekt vor allem mit Named Entity Recognition (NER) experimentiert. Im Projekt »NERDPool: Data Pool for Named Entity Recognition« (https://nerdpool-api.acdh-dev.oeaw.ac.at/) entstanden Trainingsdaten für NER. Das NER-Experiment wird auch kurz in Georg Vogelers Aufsatz angesprochen: *Vogeler*, Edition – Protoedition – Reproduktion.

45 So beispielsweise im Bericht der kursächsischen Gesandten an Kurfürst August von Sachsen 1576-07-06, Abs. 4, https://gams.uni-graz.at/o:rta1576.edd1e6d244348/sdef:TEI/get?mode=lesetext#d1t4e148 (01.02.2024).

46 Erläuterungen zum Personenregister, https://gams.uni-graz.at/o:rta1576.bt1734r1pr (01.02.2024).

Gruppen bzw. Körperschaften, die in einem eigenen Register verzeichnet sind[47], wurden nur in ausgewählten Teilen der Edition erschlossen: Als Sender und Empfänger von Korrespondenz, Berichten und Weisungen in der »Archivdokumentation«, in der Liste der zum Reichstag geladenen Reichsstände, dem Resolutionsprotokoll des Reichshofrats, in anderen edierten Protokollen, sofern es sich um Gesandtengruppen handelt, die in der Umfrage ihr Votum abgaben, und in den für die Erprobung der Erschließung der Kommunikationsereignisse ausgewählten Texten[48]. Einzelpersonen sind über ihre herrschaftliche Zugehörigkeit mit dem Gruppen-/Körperschaften-Register verlinkt, dieses wiederum listet die in den Quellen genannten Mitglieder der angeführten Gruppen bzw. Körperschaften auf.

Ähnlich wie Einzelpersonen wurden auch geographische Bezeichnungen in der gesamten Edition markiert, referenziert und mit den Normdaten von GeoNames verknüpft. Diese Zusatzinformation kann entweder direkt in der Lesefassung im Pop-up oder über die Verlinkung zum Register abgerufen werden[49].

Das gleiche Prinzip gilt für die Sachbegriffe, deren Funktion bereits im Zusammenhang mit dem Aufbau der »edierten Texte« erwähnt wurde: Sie verknüpfen diese auf thematischer Ebene mit dem Sachregister. Das Sachregister ermöglicht damit nicht nur den thematischen Zugriff auf die Beratungsgegenstände des Reichstags, sondern es erschließt darüber hinaus das Verhandlungsgeschehen als komplexen Interaktionszusammenhang sowie als Bestandteil der pluralen Verhandlungskultur des Reichs. Die Sachbegriffe ihrerseits verstehen sich als moderne Suchbegriffe. Sie lehnen sich zwar an die Registereinträge bisheriger Bände der »Reichsversammlungen« an, bündeln die Vielzahl der kleinteiligen Betreffe aber unter abstrakteren begrifflichen Kategorien wie etwa »Diplomatie« oder »Reichsgesetze«[50]. Eine Erschließung durch Sachbegriffe erfolgt nur für die »edierten Texte«, nicht dagegen für die »Archivdokumentation«.

Insgesamt wurden in dieser Edition rund 2.000 Personen, über 800 Orte und geographische Bezeichnungen, 1.200 Gruppen/Körperschaften und 170 Sachbegriffe identifiziert, markiert und referenziert.

Die Anreicherung der Texte bietet mehrere Vorteile. Zum einen können bereits während des Lesens Zusatzinformationen angezeigt und Normdaten wie GND- und GeoNames-IDs abgerufen werden. Zudem kann durch die Verlinkungen zu den Registereinträgen die Häufigkeit des Vorkommens einer Person, einer Gruppe/Körperschaft, eines Orts oder eines Sachbegriffs eingesehen werden; außerdem bieten die Registereinträge unmittelbaren Zugriff auf die Fundstellen. Vor allem aber bildet die Anreicherung der Texte die Grundlage für die Filter-Recherche.

---

47 Erläuterungen zum Gruppen-/Körperschaften-Register, https://gams.uni-graz.at/o:rta1576.bt1734r1gr (01.02.2024).
48 Dazu unten Kap. VII.
49 Erläuterungen zum Ortsregister, https://gams.uni-graz.at/o:rta1576.bt1734r1or (01.02.2024).
50 Erläuterungen zum Sachregister, https://gams.uni-graz.at/o:rta1576.bt1734r1sr (01.02.2024).

V. Suchmöglichkeiten

Gerade die Reichstagsakten-Editionen sind komplexe Publikationen mit umfangreichem Textbestand. Die edierten Texte der Historikerin und dem Historiker zugänglich zu machen und zu erschließen, ist ein wichtiges Thema. Traditionell, in den Druckbänden, wird dies durch elaborierte Inhaltsverzeichnisse und Register gelöst. In digitalen Editionen gibt es zusätzlich noch die Möglichkeit, elektronische Suchen zu implementieren, die eine erweiterte paratextuelle Funktionalität anbieten, die im Druck nicht reproduziert werden kann. Nach Patrick Sahles Definition unterscheiden sich digitale Editionen von Druckeditionen durch solche Funktionalitäten und Inhalte, die ohne Verlust nicht abgedruckt werden können (»Digitales Paradigma«)[51]. Es können zwar Suchbegriffe, das Skript, das die Suche implementiert, oder Ergebnislisten abgedruckt werden, die einer Suche zugrundeliegende Datenbasis mit allen Verknüpfungen, Filtern und anderen Interaktionsmöglichkeiten entzieht sich dem statischen Druck allerdings[52]. Einfache Suchen sind auch in PDF-Dateien möglich, der Unterschied zum Suchen in digitalen Editionen ist jedoch, dass digitale Editionen auf einem mehr oder weniger elaborierten Datenmodell basieren, welches beim Suchen und Filtern zum Einsatz kommen kann.

Oft wird zwischen der einfachen Volltextsuche und einer erweiterten Suche unterschieden. In der Edition der Reichstagsakten kommt eine Volltextsuche zum Einsatz: Bei dieser wird der Nutzerin und dem Nutzer ein einzelner Suchschlitz angeboten. Alle Inhalte der Website werden auf bestimmte Wörter oder Wortkombinationen durchsucht und die Treffer in einer Liste zurückgegeben. In der digitalen Edition zum Reichstag 1576 wurde diese Liste als ein »Data-Table« umgesetzt, dessen Ergebnisse als mit einem Link hinterlegte Titel der gefundenen Stücke angegeben und um die Informationen Datum, Ressourcentyp, Archiv und Textsorte ergänzt werden. Diese fünf in eigenen Spalten ausgegebenen Kategorien können, pro Spalte, auf- oder absteigend sortiert und weiter gefiltert werden.

Zusätzlich zur Volltextsuche testen wir in der Edition auch ein neues Suchinterface, das am Zentrum für Informationsmodellierung der Universität Graz (ZIM) entwickelt wird. Der Facetten-Drilldown, in der Edition Filter-Recherche genannt, ermöglicht über Facetten eine sukzessive Einschränkung bzw. einen Drilldown von Suchergebnissen. Der Facetten-Drilldown verbindet traditionelle Such- und Filtermöglichkeiten mit quantitativer Auswertung. Facetten sind in diesem Zusammenhang Kategorien und Unterkategorien eines hierarchischen Ordnungssystems, das die Grundlage für verschiedene Optionen zur Einschränkung der Suchergebnisse darstellt. Die bekannteste Anwendung ist die Facettensuche, die z. B. in Bibliothekskatalogen oder Portalen wie Willhaben.at verwendet wird: Ein Suchergebnis kann durch die Auswahl von bestimmten Facetten weiter eingeschränkt werden. Infolge der Einschränkung erfährt nicht nur die Trefferliste Veränderungen, sondern auch die Facetten müssen neu kalkuliert werden. Denn es werden ausschließlich jene

---

51 *Sahle*, What is a Scholarly Digital Edition.
52 Ebd.; siehe auch *Stäcker*, Creating the Knowlegde Site.

Facetten gelistet, die für eine weitere Verfeinerung der Ergebnisliste genutzt werden können. Jede Facette ist dazu mit einem Zähler versehen, der die Anzahl der Ergebnisse angibt, die bei der Auswahl einer bestimmten Facette zu erwarten sind. Dadurch wird eine Art Vorschau auf den Umfang eines Filterergebnisses unter Berücksichtigung der jeweiligen Facette ermöglicht. Es können natürlich auch mehrere Facetten miteinander kombiniert werden.

Suchen in digitalen Editionen ist aber nicht auf die Suche im Interface beschränkt. Dem Digitalen Paradigma und FAIR-Prinzipien[53] folgend sollten digitale Editionen ihre Editionsdaten in einem offenen Standard wie TEI/XML unter einer freien Lizenz für weitere Analysen und Nachnutzung zur Verfügung stellen. Historikerinnen und Historiker können damit die gesamte Datenbasis einer Edition herunterladen und eigene Suchen programmieren oder die Daten in andere Programme oder Services hochladen und dort weiteranalysieren. Voyant Tools ermöglicht etwa das Hochladen von TEI/XML-Daten und bietet auch verschiedene Natural-Language-Processing-Analysemöglichkeiten an[54]. Ein anderes Beispiel ist der Cascaded Analysis Broker des Deutschen Text Archivs (DTA::CAB)[55]. Dieses Service erlaubt das Upload von deutschen Texten in TEI/XML-Format, welche dann automatisch mit linguistischer Annotation versehen werden. Das Interessante am zweiten Beispiel ist, dass DTA::CAB die linguistischen Annotationen wieder ins TEI/XML zurückspielt und dabei die Struktur des Ausgangsdokuments berücksichtigt wird.

VI. Visualisierungen

In digitalen Editionen kommen oft Visualisierungen zum Einsatz. Mit Visualisierungen kann man sich einen Überblick über große Datenmengen oder komplexe Zusammenhänge verschaffen. In den digitalen Geisteswissenschaften sind Visualisierungen besonders durch den Begriff Distant Reading bekannt geworden, der von Franco Moretti eingeführt wurde[56]. Bei dieser quantitativen Auswertung von großen Textmengen spielen Visualisierungen eine große Rolle. Distant Reading erhielt seine Benennung in Anlehnung an das traditionelle Close Reading, eine etablierte Methode der Textanalyse in der literaturwissenschaftlichen Forschung, und wird häufig in Verbindung mit dieser angewendet. In digitalen Editionen werden Instrumente entwickelt, die es den Nutzerinnen und Nutzern ermöglichen, je nach Bedarf sowohl Distant Reading als auch Close Reading durchzuführen, was auch als Scalable Reading bezeichnet wird[57].

---

53 https://www.openaire.eu/how-to-make-your-data-fair (01.02.2024).
54 Voyant Tools Help, https://voyant-tools.org/docs/#!/guide/about (01.02.2024).
55 DTA::CAB, https://kaskade.dwds.de/~moocow/software/DTA-CAB/ (01.02.2024).
56 Vgl. *Moretti*, Conjectures on World Literature; *ders.*, Distant Reading.
57 Vgl. *Weitin*, Scalable Reading.

In der Edition der Reichstagsakten entsteht besonders in der »Archivdokumentation« eine große Menge an Daten, die durch die Hilfe von Visualisierungen etwas einfacher zu überblicken sind. Die Edition der Reichstagsakten von 1576 hat dies am Beispiel von drei Visualisierungen getestet:

Bei der Erfassung der Stücke in der »Archivdokumentation« wurden bei den Protokollen zusätzliche Informationen erhoben. So wurde etwa auch notiert, für welche Tage Vorgänge protokolliert sind und welchen Umfang (in Folio) die jeweilige Protokollierung aufweist. Zusätzlich wurde auch das tagende Gremium (aus einer Liste standardisierter Elemente: Kurfürstenrat, Fürstenrat, Städterat, Ausschuss, Versammlung/Religion, Interne Sitzungen) erfasst. Basierend auf diesen Daten, ca. 2.600 verzeichnete Sitzungstage über alle Protokolle hinweg, konnten visuelle Auswertungen erstellt werden. In der »Archivdokumentation« gibt eine Visualisierung in Form eines einfachen Kalenders[58] bei jedem Protokoll einen Überblick über die protokollierten Tage. Im letzten Projektjahr wurde dem eine umfangreichere Visualisierung hinzugefügt: In einer Heatmap[59] werden alle Protokolldaten über die gesamte »Archivdokumentation« hinweg angezeigt. Die Heatmap ist wie ein Kalender aufgebaut, auf der X-Achse sind die Wochentage verzeichnet, auf der Y-Achse die Wochen des Reichstags. Durch diese Darstellung kann man einerseits die arbeitsintensiven Tage, an denen viel protokolliert wurde, erkennen und gleichzeitig auch den Wochenrhythmus in die Analyse miteinbeziehen.

Eine zweite Visualisierung betrifft die Parallelüberlieferungen. Von Dokumenten wie den Verhandlungsakten ist bekannt, dass diese mehrfach in Archiven überliefert wurden. Wie bereits ausgeführt werden in der »Archivdokumentation« die Parallelüberlieferungen einzelner Stücke als eine Liste von Links angezeigt; als Nutzerin oder Nutzer kann man zu anderen Versionen springen. Ziel der Visualisierung der Parallelüberlieferungen war es, einen besseren Überblick über die Überlieferungssituation zu bekommen und auszuwerten, welche Texte in welchen Archiven überliefert sind. Die Visualisierung[60] wurde als ein gestapeltes Balkendiagramm realisiert, wobei jeder Balken einen Text repräsentiert. Je mehr Parallelversionen eines Texts erfasst sind, umso länger ist der Balken. Die einzelnen Reichsstände, in deren Archiven eine Version überliefert wurde, werden farblich innerhalb der Balken als Schichten angezeigt. Dadurch kann auch abgerufen werden, ob z. B. ein Text besonders häufig in Archiven von geistlichen oder weltlichen Herrschaften überliefert ist.

Drittens wurde eine Visualisierung[61] der Datumsangaben durchgeführt. Ziel war die Erstellung einer Zeitleiste. Da in den »edierten Texten« und in der »Archivdokumentation« große Mengen an Datumsangaben und unterschiedliche Datumskategorien (z. B. Ausstellungsdatum, protokollierter Tag, Ankunftsdatum eines Reichstagsteilnehmers oder Datumsangaben als Inhalte in den »edierten Texten«) vorkommen, musste es eine Möglichkeit geben, diese auf einer Timeline zu plotten

---

58 Z. B. https://gams.uni-graz.at/o:rta1576.adwn1#W1.10.5.1.1 (01.02.2024).
59 https://gams.uni-graz.at/context:rta1576?mode=committees (01.02.2024).
60 https://gams.uni-graz.at/context:rta1576?mode=versions (01.02.2024).
61 https://gams.uni-graz.at/context:rta1576?mode=timeline (01.02.2024).

Der Reichstag zu Regensburg 1576

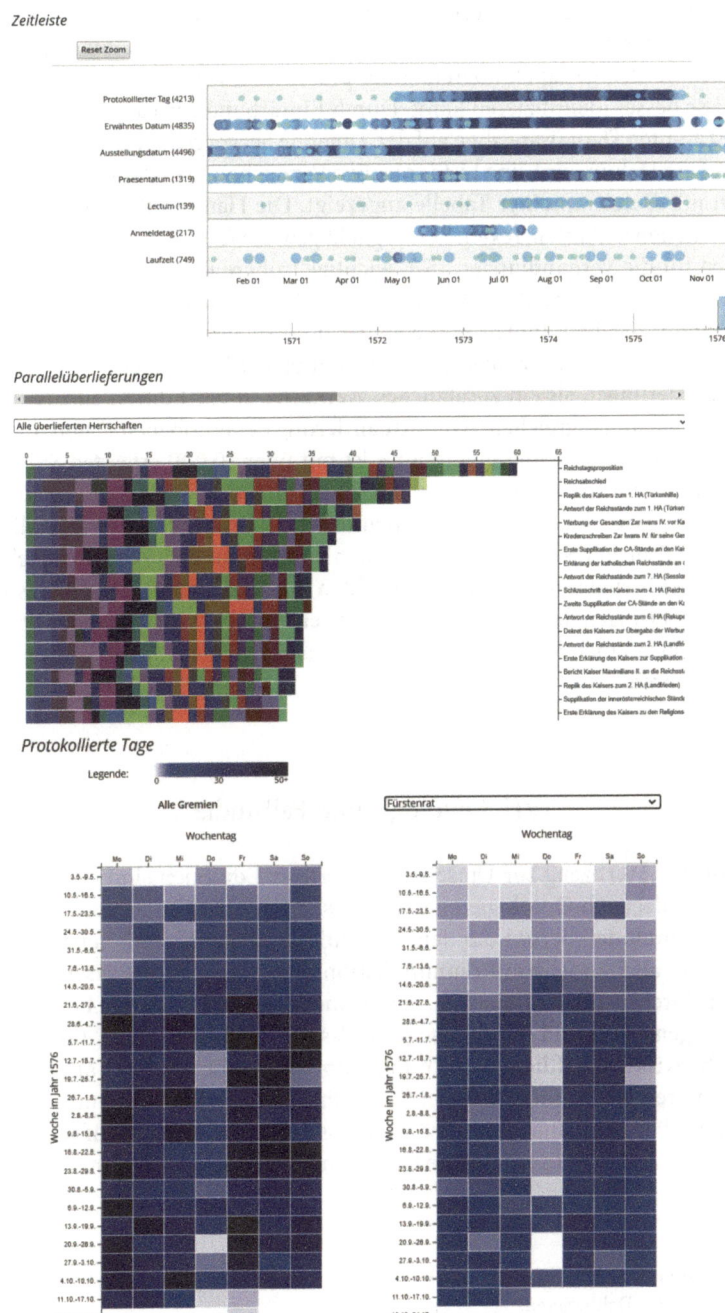

Abb. 1: Die drei Datenvisualisierungen des Projekts: Zeitleiste, Parallelüberlieferungen, protokollierte Tage.

und die unterschiedlichen Kategorien zu vergleichen. Zu diesem Zweck wurde eine Visualisierung mit parallelen Timelines für jede Kategorie von Datum gewählt. Die Timelines werden gestapelt übereinander präsentiert, wodurch man gleichzeitige Ereignisse besser identifizieren kann. Durch Einfärbung wird auch die Häufigkeit von bestimmten Datumsangaben auf der Timeline hervorgehoben und durch einen Klick auf ein Datum wird eine Liste von allen Verzeichnungen dieses Datums in der Edition mit Details in einer Tabelle angezeigt. Die Häufigkeit mancher Datumsangaben in den »edierten Texten« ermöglicht gewisse Aussagen. Z. B. werden Jahre, in denen für die Verhandlungen 1576 wichtige frühere Reichstage stattfanden, besonders häufig erwähnt. Auch kann man sehr leicht »Ausreißer«, wie mittelalterliche Datumsangaben, finden und genauer untersuchen. Das früheste Datum in unserem Datensatz stammt aus einer Erwähnung der Karolinger.

Visualisierungen als ein zusätzliches Werkzeug in der Edition einzusetzen, ermöglicht eine umfangreichere Kontextualisierung der erhobenen Daten und edierten Texte. Die »Archivdokumentation« ist mit über 10.000 erfassten Stücken zu umfangreich, um leicht einen Überblick zu gewinnen. Distant Reading und visuelle Auswertungen bieten in dieser Situation eine Lösung. Die drei Visualisierungen, die im Projekt realisiert wurden, dienen dazu, anhand von drei Beispielen das Potential der Visualisierung von ausgesuchten Editionsdaten zu zeigen. Besonders die Visualisierungen der Parallelüberlieferungen einzelner Texte und der Protokolldaten erlauben einen aus editorischer Sicht sehr wichtigen Einblick in den Überlieferungskontext.

VII. Ontologie und Fallstudie

Ein zentrales Werkzeug zur Umsetzung assertiver Editionen sind konzeptionelle Datenmodelle, auch Ontologien genannt (»shared formal conceptualizations«[62]). Unser Datenmodell beruht auf dem institutionentheoretischen Verständnis des Reichstags[63] als Bündel von Kommunikationsereignissen. Sie zu erschließen und letztlich durchsuchbar zu machen, sollte, anders als der bisherige Fokus auf Verfahrensgegenstände und -ergebnisse (das Was des Reichstags), die Edition für eine geschichtswissenschaftliche Forschung aufbereiten, die verstärkt am konkreten Funktionieren institutionalisierter Mitsprache-Formen, an Kommunikation und Verfahren (dem Wie), interessiert ist[64]. Das abstrakte und dadurch auf verschiedene Ständeversammlungen anwendbare Kommunikationsmodell wird in unserer Onto-

---

62 *Eide/Smith Ore*, Ontologies and data modeling, S. 180; *Rehbein*, Ontologien, S. 175.
63 *Haug-Moritz*, Deliberieren.
64 Eine erste, später überarbeitete Version der Ontologie wurde beschrieben in: *Bleier/Zeilinger/Vogeler*, From Early Modern Deliberation to the Semantic Web; *Zeilinger/Bleier/Haug-Moritz*, Bericht (im Druck).

logie der »Premodern PArliamentary Communication« (PPAC)[65] expliziert; ein Test seiner Übertragbarkeit steht jedoch noch aus.

Die in der Ontologie in ihren Beziehungen zueinander beschriebenen Begriffe und Eigenschaften erlauben es, im Sinne der Wissensmodellierung[66], den Quellen folgend hauptsatzförmige Aussagen bzw. sogenannte Triples zu formulieren. Etwa: »Kommunikation« »behandelt« »(ein) Thema«, ist aber auch eine Teilmenge bzw. Unterklasse von »Thema«, da sie selbst in Kommunikation thematisiert werden kann. Folglich kann eine konkrete Kommunikation X das Thema Y besitzen, aber auch Thema von Kommunikation Z sein. Deshalb müssen in dem in TEI/XML erfassten Text nur die jeweiligen Kategorien annotiert bzw. codiert werden, ihr Zusammenhang ist vom Datenmodell vorgegeben.

Um im Sinne von Linked Open Data eine weite Anknüpfung unserer Daten und unseres Datenmodells zu ermöglichen, stellen wir diese als Resource-Description-Framework-Datei (RDF), in der Standardsprache hinter dem Semantic Web[67], zur Verfügung und hängen unser Datenmodell, wo möglich, in die am weitesten verbreitete abstrakte Top-Level-Ontologie im Kulturerbe-Bereich, CIDOC CRM, ein[68]. Wie erwähnt verweisen wir zudem bei Personen und Orten auf die bereits genannten Normdateien (GND, GeoNames). Kommunikation ist in unserem Verständnis ein »event« und damit eine Ableitung der entsprechenden CIDOC-CRM-Klasse (E5), das an einem bestimmten Ort zu einer bestimmten Zeit stattfindet, ein bestimmtes Thema besitzt, aber auch selbst Thema einer weiteren Kommunikation sein kann, und an dem bestimmte Kommunikationspartnerinnen oder -partner teilnehmen. Die meisten davon sind »Political Actors«, diese sind Einzelpersonen oder Gruppen/Körperschaften. Anwesend sind die Political Actors persönlich oder durch bevollmächtigte Vertreter. Bei Kommunikation kann es sich, je nach Kommunikationskanal, um körperlich verbale (mündlicher Austausch) oder körperlich nonverbale (z. B. Gesten oder Positionen wie Sitzen oder Aufstehen) sowie materiell schriftliche (z. B. Aktenstücke) oder materiell nicht schriftliche (z. B. ein symbolisch aufgeladener Schreibtisch oder ein Schwert) Kommunikation handeln. Ferner läuft Kommunikation formal oder informal ab, wobei sich wiederum verschiedene Formen formaler Kommunikation unterscheiden lassen, die wir unter der Bezeichnung »Formalstruktur der Kommunikationskonstellationen und -akte«[69] als kontrolliertes Vokabular erfassen.

Institutionentheoretisch betrachtet war der Reichstag in der Lage, nur durch die Wiederholung früherer Praktiken, basierend auf impliziten ungeschriebenen Regeln, zu funktionieren. Eine geschriebene Geschäftsordnung gab es noch nicht, moderne Organisationen mussten sich erst noch entwickeln. Die entsprechenden

---

65 PPAC-Datenmodell, https://gams.uni-graz.at/o:rta1576.bt7825dm1 (01.02.2024).
66 *Galka*, Ontologie.
67 *Pollin*, RDF, RDFS, OWL.
68 https://cidoc-crm.org/node/202 (01.02.2024); *Oldman u. a.*, PRIMER; *Pollin*, CIDOC-CRM; *Rehbein*, Ontologien, S. 174 f.. ISO 21127:2006; *Wettlaufer*, Schritt, o. S.
69 https://gams.uni-graz.at/o:rta1576.bt78kfdm0 (01.02.2024).

kommunikativen Praktiken wurden von dem am Empirischen orientierten »Ausführlichen Bericht wie es auf den Reichstagen pflegt gehalten zu werden«[70] von 1569 oder 1577 beschrieben, dessen nicht gesicherter Autor (Simon Bagen oder Andreas Erstenberger) aus der Mainzer Erzkanzlei und somit aus der Reichstagspraxis stammen muss. Er be-schreibt das offiziell-reguläre Reichstagsverfahren, vor-geschrieben im Sinne einer offiziellen Geschäftsordnung werden jedoch keine Regeln. Genauer gesagt beschreibt dieser Traktat minutiös das Verfahren für die drei offiziellen Kurien, ihren Austausch mit dem Kaiser, die Beratung der Supplikationen, den Umgang mit Protest und ausländischen Potentaten. Die Praktiken, die er nennt, lassen sich systematisch entlang der auch für andere repräsentative Versammlungen typischen Beratungsstrukturen gliedern, die v. a. Michel Hébert[71] in seiner Studie zum spätmittelalterlichen Europa aufgezeigt hat. In Anlehnung daran lässt sich aus dem Traktat somit eine »Formalstruktur« (eine Selbstbeschreibung der Struktur) herauslesen[72].

In TEI/XML wird die Kommunikation innerhalb des edierten Texts kodiert. Dafür verwenden wir, ähnlichen ontologie-getriebenen Projekten folgend, das Attribut @ana[73], in das als Attributwert die entsprechende Referenz auf unsere Ontologie eingetragen wird (<date ana="ppac:Date" when="1576-06-28">28. Junii anno 76</date>, <persName ana="ppac:CommunicationPartner" ref="/o:rta1576.listperson#p25538112p114d100">Pfaltz vice canzler</persName> oder, für Gruppen, <rs ana="ppac:CommunicationPartner" ref="/o:rta1576.listgroup#g1913883s102e101">Sachsen</rs>). Im digitalen Repositorium GAMS[74], das wir für die Umsetzung der digitalen Edition und die Langzeitarchivierung verwenden, werden die mit @ana-Attribut ausgezeichneten Inhalte in RDF übersetzt, in dem die kommunikationsrelevanten Daten in einer expliziten, reduzierten Form enthalten sind. Dieses wird in eine Triple-Datenbank eingespeist, die für Suchabfragen und Auswertungen nötig ist.

Aus pragmatischen Gründen musste im zeitlich begrenzten Pilotprojekt jedoch von einer vollständigen Erschließung und Webpräsentation der Kommunikationsereignisse abgesehen werden – stattdessen präsentieren wir auf der Website das ausgearbeitete Datenmodell[75] inklusive einer englischsprachigen Auflistung der

---

70 https://archive.org/details/traktatberdenr00rauc/page/n7/mode/2up (01.02.2024).
71 *Hébert*, Parlamenter.
72 *Bleier/Zeilinger/Vogeler*, From Early Modern Deliberation to the Semantic Web, S. 89 f.; *Zeilinger/Bleier/Haug-Moritz*, Bericht (im Druck).
73 *Vogeler*, The ›assertive edition‹, S. 316–318; *ders./Pollin/Bleier*, Der geschichtswissenschaftliche Zugang zum digitalen Editieren; *Wareham u. a.*, The ›Confronting the Digital‹ Debate and an Assertive Digital Edition; *Pollin*, Digital Edition Publishing Cooperative for Historical Accounts and the Bookkeeping Ontology.
74 »GAMS« steht für Geisteswissenschaftliches Asset Management System. Es wird am Zentrum für Informationsmodellierung der Universität Graz entwickelt und für die Verwaltung, Publikation und Langzeitarchivierung digitaler Ressourcen verwendet: *Stigler/Steiner*, Infrastruktur zur Langzeitarchivierung und Publikation geisteswissenschaftlicher Forschungsdaten.
75 https://gams.uni-graz.at/o:rta1576.bt7825dm1 (01.02.2024).

Bestandteile der Ontologie[76], dazugehörige Regeln für das praktische Mark-up mit TEI/XML[77] und die mit den restlichen Daten als TEI/XML- oder RDF-Datei downloadbare exemplarische Annotation[78].

VIII. Fazit

Die digitale Edition der Akten des Reichstags zu Regensburg 1576 wurde im Rahmen eines Pilotprojekts erarbeitet. Ziel war es, bei der Editionsarbeit zugleich Erfahrungen für künftige Reichstagsakten-Editionen zu sammeln und damit Grundlagenarbeit zu leisten. Nachdem diese Arbeiten abgeschlossen sind, sind wir überzeugt, dass unsere Edition den Mehrwert digitalen Edierens auch für einen so heterogenen Quellenkomplex wie die Reichstagsakten unter Beweis stellt.

Ein nicht geringer Mehrwert besteht unserer Auffassung nach darin, dass durch den Wegfall der Platzbeschränkungen gedruckter Editionen auf methodisch problematische Lösungen wie auszugshaften Abdruck, Regestierungen und Quellenreferate verzichtet werden kann. Ein weiterer Vorteil sind die durch das digitale Format eröffneten Möglichkeiten, das Quellenmaterial auf verschiedene Weisen zugänglich zu machen und damit den Wert der Edition für Forscherinnen und Forscher mit ganz unterschiedlichen Fragestellungen zu erhöhen. Dafür stehen in unserer Edition die »Archivdokumentation«, die »Archivalien in Bildern« sowie die in die »edierten Texte« eingeordneten durch Schlagworte erschlossenen Texte. Die »Archivdokumentation« bietet – auch durch die integrierten Verlinkungen – mehr als ein gedrucktes Quellenverzeichnis, die »Archivalien in Bildern« können manchen Benutzerinnen und Benutzern den Weg ins Archiv ersparen, die Erschließung nicht im Volltext präsentierter Quellen durch Namen, Orte und Sachbegriffe auf

---

76 https://gams.uni-graz.at/archive/objects/o:rta1576.ontology/methods/sdef:Ontology/get (01.02.2024).
77 https://gams.uni-graz.at/o:rta1576.bt7846trk (01.02.2024).
78 Protokoll für die Religionsverhandlungen der CA-Stände (Kurpfalz), https://gams.uni-graz.at/o:rta1576.edd1e11 m515221 (01.02.2024); Bericht: Erich Volkmar von Berlepsch, Dr. Wolfgang Eulenbeck, Hans Eitel von Berbisdorff und Dr. Andreas Paulus an Kurfürst August von Sachsen, 1576-08-21, https://gams.uni-graz.at/o:rta1576.edd1e7d244433 (01.02.2024); Bericht: Erich Volkmar von Berlepsch, Dr. Wolfgang Eulenbeck, Hans Eitel von Berbisdorff und Dr. Andreas Paulus an Kurfürst August von Sachsen, 1576-08-26, https://gams.uni-graz.at/o:rta1576.edd1e6d244435 (01.02.2024); Bericht: Erich Volkmar von Berlepsch, Damian von Sebottendorf, Dr. Wolfgang Eulenbeck, Hans Eitel von Berbisdorff und Dr. Andreas Paulus an Kurfürst August von Sachsen, 1576-08-30, https://gams.uni-graz.at/o:rta1576.edd1e6d244437 (01.02.2024); Bericht: Erich Volkmar von Berlepsch, Damian von Sebottendorf, Dr. Wolfgang Eulenbeck, Hans Eitel von Berbisdorff und Dr. Andreas Paulus an Kurfürst August von Sachsen, 1576-09-04, https://gams.uni-graz.at/o:rta1576.edd1e4d244446 (01.02.2024); Bericht: Erich Volkmar von Berlepsch, Damian von Sebottendorf, Dr. Wolfgang Eulenbeck, Hans Eitel von Berbisdorff und Dr. Andreas Paulus an Kurfürst August von Sachsen, 1576-08-21 (Corrigenda: Hans von Berbisdorff), https://gams.uni-graz.at/o:rta1576.edd1e6d244447 (01.02.2024).

einschlägiges Material führen. Unsere Edition schließt dadurch editorische Lösungen mit ein, die heute unter dem Begriff der »Protoedition« diskutiert werden[79].

Diese Möglichkeiten bringen idealerweise eine größere editorische Freiheit mit sich, indem die in Druckeditionen in der Regel sehr strikt angewendeten Auswahlprinzipien großzügiger gehandhabt und damit zusätzliche Facetten des Forschungsgegenstands dokumentiert werden. So berücksichtigt unsere Edition die wichtigen Textgattungen der Berichte und Weisungen sowie der Instruktionen, die in den analogen Editionen lediglich referiert bzw. im Kommentar ausgewertet werden können. Auch die kaiserliche Rolle im Reichstagsgeschehen wird durch die Edition des Geheimratsprotokolls im Volltext und die Erschließung des Resolutionsprotokolls des Reichshofrats besser sichtbar. Der textkritische Apparat der edierten Texte kann aufgrund der anschaulichen Darstellung in der digitalen Edition viel leichter für entsprechende Forschungen herangezogen werden.

Die angesprochenen Anreicherungen und ihre Verlinkungen zu Registern mit zusätzlichen Informationen, die dadurch ermöglichten vielfältigen Suchfunktionen sowie die Visualisierungen, die erste Versuche der Datenauswertung unterstützen[80], bedeuten einen weiteren erheblichen Mehrwert der digitalen Edition. Über die Integration von Normdaten, die Herstellung von Beziehungen zu gängigen Ontologien und das Zur-Verfügung-Stellen der Editionsdaten in Standardsprachen wie TEI/XML und RDF entstehen Verbindungen und eröffnen sich Verwertungsmöglichkeiten, wie sie keine gedruckte Edition bieten kann.

Unsere Erfahrungen im Projekt zeigen aber auch, dass digitales Edieren einen nicht zu unterschätzenden Zeitaufwand bedeutet. Die Erarbeitung eines Datenmodells einschließlich der Begriffsbildung für die Suchfunktionen, die Festlegung von Kategorien für die strukturierte Erfassung der Daten und die Formulierung kontrollierter Vokabularien zwingen zu zahlreichen Entscheidungen und Vereindeutigungen, die diskutiert und in mehreren Testläufen auf ihre Praxistauglichkeit hin geprüft werden müssen. Es wäre anzustreben, dass eine solche Entwicklungsarbeit in künftige Projekte einfließt und sich auf diese Weise längerfristig bezahlt macht.

Als eine Gratwanderung erscheint darüber hinaus die Entscheidung, wie die im Fall von Drittmittelprojekten zeitlich limitierten personellen Ressourcen am besten eingesetzt werden sollen. Die Erarbeitung eines ansprechenden Interfaces, wie es von einer neuen digitalen Edition erwartet wird, hat sich als eine ausgesprochen zeitintensive Aufgabe erwiesen. Ob dieser Aufwand gerechtfertigt ist, ist angesichts des raschen Wandels der Erwartungen an solche Oberflächen eine offene Frage. Dabei ist auch die institutionelle Langzeitarchivierung zu berücksichtigen, die für Forschungsdaten leichter zu gewährleisten ist als für ihre Darstellung. Nicht umsonst wird inzwischen darüber diskutiert, was eigentlich eine digitale Edition aus-

---

[79] *Vogeler*, Edition – Protoedition – Reproduktion; *Bleier u. a.*, Mehrwert der »Archivdokumentation« als Teil einer digitalen Reichstagsaktenedition.

[80] *Bleier u. a.*, Mehrwert der »Archivdokumentation« als Teil einer digitalen Reichstagsaktenedition.

macht: ihre Daten oder das Interface[81]? Sollten die personellen und zeitlichen Kapazitäten einer Edition nicht besser in die Gewinnung von Daten investiert werden als in deren Präsentation? Oder gerät die digitale Edition damit in die Gefahr, nur noch einem kleinen Kreis technisch versierter Benutzerinnen und Benutzern zugänglich zu sein?

Eine Grundeinsicht jedenfalls hat sich bei uns allen eingestellt: Die digitale Edition ist keine Zauberformel, um das Edieren zu beschleunigen. Gut gemachte digitale Editionen können mehr als Druckeditionen, lassen sich aber keinesfalls schneller erarbeiten. Sie bedürfen der interdisziplinären Kooperation zwischen Historikerinnen und Historikern sowie Digital Humanities-Expertinnen und Experten, setzen also ausreichende Personalressourcen voraus.

Oder doch nicht? Automatische Texterkennungsprogramme machen rasche Fortschritte und für die Textanreicherung werden unter Zuhilfenahme von mehr und mehr Transkriptionen als »Trainingsdaten« automatisierte Verfahren entwickelt, die durch den Einsatz von Künstlicher Intelligenz deutlich verbessert werden können. Das muss nicht bedeuten, dass Edieren überflüssig wird. Editorinnen und Editoren tun aber gut daran, intensiv über ihre Kernkompetenzen und Konzepte langfristig halt- und gut nutzbarer Editionen nachzudenken.

Quellen- und Literaturverzeichnis

Quellen

Leeb, Josef/Neerfeld, Christiane/Ortlieb, Eva/Zeilinger, Florian/Bleier, Roman (Bearb.): Der Reichstag zu Regensburg 1576. Digitale Edition, hg. v. der Historischen Kommission bei der Bayerischen Akademie der Wissenschaften durch Gabriele Haug-Moritz und Georg Vogeler, 2023 (= Deutsche Reichstagsakten, Reichsversammlungen 1556–1662), https://gams.uni-graz.at/context:rta1576 (01.02.2024).

Literatur

Bleier, Roman/Klug, Helmut W.: Discussing Interfaces in Digital Scholarly Editing, in: *Roman Bleier u. a. (Hg.)*, Digital Scholarly Editions as Interfaces, Norderstedt 2018 (= Schriften des Instituts für Dokumentologie und Editorik, Bd. 12), S. V–XV.

Bleier, Roman u. a.: Archivdatenerschließung und -auswertung. Der Mehrwert der »Archivdokumentation« als Teil einer digitalen Reichstagsaktenedition, in: *Melanie Althage u. a. (Hg.)*, Digitale Methoden in der geschichtswissenschaftlichen Praxis: Fachliche Transformationen und ihre epistemologischen Konsequenzen: Konferenzbeiträge der Digital History 2023, Berlin, 23.–26.5.2023, Berlin 2023, o. S., https://doi.org/10.5281/zenodo.8319631 (01.02.2024).

---

81 *Porter*, What is an edition anyway; *Hiltmann*, Vom Medienwandel zum Methodenwandel; *Bleier/Klug*, Discussing Interfaces in Digital Scholarly Editing.

Ders./Zeilinger, Florian/Vogeler, Georg: From Early Modern Deliberation to the Semantic Web: Annotating Communications in the Records of the Imperial Diet of 1576, in: *Matti La Mela/Fredrik Norén/Eero Hyvönen (Hg.)*, DiPaDA 2022. Digital Parliamentary Data in Action 2022. Proceedings of the Digital Parliamentary Data in Action (DiPaDA 2022) Workshop Co-Located with 6th Digital Humanities in the Nordic and Baltic Countries Conference (DHNB) 2022, Uppsala, Sweden, March 15, 2022, S. 86–100 (= CEUR Workshops Proceedings, Bd. 3133), http://ceur-ws.org/Vol-3133/paper06.pdf (01.02.2024).

Eide, Øyvind/Smith Ore, Christian-Emil: Ontologies and data modeling, in: *Julia Flanders/Fotis Jannidis (Hg.)*, The Shape of Data in the Digital Humanities, London 2018, S. 178–203, https://doi.org/10.4324/9781315552941 (01.02.2024).

Galka, Selina: Ontologie, in: *Helmut W. Klug (Hg.)*, KONDE Weißbuch, 2021, o.S., https://www.digitale-edition.at/o:konde.151, https://hdl.handle.net/11471/562.50.151 (01.02.2024).

Haug-Moritz, Gabriele: Deliberieren. Zur ständisch-parlamentarischen Beratungskultur im Lateineuropa des 16. Jahrhunderts, in: Historisches Jahrbuch 141 (2021), S. 114–155.

Dies.: Historische Einführung: Der Reichstag des 16. Jahrhunderts als europäische Ständeversammlung, in: *Josef Leeb u. a. (Bearb.)*, Der Reichstag zu Regensburg 1576. Digitale Edition, hg. v. der Historischen Kommission bei der Bayerischen Akademie der Wissenschaften durch Gabriele Haug-Moritz und Georg Vogeler, 2023 (= Deutsche Reichstagsakten, Reichsversammlungen 1556–1662), https://gams.uni-graz.at/o:rta1576.bt3564p3 (01.02.2024).

Dies.: Reichstag des Alten Reiches, in: *Albrecht Cordes u. a. (Hg.)*, Handwörterbuch zur deutschen Rechtsgeschichte, Bd. 4, Berlin ²2023, Sp. 263–274.

Hébert, Michel: Parlementer. Assemblées représentatives et échange politique en Europe occidentale à la fin du Moyen Age, Paris 2014 (= Romanité et modernité du droit).

Hiltmann, Torsten: Vom Medienwandel zum Methodenwandel. Die fortschreitende Digitalisierung und ihre Konsequenzen für die Geschichtswissenschaften in historischer Perspektive, in: *Karoline Dominika Döring u. a. (Hg.)*, Digital History. Konzepte, Methoden und Kritiken Digitaler Geschichtswissenschaft, Berlin/Boston 2022, S. 13–44 (= Studies in Digital History and Hermeneutics, Bd. 6), https://doi.org/10.1515/9783110757101-002 (01.02.2024).

Lanzinner, Maximilian (Bearb.), Der Reichstag zu Speyer 1570, hg. v. der Historischen Kommission bei der Bayerischen Akademie der Wissenschaften, Göttingen 1988 (= Deutsche Reichstagsakten, Reichsversammlungen 1556–1662).

Leeb, Josef: Editorische Einführung: Editionsgeschichte: Deutsche Reichstagsakten, Reichsversammlungen 1556–1662, in: *ders. u. a. (Bearb.)*, Der Reichstag zu Regensburg 1576. Digitale Edition, hg. v. der Historischen Kommission bei der Bayerischen Akademie der Wissenschaften durch Gabriele Haug-Moritz und Georg Vogeler, 2023 (= Deutsche Reichstagsakten, Reichsversammlungen 1556–1662), https://gams.uni-graz.at/o:rta1576.bt2563p2 (01.02.2024).

Ders.: Einleitung. Der Reichstag 1576: Verhandlungsthemen und -ergebnisse, in: *ders. u. a. (Bearb.)*, Der Reichstag zu Regensburg 1576. Digitale Edition, hg. v. der Historischen Kommission bei der Bayerischen Akademie der Wissenschaften durch Gabriele Haug-Moritz und Georg Vogeler, 2023 (= Deutsche Reichstagsakten, Reichsversammlungen 1556–1662), https://gams.uni-graz.at/o:rta1576.bt34fgr (01.02.2024).

Liebmann, Edgar: Reichstag, in: *Friedrich Jaeger (Hg.)*, Enzyklopädie der Neuzeit, Bd. 10, Stuttgart 2009, Sp. 948–953.

Moretti, Franco: Conjectures on World Literature, in: New Left Review 1 (2000), S. 54–68.

Ders.: Distant Reading, London/New York 2013.

Oldman, Dominic/CRM-Labs: The CIDOC Conceptual Reference Model (CIDOC-CRM): PRIMER, hg. v. Donna Kurtz, 2014, https://www.cidoc-crm.org/sites/default/files/CRMPrimer_v1.1_1.pdf (01.02.2024).

Pollin, Christopher: Digital Edition Publishing Cooperative for Historical Accounts and the Bookkeeping Ontology, in: *Thomas Riechert/Francesco Beretta/George Bruseker (Hg.)*, Proceedings of the Doctoral Symposium on Research on Online Databases in History (RODBH 2019), 2020,

S. 7–14 (= CEUR Workshop Proceedings, Bd. 2532), https://ceur-ws.org/Vol-2532/paper1.pdf (01.02.2024).

Ders.: CIDOC-Conceptual Reference Model (CRM), in: *Helmut W. Klug (Hg.)*, KONDE Weißbuch, 2021, o. S., https://www.digitale-edition.at/o:konde.133, https://hdl.handle.net/11471/562.50.133 (01.02.2024).

Ders.: RDF, RDFS, OWL u. a., in: *Helmut W. Klug (Hg.)*, KONDE Weißbuch, 2021, o. S., https://www.digitale-edition.at/o:konde.131, https://hdl.handle.net/11471/562.50.131 (01.02.2024).

Porter, Dot: »What is an edition anyway?« My Keynote for the Digital Scholarly Editions as Interfaces conference, Graz 2016, http://www.dotporterdigital.org/what-is-an-edition-anyway-my-keynote-for-the-digital-scholarly-editions-as-interfaces-conference-university-of-graz/ (01.02.2024).

Rehbein, Malte: Ontologien, in: *Fotis Jannidis/Hubertus Kohle/ders. (Hg.)*, Digital Humanities. Eine Einführung, Stuttgart 2017, S. 162–176, http://books.openedition.org/obp/3397 (01.02.2024).

Stigler, Johannes H./Steiner, Elisabeth: GAMS – Eine Infrastruktur zur Langzeitarchivierung und Publikation geisteswissenschaftlicher Forschungsdaten, in: Mitteilungen der Vereinigung Österreichischer Bibliothekarinnen und Bibliothekare 71/1 (2018), S. 207–216, https://doi.org/10.31263/voebm.v71i1.1992 (01.02.2024).

Stäcker, Thomas: Creating the Knowlegde Site – elektronische Editionen als Aufgabe einer Forschungsbibliothek, in: *Christiane Fritze u. a. (Hg.)*, Digitale Edition und Forschungsbibliothek, Wiesbaden 2011, S. 123–124 (= Bibliothek und Wissenschaft, Bd. 44).

Vogeler, Georg: The ›assertive edition‹. On the consequences of digital methods in scholarly editing for historians, in: International Journal of Digital Humanities 2019, S. 309–322.

Ders.: Edition – Protoedition – Reproduktion: Der digitale Wandel, in: Geschichte in Wissenschaft und Unterricht 73/9–10 (2022), S. 498–511.

Ders./Pollin, Christopher/Bleier, Roman: »Ich glaube, Fakt ist …«: Der geschichtswissenschaftliche Zugang zum digitalen Editieren, in: *Karoline Dominika Döring u. a. (Hg.)*, Digital History: Konzepte, Methoden und Kritiken Digitaler Geschichtswissenschaft, Berlin/Boston 2022, S. 171–190.

Wareham, Andrew u. a.: The ›Confronting the Digital‹ Debate and an Assertive Digital Edition: British History and Hearth Tax Records, in: *Sanita Reinsone u. a. (Hg.)*, Digital Humanities in the Nordic Countries (DHNB) 2020, Post-Proceedings of the 5th Conference Digital Humanities in the Nordic Countries, 2020, S. 38–50 (= CEUR Workshop Proceedings, Bd. 2865), https://ceur-ws.org/Vol-2865/paper4.pdf (01.02.2024).

Weitin, Thomas: Scalable Reading, in: Zeitschrift für Literaturwissenschaft und Linguistik 47 (2017), S. 1–6, https://doi.org/10.1007/s41244-017-0048-4 (01.02.2024).

Wettlaufer, Jörg: Der nächste Schritt? Semantic Web und digitale Editionen, in: *Roland S. Kamzelak/Timo Steyer (Hg.)*, Digitale Metamorphose. Digital Humanities und Editionswissenschaft 2018 (Sonderband der Zeitschrift für digitale Geisteswissenschaften, Bd. 2), o. S., https://doi.org/10.17175/sb002_007 (01.02.2024).

Zeilinger, Florian/Bleier, Roman/Haug-Moritz, Gabriele: Bericht: Ein Pilotprojekt zum digitalen Edieren frühneuzeitlicher Quellen. Der Reichstag zu Regensburg 1576 als Beispiel, in: Zeitschrift für historische Forschung, im Druck.

Abkürzungen

Abb.	Abbildung
Abs.	Absatz
Abt.	Abteilung
API	Application Programming Interface (Programmierschnittstelle)
Art.	Artikel
ASCII	American Standard Code for Information Interchange
BBAW	Berlin-Brandenburgische Akademie der Wissenschaften
Bd.	Band/Bände
Bearb.	Bearbeiter/in/nen
bearb. v.	bearbeitet von
BMBF	Bundesministerium für Bildung und Forschung
bspw.	Beispielsweise
bzw.	Beziehungsweise
c./ca.	circa
CC	Creative Commons
CC-BY SA	Creative Commons Attribution ShareAlike
CD	Compact Disk
CD-ROM	Compact Disk Read Only Memory
CERL	Consortium of European Research Libraries
CEUR	Central Europe (Workshop Proceedings)
cf.	Confer
ch.	Chapter
CIDOC	International Committee for Documentation of the International Council of Museums
CIDOC-CRM	CIDOC Conceptual Reference Model
CLARIAH	Zusammenschluss von CLARIN-D und DARIAH-DE
CLARIN-D	Common Language Resources and Technology Infrastructure Deutschland
CMDI	Component Metadata Infrastructure
CTS	CoreTrustSeal
DARIAH-DE	Digital Research Infrastructure for the Arts and Humanities Deutschland
DDC	DWDS/Dialing Concordance
ders.	derselbe
DFG	Deutsche Forschungsgemeinschaft
d. h.	das heißt
DH	Digital Humanities (Digitale Geisteswissenschaften)
DHNB	Digital Humanities in the Nordic and Baltic Countries Conference

d.i.	das ist
DiaCollo	Collocation Analysis in Diachronic Perspective
dies.	dieselbe/n
DiLiPaD	Digging into Linked Parliamentary Data
DINI	Deutsche Initiative für Netzwerkinformation e.V.
DiPaDA	Digital Parliamentary Data in Action
Diss.	Dissertation
Dr.	Doktor/in
dt.	deutsch
DTA	Deutsches Textarchiv
DTABf	Deutsches Textarchiv – Basisformat
DTABf-M	DTA-Basisformat für Manuskripte
DTAE	Erweiterungen des Deutschen Textarchivs
d.Vf.	die/der Verfasser/in
DWDS	Digitales Wörterbuch der deutschen Sprache
ed.	edited
Ed.	editor/s
e.g.	exempli gratia
Erg.-Bd.	Ergänzungsband
engl.	Englisch
ERC	European Research Council
et al.	et alii
etc.	et cetera
e.V.	eingetragener Verein
EuReD	Europäische Religionsfrieden Digital
f.	folgende/s
ff.	folgende (mehrere)
FAIR	Findable, Accessible, Interoperable, Re-usable
fasc.	fascicle
FCS	Federated Content Search
FDM	Forschungsdatenmanagement
Fig.	figure
Fol.	Folio
frz.	Französisch
GAMS	Geisteswissenschaftliches Asset-Management-System
ggf.	gegebenenfalls
GND	Gemeinsame Normdatei
GWK	Gemeinsame Wissenschaftskonferenz
Hg.	Herausgeber/in/nen
hg.v.	herausgegeben von
HTR	Handwritten Text Recognition
HTML	Hypertext Transfer Protocol
i.a.	inter alia
ibid.	Ibidem

ICARUS	International Centre for Archival Research
id.	Idem
IDUB	Initiative of Excellence – Research University
ID.UJ	Excellence Initiative – Jagiellonian University
i.e.	id est
ISO	International Standardisation Organisation
JSON	JavaScript Object Notation
inkl.	Inklusive
Kap.	Kapitel
KI	Künstliche Intelligenz
KNAW	Koninklijke Nederlandse Akademie van Wetenschappen
KONDE	Kompetenznetzwerk Digitale Edition
LIPARM	Linking Parliamentary Records through Metadata
LOD	Linked Open Data
LOUD	Linked Open Usable Data
MP	Member of Parliament
n.	number
NER	Named Entity Recognition
N.F.	Neue Folge
NFDI	Nationale Forschungsdateninfrastruktur e.V.
NLP	Natural Language Processing
n.pag.	no pagination
n.pl.	no place
Nr.	Nummer
NWO	Netherlands Organisation for Scientific Research
o.ä.	oder ähnliche/s
OCLC	Online Computer Library Center
OCR	Optical Character Recognition
OECD	Organisation for Economic Cooperation and Development
o.S.	ohne Seitenangabe
p.	page(s)
PDF	Portable Document Format
PhD	Philosophiae Doctor
PI	Principal Investigator
PPAC	Pre-modern PArliamentary Communication
PROME	Parliamentary Rolls of Medieval England
Prof.	Professor/in
POS-Tagging	Part-of-Speech-Tagging
r	(bei Folioangaben:) recto
RDF	Resource Description Framework
REPUBLIC	REsolutions PUBlished In a Computational Environment
rev.	revised
RODBH	Research on Online Databases in History
RSE	Research Software Engineering

S.	Seite(n)
s.	siehe
sig.	signature
SKOS	Simple Knowledge Organisation System
s.u.	siehe unten
sog.	sogenannte/r/s
Sp.	Spalte/n
SUB	Niedersächsische Staats- und Universitätsbibliothek Göttingen
s.v.	sub voce
T.	Teil
Tab.	Tabelle/table
Tbd.	Teilband
TEI	Text Encoding Initiative
t.evo	Evolution von komplexen Textmustern
TGN	Getty Thesaurus of Geographic Names
tom.	Tomus
transl.	Translated
übers. v.	übersetzt von
u.a.	und andere
u.ä.	und ähnliche/s
UK	United Kingdom (Vereinigtes Königreich)
URI	Uniform Resource Identifier
U.S.	United States
usw.	und so weiter
v	(bei Folioangaben:) verso
v.a.	vor allem
vgl.	vergleiche
VIAF	Virtual International Authority File
vol.	volume(s)
W3C	World Wide Web Consortium
XML	eXtensible Markup Language
Z.	Zeile
z.B.	zum Beispiel
ZfdG	Zeitschrift für digitale Geisteswissenschaften
ZIM-ACDH	Zentrum für Informationsmodellierung Graz – Austrian Centre for DH

Autorinnen und Autoren

Ronald G. Asch war bis 2021 Inhaber des Lehrstuhls für Geschichte der Frühen Neuzeit an der Universität Freiburg im Breisgau. Seine Forschungsschwerpunkte sind die Geschichte der britischen Inseln im 16. und 17. Jahrhundert, die Geschichte von Hof, Adel und Königtum in der Frühen Neuzeit und der Dreißigjährige Krieg. Zuletzt erschien von ihm: Vor dem großen Krieg. Europa im Zeitalter der spanischen Friedensordnung 1598–1618, Darmstadt 2020.

Roman Bleier studierte Geschichte, Religionswissenschaft und Digitale Geisteswissenschaften an der Universität Graz und am Trinity College Dublin. Im Rahmen seiner Dissertation und späterer Tätigkeit als Postdoktorand entstand die Edition »St Patrick's Epistles: Transcriptions of the Seven Medieval Manuscript Witnesses«. Er war an Projekten des An Foras Feasa Instituts der Maynooth University, am Trinity College Dublin und an der Royal Irish Academy beteiligt. Seit Mai 2016 ist er am Zentrum für Informationsmodellierung der Universität Graz tätig und hat dort an verschiedenen Editionsprojekten gearbeitet, darunter am Projekt »Der Regensburger Reichstag des Jahres 1576: Ein Pilotprojekt zum digitalen Edieren frühneuzeitlicher Quellen«. Seit 2023 leitet er das Projekt »History as a Visual Concept: Peter of Poitiers' Compendium historiae«.

Elisabeth Brantner studiert Geschichte sowie die Lehramtsfächer Englisch und Geschichte/Sozialkunde/Politische Bildung an der Karl-Franzens-Universität Graz. Von 2018 bis 2021 arbeitete sie bei der Historischen Kommission der Bayerischen Akademie der Wissenschaften an dem Projekt »Der Regensburger Reichstag des Jahres 1576: Ein Pilotprojekt zum digitalen Edieren frühneuzeitlicher Quellen«. Seit 2021 arbeitet sie als studentische Mitarbeiterin am Institut für Geschichte der Karl-Franzens-Universität Graz und unterstützt den Arbeitsbereich Geschichte der Frühen Neuzeit in Forschung und Lehre.

Krzysztof Fokt (geb. 1980) beschäftigt sich mit Siedlungs-, Verfassungs- und Rechtsgeschichte des Mittelalters und der Neuzeit, sowie Quelleneditionen (inkl. digitaler Editionen im Rahmen des IURA-Vorhabens). Doktorwürde in Archäologie (2010, Universität Breslau), Habilitation im Fach Geschichte (2021, Jagiellonen-Universität Krakau), ab 2011 in der Arbeitsstelle für Quelleneditionen an der Fakultät für Recht und Verwaltung an der Jagiellonen-Universität Krakau beschäftigt. Verfasser von drei Büchern, Mitherausgeber von zehn Quelleneditionen, unter anderem der dreibändigen kritischen Edition des ältesten Stadtbuchs von Görlitz (mit C. Speer und M. Mikuła), und den Bänden 4–5 der »Volumina Constitutionum« (mit S. Grodziski und M. Kwiecień).

Gabriele Haug-Moritz, promoviert (1989) und habilitiert (1999) an der Universität Tübingen, lehrt und forscht seit 2004 an der Universität Graz. Ihr Arbeitsschwerpunkt liegt auf der Geschichte der politischen Kultur des frühneuzeitlichen Europa. Seit 2014 ist sie Leiterin der Abteilung »Deutsche Reichstagsakten. Reichsversammlungen 1556–1662« bei der Historischen Kommission bei der Bayerischen Akademie der Wissenschaften. Gemeinsam mit Georg Vogeler war sie die wissenschaftliche Projektverantwortliche des von DFG und FWF geförderten digitalen Editionsprojekts »Der Regensburger Reichstag des Jahres 1576: Ein Pilotprojekt zum digitalen Edieren frühneuzeitlicher Quellen« (2018–2023).

Rik Hoekstra is a senior researcher at DHLab/Huygens, KNAW Humanities Cluster and a digital historian. His research focuses on early modern socio-political issues and digital research methodology. He is technical lead of the REPUBLIC project and especially active in the information extraction work package.

Marius Hug ist, nach dem Studium der Kulturwissenschaft und Philosophie an der Humboldt-Universität zu Berlin, seit 2007 im Bereich der Digital Humanities aktiv. Er war bis 2015 wissenschaftlicher Mitarbeiter im DFG-geförderten Projekt »Digitalisierung des Polytechnischen Journals«, von 2014 bis 2016 Mitarbeiter im Projekt »Hidden Kosmos – Reconstructing Alexander von Humboldt's ›Kosmos-Lectures‹« sowie später an der Staatsbibliothek zu Berlin im Projekt BeWeB-3D. 2018 wurde er zu einem kulturgeschichtlichen Thema promoviert und ist seit 2019 wissenschaftlicher Mitarbeiter am Zentrum Sprache an der Berlin-Brandenburgischen Akademie der Wissenschaften und dort aktuell Koordinator des Clusters »Historische Texte« im Rahmen des NDFI-Konsortiums Text+.

Martin de la Iglesia hat Kunstgeschichte und Bibliothekswissenschaft an der Humboldt-Universität zu Berlin studiert und wurde 2021 in ersterem Fach an der Universität Heidelberg promoviert. Seit 2011 arbeitet er im Bereich der digitalen Editionen; seit 2017 als Digital-Humanities-Mitarbeiter im von der Deutschen Forschungsgemeinschaft geförderten Langfristvorhaben »Kommentierte digitale Edition der Reise- und Sammlungsbeschreibungen Philipp Hainhofers (1578–1647)« an der Herzog August Bibliothek Wolfenbüttel (https://hainhofer.hab.de). Daneben ist er ebendort als Textredakteur bei der Zeitschrift für digitale Geisteswissenschaften (ZfdG) tätig.

Paulina Kewes is Professor of English Literature and Fellow of Jesus College, Oxford, and Fellow of the Royal Historical Society. She has published widely on early modern literature, history, political thought, and parliamentary culture. She is the author of »Authorship and Appropriation: Writing for the Stage in England, 1660–1710« (1998), and editor or co-editor of numerous volumes, including, most recently, »Stuart Succession Literature: Moments and Transformations« (2019) and »Ancient Rome in English Political Culture, c. 1570–1670« (2020). She is the PI on an interdisciplinary project »Recovering Europe's Parliamentary Culture,

1500–1700« (https://earlymodern.web.ox.ac.uk/recovering-europes-parliamentary-culture-1500-1700-new-approach-representative-institutions). Paulina holds a Leverhulme Trust Major Research Fellowship (2021–2024) awarded for »Contesting the Royal Succession in Reformation England, Latimer to Shakespeare«, a book to be published by Oxford University Press.

Linda Kirsten hat Linguistik und Bibliothekswissenschaft an der Humboldt-Universität zu Berlin studiert. Ihren Einstieg in die Digital Humanities hatte sie als Studentische Hilfskraft im Akademievorhaben »Alexander von Humboldt auf Reisen – Wissenschaft aus der Bewegung« an der Berlin-Brandenburgischen Akademie der Wissenschaften. Nach Abschluss ihres Studiums 2021 arbeitete Sie als Wissenschaftliche Mitarbeiterin in dem DFG-Projekt »Die Evolution von komplexen Textmustern« (t.evo) und als Koordinatorin in dem deutsch-kubanischen Kooperationsprojekt »Proyecto Humboldt Digital«.

Marijn Koolen is senior researcher at the Huygens Instituut and the DHLab of the KNAW Humanities Cluster. He has a background in Artificial Intellingence and Information Retrieval. His research interests are information extraction from digital historical corpora, natural language processing and computational literary studies.

Josef Leeb schloss das Studium der Geschichte und Germanistik an der Universität Regensburg 1986 mit dem Ersten Staatsexamen ab und wurde dort 1993 mit einer Untersuchung im Fach Bayerische Landesgeschichte promoviert. Seit 1989 ist er als wissenschaftlicher Mitarbeiter der Historischen Kommission bei der Bayerischen Akademie der Wissenschaften in der Abteilung »Deutsche Reichstagsakten, Reichsversammlungen 1556–1662« beschäftigt und hat seither die Akten von acht Reichsversammlungen ediert. Neben der Mitarbeit am Projekt einer digitalen Edition der Akten des Reichstags 1576 erschien zuletzt (2024) die Edition zum Regensburger Reichstag 1594.

Petr Maťa hat Geschichte und Historische Hilfswissenschaften in Prag studiert und ebendort promoviert. Seit 2006 ist er in Wien tätig. Von 2008 bis 2018 war er Universitätsassistent am Institut für Geschichte und Institut für Österreichische Geschichtsforschung der Universität Wien. Seit März 2018 ist er wissenschaftlicher Mitarbeiter am Institut für die Erforschung der Habsburgermonarchie und des Balkanraums der Österreichischen Akademie der Wissenschaften. In seinen Veröffentlichungen untersucht er Kultur-, Sozial- und Religionsgeschichte des frühmodernen Adels sowie Formen und Wandlungen der regionalen Fundierung der Habsburgerherrschaft, insbesondere in der böhmischen und der österreichischen Ländergruppe. Er ist Mitherausgeber des Handbuchs »Verwaltungsgeschichte der Habsburgermonarchie in der Frühen Neuzeit«. 2021 habilitierte er sich an der Universität Wien mit einer vergleichenden Studie über symbolische Kommunikation der Landtage in sieben habsburgischen Ländern.

Maciej Mikuła ist Professor am Lehrstuhl für Verwaltungsgeschichte und Recht der Religionsgemeinschaften an der Jagiellonen-Universität Krakau. Er schloss 2007 sein Studium der Rechtswissenschaften an der Jagiellonen-Universität und 2008 sein Studium der Geschichte an der Historischen Fakultät der Universität ab. Im Jahr 2012 verteidigte er seine Doktorarbeit. Habilitiert wurde er 2018 (Monographie: Das Magdeburger Stadtrecht (Ius municipale Magdeburgense) in Polen vom 14. bis zum frühen 16. Jahrhundert: Eine Studie zur Evolution und Adaption des Rechts). Seine Forschungsinteressen umfassen die Geschichte des deutschen Rechts (insbesondere des Magdeburger Rechts) in Mittel- und Osteuropa, Quellen des mittelalterlichen Rechts und die Edition historischer Rechtstexte. Er ist Leiter des Projekts »IURA. Rechtsquellen der Vergangenheit« (https://iura.uj.edu.pl).

Tim Neu ist Assistenzprofessor für Geschichte der Demokratie und der Menschenrechte am Institut für Geschichte der Universität Wien. Er forscht schwerpunktmäßig zur Geschichte der Frühen Neuzeit, insbesondere zur vormodernen Verfassungs- und Parlamentarismusgeschichte, zur britischen Imperialgeschichte sowie zur Geschichte öffentlicher Zahlungsfähigkeit und frühmoderner Staatsschuldenregime. Einschlägige Publikationen: Inszenierte, vielfältige und vielzeitige Gefüge – Bausteine einer Theorie der Verfassungsgeschichte, in: Ino Augsberg/Michael W. Müller (Hg.), Theorie der Verfassungsgeschichte. Geschichtswissenschaft – Philosophie – Rechtsdogmatik, Tübingen 2023, S. 53–77; Die Erschaffung der landständischen Verfassung. Kreativität, Heuchelei und Repräsentation in Hessen (1509–1655), Köln/Weimar/Wien 2013; Zelebrieren und Verhandeln. Zur Praxis ständischer Institutionen im frühneuzeitlichen Europa, Münster 2009 (gemeinsam hg. mit Thomas Weller und Michael Sikora).

Joris Oddens is a research group leader at the Huygens Institute of the History and Culture of the Netherlands, Royal Netherlands Academy of Arts and Sciences and project lead of the REPUBLIC project.

Eva Ortlieb studierte Geschichte, Philosophie und Literaturwissenschaft an den Universitäten Würzburg und Münster und arbeitet seit ihrer Promotion 1999 mit einer Arbeit über den Reichshofrat in der Mitte des 17. Jahrhunderts an verschiedenen deutschen und österreichischen Forschungseinrichtungen und Universitäten. Von 2018 bis 2023 begleitete sie das Kooperationsprojekt der Historischen Kommission bei der Bayerischen Akademie der Wissenschaften und der Universität Graz zur digitalen Edition der Akten des Reichstags von 1576 in einer beratenden Funktion, von 2019 bis 2021 war sie als Projektmitarbeiterin tätig.

Constanze M. Rammer studiert an der Karl-Franzens-Universität Graz Soziologie sowie Geschichtswissenschaft und absolvierte ein Auslandssemester an der Universiteit Gent. Sie war im Rahmen des Projekts »Der Regensburger Reichstag des Jahres 1576. Ein Pilotprojekt zum digitalen Edieren frühneuzeitlicher Quellen«, unter der Leitung von Frau Prof. Dr. Gabriele Haug-Moritz als studentische Mitarbeiterin beschäftigt, bei der sie zurzeit auch ihre Masterarbeit schreibt. Daneben arbeitet sie noch am Institut für Soziologie in den Bereichen Wirtschaftssoziologie und Geschichte der Soziologie.

Ronald Sluijter is a historian and works as a senior-data manager and researcher at the department of Digital Data Management of the Huygens Institute. In the REPUBLIC project, he is responsible for the work package of text recognition and images.

Georg Vogeler studierte Geschichtliche Hilfswissenschaften, Sozial- und Wirtschaftsgeschichte, Öffentliches Recht und Mittellateinische Philologie an den Universitäten Freiburg und München. Seit 2016 ist er Lehrstuhlinhaber für Digital Humanities an der Universität Graz und leitet seit 2019 das Zentrum für Informationsmodellierung – Austrian Centre for Digital Humanities. Er ist Gründungsmitglied des Instituts für Dokumentologie und Editorik (http://www.i-d-e.de) und technischer Direktor des Monasterium-Konsortiums (http://www.monasterium.net). Seine Forschungsgebiete liegen im spätmittelalterlichen Verwaltungsschriftgut, dem Urkundenwesen Friedrichs II., der digitalen Edition, der digitalen Diplomatik und der digitalen Prosopographie. Im Bereich der Modellierung und der Anwendung von Machine Learning/Künstlicher Intelligenz auf geisteswissenschaftliche Daten ist er in führender Rolle an verschiedenen Drittmittelprojekten beteiligt. 2021 hat Georg Vogeler einen ERC Advanced Grant für ein Projekt zur digitalen Diplomatik erhalten (https://didip.eu).

Andreas Wagner ist Digital-Humanities-Koordinator am Max-Planck-Institut für Rechtsgeschichte und Rechtstheorie in Frankfurt am Main. Außerdem ist er wissenschaftlicher Mitarbeiter im Projekt »Die Schule von Salamanca« der Akademie der Wissenschaften und der Literatur Mainz. Er wurde 2008 in Philosophie promoviert und beschäftigt sich seit über 10 Jahren mit digitalen Methoden in den Geisteswissenschaften. Besondere Schwerpunkte liegen in der Digitalen Editorik, der computergestützten Auswertung von Textquellen sowie in der Modellierung von Wissensgraphen. Seine Publikationen sind unter https://orcid.org/0000-0003-1835-1653 einsehbar.

Nach dem Studium der Geschichte und Anglistik in Heidelberg hat Kevin Wunsch im Jahr 2020 seine Tätigkeit im Projekt »Europäische Religionsfrieden Digital« aufgenommen. Dort ist er für die Infrastruktur des Projekts sowie die Forschung zu den Digital Humanities zuständig. Weiters arbeitet er an seinem Promotionsprojekt zu George Ansons Weltumseglung im achtzehnten Jahrhundert. Hierin untersucht er die Möglichkeiten, die digitale Editionen für die frühe Globalgeschichte bieten.

Andreas Zecherle legte 2007 das Erste Staatsexamen für das Lehramt an Gymnasien in den Fächern Evangelische Religionslehre und Deutsch ab. Im Jahr 2017 wurde er an der Friedrich-Alexander-Universität Erlangen-Nürnberg zum Dr. theol. promoviert. Von 2007 bis 2023 war er als Wissenschaftlicher Mitarbeiter in Editionsprojekten in Erlangen, Tübingen und Mainz tätig. Seit 2023 ist er Wissenschaftlicher Mitarbeiter an der Theologischen Fakultät der Universität Leipzig.

Florian Zeilinger wurde nach einem Studium der Lehramtsfächer Deutsch und Geschichte/Sozialkunde/Politische Bildung an der Karl-Franzens-Universität Graz 2020 mit einer 2022 publizierten Dissertation über die Wiederherstellung verlorener Ehre in der Regierungszeit Kaiser Rudolfs II. (1576–1612) ebenda promoviert. 2019 wirkte er an der TEI/XML-Transkription der Briefe von Graf Ignaz Maria von Attems-Heiligenkreuz von seiner Grand Tour 1734–1738 an seinen Vater mit. Von 2019 bis 2023 war er als Mitarbeiter bei der Historischen Kommission bei der Bayerischen Akademie der Wissenschaften in ihrem Kooperationsprojekt mit dem Zentrum für Informationsmodellierung der Universität Graz zur digitalen Edition der Akten des Reichstags zu Regensburg 1576 beschäftigt.

Register

Personenregister

Agricola, Johannes, Theologe 167
Anhalt, Fürst August von 149
–, Fürst Christian I. von 148 f., 152 f., 155 f.
–, Fürst Christian II. von 13, 145–158
–, Fürst Ernst von, kaiserlicher Obrist 155, 157
–, Fürst Johann Kasimir von 150
–, Fürst Ludwig von 150
Anjou, Herzog François-Hercule de Valois, Bruder von König Henry III. von Frankreich 45 f., 67 f.
Ankenbauer, Norbert, Romanist, Germanist 197
Archibald, Christopher, Historiker 43
Azpilcueta, Martín de, Jurist, Theologe 181

Bagen, Simon, Jurist, Theologe 238
Balzer, Oswald, Editor 112, 116
Behrisch, Lars, Historiker 11
Berners-Lee, Tim, Informatiker 177
Bèze, Theodore de, Theologe 44, 47
Birtsch, Günter, Historiker 19
Blockmans, Wim, Historiker 20
Blumesberger, Susanne, Bibliothekarin, Literaturwissenschaftlerin 214
Bodin, Jean, Jurist, Staatstheoretiker 11, 43, 45–68
Börstel, Curt von, Oberhauptmann von Bernburg 151
–, Heinrich von, Regierungspräsident von Bernburg 151, 157
Boucher, Jean, Theologe 44
Bourbon, Henry II. de, Prinz von Condé 61
Burton, Thomas, Member of Parliament 106

Caesar, Gaius Julius, Feldherr, Politiker, Schriftsteller 53
Cato, Marcus Porcius, Politiker 64
Chandler, Richard, Historiker 104 f.
Charles I., Prinz/König von England 100
Charles IX., König von Frankreich 45

Cicero, Marcus Tullius, Politiker, Redner, Schrifsteller 45
Claudius, römischer Tribun 53
Clement, Jacques, Königsmörder 154
Cobbett, William, Politischer Journalist, Geschäftsmann 104
Colavizza, Giovanni, Computerwissenschaftler 136
Collins, James B., Historiker 45
Cotton, Sir Robert, Member of Parliament 104
Cromwell, Oliver, Heerführer, Lordprotector 28–30

Deleuze, Gilles, Philosoph 30
D'Ewes, Sir Simonds, Member of Parliament, Historiker 102, 104–106
Dingel, Irene, Historikerin 161
Doran, Sue, Historikerin 43
Dvorský, František, Archivdirektor 81
Dwornicka, Irena, Editorin 112

Edward I., König von England 98
Edward III., König von England 99
Eleonora Gonzaga von Mantua-Nevers, Kaiserin, Ehefrau des römisch-deutschen Kaisers Ferdinand III. 202
Elias, Norbert, Soziologe 21
Elizabeth I., Königin von England 104
Erstenberger, Andreas, kaiserlicher Reichs- und Hofsekretär 238
Evrigenis, Ioannis, Philosoph 43, 46
Ewens, Ralph, Clerk 102

Faber, Christoph, Mainzer Kanzler 230
Ferdinand I., römisch-deutscher König/Kaiser 87–89, 166
Ferdinand II., römisch-deutscher Kaiser 148, 150, 152, 155, 202
Ferdinand III., römisch-deutscher König/Kaiser 152, 202
Franklin, Julian, Politologe 47 f.

Gindely, Anton, Archivdirektor 81, 85
Gippert, Stefan, Philologe 198
Godsey, William, Historiker 76
Göhler, Gerhard, Politologe 23
Goldegg und Lindenburg, Franz von 84
Goldie, Mark, Historiker 43
Górski, Kacper, Computerwissenschaftler 114
Graves, Michael, Historiker 19
Greengrass, Mark, Historiker 43, 48 f., 54
Grey, Anchitell, Member of Parliament 103 f.
Grodziski, Stanisław, Historiker 112, 118
Guattari, Félix, Psychoanalytiker 30
Guizot, François, Historiker, Politiker 67
Gunn, Steven, Historiker 21
Gustav Adolf, König von Schweden 150, 155, 157
Gutkas, Karl, Archivar und Professor 85
Gyurikovits, György, Rechtshistoriker 84

Häberlin, Karl Friedrich, Jurist 25
Hainhofer, Philipp, Kaufmann 13, 195, 196, 199–202
Hansard, T. C., Publizist 104
Harrison, Thomas, Colonel 29
Hartley, T. E., Editor 105 f.
Haug-Moritz, Gabriele, Historikerin 21
Hébert, Michel, Historiker 21, 24, 28, 238
Helding, Michael, Theologe 167
Hendler, James, Informatiker 177
Henry I., König von England 97
Henry III., König von England 97
Henry III., König von Frankreich, Bruder von König Charles IX. 45, 57–62, 64, 68, 154
Henry III., König von Navarra (zugleich Henry IV., König von Frankreich) 60 f.
Henry IV., König von England 99
Henry V., König von England 99
Henry VIII., König von England 101
Hexter, J. H., Historiker 105
Horndacher, Martin, Reisebegleiter Philipp Hainhofers 200
Hotman, François, Richter 44, 47, 65
Humboldt, Alexander von, Naturwissenschaftler 209

Iwasaki, Shuichi, Historiker 86
James I., König von England 103

Janiš, Dalibor, Historiker, Editor 82
Japikse, Nicolaas, Editor 124

Jesus Christus 175
Jones, Elisa, Histsorikerin 49

Kameníček, František, Historiker 79
Kampmann, Christoph, Historiker 167
Karl VI., römisch-deutscher Kaiser 84
Karl V., römisch-deutscher Kaiser 166–168, 174
Karliczek, Anja, ehem. Bundesforschungsministerin und GWK-Vorsitzende 212
Kewes, Paulina, Historikerin 21
Khlesl, Kardinal Melchior 152 f.
Knolles, Richard, Historiker 46
Kwiecień, Marcin, Rechtshistoriker 112, 114

Ladislaus/Władysław IV., Kronprinz/König von Polen 156
Lamormaini, Pater Wilhelm, kaiserlicher Beichtvater und Jesuit 154
Lanzinner, Maximilian, Historiker 8
Lassila, Ora, Informatiker 177
Latour, Bruno, Soziologe 33
Le Cointe, Pieter, Kaufmann 128
Le Tourneu, Pierre „Versoris", Jurist 59
Lee, Daniel, Historiker 48
Leopold I., römisch-deutscher Kaiser 75
Louis XI., König von Frankreich 63
Louis XIII., König von Frankreich 156
Lousse, Émile, Historiker 20
Ludwig der Fromme, Kaiser 200

Maria, Königin von Schottland 100
Maria, Mutter Jesu 157
Maria Anna von Spanien, Gattin des römisch-deutschen Kaisers Ferdinand III. 152
Maťa, Petr, Historiker 32
Matthias, römisch-deutscher Kaiser 202
Maximilian II., römisch-deutscher Kaiser 221, 224–227, 229
McRae, Kenneth, Politologe 46
Michael I., Zar von Russland 157
Miglietti, Sara, Historikerin 48 f.
Miller, Georg, Doktor, Reisebegleiter Philipp Hainhofers 200
Montagu Wortley, Edward, Colonel 29
Montesquieu, Baron Charles de Secondat 67
Montmorency-Damville, Gouverneur von Languedoc 61

Naumburg, Bischof Julius Pflug, Theologe 167 f.

Personenregister

Nero, Claudius Caesar Augustus Germanicus, römischer Kaiser 53
Nezorin, Abt Florian von Welehrad in Mähren (gleichzeitig Abt von Pásztó in Ungarn) 84
Nicholls, Sophie, Historikerin 47
Noah 183
Notestein, Wallace, Historiker 104–106
Numa Pompilius, König von Rom 53

Oddens, Joris, Historiker 21
Ohryzko, Jozafat, Verleger 112
Olivier-Martin, François, Rechtshistoriker 20
Okáč, Antonín, Historiker 86
Onslow, Fulk, Clerk 102
Orzechowski, Kazimierz, Historiker 86
Otley, N. N., Colonel 29

Palatin (Fürst) August (von Anhalt) 157
Paul, Jean, Schriftsteller 209, 216
Paulus, Hl. Apostel 173, 183
Pecker, N. N., kaiserlicher Obrist 156
Pérusse des Cars, Charles de, Bischof von Langres 45
Petrus, Hl. Apostel 183
Pfalz, Friedrich V. von 149, 152
Pietrzyk-Reeves, Dorota, Historikerin 21
Plessis Mornay, Philippe du, Theologe, Politiker 44
Pocock, J. G. A., Historiker, Politologe 44

Radziwill, Fürst Christoph von 157
Ralph, James, Historiker 104
Rem, Daniel, Schwager Philipp Hainhofers 200
Renault, Rachel, Historikerin 11
Reuß-Ebersdorf, Gräfin Erdmuthe Benigna 209
Richard II., König von England 99
Rohan, Herzog Henry II. de 155
Roloff, Hans-Gert, Philologe 199
Rous, Rev. Francis, Speaker of the House of Commons 29 f.
Russell-Moyle, Lloyd, Member of Parliament 30

Sachsen (Albertinische Linie), Kurfürst August von 226, 228, 230
Sahle, Patrick, Historiker (DH) 232
Salomon, König von Israel 183
Savoyen, Kardinal Moritz von 148

Schleiermacher, Friedrich Daniel Ernst, Philosoph 209
Schlick, Graf Heinrich von, Hofkriegsratspräsident 149
Schmid zum Schwarzenhorn, Johann Rudolf, Diplomat 202
Schreiber, Arndt, Editor 146
Seaward, Paul, Historiker 21, 43
Seymour, John, Clerk 101 f.
Sigismund III., König von Polen 156 f.
Simmler, Franz, Germanist 197
Skinner, Quentin, Historiker 46 f.
Solon, athenischer Politiker 52
Sowerby, Tracey, Historikerin 21
Stäcker, Thomas, Bibliotheksdirektor 161
Stasavage, David, Historiker 21 f.
Stollberg-Rilinger, Barbara, Historikerin 23–26
Straumann, Benjamin 48
Sutter, Berthold, Editor 82
Szijártó, István, Historiker 85

Taats van Amerongen, Herr Frederik Batavodorus 128
Tacitus, Publius Cornelius, Autor, Politiker 45
Tarquinius Superbus, Lucius, etruskischer König 53
Thrush, Andrew, Historiker, Editor 102
Timberland, Richard 104 f.
Tocqueville, Alexis de, Historiker, Politologe 67
Townshend, Hayward, Member of Parliament 106
Tuck, Richard, Historiker 48 f.
Turchetti, Mario, Historiker 46 f., 66

Urban VIII. Barberini, Papst 153
Uruszczak, Wacław, Editor 112, 115

Van der Meulen, Jim, Historiker 21, 43
Van Marnix van St Aldegonde, Herr Philips 44
Villiers, George, Duke of Buckingham 100
Vergil/Virgil, Polydor, Humanist 97

Wachter, Hans, Einspänner 200
Wallenstein, Albrecht von, Herzog von Friedland 149
Weber, Max, Soziologe 19
Worden, Blair, Historiker 43

Zedler, Johann Heinrich, Verleger 25

Ortsregister

Amsterdam 21
Anhalt, Fürstentum 157
Anzenhof 200 f.
Augsburg 166

Baltikum 162
Banat 73
Bayern 152, 157
Beaulieu 45, 56
Belarus (Weißrussland)/Belarus 111
Berlin 11, 206
Bernburg 151
Blois 45, 47–50, 57 f., 61, 66
Böhmen, Königreich 72, 75, 83, 88 f., 152, 162
Böhmische Länder 74, 76
Brandenburg 152
Brandenburg-Preußen 74, 76
Breslau/Wrocław 74, 80
Britische Inseln/British Isles 107
Brünn/Brno 74
Budapest 84 f.

Cambridge 44

Darmstadt 161, 164
Den Haag/The Hague 129
Dessau-Roßlau 145
Deutscher Sprachraum 7, 146
Deutschland, Bundesrepublik 7, 195, 211 f., 214 f.
»Deutschland«, Heiliges Römisches Reich Teutscher Nation 150, 153
Dublin 113, 117, 182

Eger, Bezirk 75
Eidgenossenschaft, s. Schweiz 162
England 44, 54, 56, 67 f., 76, 97, 104, 106, 151, 163
Europa, Kontinent 9, 11 f., 21 f., 24, 53, 55, 72 f., 162

Flandern, Grenze (pays rétrocédés) 73
Frankreich/France 11, 44, 49, 53–55, 64, 66, 73, 146, 155 f., 162, 167, 221

Galizien und Lodomerien, Königreich 75
Glatz, Grafschaft 74
Görz, Grafschaft 74
Göttingen 206

Graz 7–9, 32, 82, 232
Griechenland 65
Großbritannien/United Kingdom 76, 97
Güsten 151
Guyenne 60

Habsburg-Österreich, Monarchie, habsburgische Länder 12, 32, 71–77, 79–81, 87–89, 91
Halle an der Saale 150
Hamburg 209
Heiliges Römisches Reich Teutscher Nation, »Altes Reich«/German Empire 27, 55 f., 72 f., 77, 145, 150–152, 162 f., 166, 221, 231
Hessen-Darmstadt, Landgrafschaft 149

Ilberstedt 151
Irland/Ireland 107
Italien 146, 155, 162

Jauer 83

Kärnten, Herzogtum 74, 83
Kew 103
Kolonien 181
– in Nordamerika, englische 163
Krain, Herzogtum 74, 76
Krakau/Cracow 21, 111–114
Kroatien, Königreich 75, 226

La Rochelle, Festung 155 f.
Languedoc 45, 55, 61
Lateineuropa 11
Lausitzen, Ober- und Niederlausitz 72, 74
Leiden/Leyden 128
Le Mans 11
Lettland/Latvia 111
Linz 73
Litauen/Lithuania 111
Lombardei 73
London 21, 46, 103 f.
–, Tower 104

Maastricht 128
Mähren 72, 74, 79, 83 f., 89
Mainz 161
–, Kurfürstentum 230
Masowien 156
Mazedonien 65

Ortsregister

Militärgrenze, habsburgisch-osmanische 73
Moskau 157
Moskowiterreich/Russisches Zarenreich 221
München 200 f., 229

Nantes 168
Navarra 60
Niederländische Republik/Dutch Republic, Republik der Vereinigten Niederlande 76, 122, 126, 128
Niederlande/Low Countries/Netherlands 46, 121, 162

Österreich 7
–, Erblande 72, 76, 150, 162
–, Erzherzogtum 74
–, Innerösterreich 74, 76
– ob der Enns (Oberösterreich), Herzogtum 73, 83
– unter der Enns (Niederösterreich), Herzogtum 73, 83, 89
–, Vorderösterreich 74
Österreichische Niederlande 73
Olmütz/Olomouc 74
Osteuropa 162
Ostindien 181
Ostmitteleuropa 77
Oxford 11, 21, 43

Paderborn 210
Paris 45, 50
Plessis-lès-Tours 46
Plötzkau 151
Polen(-Litauen), Königreich/Poland(-Lithuania), Kingdom 111, 114–116, 118, 156 f.
–, Republik/Poland, Republic 112, 114, 117
Posen/Poznań 113
Prag 83

Regensburg 152, 221, 229, 239
Rom 53, 153

Sachsen-Anhalt 157
Sachsen, Kurfürstentum 149, 155
Salamanca 181
Schlesien 72–76, 162
Schottland/Scotland 106
Schweden, Königreich 73, 149, 151
Schweiz, Schweizer Kantone, s. Eidgenossenschaft 55 f.
Sheffield, Universität 106
Siebenbürgen, Fürstentum 75, 80, 162, 173
Skandinavien 162
Slawonien, Königreich 75
Smolensk 156
Spanien, Königreich(e)/Spain, Kingdom(s) 44, 46, 54, 56, 67, 74, 76, 100, 155 f., 221
Steiermark, Herzogtum 32, 74, 82 f., 89
Stuttgart 229

Temesvár 73
Tirol 74
Tokaj 230
Toulouse 45
Trient/Trento 181
Troppau/Opava, Fürstentum 74
Turin 148

Ukraine 111
Ungarische Länder 76, 78
Ungarn, Königreich 72 f., 75, 78 f., 89, 226, 230
Utrecht 11

Vermandois 43, 57, 59, 61

Warschau/Warsaw 45, 112, 156
Weißer Berg/Bílá Hora, Prag 148, 150
Westminster, Palast 100, 103
Wien 73, 83, 150, 229
Wolfenbüttel 145, 147, 195, 202, 210

Yale, Universität 105 f.

Zeeland 127